PRAISE FOR

THE LADY AND THE PANDA

"Evocative and satisfying, *The Lady and the Panda* is the sort of adventure story that cries out for a film version starring Kate Hepburn. . . . Croke's book offers drama, pathos, even a doomed romance in a remote bamboo forest."

—*PEOPLE*

"*The Lady and the Panda* winds up stranger than fiction but no less poignant. . . . Like its heroine, it stakes everything on exotic glamour."

—*THE NEW YORK TIMES*

"[Croke's] arresting accomplishment is to capture the excitement of the true adventure story while dismantling the bigotry behind it."

—*THE BOSTON SUNDAY GLOBE*

"An ingenious story . . . Vicki Constantine Croke's account of Ruth Harkness' obsessional journey belongs on every animal freak's bookshelf."

—*NEWSDAY*

"Croke's research puts a human touch on a most unexpected explorer. . . . A compelling read not only on pandas, but about the person *The Washington Post* described as someone who had made the world 'panda conscious.'"

—*ALBUQUERQUE JOURNAL*

"Croke tells the story well, provides an abundance of panda lore and touches on all the relevant issues—environmental awareness, cultural imperialism, racism, sexism—without heavy-handedness."

—THE INDIANAPOLIS STAR

"[Croke] spins an engaging yarn about her intrepid hero, and does so with verve and empathy, as well as a good amount of panda particulars."

—BOSTON MAGAZINE

"Croke opens a window into China. . . . She handles a mass of historical and cultural materials, integrating it well with the narrative of Harkness' life."

—MINNEAPOLIS STAR TRIBUNE

"Thoroughly detailed and researched."

—THE OREGONIAN

"*The Lady and the Panda* presents an extraordinarily independent woman and an explorer who, herself, is well worth exploring."

—THE VIRGINIAN-PILOT

"In dusting off this exciting tale, Constantine Croke returns Harkness to her rightful place in the top rank of zoological explorers."

—PUBLISHERS WEEKLY

"Kudos are due for recovering the story of a larger-than-life woman and her tiny, famous panda bear."

—KIRKUS REVIEWS

"Croke has created an exciting tale, full of the color and spectacle of a lost, exotic era and place."

—BOOKLIST

"This well-written, exhaustively researched and documented book should be on every library's shelves."

—LIBRARY JOURNAL

"Exotic, romantic, and vivid, *The Lady and the Panda* presents a wonderful tale of a remarkable woman and her remarkable adventure. Vicki Croke takes readers on a thrilling vicarious journey through the China of a very different time."

"A remarkable journey beautifully described, *The Lady and the Panda* brings to life one of the most astonishing and overlooked stories of American adventure, the 1936 quest by Ruth Harkness to bring a giant panda to America. Vicki Constantine Croke's canvas is the mystical and wondrous China of the 1930s, her heroine a most remarkable woman, and her gift the ability to understand that this is a great love story."

"Mesmerizing. Vicki Croke has done a magnificent job of immersing the reader in an absolutely fascinating world. I found myself completely absorbed and could not stop reading. Amazing."

"Ruth Harkness, the New York socialite who journeyed into the wilds of China to bring the giant panda to America, now has the biography she deserves. In Croke's hands, the intrepid American woman and the con men, dreamers, and adventurers who joined her in the pursuit of the world's most exotic animal spring vividly to life. Part Hemingway, part *Treasure of the Sierra Madre*, *The Lady and the Panda* is a rare blend of adventure, biography, and zoology. A deeply satisfying read."

BY VICKI CONSTANTINE CROKE

The Lady and the Panda

The Modern Ark: The Story of Zoos:
Past, Present and Future

Animal ER: Extraordinary Stories of Hope
and Healing from One of the World's
Leading Veterinary Hospitals

Dogs Up Close

Cats Up Close

THE LADY AND THE PANDA

Random House Trade Paperbacks
New York

THE LADY AND THE PANDA

VICKI CONSTANTINE CROKE

THE TRUE ADVENTURES OF THE FIRST AMERICAN EXPLORER

TO BRING BACK CHINA'S MOST EXOTIC ANIMAL

2006 Random House Trade Paperback Edition

Copyright © 2005 by Vicki Constantine Croke
Map copyright © 2005 by David Lindroth, Inc.

Published in the United States by Random House Trade Paperbacks,
an imprint of The Random House Publishing Group,
a division of Random House, Inc., New York.

RANDOM HOUSE TRADE PAPERBACKS and colophon are
trademarks of Random House, Inc.

Originally published in hardcover in the United States by Random
House, an imprint of The Random House Publishing Group,
a division of Random House, Inc., in 2005.

LIBRARY OF CONGRESS CATALOGING-IN-PUBLICATION DATA
Croke, Vicki.
The lady and the panda: the true adventures of the first American
explorer to bring back China's most exotic animal/
Vicki Constantine Croke.
p.   cm.
ISBN 0-375-75970-0
1. Giant panda.   2. Harkness, Ruth.   I. Title.
QL737.C214C76 2005   599.789'092—dc22   2004051356

Printed in the United States of America

www.atrandom.com

9 8 7 6

Book design by Barbara M. Bachman

FOR MY SISTER, LINDA BIANDO

China is a country of unforgettable color, and often,
quite unbidden, come vivid pictures to my mind—
sometimes it is the golden roofs of the Imperial City
in Peking, or again it is the yellow corn on the
flat-roofed little stone houses in the country of the
Tibetan border land.

—RUTH HARKNESS

CONTENTS

AUTHOR'S NOTE

A NOTE ON CHINESE TERMS: During Ruth Harkness's time in the East, the standard method for the phonetic notation and transliteration of Mandarin Chinese words was the Wade-Giles system, which brought us Peking, Whangpu, and Chungking. Today, the standard is Pinyin, which spells those places Beijing, Huangpu, and Chongqing. This book uses both depending on the context.

PREFACE

SOME MOMENTOUS ENCOUNTERS feel that way from the start. And so it was for me and the story of Ruth Harkness. In the spring of 1993, while researching a book about zoos, I came across a tantalizing story that even in the barest outline electrified me. In a special anniversary issue of the magazine published by Chicago's Brookfield Zoo, and in a follow-up conversation with the zoo's marketing director, I learned of Harkness, a dress designer and socialite, who in 1936 took over her dead husband's expedition to the border of China and Tibet and captured the first giant panda to be seen in the West. At the time, the panda hunter was an international sensation, and the panda himself once drew more than 53,000 visitors when first displayed at the Brookfield—a single-day tally the zoo has never again matched.

Harkness's likeness would shine out from newspapers, magazines, newsreels, comic strips, and advertisements. Her panda would make the front pages of the *Chicago Tribune* for a nine-day stretch—something one newspaperman told her wouldn't have been done for anyone else, including the president. No animal in history, the lofty Field Museum reckoned, had gotten such attention. Ruth Harkness would become a hero—an unlikely one, for sure, but Americans have always liked that kind best. And her accomplishment would be so well known that *The Washington Post* would proclaim that every high school child in the land knew her name. She would succeed, the paper said, in "making the world panda conscious."

It sounded impossible—not just like fiction but like fantasy.

Yet today, few know anything of the saga.

Growing up, I had loved tales of adventure, particularly those from the animal world: Kipling's *The Jungle Book* or Joy Adamson's *Born Free*. Later, I fell for any story of westerners in the wild, frothy or fusty, scholarly or lowbrow: Osa Johnson's *I Married Adventure*, Jane Goodall's *In the Shadow of Man*, and even Daphne Sheldrick's *Animal Kingdom*, with its instructions for baking a cake while camping on the African veldt.

I really didn't have the time to research Harkness—my zoo book, *The Modern Ark*, had a fast-approaching deadline—but I couldn't stop myself. I ordered a secondhand copy of her 1938 book *The Lady and the Panda* for what seemed the outrageous price of fifty-two dollars. As soon as the volume emerged from its brown paper wrapping, though, it was clear that Ruth Harkness was a good investment. Part Myrna Loy and part Jane Goodall, by turns wisecracking and poetic, smart and brave, she was thoroughly modern in her sensibility. (Her story had none of the reflexive racial bigotry that scarred so many other first-person adventure chronicles of her time.) I felt the tug of something deep, a bond, perhaps, that had crossed the passage of time.

Meanwhile, working on my other book, I was learning that radical changes were taking place at our country's zoos, where simple husbandry had become a sophisticated science. Animal experts were employing cutting-edge technology to understand behavior and to improve zoo inhabitants' nutrition and medical care. Reproduction for captive animals had been altered by the adoption of DNA fingerprinting, artificial insemination, embryo transfers, and egg harvesting. Zoos were saving species the space-age way.

Except, it seemed, for the giant panda. The ancient, inscrutable animals were proving resistant to efforts to induce them to reproduce with any regularity outside their bamboo-covered mountains. The United

States' record was particularly dismal—at that time, not one giant panda baby born in captivity in this country had survived past infancy. (The first, Hua Mei, would arrive in 1999 at the San Diego Zoo.)

The story of Ruth Harkness, that long-forgotten panda-hunting dress designer, kept pushing its way into my consciousness. If the world's top scientists couldn't keep these panda babies alive away from their cold, wild homes, how had a Manhattan party girl managed to do it in 1936? After all, getting baby-panda formula right was something scientists were still puzzling over in the 1990s. Even by the 1980s, nearly fifty years after Harkness's accomplishment, "little was known about the species," according to the World Wildlife Fund. The more I learned about how perplexed biologists were by the giant panda, the more awed I felt by Harkness's adventure.

It wasn't just that either. Harkness was a captivating character, but her book had covered just one year of her life; everything before and after was a mystery. In fact, there was a great deal about that year in China I wanted to know more about. I had a thousand questions.

Every step of the way, as I unearthed small and large pieces of information, the story grew richer, more fantastical, and more moving. Was it true that she attended black-tie dinners at a palace far out in the Chinese frontier? Did she actually take a panda out of China by registering it as a dog? Could she really have survived a train wreck in the jungles of French Indochina while making her second expedition alone in 1937? The answers were just a sample of many surprises in store for me.

The best of them was the revelation of a cache of hundreds of letters written by Harkness—often on her portable typewriter—over three expeditions to China. Robin Perkins Ugurlu, the granddaughter of Harkness's closest friend, had read an article of mine on Harkness in *The Washington Post Magazine*. When she phoned, we agreed to meet in Cleveland, where her parents live, and where they had kept this treasure safe for more than fifty years. I received the correspondence between Harkness and Hazel Perkins in the afternoon at my hotel and read it straight through, well into the night. The letters were mesmerizing, giving the backstory on many intrigues Harkness had been too ladylike to include in her book. That summer evening, I began to know Ruth McCombs Harkness not only as a heroic character but also as a flawed, brave, and passionate woman.

Everything in this book is true; nothing has been fictionalized. The research has involved personal letters, books, histories, weather reports, miles of microfilm records of English-language newspapers in Shanghai, magazines, and archival documents from museums, universities, and the municipal library of Shanghai, and the online auction eBay (America's great yard sale).

Standing on her own two feet and saying exactly what she meant, Harkness never required anyone to interpret her words or represent her. But after years of neglect, she did need someone to revive her story. And, considering the praise that conservation insiders voiced for her contribution to the relationship between humankind and nature, I felt driven to do just that.

Harkness has been quietly canonized by the few conservationists, scholars, and zoologists who have fully studied the panda-hunting era. They know that what began in Ruth Harkness's serene mountain camp was an event that would shake the world, helping to change the way Americans perceived the widespread hunting of exotic animals.

The desire to see giant pandas survive, something we take for granted today, was a novel concept in the 1930s when Harkness brought home a little black-and-white bear, not in a cage, not on a leash, but in her arms. She told the world that this creature was not an "it" but an individual with a unique personality. The significance of this shift in perception is incalculable, as the legendary primatologist Jane Goodall realized in the 1960s with the case of chimpanzees. For if each individual matters, then each individual deserves to be saved.

Zoologist and author Desmond Morris, writing with his wife, Ramona, has said that the sight of Harkness's prize, the panda Su-Lin, was a turning point in the timeline of natural history. Blasting away at creatures and stuffing their carcasses in museums was already losing its luster. The emergence of the beloved baby giant panda would, he said, add "a very important nail to the coffin of the 'huntin' and shootin' ' epoch."

The baby panda captivated people in a way that an adult never would have. Su-Lin "was virtually changing the whole attitude of western civilization towards the species," the Morrises wrote. "In a few brief moments on the dockside, one animal did more for the cause of nature conservation than most humans could hope to achieve in a lifetime," author and nature filmmaker Chris Catton said in his book *Pandas*. The World Wildlife Fund, whose very identity is associated with its logo of a giant panda, has said that Su-Lin's arrival helped "evoke universal sympathy for the plight of the species."

Harkness spoke out about what was in her day a rather alien concept: the conservation of this species. She also did something that most of today's field biologists wouldn't even be aware of. She returned a captured panda to the wild.

At the time of her great fame, Harkness knew she had accomplished more than just winning a footrace for the title of "first." She would look at the whole matter, as she often tended to do, in a philosophical way, admitting privately that she realized she could claim a "part in giving the animal world a lift on its upward path."

THERE MAY BE about fifteen hundred giant pandas left in the wild, and the hope is that the world will not allow them to slip away. Millions of dollars have poured into China from organizations like the World Wildlife Fund and the American Zoo and Aquarium Association to help with research and conservation.

This is the legacy of Ruth Harkness. Every time a biologist treks into the bamboo forest, or a conservation group underwrites research, or a child places a nickel in a collection box for giant pandas, Harkness's mission lives on.

Ruth Harkness made history. She thrilled a country desperate for something to cheer about. She did what no other American had been able to do. And she helped a gentle, mysterious species in its fight for survival.

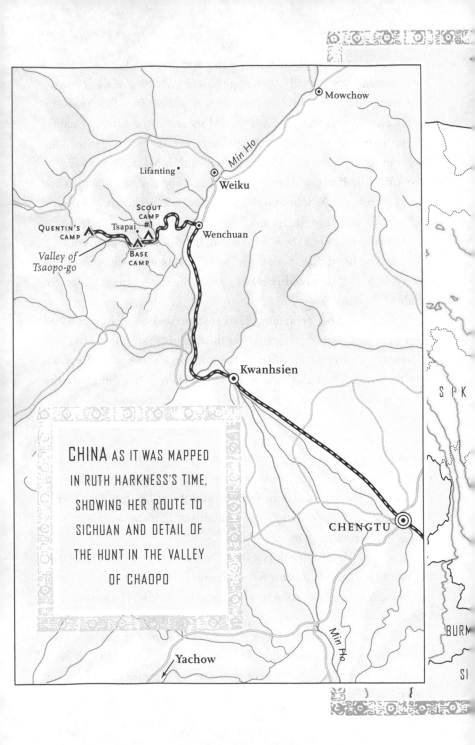

Mowchow

Min Ho

Lifanting

Weiku

Scout Camp #1

Quentin's camp

Tsapai

Wenchuan

Valley of Tsaopo-go

Base camp

Kwanhsien

SIK

CHENGTU

BURM

SI

CHINA AS IT WAS MAPPED IN RUTH HARKNESS'S TIME, SHOWING HER ROUTE TO SICHUAN AND DETAIL OF THE HUNT IN THE VALLEY OF CHAOPO

Min Ho

Yachow

THE LADY AND THE PANDA

CHAPTER ONE

DEATH IN SHANGHAI

I T WAS A BITTER WINTER NIGHT, February 19, 1936, and on the outskirts of Shanghai, far from the neon and the wailing jazz, thirty-four-year-old William Harvest Harkness, Jr., lay in a private hospital, blood-stiffened silk sutures tracking across his pale abdomen. He was dying, and alone in his agony. His original expedition mates, four adventurous men with dreams of capturing the giant panda, had all deserted him long before. Though he knew people in the city from previous trips and more recent escapades in notorious nightclubs and bars, in the end he had stayed true to some deeper nature, pushing them all away and stealing off in secret. His family, including his young wife back in Manhattan, had no idea he was even sick. With what little strength he could summon, he had been writing sunny notes home that masked his horrible condition. Perhaps he really believed his own words, for just weeks earlier he had been pressuring the doctor to release him so he could get back to his campaign. But, finally, on this frigid night, scarred by other attempts to scalpel tumors from his neck and torso and wretched from his latest incision, he found himself unable to eat or drink, then even to breathe. The sportsman who lived to rough it in the wild died under starched white sheets, in a ward reeking of antiseptic. His young life had ended in the pursuit of the most mysterious animal of his time, yet he had never managed to set a laced boot in the great snow-covered mountains that separated China and Tibet.

A world away, back in the noise and lights and rush of Manhattan, it had been an even chillier winter, one of the snowiest and coldest anyone could remember. Late in the afternoon, on the very day her husband took his last breath, Ruth Harkness was making her way home from a salon where she had enjoyed a luxurious shampoo. Bundled up, she happily picked her way along icy sidewalks that were dusted with ash for traction and walled in by freshly shoveled snow. Friends were due for cocktails shortly, and in the larger scheme of things, she had even more to look forward to. Now that things were beginning to go well for Bill, she thought, he might just be home within months. Then the two of them could travel the world as they had always imagined.

But as she stepped inside her comfortable West Side apartment, before she had time to hang up her coat, her "pretty little mulatto maid" and her houseguest, Margaret Freeland, confronted her with the horrible news: Bill was dead. A cable message had been relayed by telephone.

Her first reaction was stunned disbelief. It was too awful to accept. This must be some fantasy of the press—reporters were fascinated by Bill and the other men of high adventure, but in their hunger for sensational stories, they were always getting things wrong. It had to be one of those false bulletins. Surely, over the course of the afternoon, that would become clear.

So she waited, as the winter darkness descended and lamps inside the apartment were snapped on. But hours later a telegram from Secretary of State Cordell Hull made it official. The love of her life was gone.

The devastation of that loss would consume her for weeks, and haunt her always. "Do you have that tremendous necessity of needing one person," Ruth Harkness would ask a friend in the bruised aftermath of Bill's death, "some person who understands you and trusts you completely in everything you do and you are—and ever can or will be? Someone with whom you can let down all barriers? All pretense of any kind and still be liked or loved? . . . That is what Bill meant to me and in return I gave him what he needed."

Through their ten years together, few understood the singular nature of their bond. To the outside world, Ruth and Bill were opposites. But they were also as perfect a fit.

Both had arrived in Manhattan in their early twenties. It was the Jazz Age, when under the cover of darkness, whites began slipping into Harlem for the music. People spoke openly of birth control, and women were enticed by the makers of Chesterfield cigarettes to "blow some my way." Josephine Baker had her own nightclub in Paris. Films turned talkie. Lindbergh crossed the Atlantic. D. H. Lawrence imagined a scandalous dalliance in *Lady Chatterley's Lover,* and Margaret Mead was discussing sex among young Samoans. It was the birth of *Time* magazine, *The New Yorker,* and the Milky Way bar. For young party-minded Manhattanites during Prohibition, speakeasies were all the rage. It was no surprise, then, that the worlds of two hell-raisers would eventually collide.

Handsome, short, and slender, with slicked-back straw-colored hair and light blue eyes, William Harvest Harkness, Jr., was born to privilege. The sound of his name alone declared it. He was not a member of the famous Standard Oil Harknesses. But Bill had graduated from Harvard, class of 1924; he was a rich boy whose name showed up in the society pages, the son of a successful New York City attorney, and the scion of a wealthy New York family, as the press described him. The Harknesses were powerfully connected and accustomed to doors being opened for them.

But those points alone certainly would not have been enough to attract Ruth. Bill Harkness also had grit, and smarts, and a wry take on the world. Never arrogant, he was nonetheless sure of himself, and unconcerned with proving anything to others. His singular nature defied easy definition. As one friend pointed out, Bill had "inherited the wiry toughness of his Scotch-Irish ancestry along with a lot of mysticism, anomalously mixed with hard-headed Yankee shrewdness."

Both bookish and athletic, cynical and sensitive, Bill Harkness was a man of appealing contradictions. His complicatedness was something that Ruth would love.

In Ruth, Bill saw a novel act. She was nothing like the girls he had met at Harvard dances. With her black hair parted in the middle and pulled severely back, a penchant for the dramatic, even exotic, in her dress, and a fondness for bright red lipstick, Ruth Elizabeth McCombs stood out. She was a newly minted dress designer who possessed a rare polish and poise. Speaking with a cultured lilt, she had a deep voice and a light wit. She could fill a room with her presence, her outsized personality invariably prompting people to say that she was tall, even though she stood only five feet four. She had, according to one society watcher, "that quality which Hollywood chooses to call glamour." Over the years, her panache would carry her through lofty circles in New York City and beyond, bringing her top-notch invitations wherever she went. She appeared the ultimate city slicker but had started life as anything but.

Born on September 21, 1900, the third of four children, she came from hardworking, frugal stock in Titusville, Pennsylvania, with American roots going back to the eighteenth century. Her father, Robert, was a carpenter, lean, fit, and kind. Her mother, Mary Anne Patterson McCombs, was a bit bulky and more than a bit stern. A stay-at-home seamstress, she was as old-fashioned as the long skirts she wore. The McCombses lived comfortably, in a big brown two-story house that was more sturdy than fancy. It symbolized the McCombs way of life: solid and straightforward. The land, blessed by a nearby creek, dotted with fragrant apple trees, and able to accommodate a small kitchen garden, had been in the family for generations. Robert had been born on the very site where the big house now stood, in a log cabin, in 1872.

Though not poor, the McCombses were far from wealthy. And Titusville knew wealth—oil money, in fact. The nation's first commercially productive oil well had been drilled there, propelling a few families into an elite circle. They wintered in warm places and sent their children to private school. Their mansions were huge and ornate. But in the small-town culture, rich mixed easily with poor, and Ruth gained an intimacy with affluence, forever finding herself both repelled by and attracted to the rarefied world of the rich.

No matter where she went in life, she would always carry with her a number of family traits. Chief among them were resolve and stoicism. The hardscrabble McCombses were people who picked themselves up and dusted themselves off. Honesty was the number-one commandment. The family strengths were timeless, but to Ruth, it could also seem that her parents were hopelessly mired in the last century.

Chafing at the crabbed environment at home, where liquor and religion were shunned in equal measure, she found refuge in books, which took her to the far corners of the world. But even the family's temporary move to nearby Erie could not relieve the claustrophobia that she had begun to experience in Titusville. It was a pensive Ruth McCombs who looked out from the city's 1918 high school yearbook. Her entry, unlike the chirpy and chummy ones of her fellow students, read, "Ruth is rather hard to get acquainted with, but after you know her you find that she has many good qualities and is a friend worth having." If few people in northwest Pennsylvania really understood her, that was fine by Ruth. Like her older siblings, Jim and Helen, she planned to cut loose at the first possible opportunity.

After a semester at the University of Colorado and an experiment teaching English in Cuba, Ruth, with twenty-five dollars as her war chest, headed north to New York City.

Raven-haired and slim, Ruth Elizabeth McCombs was twenty-three years old when she first remade herself. Powdered and dressed up, she took on Manhattan, finding a job in fashion, where she could design and sew dresses for a population that bought up all the Paris knockoffs Seventh Avenue could produce. She took to her new life like a natural—utterly at ease at the center of a party, rarely seen without a smoke in one hand and a highball in the other. She became as quintessential a flapper as Clara Bow, one of the brassy, fun-loving girls in shimmering cocktail dresses who were, in the words of F. Scott Fitzgerald, "impudent" and "hard-berled," who flouted convention and danced with abandon. Ruth said there were only two things in the world she hated: going to bed at night and getting up in the morning.

She might have been in great demand, but it wasn't because she was pretty (she always said her face was not her fortune, and that it took an expensive photographer to bring out her best). She was so striking, though, that when she walked into a room, men noticed, and Bill Harkness was no exception.

Ruth Harkness could fill a room with her presence.
LOTTE JACOBI/COURTESY MARY LOBISCO

It didn't matter that she came from working folks in a small town, and he from big-city upper crusters. It meant nothing that she "had to work like the devil for a bare living," and that he maintained his comfort without a thought to employment. He was intrigued.

Together, they knew how to enjoy themselves, to kick up their heels at naughty, high-toned soirées and low-down speakeasies alike. During the postwar era of sexual freedom, the two bohemians became a full-

Bill Harkness, Ruth said, "spent most of his life on game trails in remote corners of the globe." COURTESY MARY LOBISCO

fledged couple. They were as good as married, without the traditional, stodgy sanctity of a wedding. Neither was a prude, and both loved physical pleasure. Ruth even joked about scandalous notions like being spanked on "a bare derriere."

At the beginning of their courtship, they found themselves constantly tucked away in some corner, slugging back bootleg booze and lost in intense conversation. Addicted to reading, they soon began swapping books on their favorite subject—exotic travel. Their leather-bound volumes were filled with high adventure and glimpses of strange cultures. Often they contained delicate fold-out maps shaded in beautiful colors, veined with blue rivers and dappled by the shadowy wrinkles of mountain ranges. The most captivating among these atlases were the half-finished ones, those in which the dense, busy portions would end abruptly, leaving blank whole uncharted territories—regions of the world still steeped in mystery. Here were the places that had not given up their secrets to Western travelers and mapmakers. Sitting together in the haze of cigarette smoke, warmed by a glass of whiskey, their imaginations racing, Bill and Ruth always found themselves drawn to those patches of the unknown.

Bill had spent most of his short adulthood "on game trails in remote corners of the globe," Ruth said, visiting India and China, Java, Borneo, and other islands of the Dutch East Indies. He thrived on the rough-and-tumble life in the field leavened by stints of footloose merriment in exotic cities. In long letters home, and then in intimate getting-reacquainted sessions on his return, he entranced Ruth with his tales of treks abroad.

His accounts, no doubt, were as gracefully told as the sagas the couple read together. For Bill was the romantically literary type with a classical education. He had passed college-entrance examinations in Latin, Greek, French, English, and ancient history. He described himself as an author and a man of letters and was an American intellectual in the mold of Teddy Roosevelt—the brave outdoorsman, as familiar with Milton as with a "Big Medicine" .405 rifle.

He and Ruth spent weekends at his family's estate in Connecticut, and sometimes slipped off for tropical romantic getaways to places like the Virgin Islands. They drank and philosophized. "A dash of absinthe," Ruth said, "and you analyze the hell out of everything." They read books, walked on the beach, and poured their hearts out to each other.

And there was so much to talk about. Each of them was haunted by a penetrating, persistent loneliness, suffering bouts of it even in a crowded room. Yet they craved solitude. To Bill and to Ruth, being alone was a complex state: the satisfaction of solitude played against a chronic sense of loneliness.

As they settled into a life together, and even after they were married, their rather elastic relationship was marked by intimacy and long periods of separation. Paradoxically, they seemed to grow closer while apart. When traveling, Bill found he could be utterly open with Ruth. In addressing her, he wrote more easily, and with greater clarity, than when scribbling in a private journal. Her intuition, her understanding of his very nature, was so complete, that just placing her name at the top of the page, he said, drew him out. He was so certain of a mystical connection between them that he never worried about how they would keep in touch despite the vagaries of international mail service and the fluid nature of his itineraries. "He had a divine faith," Ruth explained, "that I'd somehow know how to get letters to him and strangely enough I did."

Her responses were encyclopedic. She couldn't help "rambling"— telling him every detail of her activities and thoughts.

For Ruth, who would always feel that her family misunderstood her, there was, in this distant intimacy, a familiarity. She was accustomed to physical and emotional separations, and as Bill continued a life constantly on the campaign, his presence was a palpable part of her life.

SO ON THAT WINTRY February afternoon when Ruth found out that Bill was dead, her emotional loss was profound. She felt in a fog—incoherent and, she would reflect later, impossible to deal with.

The friends who rallied around her quickly became concerned about a practical matter. It was clear that the widow would receive a relatively small inheritance. With Bill and his father both dead, Bill's stepmother, who had inherited about $150,000 two years before, was the keeper of the estate. Ruth would always say that money didn't matter to her, and she proved it now as her financial state changed drastically. Facing life without Bill's purse, she didn't lift a finger to fight for a scrap of it. She was to receive about $20,000—a not-unpleasant sum in 1936, but not enough to last much more than a year for a Fifth Avenue address. It was for a young woman perhaps sufficient to live on for some time if she scrimped and lived a small life. But "small" wasn't in Ruth Harkness's vocabulary.

Her friends were distraught over the inequity of the distribution. And they saw that the apartment, the maid, the expensive portrait photographers, the luxury Ruth Harkness had been enjoying, would all go. In no time, she would be in the same pickle as everyone else living through the Depression.

She left it to her dearest friend, Hazel Perkins, an industrious and ambitious woman raising two boys alone, to negotiate and sometimes spar with Bill's stepmother to retrieve some of his personal effects from the family home—furniture, books, and his mother's jewelry.

Security wasn't Harkness's passion; in fact, it would be the last thing she would spend time dwelling on now. Over many chilly days and nights, she was drinking through teary-eyed reveries. In those sad, quiet hours she might even have heard echoes of a jaunty, bittersweet rendition of "Vilia," the signature aria from *The Merry Widow*, about a forest nymph who falls in love with a mortal man. Bill used to absentmindedly whistle the tune, which now could serve as a melancholy anthem for the couple.

Already in the numbed ache of those days, though, she had an inkling of what she wanted to do, and the twenty grand would be just the ticket. The rage of emotion that welled up inside her was being marshaled into conviction, a resolve that was probably too outrageous to say aloud. She decided that she wouldn't leave Bill's mission incomplete—she would pick it up and carry it to victory. After all, she reasoned, exploration was in her blood as much as it had been in his. She had spoiled for the voyages into the unknown just as Bill had. And at this point, who knew what the future would hold, so why live a modest life when she could have herself "one grand adventure"? She had the money, the purpose, and, with her husband's death, something else, something surprising. As she sent instructions for Bill's body to be cremated, her own freedom began to emerge from his ashes.

Like a swimmer who dives to the bottom of a pool and pushes off, it was often from the position of lowest circumstance that Ruth would rebound with enormous energy. Now she'd need it. For her to enter Bill's realm would be considered heresy.

Bill Harkness's background and exploits had placed him among an elite group of the time—wealthy lads with a taste for adventure, a cocktail shaker in one hand and a pistol in the other, as comfortable in black tie as they were in field khaki. Teddy Roosevelt's sons Theodore and Kermit described their brethren as the "brown lean men who drift quietly into New York" making plans to launch great expeditions, trekking "to lonely places where food is scant" and "danger a constant bedfellow."

It was a time in which seekers in science didn't need advanced degrees or rigorous course work. Bill and others like him were amateur zoologists of fine breeding, with solid Ivy League educations, who enjoyed the privileges of good standing with the heads of natural history museums and zoos. Funding was effortless—they either underwrote their own expeditions or used their status to hustle sponsors, always in the most gentlemanly way.

Handsome, articulate, well-educated daredevils, they made great copy, and the market for their wares was phenomenal. The cavernous, echoing halls of museums of natural history were still in search of new exhibit specimens, while the zoos that had sprung up across the United States were on the prowl for anything new or unique. In Bill and Ruth's young lifetimes several large mammals had just been described for the first time, including the mountain gorilla and the velvet-coated cousin to the giraffe, the okapi.

Zoos were seeking more than just the novel; they were also desperate to maintain their collections of better-known animals, which in some cases suffered very high mortality rates. In 1931, gorillas were as scarce and perishable as wild orchids. The Bronx Zoo assured visitors that "the agents of the New York Zoological Society are constantly on the watch for an opportunity to procure and send hither a good specimen of this wonderful creature." But it also warned that the viewing opportunity might be short. "Whenever one arrives all persons interested are advised to see it *immediately*,—before it dies of sullenness, lack of exercise, and indigestion," the guide read.

Demand for animals was strong enough that the dashing boys of high adventure would never fill a fraction of the orders. There was work enough for an army, but a definite caste system was established. Bill's crowd was at the top; below them were many other men from all walks of life, driven by every impulse imaginable: scholarly inclinations, a love of wildlife, greed, or a hunger for fame.

If in Ruth's zeal to join Bill on his treks, she had noted the presence of those few women who were in the game, there couldn't be a more obvious example than Osa Johnson. Flying zebra-striped and giraffe-spotted his-and-hers Sikorsky amphibious planes, Martin and Osa Johnson thrilled Americans with the movies they produced of exotic people and animals around the world. By filming naked "savages" and charging rhinos, and in exploring places rarely penetrated by westerners, the Johnsons were able to command $100,000 speaking tours. In the dark times of the Great Depression, the American public couldn't get enough of their derring-do. There were documentary films made for the American Museum of Natural History in New York, popular big-screen movies such as *Simba* and *Baboona*, and later, Osa's bestselling books, including *I Married Adventure*. Audiences and readers thrilled at the couple's stories of cannibals and cobras. In various scenes, Osa could be seen playing "Aloha" on the ukulele for a "cannibal king" or riding a zebra. Diminutive though she was, she once managed to pose carrying a full-grown Pygmy woman in her arms.

The Johnsons' keenest competition came from Frank "Bring 'Em Back Alive" Buck. In his own crowd-pleasing books and films, he battled man-eating tigers and venomous snakes. He was suave and dashing and was always able on film to emerge from seething jungles with his khakis still sharply creased.

Out of sight of the movie cameras and far below these high-toned characters were countless collectors working without advance pay and lacking formal association with any large institution. They were truly in the trenches, sweating it out in the tropics, freezing on snowy massifs, and always hoping for a big windfall. They often traveled on the cheap, trying to peddle whatever they had.

In newspaper stories, these exploits were portrayed as thrilling—crowded with bloodthirsty natives, marked by hidden peril at every turn. Rarely in the recounting was the casual cruelty of the actual captures related in detail.

Adult elephants often had their Achilles tendons slashed in order to let hunters collect the babies. If done correctly, the bleed-out would be painless, the men claimed. Distressed captive baby giraffes would often just crumple and die, despite the whole herds of goats employed to supply milk. Baboons would be tied, muzzled, and nearly mummified in cloth. Zebras might be whipped to exhaustion.

Over the course of his career, Buck boasted that he had delivered 39 elephants, 60 tigers, 62 leopards, 52 orangutans, 5,000 monkeys, 40 kangaroos and wallabies, 40 bears, and 100 snakes—in all, 10,000 mammals and 100,000 birds. The numbers that died along the way were incalculable, with the loss viewed not in moral or ethical terms but as a monetary issue. "If enough specimens die en route, the collector finds himself 'in the soup,' " Buck wrote.

While unaware of these horrible practices, Ruth certainly had been versed in the game's colorful cast of characters. And in 1933 one player had come knocking. Well over six feet tall, with a receding hairline and a devilish goatee, Lawrence T. K. Griswold was an old Harvard chum of Bill's, who pitched a proposal that would change the course of both Bill and Ruth's lives. He had an expedition in mind as he traveled to New York searching for a partner who had not only the backbone and temperament for such arduous travel but also the cash to float it.

Since Bill was the obvious first choice, Griswold went looking in the speakeasy district of New York at a little joint called Emilio's. As it turned out, he found Bill, who "was fortunately furnished with enough money to do whatever he wanted within reasonable bounds," idle at the moment and eager to go. And with Bill "in," it was easy to recruit the rest of the party.

Ruth Harkness wasn't impressed with Larry Griswold; she thought he was a bit of a sponger and a pretentious one at that. She also may not have cared for the way he took Bill away for such long periods on adventures that excluded her. She wanted to jump into the action herself. Alone, maybe Bill would have capitulated, but the team of Bill and Larry wouldn't budge: it was boys only.

The first Harkness-Griswold expedition targeted the Indonesian island of Komodo. They were in search of the biggest lizard on the planet, the elusive Komodo dragon, which had been introduced to the world in a scientific paper the decade before, and was one of the most sought-after creatures in existence. Weighing up to three hundred pounds, the Komodo has huge, curved, serrated teeth, perfect for tearing flesh. Great head and neck muscles and a jaw hinged for extra-wide opening aid the animals in bolting massive amounts of meat. The modern-day dinosaur would be a provocative prize.

Through the campaign, Bill and Larry depended on each other, confident enough in their own fortitude to always find humor in the face of mortal danger. Gaining success with their particular style of careless rich-boy swashbuckling, the team came away from the island in possession of several fine live specimens. But in Shanghai, on the way home, there were more high jinks to come.

Too busy romping in the most notorious city in the world, Bill was not aboard the ship, the *Empress of Asia,* as it pulled away with the rest of his party. Realizing the clutch he was in, he cabled Griswold with a one-word message—SKILLIBOOTCH—which reached the *Empress* as she entered the harbor of Nagasake. It was "Bill's own invention," Griswold would explain later, "and used to indicate an attitude of encouraging nonchalance." In a series of maneuvers worthy of Errol Flynn, Bill Harkness quickly grabbed an express boat out of Shanghai and hopped a train at Kobe, calmly materializing in Yokohama in time to meet the ship.

Bill was at the top of his game. At thirty-two he was fit, happy, and, having pulled off the trapping of the great Komodo lizards, successful. He had now established himself as a gifted hunter.

Back in New York in May 1934, showing off what *The New York Times* called three "Big Dragons," the Ivy League adventurers found that the experience had only whetted their appetite. They began plotting their next collaboration.

With "a yearning desire to blaze new trails in the field of zoology," Ruth said, Bill next made a plan as dangerous and exotic as they come. He and Griswold intended to travel to the other side of the world to capture the biggest prize of them all—a live giant panda. Very few people had ever seen one of these animals alive. Most of the population beyond the Tibetan borderland had never even heard of one. The animal was so little known, in fact, that when Bill first mentioned it to Ruth, she thought he had intended to say "panther," not panda.

HE MEANT PANDA all right, and that summer of 1934, he brought Ruth up to speed on the animal that was the hottest treasure in the world. Even in its native haunts, where animals were seen as sources of medicine and myth, symbols for poets and artists, little had ever been written about the panda. It was a living mystery in a mysterious region, a place that in the twenties and thirties was absolutely fascinating to Americans. And as intriguing as China was, high Tibet tantalized imagination even more, seeming as much fancy as fact. Everything related to the search for the giant panda appeared rather otherworldly, as decade after decade, the animal dodged Western stalkers with an uncanny, some would say supernatural, skill. Yet each passing year, the brutal and punishing competition was becoming more of a siren call, one that often led to death, ruin, or disappointment.

It had all begun in the spring of 1869 with the journey of a French Lazarist missionary, Père Armand David, through Baoxing, or what was then known as Muping. The holy man, who was also a naturalist of some repute, was invited for tea and biscuits at the home of a local landowner. When he noticed a great woolly pelt of a black-and-white bear, he immediately grasped its significance. Though he would go on to be the first to describe much of this portion of the natural world to the West, and have many species named after him, nothing in his illustrious career would compare to this one dazzling moment of discovery.

Commissioning a group of hunters, he would within weeks have two skins of his own—one of a young bear, another of an adult. He wrote in his diary that this "must be a new species of *Ursus*, very remarkable not only because of its color, but also for its paws, which are hairy underneath, and for other characters."

He named the species *Ursus melanoleucus*, or black-and-white bear, and shipped the pelts off to Alphonse Milne-Edwards at the natural history museum in Paris, gushing that this new creature was "easily the prettiest kind of animal I know."

While Milne-Edwards may have agreed with the assessment of the animal's beauty, he objected to the missionary's placement of it within the bear family, launching a debate about its classification—and whether it was closer to a bear or a raccoon—that would live on for more than a century. At the time, there was already one panda known to science, the little raccoonlike red panda. Milne-Edwards wanted the new animal to be called *Ailuropoda* (panda-foot) *melanoleuca* (black and white).

The creature would come to be known as the great panda, then the giant panda, and very quickly, in the assessment of historians, "the most challenging animal trophy on earth."

The appraisal of experts in the field only made it more mesmeric. In 1908 famed botanist Ernest Wilson spent months surveying the kingdom of the panda. "This animal is not common," he wrote, "and the savage nature of the country it frequents renders the possibility of capture remote." Despite his extensive wandering in the heart of this habitat, Wilson himself never saw any more of the panda than its dung.

Still, he would consider himself lucky, for one could encounter worse things than failure when looking for pandas. There were natural calamities, injuries, and often confusion, as the men who came to hunt the panda would find themselves utterly lost in the unforgiving terrain. The best known cautionary story was that of J. W. Brooke, a contemporary of

Wilson's, who was killed by Yi tribesmen, then known as Lolo, during his hunting expedition in search of giant pandas and other trophies. Brooke had been arguing with a local chief, and in a Western gesture of conciliation, which did not translate, he reached out to touch the man's shoulder. His faux pas was met with a slashing sword. Injured and shocked, the explorer reflexively shot and killed the chief and then was killed himself by the outraged Yi.

So elusive was the panda at this point that even "possibly" being the first westerner to see one alive in the wild was an honor. And over the next few years, two men made that claim: brigadier general George Pereira, the British military attaché in Peking, and J. Huston Edgar.

Spotting something that looked like a giant panda in the fork of an oak tree a hundred yards away inspired Edgar to write the poem "Waiting for the Panda," which read in part:

"You may wait 'till doomsday,
Yes, and miss him then."

Considering how many people had tramped through bamboo forests without coming upon a giant panda, it was natural for some to wonder if the animal had gone extinct, or perhaps never actually existed at all. Perhaps it was just "a fabulous animal," *The New York Times* speculated, "like the unicorn or the Chinese dragon." As doubtful, *The Washington Post* said, as a sea serpent.

By the time Teddy Roosevelt's sons Kermit and Theodore decided to step in, "the world was agog with expectation."

In the late 1920s, just returning from a central Asian expedition, the brothers reported hearing a seductive summons. "Spirits of the high places of earth, from the barren boulders and snows, hinted of days when the driving storm caked the ice on beard and face; spirits from the desert sang of blowing sand and blinding sun," they wrote. Vowing not to return empty-handed, the brothers decided to head east in pursuit of the animal that had "never been killed by a white man."

Funded by a generous patron of the Field Museum, to the tune, it was reported, of $100,000, the Roosevelts traveled to panda country via French Indochina with a strong crew that included a handsome young Chinese American named Jack Young, who would go on to conduct many expeditions himself and play an important role in Ruth Harkness's life.

Grueling as the Roosevelts' journey was, the two brothers were successful, shooting a giant panda on April 13, 1929. In an impressive show of fraternal loyalty, they would always claim to have fired simultaneously, killing the animal together, and sharing the credit in equal parts.

As their panda, as well as the purchased skin of another, went to the Field Museum for examination, stuffing, and exhibition, envious natural history museums all over America began to pine for their own pelts. The Roosevelt triumph opened the floodgates, inflaming "the imaginations of the younger generation of American would-be explorers," *The China Journal* would write, launching waves of daredevils in "expedition after expedition" that marched into "panda country along the Tibetan borders of West China after this rare and elusive animal."

In New York, in the summer of 1934, as Bill spoke to Ruth about his own plans for a new expedition, the bar on panda hunting had been raised even higher. Killing a panda could still bring glory, as it had for the Brooke Dolan expedition in 1931 but capturing one alive would be a historic achievement.

Noting the competitive climate, *The Washington Post* predicted a gold rush. "Want to make a small fortune—perhaps as much as $25,000?" it asked. Nab a giant panda, and "the heads of all the zoos in the world will beat a path to your door to bid on it." It warned, however, that if hunters wanted that cash, they would have to be quick, for it would be only the very first live panda that would warrant such a large payday.

Bill Harkness and Larry Griswold did hurry, making plans to leave by the end of September. During the frenzied preparations, however, Bill found himself overtaken by something beyond expedition fever. At the very last moment, he and Ruth decided to marry.

In a civil service in Rye, New York, on Sunday, September 9, 1934, Ruth Elizabeth McCombs and William Harvest Harkness, Jr., made their relationship official. Plain and simple, the ceremony was held in a municipal building. There had been no ambition for a proper wedding, and now, with the latest news from the field coming in, there was no time for a traditional honeymoon. Just two days before Bill and Ruth's vows, explorer Dean Sage had reached one of the farthest outposts in China in his quest to land a giant panda. The race was on.

Heading up what newspapers loftily referred to as the Griswold-Harkness Asiatic Expedition, Bill and Larry, along with two friends, headed out on September 22 for what they said could amount to a three-year endeavor.

That meant that within two weeks of her wedding, Harkness was anchored at home in New York City, sitting vigil for a man who had darted to the other side of the world in the company of his little hell-raising fraternity. Before marriage, she would have been free to travel, but now, with a husband gone on a major expedition, her duty was to sit tight.

AFTER A FEW WILD adventures in and around Borneo, and some high-class socializing with Hollywood leading man Ronald Colman in Indonesia, Bill Harkness and company finally reached Shanghai in January 1935. Within weeks, everything began to deteriorate.

First of all, the members of the Griswold-Harkness Asiatic Expedition were bailing out at every turn, leaving only Lawrence Griswold's handsome and wild-hearted cousin LeGrand "Sonny" Griswold and Bill to carry on. Or attempt to carry on. They could go nowhere without permits, and the documents weren't materializing. Through charm and bribery, Bill Harkness had nimbly secured visas, permissions, and transportation in many countries. Here in China the bureaucracy wouldn't yield. His advancement was opposed by the all-powerful science bureau, Academia Sinica, and also by both national and provincial agencies concerned by the movement of Communist troops.

Nonetheless, *The China Journal*, a well-respected magazine with a scientific bent, reported that given Bill's experience and the time he had allowed himself for the hunt, his chances for success were good.

Early on, Bill met up with an interesting character, nearly a generation older than himself, named Floyd Tangier Smith. Bill had money and no expedition, and Smith had expedition camps established in panda country and experience with Chinese officials, but no money. A partnership of mutual need was suggested. Ignoring his doctor's orders for three months of complete rest followed by a year of reduced activity, Smith signed on. Each man thought the other just might get him on track; neither had any idea of the deep and long-lasting consequences of their association.

The commencement of the new affiliation with Smith didn't seem to budge the permit process one bit, which led a frustrated Bill Harkness to begin a strange series of disappearing acts. The Shanghai papers just then were filled with stories of kidnappers and ransom schemes. Bearing a draft for five thousand dollars at the time of his first escapade, Bill seemed a likely target.

On March 18, United Press carried a dispatch about him headlined SCIENTIST VANISHES FROM TRAIN IN CHINA: POLICE DOUBT THAT W.H. HARK-NESS HAS BEEN KIDNAPED. The story said the "seeker of wild animals" was reported missing "under mysterious circumstances," having somehow evaporated on the train between Nanking and Shanghai four days earlier. The next day, UP announced that the "famed American naturalist" was just fine at the Palace Hotel, but that he was not forthcoming about what had happened.

Weeks later Bill went missing again. WILLIAM HARKNESS HUNTED IN CHINA: SHANGHAI POLICE SEEKING NEW YORK CLUBMAN ran the headline over an Associated Press report. It seemed that Bill was back on the lam, falling out of touch with his Western friends. His one original remaining expedition member, Sonny Griswold, confided it was clear that Bill had not been taken by bandits as had been reported. This time, Bill was found holed up in a hotel under the name Hansen.

When the frustrated explorer was dragged before the district attorney, he explained that he was trying to "forget" his great disappointment over failing to secure a permit for his expedition.

Worse, that same month, Bill slid further behind in the panda-hunting roster. The fourth panda to fall to a westerner was claimed by Captain

H. Courtney Brocklehurst, a Brit who had been a game warden in the Sudan. Yet, the tally of giant pandas taken by westerners was still, according to historians, remarkably low.

More than ever, big museums in America were in a froth to get their own specimens. "As a result," historians have noted, "these hunting parties began to overlap with increasing frequency."

It was an exciting time to be in the field. But that was the problem. Bill wasn't in the field, he was stuck in Shanghai. And there was a further humiliation in store, as the authorities decided to monitor him. He was ordered to report personally to the district attorney's office every three days to ensure that a U.S. marshal wouldn't have to go looking again. A dejected Bill Harkness declared he would leave soon for home.

FOR NEARLY TWO YEARS, Ruth Harkness's only glimpse of the Far East had come through her husband's correspondence—tissue-thin envelopes with their exotic stamps and datelines: the South Seas, Tawi-tawi, Zamboanga, the Dutch East Indies, British North Borneo, Shanghai. She eagerly tore into them, craving news of the man she loved, hoping always that one would contain an invitation to come join him.

Through overtures in her own letters, Ruth managed to extract an offer from him; instead of having to wait for the next expedition, there was a chance that she could actually join him in China. Together, they would reach those mysterious places on the map whose very names, she said, "stir the imagination." As it turned out, though, the tantalizing proposition was quickly rescinded when Bill suddenly received permission to travel, allowing him to head up-country immediately.

By this point, Harkness and Smith had been joined by a latecomer. Just weeks before, an adventurer Bill had not known previously came aboard—Gerald, or Gerry, Russell. He was of Bill's ilk—a young, Cambridge-educated Englishman—though one who had not so far proved himself much of a player. The press accounts of this expedition barely mentioned Russell at all, yet he would play a role in Harkness matters for quite some time.

Although one important government permission had been granted, many others were not in place as Bill began the journey to Chengdu, where Smith was waiting with the equipment. The three had decided to gamble that the rest of the authorizations would come through while they traveled.

Despite the uncertainty, as he flew over the great yellow waterway, the Yangtze, Bill must have been relieved to finally be on his way. In July 1935 *The China Journal* was reporting that the "Harkness Expedition" was in the field. But it wasn't to last. Right at the threshold to panda country, near Leshan, in Sichuan, the party was rebuffed because of unresolved permit problems. By September 30, Bill was right back where he started—in Shanghai.

There was no mention of failure, and hardly any acknowledgment of Bill Harkness for that matter, in an interview Smith gave to the *China Press* shortly afterward. Though Bill was underwriting the endeavor, his partner said only, "I always take a group of trained men, while on this next trip I have the good fortune to be accompanied by Mr. William H. Harkness, who is interested in collecting live animals from the interior." Later Smith would even say that aside from the money, Bill had only been a handicap. At the moment, Smith professed optimism, telling the press that the two would be up-country again soon, with plans to be back in Shanghai by February or March. He hoped to have secured a panda carcass by then.

Instead, Harkness and Smith would be dry-docked for months, awaiting permissions that did not come through until January. And by then it was too late; Bill Harkness had fallen ill. The heavy smoker and drinker was being ravaged by throat cancer.

CHAPTER TWO

INHERITING AN EXPEDITION

UT OF THE BLUE, before winter had changed to spring, a young British aristocrat presented himself to Ruth Harkness. Fresh-faced, impeccably mannered, and idealistic-seeming, Gerald Russell was the British junior partner from Bill Harkness's last expedition. Having been traveling for some length of time, he was unaware of Bill's death. Ruth was living in a flat in a remodeled house at 333 West Eighteenth Street when Russell sat talking to her, making clear that he had been immensely impressed by her husband. He found him to be "tough and determined," two characteristics that were vital in a field companion. In China Russell had been sure there were great things in store for Bill Harkness.

As terrible and hard to take in as the news he heard now was, a redeeming thought surfaced in his mind while they spoke: why shouldn't Ruth "continue the expedition her husband had started"? It seemed unfair, wrong even, to let Bill's legacy trail away into oblivion. "After Bill's death," Russell said, "someone bearing his name should get the first giant panda."

Ruth had already been thinking just that. Bill's remains were to be burned to ash, but not his hopes and dreams. She had the will to do it, having always longed to make the trek herself, and with no one else to stand in for him, she felt a moral imperative. Practically speaking, with Bill's gear and bank accounts left behind, the foundation for a new expedition was already in place.

With Russell's encouragement, Ruth Harkness's desires didn't seem so preposterous. And additionally, he provided concrete information about how she should proceed.

Right off, he urged her to join forces with Floyd Smith. Harkness had already been in touch with Smith, who was waiting for her decision about the distribution of Bill's effects, though she didn't know much about him outside of the references to him in Bill's letters.

The bare details were that he was in his fifties, "an old China hand," as they used to say, a man who had spent the bulk of his time in the East. Russell, who thought Smith "the cream of the earth; a great gentleman, esteemed and loved by all," endorsed him now.

At the same moment that Russell was singing his praises, however, Smith was in a fix in Chengdu, where he had been stationed waiting for Bill's arrival. Bill's death had knocked the legs out from under him. It might not have affected him emotionally, but it did, as Smith put it, "upset all calculations." Forever racing to stay one step ahead of financial ruin, Smith now found himself stranded in western China, flat broke, and reduced to eating cheap "coolie food." He needed to extricate himself from this predicament as quickly as possible, as he set about his new dealings with Bill's widow. He had made an agreement with Bill from the start that Ruth Harkness would receive Bill's half of any proceeds the endeavor produced. Whether he liked it or not, she now represented Bill's interests.

From her perspective in New York, no matter what Smith's character or worth, Harkness would need to make some momentous decisions. Bill had bank accounts and a tremendous amount of accumulated gear in Shanghai. It was up to her to determine what should be done about them.

Russell could be of enormous help. He vowed his allegiance to the cause, offering to sign on to the expedition himself, and take up with Mrs. Harkness where he had left off with her husband. It seemed like a windfall to Harkness, and it must have to Russell too. For when he next revealed that he was financially embarrassed, she agreed to underwrite him.

The two set a plan. They would meet in Europe to solidify arrangements, then get an expedition together in Shanghai. Once Ruth picked up Bill's ashes, she could head toward the frontier. It all seemed so perfect.

But, of course, it was madness. Without one factor in her favor, Ruth Harkness had decided she was the one to capture the giant panda. And she was totally out of her league.

ON FRIDAY, APRIL 17, 1936, Harkness boarded the Dollar liner *American Trader,* along with a raucous mob of her dearest friends, who had all come to see her off. In the close confines of her little cabin, the air was blue, she said, with the haze of cigarette smoke. Cocktail glasses clinked, bodies spilled out into the passageway, and waves of laughter erupted.

To many of those present, this was one jolly good joke. Harkness didn't mind the ribbing—in fact, she laughed right along with them, only too happy to list her inadequacies as an explorer. She knew nothing of expeditions, hunting, or working with native trappers. She had no idea what to expect of the rough terrain or reports of murderous bandits deep in the interior of China. She wouldn't even walk a city block if there was a taxi nearby to be hailed.

"She's as mad as a hatter," her brother, Jim, had announced from his uncomfortable position wedged on the lower berth. His sister's sinking her tiny inheritance into an effort to capture a live giant panda was preposterous. None of the he-men who had gone off to do it had come close. And besides, what the heck was a panda, anyway?

Harkness's best friend and staunchest ally tried to defend her. Hazel Perkins responded that had she no children herself, she too would take up such an adventure. "I'd probably do wilder and more impractical things than hunting pandas," she said loyally to the gathered crowd, but then added, "if there is anything more so."

Perkins may have been the only believer. The rest of the friends around Harkness that day would certainly not be the last to underestimate her in this venture. They and so many others could not see past the gaiety and good humor to the resolve that was as much a trait of Harkness as her trademark glossy black hair.

Under cloudy skies, Ruth Harkness set off for adventure that late Friday afternoon aboard an oceangoing liner. She was among a throng of giddy passengers, many of whom stood huddled against the biting sea wind, watching the Statue of Liberty grow dim in the distance.

The crossings to Europe and then China, the stays in London and Paris, would be a blur of late-night cocktail parties, masquerade competitions, and shipboard pranks. Harkness would keep the bars open till nearly dawn. She would throw recorked bottles containing funny notes overboard. And once, she and a group of revelers would even trap the ship's captain inside his sleeping cabin, staking a threatening pirate's note complete with skull and crossbones on his door with a big knife.

Russell met her in London and then the two left for France, to join his family. At a magnificent château in the Rhône Valley, she discovered that the same Gerry Russell who needed her money to cover his trip to China was from a clan of titled parents and stepparents, whose friends were all a mess of "princes—counts—viscounts—marquises, etc, etc." The country life of swimming, riding, and tennis reminded her of days with Bill's family, but then, anything and everything reminded her of him. "More than ever am I missing Bill," she wrote.

She was, by the time she boarded the *Tancred* in Marseilles and settled into a luxurious cabin, feeling unsure about Gerry Russell. "Sometimes I think I'm rather fond of Gerry in a protective way and then again I don't like him much," she mused. He was outwardly courteous and considerate. But she began to wonder if he actually had "any depth of character." He seemed to be missing a sense of determination.

She had plenty of time to mull everything over as the *Tancred* plowed its way east over the next two weeks. From Suez on, she found herself in what she called a Somerset Maugham frame of mind—sipping cocktails on deck while being mesmerized by the "disturbingly beautiful" scenery that passed before her. At Port Said she watched the sun become an enormous red ball sinking lower and lower down behind the marshes. She stayed up on deck for hours, and long after darkness had fallen, she remained as the ship's powerful searchlights scanned the shore. Long after midnight, when the captain came out in his pajamas to sit beside her and speak of the solitary nature of a sailor's life, she couldn't help thinking of the loneliness of "all life."

The fabled Orient was striking a deep chord within her, one that intensified with the passing of each nautical mile. Every port seemed to strengthen a mystical connection, especially in Hong Kong, which was nothing short of a spiritual revelation.

A WHISKEY SODA in one hand and a Chesterfield in the other, Ruth Harkness stepped from the shipowner's home out into the nighttime darkness of the tropical lawn. Her friend, the captain, had taken her swimming and shopping during the day, and then after a change of clothes to this small dinner party. The city was sweltering, but here, high on one of Hong Kong's magnificent peaks, the air was balmy. Harkness knew she was in for a beautiful view of the bay, for when they had arrived at the house earlier she had glimpsed the warm colors of the sunset in rippled reflection below. Nothing, though, could have prepared her for what she was about to see. As she made her way out to the edge of the yard, she gasped. She simply could not at first comprehend what she saw before her.

Above were moon and cloud, and the millions of stars of the night sky. Below, the sea had been transformed into its own glittering, dancing galaxy as hundreds of boats—flat-bottomed Chinese junks—crowded together to fish by torchlight.

Boundaries vanished as sea and sky appeared in mirror image. She was now in the land of yin and yang, unity and separation. In this realm, opposites fit into each other, hold the seed of the other, become each other. It is where light and dark, male and female, heaven and earth, are reconciled.

Ruth Harkness experienced a strange sensation that would never leave her—that here, on the other side of the world, she was "in some inexplicable way—home."

PAST OIL-SUPPLY DEPOTS, repair docks, dilapidated warehouses, and factories belching black smoke, the SS *Tancred* cut velvety furrows through the silted waters of the Huangpu River. Coming on the heels of the most sweeping vistas imaginable, the approach to Shanghai was dirty and ugly. Oppressively hot too, for this was one of the most miserable days the steamy port had to offer. Harkness couldn't help feeling let down. If Hong Kong had been celestial, Shanghai, "the Whore of the East," was truly of the earth. Harkness would thus be surprised at how quickly she grew to love Shanghai, to embrace its very filth and to recognize the divine not just in the stars above, but in the ground below her feet.

But at that moment, even as the ship took a sharp left turn with the bend of the waterway at Soochow Creek and the scene changed to opulence, she still had her doubts. Here, amid the architectural magnificence that marked the beginning of what Europeans and Americans would consider the city proper—the steel-and-concrete dynasty of the International Settlement—was the Shanghai of movies and novels.

Harkness took in the handsome buildings that lined the shore. Possessing what had been described as a "distinctly skyward" inclination, each tried to outdo the next for stateliness and panache. There was the posh Shanghai Club, the domed Hong Kong and Shanghai Bank building, and the grandest structure of them all, the pyramid-capped Cathay Hotel. All the marble and granite, columns, bas-reliefs, flying buttresses, and tile mosaics made it resemble London or Paris or New York—an effect the Western businessmen were aiming for. But China wouldn't be submerged so easily, and fluttering incongruously in delicate motion before the massively built-up shore were the great poetic junks—hundreds

Harkness stayed at the Palace, across Nanking Road from the pyramid-topped Cathay along the Bund. COURTESY MARY LOBISCO

of them, clustered like butterflies, their sails veined by seams, many of their prows decorated with alert eyes.

East really did meet West here, though it wasn't always an easy fit. In order to erect these Western skyscrapers—at ten to twenty stories high some of the tallest in Asia—earth, if not heaven, had to be moved. Concrete rafts were constructed to steady the structures in the shifting muck. Raised up from marshland and mudflats, Shanghai was the convergence not just of East and West but also of water and land, Occidental and Oriental, rich and poor. It was paper lanterns and neon lamps. It was civilized and barbaric. And anything was possible—poor men could become wealthy overnight. Chinese communism could be born in this enclave of Western capitalism. Shanghai was fluid and ever changing, a robust half-breed throbbing with its own hybrid vigor.

It was like nothing else in the world. In this notorious town, brine, fish, acrid factory smoke, ambition, sorrow, and hope all blended together in a great gurgling and vivifying ooze. The place reeked of it, and the smell was noted by every writer who passed through. It was thick and heavy, according to one, mixing the scents of "open-air cooking, offal, pissoirs, the fumes of opium, and decaying food." Shanghai possessed what the Chinese called *rinao*, a dizzying assault of the senses that could choke—or resuscitate—a person. At the moment of her arrival, Ruth Harkness wasn't so sure which it would be for her. It was a test of character—even the mighty generalissimo, Chiang Kai-shek, had said the city was "a furnace for the making of men." And Harkness herself would soon feel that heat facing some of the toughest trials of her journey.

As the *Tancred* slowed and came to a stop, the heavy air draped itself over the passengers. At least Harkness could be grateful that she had tanned herself while out at sea precisely so she could forgo silk stockings on days like this. Swarming the railings, the passengers now squinted through this fevered, hazy blur for a closer look at the famous city.

Thousands stood along the water, carrying flowers, waving hats, and craning their necks to catch sight of a fiancée, a brother, a classmate. There were men in business suits, women in kimonos. Clamoring for work were half-starved coolies in blue, loose-cut trousers, Japanese cabdrivers in white. Missionaries jostled with millionaires. With Americans, Chinese, Russians, English, Japanese, French, and German Jewish refugees—fifty nationalities—it looked as though half the world's population had turned out carrying the entire world's expectations. Shanghai might have been known for its vice, but high hope was truly its chief commodity. Nowhere was that feeling more raw than down on the waterfront where the waiting crowds sweltered.

Pressed among the colorful and expectant crowd that day, fresh from his debacle in Chengdu, was the gaunt and sallow Floyd Tangier Smith, with his beautiful half-Scottish, half-Japanese wife, Elizabeth. Known as "Ajax" to his friends, and "Buster" to his family, Smith was a man with more than his share of expectation. The tall, bespectacled banker-turned-adventurer, now fifty-four, had still not landed his one big fortune. He wasn't averse to accepting handouts from his family back in the States, however abashedly. For Smith, there was always tomorrow. Over the years, his letters home had been filled with optimism about his next big break and future expeditions that would surely bring "honest to goodness money." While he had been hoping to find just that the year before with the Bill Harkness partnership, that enterprise, like many of Smith's previous ones, hadn't panned out.

Now, as sweat trickled down the backs of those standing by at the waterfront, the hunter patiently lay in wait for the one person who could get the expedition's finances back on track, who might even, if everything went just so, change his fortunes for good.

If God lets Shanghai endure,
He owes an apology to Sodom and Gomorrah.
—A CHRISTIAN EVANGELIST IN THE EARLY 1920s

It took a small international caravan—Smith, his wife, and several coolies, with a few Russians thrown in—to transport Harkness and her belongings to the hotel. They squeezed through the crowd, navigating the fantastic chaos of the Shanghai streets. There were rickshaws, automobiles, buses, trams, wheelbarrows, bicycles, and carriages; streetside market stalls were piled high with melons and onions; children shouted themselves hoarse, hawking English-language newspapers such as the *Shanghai Times*.

Harkness's group negotiated the short but tumultuous length of the waterfront up to the calm of an American favorite, the Palace Hotel. The conservative old Palace, white with red trim, was handsome and more than respectable, though its day as the best hotel in the ever-changing Shanghai had come and gone. The Palace was now dwarfed in stature and style by others, particularly its neighbor across Nanking Road, that luxurious wonder, the twenty-story, air-conditioned Cathay. Inside the Palace's gleaming mahogany-paneled lobby, as was painfully obvious on this day, the modern marvel of air-conditioning had not been installed. It didn't matter. Harkness was on a budget, and at twelve dollars a night, the little hotel that had been good enough for Bill during his long stay in Shanghai was good enough for her.

From the moment she settled in to Bill's old digs, the introductions and invitations poured in, and she wrote home immediately, frantic for the satin evening slip she had forgotten to pack.

Within days, a fleet of pilots from the China National Aviation Corporation, or CNAC, which was a partnership between the Chinese government and Pan Am, began to court her. There was a Frenchman in hot pursuit, a German Jew, and a "darling" young pilot in his twenties who buzzed around, taking her out often. Speaking of her youngest suitor, she joked to friends that she'd "like a son to be like him." Among her many new pals was an American newspaper reporter named Victor Keane, a fun-loving graduate of her own alma mater, the University of Colorado. The two fell in tight with each other, and the hard-drinking, wisecracking Vic showed her the town.

Certainly there was plenty to see. The first word under the "nightlife" section of one mid-thirties guide to Shanghai was "WHOOPEE!" And if the reader required more of an explanation, it was provided: "High hats and low necks; long tails and short knickers; inebriates and slumming puritans . . . When the sun goes in and the lights come out Shanghai becomes another city."

At about seven in the evening, Harkness would find herself sitting in a low wicker chair on the great verandah of the Race Club, sipping gimlets and chatting up a whole new smart set. The club was a lush, green twelve-acre oasis in the heart of Shanghai, and as night closed in and the sky darkened, Harkness could watch the surrounding city begin to blaze with light, its candy-colored neon signs snapping to life with luminous threads of violet, magenta, and fuchsia braided into Chinese characters.

At the Chinese clubs, local gangsters danced the rumba to Russian orchestras. Chinese rich boys with jet-black hair, brilliantined to a lacquer finish, squired modern Chinese girls in stiletto heels and high-necked brocade silk sheaths slit up to the hips. Revelers could try a Polish mazurka or the Parisian Apache, the carioca, the tango. Crooners and torch singers bawled American jazz through the night.

Harkness and Keane would commence with drinks in the afternoon, sometimes finding themselves having "closed up Shanghai at six the next morning." Cocktail hour, it was said, ended in Shanghai "anytime between 2 A.M. until Breakfast," and then for most it was off to Delmonico's, in the Chinese territory, for a plate of scrambled eggs just before dawn. Exhausted partygoers then would head back to their hotels, where the early-morning vacuums would have already started humming.

Harkness couldn't have asked for a better guide than Vic Keane. He was the picture of the suave, good-natured American in Shanghai. He lived amicably away from his wife, while in a large, handsome apartment he kept a beautiful and possessive White Russian mistress, whom Harkness described as "a really entrancing creature who speaks practically no English, but enough I gather to make his life fairly miserable." When he had to make trips out of town, his wife not only took over the reporting job for him but also assumed guardianship of the mistress, who was "as helpless as a kitten."

Shanghai was a place of serious debauchery and vicious crime.

Because Western nations had carved it up into three distinct sections—the International Settlement, the French Concession, and the Chinese area—there were ample cracks in the system, allowing crime to fester. A lax moral atmosphere, multiple jurisdictions, and incredible wealth combined to make Shanghai "an outlaw's haven." And the riches were truly enormous. Six million dollars a month was paid out in protection money in the opium-distribution rackets alone.

Curious about the notorious drug, Harkness found someone who could take her deeper into the hidden side of Shanghai for a better look. In her letters home, she described him only as a Norwegian newspaperman, hard at work on an exposé of opium use in the city. He may very well have been Henry Hellssen, "Denmark's globetrotting journalist," who was in and out of Shanghai during that period. The two explored the dark, narrow streets of Chapei, the old Chinese City, which was rarely seen by westerners, who found it repugnant and frightening. The few who did venture this way were likely to be addicted to "the pipe" themselves.

In the Chinese parts of Shanghai, Harkness saw beauty and a vibrant history. "All of China, eating, sleeping, living, and loving there as they have for thousands of years—all in the dirty, and airless streets," she wrote. Harkness pressed on, game to infiltrate even the most wretched dens. With her newspaper chum as guide, she made her way into a filthy, ramshackle building, where the air was redolent, Harkness said, with the sweet and sickening scent of opium. The westerners stayed to observe a Chinese man and woman as they lay on couches smoking long pipes filled with the drug.

Through such wanderings, she was discovering that there were two Shanghais, and that it was the Chinese one that beckoned to her.

THE WESTERN-RULED SHANGHAI that Harkness saw in 1936 had been in the making for centuries, but it really got into gear over a British trade imbalance that built throughout the 1800s. English merchants were buying up silk and tea from China but selling little or nothing in return. The self-reliant Chinese didn't want anything, and were pleased with the way trade was going—their goods heading out, silver flowing in. The Brits eventually came up with a commodity that they could sell—cheap opium from India and Persia. Once only the drug of the wealthy in China, it could now be sold inexpensively for a mass market. And the populous country made for one hell of a mass market. In the 1830s, enough opium poured in to keep twelve million inhabitants smoking. Not wanting their citizens addicted to the drug, Chinese officials attempted to keep it out.

The livid opium merchants were able to press the British government into putting its guns in the service of their cause, with an outcome that was entirely predictable. With no comparable army or navy, China lost the 1839–1842 Opium War. In victory, the British crafted an incredible agreement, the Nanjing Treaty, which granted them unrestricted trade, as well as land rights in five major ports. Quickly, the United States, France, and other countries demanded their own table settings for the feeding frenzy.

It was all a shock to China. Traditionally, the country had been able to maintain an exalted position nearly on reputation alone. Its strength was in moral, not military, standing. In dealings with fellow Asian countries, China, with its ancient civilization and Confucian canon of honor and ethics, had always been treated with respect. It called itself *Zhongguo*, the Middle Kingdom, the center of the world, ruled by the Son of Heaven. And indeed, the Japanese, Vietnamese, and Koreans all seemed to agree, incorporating the best elements of Chinese culture into their own.

The inherent dissonance between China and the Western world would have terrible consequences. The Chinese viewed foreign relations not as a commercial opportunity but as a cultural endeavor. Self-sufficient and revered, China was accustomed to courtly and rigid formalities. All strangers were barbarians and were expected when approaching the emperor to humble themselves by bending down and performing the "kowtow." The country's high-ranking, well-educated envoys and emissaries would never debase themselves by undertaking issues of trade and money. To the crass, tough, and greedy westerners, it all added up to an unlocked storeroom.

Now the culture that had invented both paper and printing was being handed documents containing insulting demands. The country that had produced the first compass and gunpowder was at the mercy of bullying foreign fleets, which used these inventions against it. Worse, under the new rules of extraterritoriality, foreign nations had the unlikely right to abide by their own laws in certain designated places, such as the busiest and most lucrative ports in the nation. "We are being carved into pieces like a melon!" was a common cry. The occupiers developed a sense of entitlement and superiority that Harkness found offensive.

The funny thing was that much of the snobbery was affected. People became whatever they wanted in Shanghai. In this city, it was impolite to ask about someone's past because it was assumed there *was* something to hide. As in American gold-rush towns of the 1800s, what counted here was drive and ambition, not family connections. For most, Shanghai was a temporary stop—and the more temporary, the better. The point of coming here, according to one newspaper, was "to make money and get out." Yet many foreigners stayed, decade upon decade, joking that they couldn't go home because they wouldn't know how to get along without five servants anymore.

IT WAS TOO EARLY in her trip for Harkness to have developed a routine. In the drenching, one-hundred-degree heat of that summer in Shanghai, she sometimes found herself holed up in her hotel room, sitting naked on her bed, banging out letters home on her portable typewriter.

Some days she would pinch pennies and have the thirty-cent lunch served at the YMCA. For low-key socializing, she'd go to dinner with Elizabeth Smith at a favorite little sukiyaki restaurant in Japantown. Within a small, screened private room, they would sit on cushions before a low table and enjoy fried prawns and seaweed. They drank hot sake from tiny blue bowls and watched as the food was cooked right before them.

The dress-designer-turned-explorer also discovered the most talented tailor in the world here in Shanghai. "ZIANG TAI: Any Kinds of Ladies Tailor and Skin, Etc" read his business card. Ziang would conjure perfect dresses with matching jackets from the sketches that Harkness drew for him. Each would cost the equivalent of two American dollars. Playing the part of the oblivious socialite, Harkness would write, "There is really nothing like the stimulus of a new dress to brighten the atmosphere."

There were days when she would take an aimless ride in a rickshaw, immersing herself in the choreographed commotion of the streets, where banners in bold Chinese characters waved down through shafts of sunlight, advertising sales, silks, mah-jongg sets, live birds, ivory. She found Shanghai to be "a great sprawling rambling" place filled with beautiful faces.

How preposterous, she wrote home, that westerners say the Chinese all look alike. The people she saw on Bubbling Well Road were as different from one another as the pedestrians on Fifth Avenue in New York. And in those faces she rarely, if ever, detected anxiety. She came to be-

Harkness saw there were two Shanghais, and it was the Eastern version she was drawn toward. ALFRED T. PALMER/COURTESY JULIA PALMER GENNERT

lieve that the poorest Chinese peasant had something most Americans, even the richest—perhaps particularly the richest—never knew: inner peace.

Just down the street from her hotel, she could shop on the ultra-cosmopolitan Nanking Road. Every luxury item in the world was carried here. There were goldsmiths, silversmiths, silk emporiums, and shops carrying sandalwood carvings. Several blocks west of the Bund, the waterfront promenade, were the top Chinese department stores, Sincere and Wing On, in whose food sections one could "buy 'thousand-year-old eggs,' dried grasshoppers, Russian caviar, Camembert cheese, and Hormel's soups."

In order to negotiate her way, Harkness began to pick up the bastard language known as pidgin English, a trading tongue that mixed English, Chinese, Indian, and Portuguese and followed the pronunciation, idiom, and grammar of Chinese. Pidgin English solved one problem, that of basic communication, while creating another, making Chinese speakers seem simpleminded. According to the guidebooks, "Catchee one piece rickshaw" meant "get a rickshaw." "Talkee my" was "Let me know." "Chop chop" meant "quickly." "How muchee?" was "How much is that?"

In all of her rambles, Harkness was never afraid, although some crimes, such as armed robbery, were so commonplace that Ralph Shaw, a British journalist in Shanghai, reported that they weren't worth coverage. Kidnappings too were so frequent that most wealthy Chinese employed bodyguards—often big, strapping Russians—for protection. There were "more gangsters in Shanghai than Chicago ever saw in the heyday of Capone," Shaw claimed.

The headlines in the city's papers screamed of suicides and gruesome crimes, and while Harkness was in town, there were plenty. Within days of her arrival, an American military officer leaped to his death from her hotel. A Chinese man's head was found near the Moon Palace Hotel. And the headless, nude body of a Chinese woman was discovered chopped up and stuffed into a leather suitcase near the Shanghai Rowing Club.

Drugs, gambling, prostitution. Chinese gangsters in pinstriped suits carrying tommy guns. Triad bosses displaying long, opium-stained nails and wearing silk brocade gowns. International con men who found refuge in the city that didn't require a passport. Shanghai was a hideout for criminals of all countries. In this wild town, the top bad guys were colorful celebrities, with schemes that could exist only in Shanghai. Huang Jinrong, or "Pockmarked Huang," not only ran the biggest racket going—the notorious Green Gang—he was also a high-ranking Chinese detective with the French police. He and his associate Du Yuesheng, or "Big-Eared Du," wielded power equally with municipal officials, gangster kings, and more. With their henchmen they were guns for hire in the massive political upheavals that would change China forever. When Chiang Kai-shek's Nationalist government wanted to teach a lesson to organized labor or Communists, Huang's bone breakers were called in.

Along with crime, there were ample doses of vice. Shanghai boasted the longest bar in existence. And by 1930, it possessed more prostitutes per capita than any other city in the world. Here, the most depraved people from all walks of life came to satisfy their urges. One particularly twisted warlord from Shandong Province, a six-foot-seven maniac with a shaved skull, loved to sweep into Shanghai surrounded by soldiers numbering in the thousands. Fond of decapitating enemies and posting their heads on telegraph poles, Chang Tsung-chang played as hard as he butchered. He was said to keep forty-two concubines, and he once sodomized a teenage boy during a dinner party as all the guests and sing-song girls looked on.

Shanghai debauchery was legendary, but for the foreigners the city was not quite its lively self in the summer of 1936. Western residents traditionally decamped to cooler country places for the hot season, and the exodus was especially noticeable in this brutally steamy year. Harkness saw that "everyone who can afford to leaves Shanghai during July and August; they go to the hills, they go to Japan, they go North." The deflated party scene, though, was of no consequence to her. Harkness had already begun losing interest in it all anyway. Something surprising was happening. As the hard-drinking dress designer became more and more intoxicated with China, she found herself indulging less and less in cocktails. She wanted to keep fit for the expedition, and she was starting to have a sense of how she could chart her own course. Deliriously, she wrote, "I think I am happier here than at any time since I left home."

DURING THE MONTHS in Shanghai, Floyd Tangier Smith behaved like an ardent suitor. He cleared the decks for Harkness, making himself available to her at all hours, enjoying everything from prelunch drinks to meals and late-night talks. It made his wife, Elizabeth, "jealous as hell," Harkness knew, to sit at home night after night while her husband was out with the woman who seemed to have attracted every married and unmarried man in Shanghai. "The talk usually started with previous expe-

Floyd Tangier Smith done up in traditional Chinese silk. LIBRARY OF CONGRESS

dition affairs, and ended always, no one knew quite how, with Buddhism, or Tibetan mysticism and adventure," Harkness said.

Sometimes tucked away in her hotel room, with the sounds of the river traffic wafting through the windows, the careful listener and the tireless yarner would sit sipping whiskey sodas and talk about China's distant borderland. The darkly attractive widow had no trouble drawing out the homely, rawboned older man. He was all too eager to pontificate, even though he must have looked and felt awful—suffering as he was from sciatica and a recurring case of malaria. But nothing, it seemed, could keep him from these all-important talks with Harkness.

She was just as eager to have them, for it was time to get down to business. The first step—before organizing the expedition, applying for permits, or mapping out the journey—would be making a decision about partnerships. She had scores to settle, and Bill's ashes to collect. She wanted desperately to untangle the mystery of his death and his finances. All roads led to Floyd Tangier Smith, who in turn stood at the fork of another, the one leading out of Shanghai and into the wild. Harkness would have to tread carefully. She had to be tough-minded and pragmatic, particularly where Smith was concerned, since he was the biggest question mark. She would assess him entirely on her own—from what she herself saw and heard.

Once lubricated with a few cocktails, he could be quite expansive. "He has been here for twenty-five years or more," Harkness said, "and the tales are wonderful. The Panchen Lama of Tibet, the animals he has collected, the racehorses he has owned, gold in the high mountains, Chinese civil war and bandits." Smith was a practiced storyteller who in previous trips to the States had told reporters many of the same chestnuts—how he had been the only white man for scores of miles in "barbaric" regions; that he had lived for weeks on cornmeal and game, how he had been snowbound for months on end in below-zero temperatures.

For those first few days in Shanghai, Harkness savored the accounts. They were glimpses of the rough life of adventure she intended to have for herself, even while giving her cause to have doubts about this old China hand. For Smith never tried to disguise his contempt for the Chinese. "It was a long job teaching these hunters that there is a difference between a live animal and a dead one," he wrote of the native workers in western China, "for they are primitive, stupid and deceitful, and they lie with the greatest of ease."

Harkness, on the other hand, found the Chinese to be an amazingly honest people. Here, her hotel room remained unlocked and nothing, down to the "little pile of coppers" left on her dresser, was ever taken. "I divide the whites in two classes out here," she would write, "those with the superior attitude toward the yellow races, and consequently hating them and being cordially hated in return, and those who like the Chinese, try to understand them, and in turn receive the same treatment with at times a great deal of service and unbelievable loyalty thrown in."

Smith was also a product of his age and time. The notion of a woman in command of an expedition irked him, and his irritation occasionally surfaced in negotiations. But he needed her money, and in courting her as a financial partner, he must have labored to keep those views in check.

Harkness and Smith did find common ground in their interest in animals. Smith even loaned her a fairly tame large Indian civet. The size of a small dog, the exotic animal had the coat of a raccoon, complete with a magnificent striped tail. "Noctivorous," Smith had said of him, and Harkness discovered that indeed "Szechwan" was like a typical Shanghai citizen, wanting to sleep all day and play all night.

Even on this front, though, the two were miles apart. Smith was the kind of animal lover who could unload the barrel of a rifle on a creature as easily as he could scratch its haunch. He wanted the glory of capturing a live panda, but nearly as good, he said, would be snagging one to "pickle." Toward the unfortunates he collected and shipped out, he felt no sorrow. "Those who think that the animals chafe at their captivity do not realize that with a regular supply of food and freedom from the fear of attack, most of them are 'in clover,' and they know it," he wrote.

Harkness was a sentimentalist through and through. She was forever rescuing stray kittens, falling in love with dogs, and even keeping a pet monkey in New York. In France, a live pigeon shoot she witnessed was "atrocious." "I don't know how you feel about animals," she once told a crowd, "but I develop a terrific inferiority complex when dogs look askance at me, and to have a cat sneer at me will depress me for days."

As mismatched as they were, both Harkness and Smith were determined to capture a giant panda. And as they sized each other up over those steamy summer nights, each thought the other was wholly incapable of accomplishing the task.

Despite Harkness and Smith's building wariness, the marathon sessions did not slow down. Smith couldn't afford to let Harkness go—he was trying to reel her in, and he had laid out what he thought was the most practical strategy, a scheme that he reasoned would appeal to a city sophisticate like Harkness. If she would simply bankroll his operation, not participate in it, the two of them could stay in Shanghai, letting his hunters do all the work.

Harkness was appalled. She began to feel she knew where the trouble in Bill's blighted expedition had lain. Here was Smith selling himself as an experienced resident collector—he knew the ropes, had the contacts, the infrastructure—yet he simply never produced. Poor Bill had made it out to the edge of panda country, only to be wrenched back because Smith had not managed to obtain permissions. Even now, at the time Ruth Harkness came into the picture, Smith was trying to revive his operation in Sichuan, still finding it impossible to secure those permits.

Through all Smith's reminiscences, she had been reading between the lines. The arc of his life story was a troubling one. Even though he had managed some important specimen hauls to places like the Field Museum in Chicago, he ultimately appeared either the unluckiest or most incompetent collector going. As she reviewed the mishaps of his long career, the portrait that emerged was of a man always ready with a justification, eager to point a finger, to play people off one another, to scam a little extra cash, and to skirt a code of ethics he claimed to live by.

Born in Japan in 1882 to missionary parents, Smith had gone west for college—attending four schools in four years before graduating from Bowdoin. His professional life began in banking and business on Wall Street, then continued in London, Bombay, and Shanghai. Here he wore suits and toiled over smudged figures on bank ledgers, all the while pining to join the ranks of young men from the West who raced through the city on their way to exotic adventure in the borderland with Tibet.

He went on expeditions when he could, but his big break eluded him until he was nearly fifty, when the Field Museum sent him out to gather specimens of the still little-known fauna of western China. The assignment, initially conceived as a ten-year survey, was a windfall for Smith, who hungered to make a name for himself in the field.

From 1930 to 1932 he was able to live the life of a collector. During this period he provided the museum with seven thousand specimens, or "deaders" as he sometimes referred to them: mammals, reptiles, birds, and fish. It was a sizable catch, in keeping with that of similar expeditions. But the exhausting work certainly wasn't making him rich, and his desire for a panda began to burn early. Even though the Field Museum told him to forget about the animal in order to concentrate on other wildlife, a panda, he wrote to his sister on Long Island, would be the ultimate prize.

Smith hoped to accomplish the goal the way he did all his hunting—not so much by chasing animals himself as by setting up an elaborate network of camps—seven in this case—staffed by teams of local hunters. He maintained throughout his life that this was the only sensible approach to wildlife collection in China. It was part of the reason he never had the allure of some of his more charismatic contemporaries, who thrived on field life and enjoyed the actual hunting.

His long typed reports to the Field Museum over several years read like an encyclopedia of excuses. Nearly every single one informs his handlers of new, unexpected delays in progress, in shipping, in permits—blaming them on a running catalog of difficulties: rain, bandits, inept or treacherous hunters, political upheaval, "certain reactionary elements," dissension among hunters, official obstruction, and betrayal.

He lost hundreds of specimens to marauding bandits. When his camp was burned, he also lost chemicals for specimen preservation. It was at a critical moment too, for shortly afterward, a coveted giant panda was shot by his men. The specimen moldered in a charcoal burner's hut for seven long months, emerging in very poor condition. Hundreds of beautiful bird trophies he reported collecting often vanished before he had the chance to ship them out to those who had commissioned them, though, of course, he may have exaggerated the size and quality of his losses to his bosses.

Added to all that, his health often gummed up the works. Rotted teeth needed extracting. Intestines, heart, and nerves were shaky. There were battles against tuberculosis, headaches, and raging infections. He was as familiar with the hospitals of Shanghai as with the routes that led west.

It appeared that whenever big events occurred in the field, Smith was absent. He was away "in quest of supplies" the time bandits burned down a major part of his operation. He was not with the men when that giant panda was shot. The worst debacle of the expedition occurred when a huge cache of specimens for the museum languished in-country, unbeknownst to Smith, because of a shipping mix-up. Smith felt terrible about the problem when he learned of it, coming to believe later that the repercussions were dire. Though the Field Museum had contracted him for a decadelong survey of Chinese animals, the project was abruptly curtailed. About a year and a half into the endeavor, Smith was told to have his work wrapped up in six months. The museum cited the financial strain of the Depression as the cause.

Smith was stunned. This should have been the period of high payoff for all the foundations he had laid. Now he was being suddenly recalled. It was unfair. He fretted that the shipping fiasco, which was not his fault, had prompted the museum to drop him.

Ultimately, Smith was able to continue his association with the museum, if on a less formal basis. He would be freelancing, which would allow the institution to choose his offerings à la carte rather than having to underwrite the entire tour. Who wouldn't stew? He was dumped off a secure payroll only to endure the sight of others, who were bankrolled by museums and academies or could finance their own way, launching lavish expeditions from Shanghai, which were covered by an adoring press.

In the words of one associate, Smith "lived precariously." The haggard and luckless adventurer would forever be chasing after the next check, straining to maintain a high profile while an army of Ivy League boys paraded through town. So, now, in the summer of 1936, Smith kept at Harkness, pushing the notion of running an expedition from Shanghai. He could not see that she was repelled by the arrangement he doggedly pursued. For her part, she was rather more astute about him. She saw that for Smith "fame and fortune" were "always just around the corner. The next trip will surely make him wealthy." In fact, Smith, counting on Harkness's money, had already written to the Field Museum claiming he would be back in action very shortly.

Smith had faced one disappointment after another, according to his wife. And he would soon reach a breaking point. Harkness would later see clearly what she suspected then: Smith wasn't up to the task.

Despite all his experience and big talk, Smith would just be a liability. "I think Ajax is out," she wrote home within a week of her arrival, on July 25. "He is anything but well, and as much of a dear as he is, is totally impractical in many ways, and I cannot afford to take chances of any kind."

WITH THAT SETTLED in her mind, Harkness moved forward. On a hot, rainy Sunday, just after dawn, she flew to the American embassy in Beijing, where the diplomatic corps was reluctantly in the process of shifting power over to Nanking, the old Ming capital, now the seat of government under Chiang Kai-shek. Harkness had hatched her own strategy, and teaming with Smith was just one of her husband's mistakes she planned not to repeat. The other was getting tangled in the legendary Chinese bureaucracy that had left Bill languishing in Shanghai for months on end. To conduct a scientific expedition into the Chinese interior, one had to appease many governmental agencies. It was a tedious, capricious, and time-consuming process. That just wasn't for Ruth Harkness.

From high in the air, on her first flight ever—"and how I adored it!" she reported—she looked down with wonder at the endless miles of lush farmland in "every conceivable shade of green velvet." The whole country seemed to be a garden segmented into a thousand irregular shapes and sizes. She peered out the window, mulling over what she was about to do.

She had had a flash of insight into how to circumvent all the predictable problems. She would use the great wall of skepticism that always greeted her to her own advantage. Everyone kept reminding her that she was not a scientist, not a zoologist, just a dress designer. Fine, she thought. If I'm not a scientist, why should I apply for scientific permits? Why outline a collecting blueprint? If she got none of the benefits of a big, sanctioned expedition, why should she be saddled with its strictures?

She could think of it all quite philosophically, and see it through the prism of yin and yang: in weakness there is the seed of strength. From a position of powerlessness, Ruth Harkness drew power. She turned the dynamic she was presented with on its head. She would not rouse the dragons who guard forms in triplicate. She would tiptoe by them. She would go on record with the embassy about her destination, and she would even mention her silly little panda dream, but she would leave it at that. For Harkness, the fact that it meant breaking the rules wasn't a problem; it was more like an added benefit.

Once her mind was made up, things happened quickly in Beijing. The moment Harkness presented letters to the legation, she was ushered in to see Ambassador Nelson Trusler Johnson. The portly middle-aged official knew a great deal about previous panda hunters, including Bill, whose exploits made up "a rather extensive file." A good part of that sheaf of papers would, no doubt, have concerned her husband's propensity to disappear without a trace. But Ruth Harkness liked the ambassador. He had a reputation for being knowledgeable about the East, and most important, Harkness heard that he possessed a rare understanding and sympathy toward the Chinese.

Johnson advised her to travel to Nanking. There she could find out more about the turbulent conditions in Sichuan, and she could begin applying for scientific permits through the Byzantine bureaucracy of the Academia Sinica. Harkness kept mum. In a way, she would be following the Daoist edict of effortless or right action, which Johnson himself had displayed in calligraphy up on the wall of his office: WU WEI ERH WU PU WEI, Through not doing, all things are done.

If she needed a sign that she had made the proper decision, she got it at the end of the interview. As the ambassador ushered her out, he couldn't resist a parting remark about catching a panda. "Now be sure to take plenty of salt to put on his tail," Johnson said patronizingly, "and do let me know when you've got him."

She must have smiled to herself as she stepped over the official threshold and out into the ancient streets of what was no longer being called Peking, or "northern capital," but, under its changed status, Peiping, or "Northern Peace." Sunlight and the dust blowing in from the Gobi formed a scrim through which Harkness felt she passed into another dimension. Again, just as in Hong Kong, there was an overwhelming sense of familiarity, a spiritual tug that she could not explain. "A sudden feeling swept over me that all this was not new in spite of the fact that I had never been in Peiping before," Harkness wrote, "that I had seen those great walls that are fifty feet high, and sixty feet thick at the base, that I had known the dull red of the bricks, and the massive watch towers." In the filtered light, the sounds of hawkers' cries, the tinkling of barbers' bells, the sight of camels burdened with produce, all seemed comfortingly familiar.

With the exception of one acquaintance, an American woman, Harkness avoided her countrymen. All the letters of introduction to fellow westerners remained unopened inside her purse. Instead, she hired a tall rickshaw driver named Gao for the fortnight she would be in the city, bristling at the Western custom of calling someone like him "boy." She said he was for her "horse, guide, and mentor." Through the arid hot city, she saw the Temple of Heaven, the Forbidden City, the Temple of Confucius—ancient gnarled cedars, brilliant yellow enamel-tiled roofs. She met silversmiths and embroiderers and admired their exotic jewelry and silks. There were the dazzling greens, blues, and yellows of the huge glazed ceramic Nine Dragon Screen, its great twisting monsters frolicking in foamy surf. Gao even took her to meet his wife and family at home, serving her tea and moon cakes. It was all so beautiful. From the first shafts of morning sun until dusk, when "the shadows rise like purple ink drowning the Imperial City," the trip had taken on the slow-moving and fateful feeling of a dream.

From Beijing, Harkness followed Johnson's instructions and flew to Nanking, but her visit was cut short because of illness. With a bad case of bronchitis developing, she nearly lost her hearing during the high-altitude plane ride. She abruptly returned to Shanghai, where surprises were waiting to explode like firecrackers in a barrel.

CHAPTER THREE

GAINING THE WHIP HAND

ERRY RUSSELL FINALLY ARRIVED in late August, taking a room at the Palace Hotel across the hall from Harkness. Initially Harkness was overjoyed by his presence— "we are clicking beautifully," she said. Their planning sessions jumped into high gear, with both constantly dashing across the hallway, throwing open each other's doors, and charging in— despite the fact that due to the heat, each was often in a state of near complete undress.

The weeks before his arrival had been tough for Harkness. A case of dysentery, complicated by colitis, had landed her in the same hospital where Bill had died. The illness was potentially fatal, and common to any area, like China, that used human feces as fertilizer. Doubled over with intestinal spasms, spiking a high fever, and suffering from dehydration, Harkness was told, she reported, "that an operation is the only thing that will fix me up."

She didn't have time. The amoeba did keep her running back to the hospital over the first weeks of August, but, she said, surgery was "out of the question. The panda won't wait." She agreed to go under the "gas" for "a minor repair job," coming back to the hotel the same day she was admitted. By the time Russell landed, the problem had subsided.

Now, though, she would have to face another dark cloud. However gently Harkness might have broken the news to Smith that she would not be partnering with him, things began to unravel. Their point of contention was Bill Harkness and his money.

Russell, Harkness, and the Smiths saw one another nearly every day in Shanghai. For Smith it was an opportunity—every meeting was another pitch session. Too broke to carry on his own work, he was becoming desperate at the thought of losing access to the Harkness till. Both Smith and his wife resented Harkness, believing she had strung Floyd along by expressing interest in taking over the expedition.

It had to have been stifling for Harkness. "Ajax is being rather difficult," she wrote home, "and more or less putting it in the light of a moral obligation that I take him."

The dinners and socializing would have been trial enough in the face of the growing tension. Then Smith decided to expand his subject matter beyond expedition talk into an area that would wound Ruth Harkness beyond measure. In his conversations with her, he began to paint a vivid and grim portrait of Bill Harkness's last year of life.

There had been seven bouts of catastrophic illness and four operations, Smith told her, which began in the spring of 1935, right after Bill had signed on with him and then gone missing. The early manifestation of his disease may well have prompted Bill's odd disappearing acts. When several growths appeared on his neck, he was admitted to the hospital for an operation. Even though his recovery would take some weeks, he, Smith, and Russell were eager to get started. Optimistically, they agreed that Smith would proceed to Chengdu on June 3 with all the gear, and Bill would follow shortly after by plane. Remarkably, it went off as planned.

Once they were out west, however, things spiraled downward. As Ruth Harkness had understood previously, permit problems caused them to return to Shanghai in September. What she didn't know was that they had to go back east anyway because new tumors had begun to surface on Bill's neck.

Bill Harkness and Smith carried on as though this were just another simple delay. On October 13 Smith left for business in Nanking, on the understanding that that night Bill would check in to the hospital, where he was scheduled for another surgery. But when Smith returned he discovered that Bill had cabled the hospital at midnight saying he would postpone his treatment by twenty-four hours. The following day came and went without Bill checking himself in. The doctor now revealed to Smith what he had withheld from Bill: the tumors were malignant, and the young man was suffering from a ravening cancer. Perhaps Bill's behavior indicated that deep inside, he already knew. He spent the next five weeks doing as he pleased—checking in to four hotels, reading innumerable books—and ditching the authorities who had been notified by Smith to search for the missing man. Smith, worried that Bill was "unknowingly committing slow suicide," combed the city for him. At last he caught Bill in broad daylight, casually strolling out of his bank accompanied by Russell. Smith explained to Bill that the doctor said any procrastination would have serious consequences. So the next day, accompanied by Smith, Bill checked in to the hospital.

Torturous as the operation and recovery must have been, the doctor was pleased with the results and hopeful when Bill was released on Christmas Day 1935. The embattled explorer felt well enough shortly afterward to make plans with Smith to head up the Yangtze by steamer for Sichuan. But no sooner had reservations been booked than Bill began to shed weight alarmingly, ultimately not even having the strength to get out of bed.

By late January, Bill was readmitted to the hospital, diagnosed with a serious colon condition. Clearly, the cancer had spread, but somehow the doctor was upbeat, saying the new problem could be treated with radiation. In the face of the latest affliction, Bill was more desperate than ever to get himself back into the frontier. The doctor reassured him that if the treatment went well, Bill might just make it to Chengdu within a week; there he could finish out the course of therapy. Again, there was a setback. The doctor reneged on the proposal, insisting that

Bill stick to Shanghai for the full set of treatments. The ailing American couldn't stand to cancel plans completely, so it was decided that Smith would get up-country by boat on February 14, with Bill grabbing a plane to Chengdu when he was fit enough.

At the end of his river trip, Smith found an airmail letter waiting for him with the news that forty hours after an emergency operation on his stomach, at 4:45 A.M., February 19, 1936, Bill Harkness had died.

The story devastated Ruth. "The poor lad was apparently in dreadful condition," she wrote home, "full of sarcoma that never could have been cured, jaw infections, and too many horrible things to talk about. He was just skin and bones when he died." Although Smith told Harkness her husband had been unaware of the gravity of his condition, he did not pretend the end was swift. Apparently it was lonely too, for Bill had refused help from friends in Shanghai. It was crushing for Ruth to hear of Bill's torment and isolation.

But there was more. Smith couldn't or wouldn't stop himself. He began to tell Harkness secrets of Bill's that she said "no man ought to tell his wife." There was a rumor that Bill kept a White Russian mistress. Fueled by whiskey sodas, Smith unloaded everything on Ruth, telling her things, she said, that she wouldn't even repeat in letters home. And somehow—it may have been the McCombs stoicism—she sat through it.

It maddened her that he couldn't shut up about what she didn't want to know, yet would not come clean about the things she was impatient to discover. The details of the financial arrangement between her husband and Smith he refused to reveal. Ruth Harkness would always believe that Smith still had much of Bill's money—and she wanted it back. Smith not only rebuffed her, protesting that all of Bill's money was already gone, but he also wanted more from her. He maintained that the "joint account" arranged between him and Bill was that Smith's own stake in the partnership consisted of his bush knowledge and the use of his well-established camps and the hunters he already knew. Bill's contribution was all the fresh money to underwrite the expedition itself. But Smith also contended that "my investment in cash alone was a very great deal more than Mr. Harkness was called upon to pay."

Fed up with what she thought were Smith's evasions, she began to sift through Bill's papers for answers. Although she joked that she couldn't count higher than ten "unaided by pencil and paper," she was appalled by what she unearthed. There was Smith, all right, on Bill's payroll, but he wasn't the only one. She wrote home to Hazel Perkins. "My God, Perkie, the things I have discovered. Bill at one time carried Larry [Griswold], Sonny [Griswold], Bryon, to say nothing of Ajax and God knows who else. And there is expedition stuff from here to Tibet."

She believed that Smith was one of many who had been siphoning off Bill's money. Harkness now sized the matter up: Bill had put in plenty of cash, but what had Smith provided? No permits and no time in panda country. She was not impressed. As she scrutinized the partnership's records, she found Smith's organizational skills utterly lacking. Receipts, equipment lists, and the equipment itself were in disarray. Harkness felt that the chaotic condition Smith kept things in confirmed her earliest impressions. "The messed up lists clinched the matter in my mind. I had definitely decided before that I could not take Ajax, merely through working on instinct—now I know that I am right. I do not think that Ajax is capable of organization, executive direction or concentrated effort in one direction," she wrote.

That was fine by Russell. Apparently, he had no qualms about Harkness's decision to cut Smith out. But years later he would not recollect any of the unpleasantness, only that Smith's permit problems were too much to take on.

JUST AS HARKNESS was feeling so disenchanted with Smith, she met three other men who would spin the plot in a whole new direction.

First, she got a call from the charming and well-known explorer Jack Young in Shanghai. Young was funny, confident, spirited, and shrewd. He was so dashing that he sometimes referred to himself as the Chinese Tyrone Power. Only twenty-five years old, he already had a significant reputation in the exploring game. He had been on the Roosevelt expedition that shot the first giant panda for the West, and by 1934 he had struck out on his own, staying in the news with other expeditions, such as the one in which he scaled the 25,000-foot Minya Konka, today called Gongga Shan, in Sichuan, with Americans Richard Burdsall and Terris Moore. Most recently he had created something of an adventuring dynasty for himself. With his beautiful and vivacious Chinese American wife, Adelaide "Su-Lin" Chen Young, and his brother Quentin, he had ranged over much of western China and Tibet.

Offering his help, Young met with Harkness for a long discussion about her expedition. She liked him immediately and loved the great zest he seemed to have for adventure. Jack Young, she realized, would make a perfect expedition partner. Unfortunately, he was already booked. He was setting out for the Himalayas in India with some Harvard grads to scale the mighty Nanda Devi.

Quentin Young in a Western-style suit.
COURTESY JOLLY YOUNG

He did have an alternative, though. Jack Young recommended his brother Quentin, saying he could arrange to bring him by right away. At twenty-two, Quentin was younger and less experienced, having never captained his own team. He had traveled extensively with Jack, however, and was strong, smart, and eager to prove himself.

He had something else going for him, as Ruth Harkness saw that hot summer day when he and his brother walked toward her in the mahogany-paneled lobby of the Palace Hotel. Quentin Young was stunningly handsome. Nearly six feet tall and rail thin, dapper in Western-style suits, he had thick jet-black hair that he wore slicked back, though a lock of it often fell rakishly loose across his forehead. Despite his urbane look, he was unaccustomed to dealing with foreigners, and as the three sat together sipping fresh lemonade in the lounge, he seemed awkward and uncomfortable. During the meeting, he allowed his older and bolder brother to do all the talking. Harkness may have been dealing with Jack Young, but it was Quentin, with his shy smile, who made an impression.

Quentin was startled by Harkness's cool confidence. With her hair tucked up under a turban, she sat casually smoking cigarettes while talking expedition. There was nothing demure about her. She was straightforward and relaxed, clearly comfortable speaking with men.

So they talked. Jack Young tallied his brother's field strengths. Quentin was a crack shot and an accomplished hunter and trapper. He spoke English as well as Chinese and was fluent in the Sichuan dialect; there would be no need for an interpreter.

Furthermore, Quentin was willing to accept a small salary with expenses so that he would have the chance to do some hunting for himself. He was hoping to shoot a giant panda for the Nanking Museum. Despite Quentin's reluctance to speak, it was clear to Harkness that he felt a strong rivalry with his brother and was eager to do some catching up.

Neither side really needed to be sold on the other. "If much of young China is like Quentin and his brother Jack, it seems to me [a] very hopeful outlook," Harkness wrote. By the next day, a deal had been struck with the Young brothers, who returned to the Palace Hotel armed with stiff linen maps, some in Chinese, some in English, all with large blank areas indicating uncharted territory. Harkness's eye, as usual, was drawn to those mysterious open spaces. The notion of finally being free to march into the unknown thrilled her.

That they would travel fifteen hundred miles along the Yangtze was understood. But there were many routes from Chunking (now Chongqing) inland to panda country. As Harkness discussed the options with the Youngs, she was astounded by the exotic details they mentioned casually—a lamasery where they could find accommodations from friendly monks, a lake they had discovered that was not charted by any cartographer. Shortly, a plan was in place: Harkness, Quentin Young, and Russell would leave Shanghai on September 19, headed for a region that Jack Young knew well, the area southwest of Chengdu, close to where the Roosevelts had gotten their panda. At the city of Kiating (modern-day Leshan), Russell would split off to Chengdu to organize equipment, afterward meeting Harkness and Young in the field. In the meantime, Gerry Russell's presence in the planning stages was being nudged to the back burner, as each day was filled in collaboration between Ruth Harkness and Quentin Young.

THERE DIDN'T SEEM to be room in Harkness's life for any more characters at the moment. And yet an American with a personality as grand and brawny as a bison came charging in.

Dan Reib, an executive with the Shanghai branch of Standard Oil Company of New York, or Socony, had heard through mutual friends about Harkness's plans to launch an expedition. Ringing her up, he explained that because he had spent so many years in western China, he thought he might be of some help. He even had a few books on the subject that she might find interesting.

She was delighted. They both had other lunch plans that day—hers with Russell, in fact—but she squeezed Reib in for what was a popular practice in Shanghai: a before-noon drink.

Reib was a *taipan*, all right, a great captain of commerce, but he was also clearly his own man. He warned Harkness on the phone that he was a "barbarian," and would be wearing shorts in this hot weather, not giving a damn about the Bund's rigid decorum. No doubt, that alone had appeal for Harkness.

She had a caution of her own. Considering the constant barrage of

Dan Reib in Shanghai. COURTESY JANE POLLOCK

headlines like MRS. HARKNESS AIDS COLLEGE, which made people very confused about her identity, she informed him that she wasn't of the Standard Oil Harknesses but just "a poor working girl who is on a madcap errand." He responded that he wouldn't have bothered with her otherwise.

When Reib showed up at the hotel, Harkness was swept up in the surging momentum of his vitality. He was only about five feet nine, but there was a rare and purely American "bigness" about him in every sense, she said. Stocky, husky, and outspoken, he was a "cyclone" who radiated energy and generosity. He had black curly hair and dark, deep-set eyes. His gaze was clear and level. Most of all, she said, he had a big soul, just like that of her dear friend Perkie back in the States. They had their cocktails as he told her all about the Chinese frontier. His stories of adventure were like none she had ever heard. He had spent months on end living in faraway places that no other foreigner had ever penetrated. He had even been captured, tortured, and held for ransom.

His whole life, really, had been one big adventure. Raised a rich prep-school boy off an uncle's inheritance in Texas, he had joined the circus for a time at the age of thirteen. In his midteens, he had split off during a school trip to bum around Europe for two years, quickly learning to speak like the natives wherever he went. Despite his footloose ways, he had passed the rigorous admissions exams to Cornell University, where he received a degree in engineering. His facility with languages came in handy in Shanghai, where his bosses, in an effort to get him up to speed, put him on a boat traveling the Yangtze with no fellow westerners. He returned weeks later a fluent speaker.

Here in Shanghai, he was known as a stand-up guy, fond of wearing a cowboy hat while scaring everyone off the bridle path as he charged down on his big Russian mount. He adored women and was fast with his fists if he felt their honor needed defending.

Harkness and Reib connected immediately, and their quick drink turned into two, and three, until the meeting stretched on without end, both of them standing up their "tiffin," or lunch, dates. Before they finally parted, Reib had set plans for their next session.

The second time he came to her hotel, he brought "armfuls of maps, books, lists of things to take and many other things." It was another incredible visit. They would meet again and again, Reib providing her friendship, guidance, and a remarkable amount of logistical support. He would purchase food and medicine for the field. He negotiated her banking and mail delivery. As an executive of Standard Oil, he authorized all kinds of free transportation—by boat and car—for her. It was an enormous gift, since Standard Oil, like tobacco companies and the missionaries, seemed to be everywhere in China. In fact, *Fortune* magazine referred to the triumvirate as "the Gospel of the three lights: the cigarette, the kerosene lamp, and Christianity." Reib also gave the American widow important letters of introduction to comrades all along her route. In helping her, no task was too small or too large for him. He had, she said, provided her with "everything from maps to brandy and crab meat" for what he had come to call her "experdition."

Reib particularly loved telling Harkness stories of a little brotherhood of his, a unique band of fearless westerners spread throughout China who referred to themselves as "the Hard-Boiled Eggs." Two of them Harkness would meet. One was the frail, elderly, and kind Sir Merrick Hewlett, who was about to retire after a long career. The other, E. A. Cavaliere, lived in Chengdu, where he served as postal commissioner for Sichuan; he would come to play a major role in Harkness's life once she was up-country.

Reib, Harkness wrote home to Perkie, "makes this China trip, just by knowing a man like that, a success if nothing else does." With all his achievements, Reib could have been arrogant or egocentric. His stories might have been exciting but empty yarns. Instead, he always saw the deeper shadings in life and spoke poignantly of what he had learned in the East. Reib had been beset by problems but was not bitter, in fact he felt he had benefited from his experiences. He told Harkness, "One gains sometimes only through loss."

Harkness felt humbled by him, though she was secure enough to know, she said, that "I have given him something too." Reib liked strong women—his own mother had fought the system all the way up to the Texas Supreme Court for her rights in her divorce. He made clear his desire to see Harkness succeed. Twice he even dreamed of it—his friend returning with a giant panda.

Harkness would later describe this relationship with Reib as "a marvelous companionship while it lasted." Far from New York, and years after having last been with her husband, she felt a luxurious contentment with this "real man." Together, she and Dan Reib "had found the rare and beautiful." Despite the ardent description, Harkness characterized the relationship as platonic. "I suppose this almost sounds as if I were in love with him, which I am not in the least," she wrote home to her pal Perkie. "I feel much the same [about Reib] as I do you without a lot of sex nonsense mixed up in it." Of course, the funny thing was that the correspondence between Harkness and Perkins sounded passionate too—full of "darlings" and closings of "much, much love." The connection between the adventuress and the *taipan* looked and sounded like a romance to everyone around them, especially Reib's girlfriend. He was a divorced man but involved with a British woman, who, Harkness said, was "at great pains to let me know that Dan is hers and hands off."

Shanghai thrived on secrets and gossip. "The speed with which rumor spread in Shanghai bordered on telepathy," author Vicki Baum noted. *New Yorker* writer Emily Hahn concurred: "Shanghai gossip was fuller, richer, and less truthful than any I had ever before encountered." In her relationship with Reib, Harkness found out how true this was. "The most intimate pieces of knowledge are common property," she said. But it didn't matter. "I am becoming reconciled to being thought a little mad," she reported, "and perhaps not quite nice." She was determined, she told Perkie, to be "callous to people's curiosity about me." And, boy, she wrote, were they ever curious.

IN SEPTEMBER, HARKNESS worked the days through with Young, met with Reib at any hour, then shared sukiyaki dinners with Russell, who was still quietly on board. By now, nightlife had lost its appeal for her. "I shall be glad to get out of Shanghai," she wrote home. "It is rather uninteresting for a place that is supposed to be so wicked and gay, etc. etc. Perhaps it is, but I assure you I can think of nothing that interests me less than night clubs and that sort of thing. And serious drinking certainly has no charm either." There was so much to do that some nights, back in her room, she was too exhausted to sleep.

One of her biggest tasks was sifting through the enormous amount of equipment Bill Harkness had amassed. In the lingering summer heat of early September, Harkness and Quentin Young headed to the French Quarter, where Bill had rented a garage for storage. They stood before the building, pulling open its huge creaking doors, releasing the terrible musty odor of long-stored equipment to sun and air.

What they found inside was stunning. It looked like provisions for a well-heeled army. The sheer bulk of the boxes, bundles, bales, and trunks was staggering. Bill was to have enjoyed a proper gentleman's expedition with enough porters to heave every imaginable supply, including hammocks, folding stoves, nine saddles, and 336 pairs of thick wool socks. There was, she said, "an armoury of guns": rifles, shotguns, pistols, and

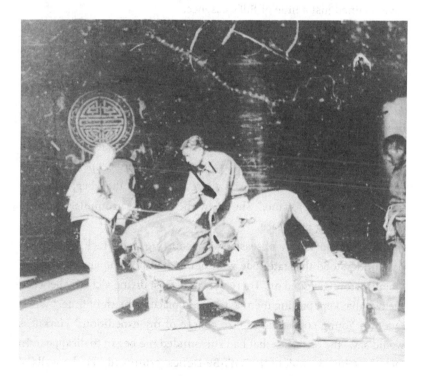

Quentin Young packing for the expedition. COURTESY MARY LOBISCO

bayonets. There was clothing, medicine, surgical equipment, and food. And everything came in multiples.

Harkness and Young got started, prying off lids and investigating each container. Harkness found here the intersection of two great passions—adventure and fashion. Among the supplies were the makings of her own expedition wear. Beyond the great piles of clothing for Bill's gargantuan companions, there were the things he had stowed for himself, which were small enough to be cut down and refashioned to suit a woman. Ruth Harkness knew that her favorite tailor, Ziang Tai, was up to that task, with a "Yes, missy, can do." Here she put her hands on woolen long johns, jodhpurs, slacks, and shirts, every one of them belonging to the man she missed so much. She wrapped herself in a nicely broken-in tweed jacket that despite the miasma inside the garage must have retained just a little of Bill's essence.

Having taken over his mission, she would now literally be walking in his shoes. She plucked out the smallest pair of hobnailed boots, each with two and a half pounds of hardware in it, to be shrunk by a resourceful Chinese shoemaker.

The expedition seemed so seductively real and precious that Harkness feared it would be taken from her. She found herself gripped by a strange anxiety and experienced a recurring nightmare, in which she had been transported to the United States and was trying desperately to get back to China, "the country," she wrote, "that even then began to have untold fascination for me." She knew the fear was groundless—everything was falling into place.

In this land nearly obsessed with courting good luck, she somehow understood that fate rode with her. It had become apparent when Quentin Young signed on. There was an almost divine alchemy between the two that kept putting them at the right place at the right time. "When Quentin Young consented to take charge of my expedition," Harkness would say, "the obstacles that had surrounded me began to disappear. In fact, the Chinese Wall of 'It-Can't-Be-Dones' crumpled like the walls of Jericho."

There was some irony in this, since no self-respecting Western expedition force would have put either Harkness or Young in command. Without her money, they wouldn't have taken Harkness on in any capacity. She had, of course, her sex going against her, and a lack of experience. Young was not so green, but he was Chinese, and barely past his teens. They were both so far outside the elite inner circle of wealthy well-known adventurers that their "much hooted-at expedition," in the words of The New York Times, wasn't even worthy of the kind of interest these gentlemen took in one another's business.

Between Harkness and Young, though, respect grew during the long days of collaboration. Harkness was touched that Young sought her opinion on all expedition matters, including things she had no knowledge of, such as what types of traps they might set. For his part, Young, accustomed to the bigotry of foreigners, was surprised by Harkness's utter lack of it. She hardly saw Young as "other." In fact, his slouchy stride and shy expression reminded her of her beloved brother, Jim. She found in him "an innate dignity" the likes of which she had never witnessed before.

The quiet explorer worked out a Chinese name for Harkness, as was the custom, revealing something of how he perceived her. "My name in Chinese means 'silky dew,' all of which is pretty fancy," Harkness wrote home. "Quentin says I must have a title as well. He is thinking up one. Now I wonder if I will be Lady Silky Dew or just plain Duchess. I think myself it should be Heavenly Princess Silky Dew etc etc." She got a kick out of Young's image of her, but she must have thought Reib's more accurate. He too had conjured a Chinese name for her: Ha Gansi (at the time spelled out as "Ha Kan Sse"), which translated as "laughing with courageous thoughts." It was Reib's version of her Chinese name that she had printed up on cards. The characters were lovely, she thought, particularly the last, which was represented by a field of rice with a heart below it. "To cultivate your rice field with your heart is to think," it was explained to her.

A dinner was arranged so that Harkness could meet Jack Young's wife, Su-Lin. As a newlywed two years before, Su-Lin had accompanied Jack and Quentin on an arduous nine-month expedition from China into Tibet, where it had been her job to preserve botanical samples. She was from then on considered the first Chinese woman explorer, even though she was actually Chinese American.

Barely coming up to Harkness's shoulder, Su-Lin certainly did not look like a mountaineer. Pretty, with shoulder-length black hair parted on the left, she was clothed in the style that was all the rage in Shanghai—a long silk overdress, slit to the knees, exposing matching silk petticoats underneath. At the time Harkness met her, Su-Lin was working as a reporter for several publications in Shanghai, including *The China Journal* and the *North China Daily News*. Her name was always popping up in the society columns, and Emily Hahn, that hard-to-please party girl, would later pronounce her "glamorous."

Harkness was thrilled that this pampered daughter of a New York nightclub owner had climbed to elevations of over fifteen thousand feet, tracked bears, and endured nights on her own in the field while Jack and Quentin were off hunting. Su-Lin told her she had long ago been diagnosed with a heart murmur and that her only previous camping experience had been in the White Mountains of New Hampshire.

She had some admonishing advice for Harkness. The travel would be dirty and uncomfortable. In Tibet, Su-Lin had sometimes stayed in yak-hair tents, drinking yak-butter tea, warmed over a yak-dung fire. Everything she ate was suffused with stray strands of yak hair. The smell of it all was unfortunately unforgettable to her. Everything she did drew an audience—she could never bathe in a river or brush her teeth without attracting a crowd—and the curiosity would be magnified for Harkness. Besides that, fleas and lice infested the little ramshackle inns along the route.

That evening, as Jack and the others laughed and told stories, Quentin looked on shyly. Across the table, his sister-in-law was keeping an eye on him. He did not need to speak for her to guess what he was feeling. She saw what was passing between her young, virile brother-in-law and the free-spirited Harkness. A flirtation, however subtle, was simmering. Once they were in the snowy wilds of Tibet, a love affair between Quentin Young and Ruth Harkness was, Su-Lin believed, "inevitable."

HARKNESS SENSED she was walking with destiny—her destiny, and it seemed to have been waiting here for her forever. Curled up in a big chair in her room at the Palace, she contemplated these matters endlessly. She could meditate "by the hour," she said, "with a feeling of the universe . . . and that there was just one little door to which if I had the key would unlock the mystery . . . a strong, strong feeling. The whole atmosphere of the Orient—particularly China—is spiritual. You can almost feel it."

She felt so perfectly aligned on the rails of her own fate that even when those who would be revealed as enemies leaned on her, they seemed to be pushing her further in the direction of her goal.

"I am looking for something," she reported home. She was searching for "the Way," she said, but not in a strict religious sense. "I have discovered this much at least—that as long as one is 'earthbound' by the desire for possessions (that aspect does not worry me) and also by people, one will never get anywhere. I am convinced that the human mind is capable of anything—absolutely anything." But to achieve something, a person must, she said, "arrive at a definite spiritual basis of thought."

Coming to China had been less a decision than a command. It was like a story that had already been partially written. Perhaps this country felt so much like home because she was being reborn here. As she struggled to express all that she was feeling, she could only laugh at herself. She wrote to Perkie, "You are probably saying the girl is either tight or tinged with the madness of the East."

What she could say with absolute clarity was that it had all brought her a profound happiness. "China has given me a peace of mind that I never had before, and a calmness that is a great relief after the tumult of the last two years." Following her bout of gloom over Smith, in a cycle she would often experience, she felt euphoric. "After mature thought and deliberation, and a journey half way round the world," she wrote, "I have come to the profound conclusion that this world of ours is the most fascinating of all possible places to be, and my God, Perkie it's full of wonderful people. I am so dam glad to be alive, and in China, and about to stalk a Panda, I could scream and yell and howl for joy in spite of the fact that I am clutching a thermometer in my mouth and the temperature seems to be 100. Dam bugs aren't out of my system yet."

BESIDES THE LINGERING effects of her illness, there were a few other annoyances dragging on Harkness's elation. Gerald Russell was one of them. Some of the old issues were resurfacing between them, plus he had started in on her about "dealing with the Chinese." He distrusted the Young brothers. She sputtered about this in a letter home: "Jerry [sic] says, 'It is possible that Jack wants Quentin with us to protect his future interests in Szechuan. Perhaps he himself wants, when the time is ripe, to be the first to secure a panda. Quentin, not dishonestly of course, will simply see that we have a nice trip but that we just never get the Panda. A procedure that would not to the Chinese mind perhaps represent dishonesty.' "

Russell may well have come under Smith's influence on this score. Not only was Smith suspicious of the Chinese in general, but he had a grudge against Jack Young in particular. Smith had accused him of stealing birds and business from him before. While complaining to the Field Museum earlier, he had made the preposterous claim that he had taught the youthful adventurer everything he knew about hunting.

As Russell raised his concerns, Harkness strongly disagreed. "My personal feeling is that Quentin loves this sort of thing for itself," she said. In Quentin Young, she saw a youth in love with adventure.

But the problems with Russell gnawed at her for weeks.

On what would have been her second wedding anniversary, September 9, she had tea with Gerry. It was "a day of Chinese rain and dampness, lassitude, and wondering," she said. The young Brit was a killjoy. "We are like two dogs always sniffing each other, and never making up our minds whether we like the smell or not," she said.

Soon enough, she would know for sure that Russell was not for her. The fact was that the more time she spent with Reib and Young, the more Russell suffered in comparison. With Reib, the world was an expansive, wondrous place; Russell, on the other hand, she said, "simply crushed every ounce of naturalness I had and depressed me to the Nth degree." She had brought him on board to begin with only out of insecurity. Before she ever got to China, she had thought—foolishly, she realized now—that she "must have a man with me." Russell had been to China, was willing to go, and had seemed so fond of Bill. But now her eyes were open. The trip wasn't a lark. It was no typical expedition with jobs for men to sign up for. It was a mission. She didn't want anything or anyone slowing the momentum or sullying the spirit of it all.

And there was so much threatening to pull it down. In addition to Russell, somehow Smith was still in the picture. He was a broken record, visiting her in her room, which by now was filled with expedition gear, steamer trunks, and maps, drinking whiskey sodas, and warning her darkly of the calamities that awaited her. Over and over, he pointed out that she knew nothing of the language, the people, the terrain. He told her that hunting a giant panda exclusively without gathering other wildlife was naïve and impractical. Smith, or "Zoology Jones," as she would later refer to him in a book about her experiences, "wanted, of course, to continue the arrangement with me that he and Bill had," Harkness wrote, "but in the first place I couldn't afford to finance another person, and I had the utmost confidence in Quentin. He knew the country, the language; I felt that I did not need a foreigner; in fact, I did not want another foreigner, for by that time I had seen enough of the attitude of most Westerners in China to heartily resent it."

That little bit of attitude must have galled Smith, and Russell too. They would have had more than a few private words over it. But Harkness stood her ground. Her new, tougher stance meant Russell would be out also. Their differences had been making her miserable. And all efforts to hash things out with him had failed. By the second week of September, she had made up her mind.

"The VRYENGLISH GENTLEMAN is no longer with the Harkness

Asiatic Expedition," she wrote home. Her dealings with Smith in partic-ular had led her weeks before to steel herself. "I've decided that for a while at least that I am taking what I want, and not considering every body else." She'd come to the conclusion that "one ought to be a bit hard boiled to get along." Now she could be. She had the strength and the goods. "Sometimes it helps to have the whip hand that even a small amount of money gives one," she said.

It didn't mean that Harkness intended to be overbearing or unprin-cipled. She felt that since she had underwritten Russell's travel to China, she was obliged now, in fairness, to hand him the money for his return ticket. She thought he loathed her for causing him to lose "a hell of a lot of face with his friends." And when Russell dealt with the blow in the supremely British way of becoming even more polite, she took it as the most obvious sign possible that he was "just hating my guts."

In the process of negotiating her course in Shanghai, she had, no doubt, made enemies. She had also picked up enough of the philosoph-ical attitude she admired in the Chinese, so that all this wrangling did not distress her. Yes, she said, "Jerry [sic] I think behaved rather badly, and Ajax very much so, even trying to get money from me. . . . But it is all to the good, in a way, and all to be chalked up to experience, with out which life would be flat and dead." Russell was about to provide even more excitement, though Harkness would not learn of it until she was far up the Yangtze.

SOMETHING ELSE, of a very practical nature, was bothering Harkness—how would she and Young keep a captive four-hundred-pound bamboo-eating bear alive? Just how much of the specialized grass would it take? Once outside the area where bamboo thrived, what would they do? The scientific literature was of no help. Very little was known about pandas.

Late one night, restless with worry, she had an epiphany. It was some-thing none of the old-hand experts had ever contrived. She wondered about finding a baby panda instead of an adult. It would solve all logisti-cal problems—the animal would feed on formula, not bamboo, and would be much easier to transport. It was preposterous enough to dream that she might find any panda, but a baby? "That was sheer, unadulterated madness," she said. And yet it was a hunch. "A small voice, deep within me," she said, "told me to prepare for that eventuality." She got out of bed and by lamplight jotted down a note for herself: "Nursing bottles, nipples and dried milk," she wrote, then turned out the light. It would be the most providential shopping list of her life.

AS HARKNESS SLEPT IN SHANGHAI, far away in the Qionglai Shan, or mountains, of Sichuan, a pregnant giant panda was steadily consuming bamboo. Sitting upright, the great black-and-white bear, known as *beishung* to the Chinese, grabbed branches within easy reach of her big paws, which looked, with their wrist-bone-turned-thumb, like mittened hands. Placing the largest end in her mouth, she pulled the sprigs through her lips sideways, stripping the green leaves and discarding the denuded branches. It was the end of summer, still a lush time when she could eat her fill of the succulent foliage.

As she ate, the only sound in this quiet mountain home was the snapping of the bamboo, the rustling of the leaves. It looked like a placid life. But like all giant pandas, she was living on a knife edge.

She was a bear, after all, and built to eat meat. But like the rest of her kind, she was feeding almost exclusively on bamboo. This grass gives pandas so little nutrition that they must stuff themselves nearly round the clock to meet even a low threshold of energy. Certain animals, like cows, have systems that are designed to batter tough plant-cell walls and absorb plenty of nutrients. But not giant pandas. Some of their teeth evolved over time to crush plants better, but their stomachs remained steadfastly that of a carnivore.

It looked to one zoologist of the time as though pandas simply had "little interest in evolution." These magnificent animals seemed so impractical, in what they eat, in the way they mate, and even in their flashy coloring. And yet whatever they've done has worked. They have roamed this planet far longer than man. It is the mystery of the giant pandas—

they have survived over millions of years even when other, seemingly more fit species have not.

So much about the panda has seemed so paradoxical that the animal appears the embodiment of yin and yang. Somehow the bear with a tenuous grasp on existence has lived longer than humankind, the animal built to be a carnivore lives as an herbivore, and the solitary creature so adept at hiding from the world displays the most colorful of markings.

To Ruth Harkness, there was an appealing integrity in the panda's existence. "They had lived through a world with such changes as we have never seen, and they had remained themselves," she wrote.

In their day-to-day lives pandas embrace solitude—except for a very few days when, driven by a reproductive urge, they mate, and in the months devoted to raising a cub. This giant panda was going about just such a solitary life, though her baby, a tiny intruder, would emerge soon enough. She had chosen her small territory carefully—it was dense with bamboo, had drinking water close at hand, and contained within its boundaries large and old rotting trees that would provide her a hollowed-out trunk roomy enough to den in at the time of her labor—an event that would, as these births had for thousands of years, take place in secret and in solitude. This particular baby, though, wouldn't remain hidden for long.

LATE AT NIGHT, far outside the city, at the Spanish-style Columbia Country Club—about the only place where there was a prayer of catching a breeze in the interminable Shanghai heat—Ruth Harkness sat with Dan Reib and a lively gang of executives and pilots. The posh cocktail lounge was a popular summer watering hole, known for its open and shaded natural setting, its wide verandah built under the stars, and its cool swimming pool. On a night like this, the room would have been filled with well-dressed sophisticates. At the Harkness table, the conversation had just turned to expedition when a young pilot, James McCleskey, and his wife, Peggy, were invited to squeeze in. The raucous group hushed as Harkness in her deep, resonant voice unfolded the story of Bill's disastrous efforts to capture a live giant panda, and her own decision to carry his torch. She laid out her plans to head toward snowy Tibet.

It wasn't just the thought of those cold mountains on this hot dreamy night that bewitched Peggy McCleskey. There was also such radiance from this brave woman, her mission was so romantic, and she possessed such obvious strength, that Peggy, the mother of a newborn baby, surprised herself by asking to come aboard. As soon as the words left her lips, there was, as expected, a loud, overwhelming objection by the Shanghailanders gathered around the table. The men admonished McCleskey to stick to the safety of the city and not consider entering the country, where God knows what could happen.

No one needed reminding of the danger swirling throughout this country. In America and England, people were spellbound by the breathless dispatches. Here in Shanghai, there was no escaping such talk. The news of fighting between the Kuomintang and the Communists, and the danger it posed for foreigners, was so dire that it made men shrink from the thought of such travel, never mind women. Shanghai's papers that summer were full of bulletins on the whereabouts of the Reds. The stories were always conflicting and often, it seemed, exaggerated to the point of hysteria. The headlines told of cities under siege, harrowing escapes, and the generalissimo's victories: COLLAPSE OF REVOLT IN SOUTHWEST: GEN. CHEN CHI-TANG ABANDONS CANTON AND FLEES TO HONG KONG: CITY UNDER MARTIAL LAW; *Keeping the Reds on the Run.* Especially hairraising were the ones about obscure, ordinary westerners caught in the turmoil, such as, MRS. OGDEN'S SOLITARY FLIGHT FROM BATANG [TIBET].

Panda country seemed especially vulnerable. Shanghailanders were fed a steady diet of accounts about Communists menacing villages near the border. Described as marauders and outlaws, the Reds and the trajectory of their movements were tracked closely in the papers. Thousands of Communist soldiers on the move in western China were said to have become nothing more than "roaming bandits."

Like everyone else in Shanghai, Harkness had pored over the stories. But, unlike most, she relied on her own counsel. The only prospect that had her "scared to death" about the trip, she said, was the thought of what her permanently waved hair might look like up-country. For now, sipping a cocktail and taking a drag from her cigarette, she sat listening to these men. She couldn't help it—to her, most of the talk seemed like unadulterated foolishness.

The newspaper dispatches may very well have been sensational. But there was no getting around it: Harkness's great adventure was playing out against the backdrop of what Pearl S. Buck called "the most dreadful upheaval of our age."

The trouble had been coming on for a long time. To a certain extent, the roots of it could be traced to the turn of the century, when uprisings and rebellions had begun to boil up with some force. At that time, there was poverty, unrest, and also a growing anger over the injustices of the westerners who were looting the country's resources. In 1900, the year Ruth McCombs Harkness was born, the antiforeign Boxer movement exploded with unexpected ferocity, in widespread, panic-inducing attacks on Western missionaries that killed about two hundred in all. The adherents of the cause, peasants who initially called themselves "Harmonious Fists" but were dubbed Boxers by the foreign press, practiced ritual boxing, a kind of martial art they believed endowed them with special powers. Though they were eventually suppressed, the strains of a lingering nationalism continued to gather strength.

Whether of the reformist or revolutionary variety, much of the discontent was directed against the Manchu leaders of the Qing Dynasty. The Manchus, who had been in power for centuries, were foreigners themselves—not ethnic Chinese like the vast majority in the country but nomads from the northeast. In fact, the long queues Chinese men wore their hair braided into were a symbol of their subjugation to the Manchus. In the eyes of the Chinese, this dynasty was making no effort to protect the country from foreign bullying, if indeed it was capable of doing so. For in the early part of the twentieth century, the few shreds of the once glorious Qing were held together, improbably enough, by a frail old woman and a little toddler—the ineffective empress dowager and the boy emperor, Pu Yi. The court tried in its last gasps to institute government reforms. But it was far too late. The virtual end of dynastic rule in

China came in 1911, as several revolutionary forces, many aligned with the more modern-thinking, Western-educated Sun Yat-sen, rose up.

But even that movement imploded within five years, failing, as historian Barbara Tuchman put it, "to fill the void left by what it swept away."

Without a unified government, the country reeled. For one long, chaotic, and turbulent decade, brutal *tuchuns,* or warlords, ruled, held in check by no government. Warfare fanned across the provinces, and poverty crushed the peasant. Seventy to eighty percent of the Chinese people were illiterate and had no sanitation, running water, or electricity. As a leaderless China stumbled back in time, the rest of the world surged forward, modernized, and then, scenting the unmistakable odor of distress, took advantage of this vast and vulnerable nation.

Inside the country, two rival Chinese powers emerged in the 1920s. Initially yoked together, counseled and encouraged equally by the meddling Russian Bolsheviks, they would ultimately be locked in a long, savage battle. They were the Communist Party with its headstrong, idealistic soldiers such as Mao Zedong and Chou En-lai, and the Nationalist Party or Kuomintang, first under Sun Yat-sen, and then, quickly, his charismatic and straight-spined military aide, Chiang Kai-shek.

Throughout the 1920s, strikes, boycotts, and demonstrations against foreign powers brought to the surface hidden hatreds. In Nanking, Nationalist soldiers rampaged through the city, terrorizing the white community, which at the time included Pearl S. Buck, and killed six foreigners, including a university vice president.

In 1927, a pivotal year of brutality and betrayal, the uneasy alliance of the Communists and the Kuomintang ruptured, and in 1928 Chiang made Nanking the seat of his own government. Better funded and better organized than the Communists, and with the blessing of Western powers, Chiang proclaimed himself president of a unified China. The generalissimo, as he was dubbed by the government in 1932, may have run a corrupt, repressive government, but he was perceived by the West as standing against the godless Communists, and was friendly to big business to boot. Making Chiang even more attractive to Americans and

Europeans would be his marriage—celebrated in the ballroom of Shanghai's Majestic Hotel—to a rich Christian girl, educated at Wellesley College and part of an enormously influential family, which was referred to as the Soong Dynasty. By 1930, Madame Chiang had even persuaded her husband to convert to Christianity.

Whatever his religious leanings, Chiang's hatred for the Communists burned so hot that he would concentrate his soldiery against them, ignoring the belligerent, land-grabbing moves of the Japanese, who seized Manchuria in 1931. To critics, he explained the choice by saying that the Japanese were a disease of the skin, but Communists—who had targeted the enemies of the suffering masses, the landlords and tax collectors—were a disease of the heart. The Communists saw tiny little Japan not as a disease at all but as a predator positioning itself to swallow China whole.

By the time Harkness came on the scene, the country was well into a period of great tumult, for it wasn't just the Nationalists against the Communists. Independent provincial leaders and private armies shifted their loyalties as they pleased, spawning discord and bloodshed, coups and uprisings. Students could gather in demonstrations numbering in the tens of thousands, or commandeer trains. Where soldiers fought, the brutality was unspeakable, with tactics that included burying people alive or beheading them.

One of the most important events during this time was the legendary Long March of 1934–1935, through which Mao Zedong rose to power. Dodging the Nationalist Army in southeast China, he led some eighty thousand people on a trek that covered six thousand miles and concluded a year later with about nine thousand exhausted survivors. Unlike many of his urban rivals, Mao believed that political success would come in this agrarian society only through the support of the millions of rural people. He predicted that "in a very short time several hundred million peasants . . . will rise like a tornado or a tempest."

Harkness knew the history, the politics, the dangers. But it wasn't enough to intimidate her.

"I was told that I was playing a million to one chance," Harkness would say. "I knew it. I was told that Western China was no place for a lone, white woman—especially a woman with no experience in the business of exploring. I did not believe it. I was warned of the ever-present possibility of running into bandits in the interior of Szechwan and reminded that Bill had been compelled to run back. Well, I was willing to take a chance. In short, I had journeyed too far and gambled too heavily on my hopes to admit defeat before I started."

WEST TO CHENGDU

WELL AFTER MIDNIGHT, Ruth Harkness stood alone on the deck of a "darling little river boat" cruising up the great Yangtze. The breeze against her skin was gentle in the mild fall evening. Taking a drag from her cigarette, she looked out at the lighted banks, crowded with coolies loading and unloading ships, singing out their rhythmic work chants— "Ah ho! Ah ho!"

At last headed for deepest China, she could not close her eyes and allow the evening to end. Soon Shanghai, the city so dominated by foreigners, would be behind her. According to the compass, the boat was moving west, but it was, Harkness knew, to a truer East.

It was September 27, 1936, the official launch date of the Ruth Harkness Asiatic Expedition. The steamer *Whangpu*, which would be her home for the next eleven days, was headed up the longest river in Asia, simply called by the Chinese *Chang Jiang*, the Long River—in the direction of its source in the Tibetan highlands. She would travel the sometimes turbulent, sometimes serene waterway that cut through the center of the country and was the very heart of the Middle Kingdom.

As was so often the case with her here, she was in a philosophical mood, her thoughts at the start of her great venture centering on the belief that something miraculous was happening to her. She would write home to her best friend, "dear, dear Perkie," that during her time in Shanghai she had come to know herself as never before. She felt that "China can in some way sharpen and clarify a personality much as a good photographer retouches a cloudy film." The transformation startled even her. "I sometimes wonder if this is the same person who once lived on 18th Street in New York and designed clothes," she mused. "I doubt it."

The expedition's start had been marked hours earlier by a party on the aft deck held by several Shanghai friends, including Gerry Russell and Elizabeth and Floyd Tangier Smith. But as they sipped highballs and offered polite conversation, this trio couldn't have felt much goodwill toward Harkness. The rest of the crowd toasted and teased her, spinning fantasies of her being lost forever in the wilds of Sichuan. She laughed right along with them. Just as she had when leaving New York months before, she kept her optimism to herself.

She did tune out all the joking at one point, though, stealing a moment to watch Young's own bon voyage party, which was under way nearby. She was seeing him in a very different context this evening—surrounded by his own smart set, westernized college kids, all looking athletic and sophisticated. In Shanghai, the trendsetting boys sometimes wore horn-rimmed glasses, and the girls might have their hair "permanently waved." Among Young's clique, one figure stood out. Maybe it was her good looks, or the way she stood near Young, or the manner in which they spoke to each other that made Harkness immediately take note of this strikingly beautiful young woman in a bright red sweater. Her hair was sleek and dark, cut into a fashionable bob. She was the picture of modern Shanghai. Despite the amount of time Harkness and Young had spent together, he had divulged nothing about the wealthy and athletic Diana Chen. She and Young were secretly engaged. Even their families didn't know. Undoubtedly, Chen's powerful parents would have been astonished to discover that their daughter was not only betrothed to this adventurer but using her extra cash to help finance his college education. All of that would come out in time.

HARKNESS HOPED to use her interval on the river to acclimate herself to more homespun Chinese culture and to learn something of the language. Of course, she would also get to know Quentin Young better.

He was berthed belowdecks with hundreds of other Chinese passengers, while Harkness and six other foreign passengers had cabins above. "First class accommodations on this boat are marvellous but you should see first class Chinese, not to mention second, and my God steerage!" she wrote. Young, she reported, was "first class Chinese—a tiny bunk with no mattress (which he doesn't seem to mind)."

The two groups were to do everything—eat, drink, relax—in total isolation from each other. The *North China Daily News* recognized the split, printing only the names of the foreigners in the list of passengers it routinely published in the shipping pages.

The "upstairs/downstairs" protocol separating whites from Chinese was one more rule for Harkness to break. She repeatedly had Young to her cabin, and trotted down into the Chinese area whenever she pleased. Young gave her Chinese-language lessons, plotted strategy for the expedition, and spent hours conversing with her. "People are very curious as to what I am doing, and I am saying not a word about panda, and being a rather bad liar, I suppose that there is an air of mystery about it all—but it's a hell of a lot of fun anyway," she said. She wanted to maintain a low profile, "slipping upcountry" as quietly as possible, because she feared that publicity might ruin her plans.

Nonetheless, the lives of the Chinese passengers were an irresistible draw. "It is unbelievable how they live and travel," she wrote. Crammed into small compartments, they were able to cook and eat and sleep, to nurse children, to smoke pipes, and to chat as though they had all the space in the world.

Harkness marveled too at what seemed to her the natural and enviable Chinese serenity. The confinement, the noise, the lack of privacy, would have made westerners short-tempered. Instead, she noted, here in the center of the commotion, in the cubicle next to Young's, an elderly Chinese man "with a long beard of seven hairs, cross legged with his eyes closed in contemplation (Buddhist with everything from cooking to childbirth going on around him) and you knew that his mind was not in his body—on the deck babies being nursed, men weeweeing over the rail and a few smoking opium." Harkness thought to herself that if there really were such a thing as a soul, his was traveling far from the cacophony about them. "I knew to look at him that he was not of this world," she wrote.

As she journeyed up the most famous river in China, Harkness began to discard her Western ways. Her American clothes were long gone, left behind in Shanghai, in favor of an Eastern-accented expedition wardrobe her Shanghai tailor had fashioned for her—loose-cut, boxy jackets and matching trousers made out of the durable blue cloth the coolies wore. She would rebuff most social invitations from foreigners during a layover in Hankou, saying she didn't have anything to wear. The truth was that she just didn't want to dilute her expedition time with non-Asians. She hoped that now that she was on her own, she might "forget all things Western and absorb things Chinese."

Not wanting to miss a moment of it, she would often spend the night up on deck wrapped in her silk-stuffed sleeping bag, watching the stars in the black sky, and waking to the morning sun.

All along the waterway, she would rush from the boat at every stop in little river towns to scout what seemed to her, with each passing *li,* or third of a mile, more and more the real China. She found dusty streets lined with treasure-filled stores. "Shop after shop, open to the street, full of the most beautiful paper-thin bowls of unbelievable color, square plates with magnificent dragons, patient artists painting feathery bamboo on teapots and cups, and all for just nothing in our money," she wrote. Always, throngs of curious people trailed her every step. Without fail, she discovered, her smile was always returned.

She passed through the more-than-hundred-mile stretch that contained the great gorges of the Yangtze, where rough cliffs rose straight up from the water for a thousand feet. She could sit for hours as the boat chugged through these breathtaking channels—the very same that eighth-century poet Li Po had described as the countless folds of hills—and watch the changing panorama of jagged cliffs set in deep shadow, veiled in clouds and mist, or awash in the amber of the setting sun.

Along the way, there were flimsy, crooked little peasant huts that seemed no bigger or more secure, she said, than swallows' nests perched precariously on the little ledges of rock. She passed terraced fields of rich green for mile upon mile, flooded rice paddies, old women balancing painfully on bound feet as they pulled along tethered geese or pigs or goats. Cows carried baskets of coal. It seemed as if every inch of soil that could be tilled was. One of the panda hunters, Dean Sage, had noted that the people here managed to farm on the kinds of cliffs that would make goats "think twice before climbing."

One day at dusk Harkness looked out from the deck to the shore. To her, it was always a magic time, for she said, "as evening falls, there is a strange feeling of nostalgia for something unknown." In the deepening darkness along the banks she spotted "a reed hut, in the distance." It "blended with earth, sky and water, with only a point of yellow light showing through the flimsy structure and a wisp of smoke to make you know that it was home—to someone." The little light kindled a longing. Here, in the half-light where the impossible takes place and day meets night, the dwelling place of one family became as elemental as the earth and sky and water around it. Harkness wrote: "China gets to you, my dear."

"I wonder when, and sometimes if, I will ever get back to America," she told Perkie, not with dread but with some mystical affirmation. Death and eternity, and the thought of belonging, were on her mind, not in the least because she now had possession of Bill's ashes. Young had taken them from the bronze urn and transferred them to a more portable cardboard container, which he placed inside their steel cash box. "I have told Quentin," she wrote to Perkins, "if any thing happens upcountry to me that I want to be put away there." She was quite clear about her wishes. Should she die while out on expedition, her body—and no doubt her soul—would stay forever in China.

IN YICHANG, HUNDREDS of miles west of Shanghai, Harkness and Young transferred to the *Mei Ling,* which would ferry them into the great cliff city of Chongqing, then known as Chungking. The 150-mile portion of the Yangtze they were approaching was notoriously dangerous, a stretch that Sage said "boils a tortuous course through a deep, cañon-like channel, which it has cut in a rugged, mountainous country."

As usual, though, Harkness was only feeling more and more secure, no matter what they confronted. Part of it had to do with Quentin Young. On board the boats, or wandering ashore, she was obtaining a most promising preview of his field persona. "It will not be a matter of surprise to me if Quentin is some day one of the men with the power and thoughtful intelligence to help in the shaping of his country's destiny," she wrote.

Her opinion was shared by an important group. Everywhere, dogs, pigs, cats, even roosters would sidle up to Young looking for attention. The mascot aboard the *Whangpu,* for instance, a little calico cat, would seek him out, crawling up onto his shoulders, rubbing against his ears and playing with his hair. "He seems to have a rare and strange attraction for any animal," she wrote. "There are some people—not many— who understand animals and are almost able to talk to them in some silent fashion."

She decided during the river trip to turn over all the expedition's finances to him. This way he would not have to ask her for money each time the coolies were to be paid, or when the bill was due at an inn. He would carry the cash, doling it out as needed. It was an enormous gesture of trust—and an interesting one. Up-country with Quentin Young, who by any Western standard of the day would have been expected to be her subordinate, she did nothing but treat him with respect, viewing him as a full and equal partner.

She came to another conclusion too, a point of honor for Young: even if she could not bring a live giant panda out, it was essential for him to accomplish his goal. He had taken this expedition on for very little money so that he would have the chance to shoot a panda and present it to the Nanking Museum. She perceived it as a matter of nationalistic pride to him. With natural history museums in the United States displaying stuffed giant pandas, China, obviously, should have its share too.

Harkness insisted on one proviso: the panda hunting had to follow the trapping, not because of any hierarchy, but she just couldn't bear to take part in killing an animal.

She never could have fit in on a traditional expedition like that of the Dean Sage party, which had skinned its trophy in only an hour, indulging in a grilled giant panda "sirloin steak" the next night for supper.

Young was managing everything like a seasoned professional and with a style all his own. Arriving at the forbidding cliffs of the five-hundred-year-old city of Chongqing on October 11, they had stayed on board overnight to reorganize. As they headed out late the next afternoon, they were surrounded by a mob of desperately poor coolies. Aggressively jostling one another, they fought for the work of transporting the expedition's equipment up the frightfully vertical pathways cut into stone and leading from the shore to the high city. With mounting combativeness, the men shouted angrily, closing in around Young and Harkness. Young had a revolver with which he could easily have threatened the group. Instead, standing so tall over them, he made a joke. Though Harkness could not comprehend the words, she did understand when the faces of the angry men turned into grins. With the situation defused, they and their luggage were bundled and carted upward, along the steep and narrow footpaths. Harkness and Young rode in plush sedan chairs, set on poles and carried aloft by coolies, up the precarious route.

Darkness was falling by then, which meant they would arrive at the gates of Chongqing at just the right moment to experience its great wonder. Harkness, having been slowly carried step by step up a dim, ancient stone path, emerged at the top only to be overwhelmed by a fantastic vision—a riot of neon lights, signs, banners, and the crowded streets of a busy, modern metropolis. It was a wild electric Broadway, she said, "here at the end of the world."

Harkness loved the vivid intensity of Chinese urban life—including the scents that most foreigners dreaded. "The smells of a Chinese city are indescribable," she wrote from Chongqing, "the incense, the food cooked on charcoal in the streets, just the burning charcoal itself in the dusk—and of course the odor, horrible at times, of the open sewage."

Once they settled in, they encountered other, less pleasant, surprises. First, their accommodations were with, as Harkness delicately put it, "some goddam missionaries." She grumbled, "How I hate the breed." There was much about their lives and beliefs to rub her the wrong way, especially their attitude toward the Chinese. She saw so many poor Chinese, their children wretched with disease, running eyes, and open sores; their animals so ill, the sight of them turned her stomach—all kinds of problems that Western medicine could cure. Half the people in China at that time would never reach the age of thirty, and preventable diseases were to blame for three quarters of the deaths. "When I see missionaries here living in a style that rich people can't afford at home, in point of servants at least, with a home leave, expenses paid, and then to learn that they [give] no free medical service at all—it is not a pretty picture," she said.

Then word came in of a rival panda-hunting party, way ahead of her own. Unbelievably, it was being led by Gerry Russell.

Rather than sailing to America, he had formed plans in secret, waved Harkness off on her boat, then grabbed a plane the next day to start his own expedition, beating her to Chengdu by weeks. He must have been making those arrangements for some time before his departure, sneaking behind Harkness's back.

"He is trying to best me at my own game," she fumed. And considering his comfortable lead, he had a good chance at it. She would discover later that upon landing in Chengdu he had even gone straight to Dan Reib's friend Cavaliere with an old letter of introduction Harkness had secured at the time their expedition was to be a joint one. "I think it was a bit unsporting of him when he saw me off in Shanghai not to tell me that he was flying here the next day to go after Panda too," Harkness wrote home. It made her want to "wring his redheaded neck."

Russell hadn't come all the way to China for nothing—with or without Ruth Harkness, he decided, he would head into the high country.

The more she thought about it, though, the less it got to her. "A little competition will make it more exciting," she said. In her well-loaded arsenal, her top weapon was Quentin Young. "I have the much better chance of getting the beast because I have the best man in China for the purpose," she reasoned.

Always generous in spirit, even to those who wronged her, Harkness conceded, "I can see Jerry's [sic] side to a certain extent." He had come an awfully long way only to be turned back. It was the deceit of it all that would never sit well with her, though. She could not fathom how a "so-called gentleman's so-called sense of honor" could have allowed such dishonesty. What she didn't know was that the worst was yet to come.

WHEN IT CAME TIME to leave Chongqing two days later, Harkness and Young did so in style. Reib had arranged a Standard Oil company car to ferry them two hundred miles over rough and rocky roads to Chengdu— a windfall in this tract where transportation was so hard to secure.

THE FIRST GLIMPSE of Chengdu late the next day was staggering. Completely protected by formidable stone walls, forty feet high and just as thick, the great two-thousand-year-old city was an impenetrable fortress constructed against threatening barbarians. Entry was negotiated through massive gates positioned at the four points of the compass, to its Tibetan neighbors the four sacred directions. At the very frontier of Chinese civilization, it was a portal between ancient and modern worlds, serving as a staging area for wanderers, soldiers, and merchants.

To Harkness, Chengdu would for a time feel like the center of the world. She would be landing now in a home that couldn't exist anyplace else on earth. It was a sprawling walled estate, within the walled city, that was part Chinese pavilion, part Italian villa. Behind the grand front gate trimmed in gold Mandarin characters were many tile-roofed buildings overlooking lush, landscaped courtyards. Once the residence of the provincial governor, it had enough bedrooms to accommodate one hundred guests comfortably. During Harkness's stay, several of them would be filled. And nearly every dinner would be an event.

At seven o'clock, on one of her first nights, an international lineup of guests occupied E. A. Cavaliere's immense, "haphazard" living room. Ruth Harkness stood before the fire, holding, as usual, her cigarette and her drink, served neat. The scarcity of evening wear in her luggage was not apparent, for she possessed a knack for throwing together dashing outfits, and she had stowed away one knockout—an embroidered, padded Japanese dressing gown. This night, as the only woman entertaining a buoyant and eclectic crowd, she was in her element.

The lavishness of the affair was business as usual for Cavaliere, a man of about sixty who was as generous as he was social. Small and dapper, with gray hair and blue eyes, Cavaliere was a courtly bohemian who spoke eight languages, including Chinese. He declared that, after thirty-six years in this country, he felt more Chinese than Italian. He lived his life as he pleased, keeping a White Russian mistress and befriending a wide assortment of characters, many of whom he came into contact with in the course of his work as the province's postal commissioner. Cavaliere had created a world of comfort and refinement, and guests arrived in a steady stream from the rugged lands that stretched for hundreds of

The cultured and kind E. A. Cavaliere.
COURTESY MARY LOBISCO

miles around Chengdu. Pilots, explorers, ambassadors, officials, specu-
lators, musk merchants, and even missionaries came to stay.

In this wilderness outpost, his home was an elegant oasis, filled with
fine food, wine, and song. "Kay" had two fine Victrolas and an impressive library of albums, heavy on opera. He was partial to Italian com-
posers, and particularly savored the recordings of Enrico Caruso. On a
given evening the whole Chinese estate might echo with the beauty and
power of the tenor's voice as he sang of the sorrow that twilight brings
in the haunting "O Sole Mio."

Cavaliere never turned a traveler away—or hardly ever. Harkness discovered at the outset that some sharp instinct on Cavaliere's part had
prompted him to send Russell packing weeks before. For everyone else,
though, the generous Italian had the room and the resources to entertain in high style. The constant airlift service of the pilots of the CNAC
kept him well provisioned with fare from the wine cellars and gourmet
markets of the world.

The pilots were grateful to Cavaliere on two fronts: they always found
free quarters with him, and, rather amazingly, Cavaliere also fixed their
planes. A mechanical savant who loved to tinker, he proved himself one
of the most able aviation mechanics the men had ever known, though as
a gentleman, he never accepted payment.

Kay had settled Harkness and Quentin Young in large, beautiful
rooms off a sunny courtyard filled with dahlias, zinnias, and flowering
trees. He provided Harkness with her own dedicated rickshaw boy, who
was always at the ready outside her door. And he arranged all her banking, including postal orders to the towns on her route so she wouldn't
have to carry much cash in the bandit-riddled territories. It took her no
time to feel that she knew her host well—within days, he was already
"dear Cavaliere," a man whose doting friendship would not end once she
was out of his house and on the road to the border.

Cavaliere couldn't have been more different from the expats she had
disliked elsewhere in the country. He seemed in harmony with China
and possessed a European's shrugging acceptance of human nature. He
also knew firsthand about the terrain in this mystical part of Asia, where

the green Sichuan Basin met the snowcapped mountains marking an ever-shifting border between China and Tibet. Here the hot winds of the plains barreled into the mountains, condensing the moisture and shrouding the world in a dreamy mist. From his living room, warmed by a fire, Kay could serve a tumbler of strong spirits to guests like Harkness and paint a vivid picture of this exotic land so little known to the outside world. In fact, he did sit with her at length, cautioning her about the savage beauty of this lost part of the world.

Not far beyond the ramparts of Chengdu existed land, mile upon mile of it, that was uncharted and filled with peril. The mountain chain that separated the Sichuan Basin from the Plateau of Tibet was crowded with unnamed peaks, among the steepest and tallest on earth. The mountains of Tibet were formed tens of millions of years before in some spectacular slow-motion collision between landmasses. Sheer, breathtaking, and punishing, the jagged ridges of the Qionglai Shan could reach heights of twenty-five thousand feet. There were wet, dense, nearly impenetrable walls of bamboo; deep, plummeting gorges; bone-numbing cold. The Chinese had marveled at this forbidding place for millennia. "It is more difficult to go to Sichuan than to get into heaven," the poet Li Po, who would become one of Harkness's favorites, had mused.

Even where the mountains could be breached, bandits and fierce tribes served as human barriers. In 1925 the famous American botanist Joseph Rock had witnessed men impaled, others hung up and disemboweled alive, and severed heads used as decorations for barracks. By repelling the outside world, the region had sheltered many mysteries within, including what was now the most sought-after animal in the world. The enigmatic panda roamed across this front, which was neither China nor Tibet. A no-man's-land absent from maps and beyond the reach of law.

Panda hunter Dean Sage wrote of "winds that howled wintrily through the crags, and chilled us to the bone," of mountains that "seemed fairly to hurl their jagged peaks against the sky," of trails up mountainsides "about as steep as it was possible for a man to climb," and of the backbreaking work of "thrashing through bamboo jungles of unbelievable density," of "wading through snow" and "creeping over ice-covered ledges."

For Harkness, always tantalized by the forbidden and forbidding, the dark descriptions would only have sent her imagination galloping and sharpened her determination. And who knew? Beyond all the danger just might lie a magical dominion. If Western experts were mystified, all the better, for past the realm of science lay that of spirits and poets; beyond calculation was belief. Many Chinese artists and thinkers held that in these mountains were glimpses of the infinite. Even Western climbers, now increasing in number, had often reported experiencing a spiritual ascent along with the physical one.

This borderland and all of inner Tibet—"the Roof of the World," as Victorians had dubbed it—had by now gained a reputation for possessing a sacred dimension unknown in the West. Explorers claimed to have witnessed the queerest phenomena—Alexandra David-Neel, the intrepid Parisian who had spent years there, chronicled lamas who had perfected something called *lung-gom*, the ability to fly while in a trance state, and monks who could produce great body heat in freezing temperatures through the practice of *tumo*. Writing for *National Geographic* magazine in 1935, Dr. Rock described the shamanistic rapture of an oracle in Tibet who displayed seizurelike convulsions when possessed by a deity, his face turning purple, blood oozing from his mouth and nose. While in this state, the man took a strong Mongolian steel sword and, Rock reported, "in the twinkling of an eye he twisted it with his naked hands into several loops and knots."

At the approach to Buddhist Tibet, in the folds of these mountains, there was a wrinkle in time and space. Distances could not truly be measured in miles or kilometers. In such a place, a traveler might be tempted to believe in the Tibetan legend of Shambala—a mystical realm hidden away in the mountain passes, where even the air was different—bringing clarity to thoughts and spiritual feelings. The story was persistent, told in many cultures, in many lands. It was even the center of the world's first paperback book, *Lost Horizon*. In 1933, the author James Hilton foretold the calamity of World War II, "the Dark Ages," which would "cover the whole world in a single pall." And he wrote of the sweet utopia of Shangri-La, which would remain immune to it all.

The rest of the world did seem to be going mad, with the threat of war growing and the global economy deteriorating. Yet there was a glimmer of hope in this sheltered land that existed on a higher, more benevolent plane. For Ruth Harkness, it was no fantasy. In this place, she would discover for herself "a beautiful forgotten world."

IN CHENGDU, it was time to finalize plans.

Quentin Young, in consultation with an elderly, gray-bearded servant of Cavaliere's, hired sixteen coolies and Wang Whai Hsin, a happy, quirky cook whom Harkness loved from the start.

The most important decision was where exactly they were going. Since panda country was all around them, Harkness discussed possibilities with Cavaliere. He agreed with the advice of Jack Young—that she should travel southwest along an old trade route toward Kangding, then called Tatsienlu, and make more than a week's journey still southward from there. This was the area that had provided the Roosevelt brothers with their panda and, before them, that famous panda skin of Père David's.

But for Harkness, in 1936, the first choice wasn't meant to be. The Kangding plan unraveled quickly because of logistics. The only road in this direction was "a government monopoly," restricted to official vehicles and a single sanctioned bus that was supposed to make the run once a day. Harkness had piles of gear, at least thirty pieces of cargo, which would not fit on the bus.

It was decided that she was better off heading northwest instead, to the Qionglai Shan range. All recent panda successes had come out of the northwest, in what was known as Wassu land or Wassu country. That was where Floyd Tangier Smith had set up hunters, and where Bill Sheldon of the Sage expedition felt he had found "the best wildlife country in Western China." The region was much easier to reach, with the line of the mountain chain slanting toward Chengdu at its northern portion, and beginning just sixty-two miles (one hundred kilometers) from the city.

Throughout this time, Cavaliere threw one dinner party after another. "If I spend everything I have—what an experience it will have been—even till now," Harkness wrote home. "Can you imagine having left my few dollars in investments, and having a few miserable pennies every month when I can have this?"

With everything set, Cavaliere orchestrated another gathering. This one included, along with "the usual assortment" of guests, W. H. Campbell, a blue-eyed and very British representative of the League of Nations; a "charming" German engineer; and a glum American pilot.

Right away, the German bore in on Harkness; he couldn't understand what such an urbane and sophisticated creature was doing in this outpost. As they dined, he interrogated her about her plans. Still wanting to keep a low profile on the expedition, Harkness answered vaguely about having come for the hunting. She couldn't have picked a worse cover. Hunting was the German's passion, and he wanted details on her shooting ability and the arms she had in her possession. Realizing that she wouldn't be able to sustain the ruse—of all the equipment for the trek, the guns had interested Harkness the least—she confessed. She was headed deep into the mountains in pursuit of the giant panda.

The German—and everyone else, for that matter—was truly baffled. The whole gathering erupted in protective objections from the men. Oh, you'll never come back alive, the pilot warned, backing up his prediction with gruesome tales of other would-be explorers who had vanished in this unforgiving land. The *China Press* had reported on the warlike people here: "Any man who ventures into their territory may expect to depart therefrom in two sections. It is no wonder that the Lolo country is represented by a blank space even on the best of maps."

Wearily, Cavaliere informed the guests that, if he could, he would prevent Harkness from setting out. He had told her it was "foolhardy" to go on. But it had done no good.

Only reinforcing the skepticism of her dinner companions was Harkness's behavior one night. Irate over animals loosening the gray tiles of his roof, and hearing footsteps above, Cavaliere, in the middle of a party, ran outside with a gun. Taking aim at the culprit, he shot dead a small silver cat, which skidded off its high perch, fell, and crumpled on the walk. Harkness, who was so dedicated to her own cats that she often took them on exotic vacations with her, ran inside the house in tears.

AT THE WESTERN GATE of Chengdu, a ragtag caravan emerged from the curtain of dust rising in the hazy sunshine. It was made up of sixteen coolies, the rounded form of Wang Whai Hsin, the raven-haired Ruth Harkness (already wearing her blue cotton expedition suit and bamboo rope-soled sandals in place of her walking oxfords), and the dashing Quentin Young, who, throughout the expedition, "was smart in his well-cut breeches, his red-topped socks and little cap that matched."

It was eight-thirty on the morning of October 20, and the streets were already choked with travelers. Sichuan, the largest province in China, matching the size of France, had one of the densest rural populations in the world. That was obvious from the foot traffic coming and going to market, the peasants pushing wheelbarrows heavily laden with goods like stones or salt, pigs, and even people. Through this steady stream of humanity, the Harkness expedition aimed itself away from the heat of Chengdu and toward the snowy mountains of Tibet.

Revitalized by their morning smoke of opium, the coolies worked in twos, each pair lugging as much as 160 pounds between them in a Sichuan-style bamboo contraption called a *wha-gar*. Basically slings tied between two bamboo poles, *wha-gars* could hold gear or human riders. Harkness, like many foreigners before her, had at first been troubled by the concept of being carried aloft by the poor men who were smaller than she was and often appeared barely able to stand. But it was common practice, ultimately providing much-needed work for desperately poor people.

Nonetheless, she decided to walk on that first morning's hike, reasoning that she had better get in shape for the arduous mountain trails ahead. In the slippery bamboo forests she would have to be able to manage on her own. The plan from the start was to cover up to thirty miles a day.

It took no time at all during this first clip for the caravan to break apart. The long-limbed Young was striding out front, with Harkness bringing up the rear about a mile back and all the coolies somewhere in between. She might not have looked like it right then as she struggled to keep up her pace, but the would-be explorer had become a genuine explorer. Out of Chengdu, with every step, Ruth Harkness was overtaking her husband's progress, drawing ever closer to what she called "the real adventure."

Straightaway, Young and Harkness confronted a problem: opium addiction in the ranks. It was the bane of China. Hungry coolies, who earned so little, would forgo food to spend their small wages on the drug aptly called "black rice." These unhappy souls did the work that strong draft animals would take on in other parts of the world, for here it was cheaper to hire a coolie than to feed a donkey. What it took to survive this lot in life was expressed by the very name "coolie," which meant "bitter strength."

Coolies were considered the lowest of Chinese society, beneath the peasant class, even, which possessed its own kind of spare nobility. These men owned nothing but the tattered blue trousers tied at the waist with rope, straw sandals, a threadbare blue jacket, and the pipes they used to smoke. On frosty nights at higher elevations, they would have to spend some of their few coins renting filthy blankets to pull over their bony, wasted frames. Miserable, wretched, with no hope for a better life and only the fear of their bodies failing them, they found in opium the serenity and the stamina to go on.

Each day the men were paid a small amount to buy food. Generally, opium would be purchased in three intervals with meals—morning, midday, and midafternoon. The Great Smoke provided calm and clarity, and for the godforsaken coolies there was, after just a few puffs, a release from physical pain too. Harkness saw the transformation herself. One miserable young coolie who had collapsed under the weight of his load in the morning became, following his afternoon smoke, a swaggering strong man hauling the same burden. "How shall a coolie endure life if he has no opium?" a downtrodden character in the novel *Shanghai '37* asked. "Life is too hard without dreams." Though their behavior was understandable, addicts made for irresponsible workers, often disappearing out from under their loads, never to return.

Right after lunch this first day, Young had to contend with a porter who decided he wouldn't work anymore. The group had already started back out on the road when Wang came racing up to Harkness, who had given up her march for the comfort of the *wha-gar*. "One piece coolie no good; he run away," Wang breathlessly reported. "Too much opium."

Furious about the problem this presented to the expedition, Young was also provoked by the issue in general. He was ashamed of the addiction of his fellow countrymen.

Harkness didn't feel that stigma, obviously, and she would go on to enrage Young during the trip by trying opium herself. In the case of the missing coolie, she saw the problem only from the worker's point of view. Here she was barely managing to carry her own camera, while the porters, all shorter than she, outstripped her with their quick, short-stepped strides, under massive weights. How could she not feel for them? If she were in their situation, she said, she'd "do worse than smoke opium."

There was nothing to be done now but redistribute the cargo and go on. Down one coolie, the group continued. That evening they lodged in a dark, low inn with a dirt courtyard. After dining on a hearty bowl of sour egg soup, an exhausted Harkness turned in shortly after sundown. "Last night's Inn was a beauty," she wrote home the next day. "The 'rooms' were indescribable (our coolies slept in them) but Quentin barricaded a corner of the courtyard with our loads, put my camp cot behind, two tables in front on which he slept, all of which did not keep all manner of Chinese from wandering in and out all night—but I slept well and largely from 7:30 to 5:30. It is all very wonderful—even the appalling 'terlets' which both men and women use, which are nothing more than pits can't dim the lustre of this particular expedition."

It was the life of a soldier now, with the team rising at dawn to head back on the trail. As Harkness stepped along that warm morning, focused on the gleaming clouds on the horizon, it dawned on her that the billowing whiteness wasn't cloud at all but her first glimpse of the great Qionglai Shan, the snowy mountains that she had dreamed of so often in the sweltering heat of Shanghai.

Her reverie was interrupted, however, right after the midmorning breakfast stop, when two more coolies ran away, forcing the caravan to rely on Sichuan-style wheelbarrows. Out of sixteen porters, three had

"Our porters take time out for opium," Harkness wrote
on the back of this snapshot. COURTESY MARY LOBISCO

vanished within forty-eight hours of the expedition's start. Since it was Young's job to manage this campaign, he became grim, realizing that if the defections persisted, the venture could be derailed. He gathered the remaining porters and, brandishing a revolver to punctuate his remarks, told them that if he had to, he would withhold the daily food advance to prevent them from purchasing opium. He made certain that the desperate men understood his authority and the consequences of their actions.

Just miles out of Chengdu, other realities were closing in. Throughout the day, groups of soldiers, some carrying submachine guns, overtook them on the road. Amid reports of bandits in the area, a cluster of military men passed by with two prisoners tied in ropes. Young was alarmed by the steady procession. Bumping along in one of the wheelbarrows, the Sauer rifle cradled in his lap, he begged Harkness to arm herself with any of the other guns. Not only was Harkness untroubled by the bandit report, she thought Young's concern was adorable. What a picture he made, with the gun, the wrinkled brow on that handsome face, and the unruly lock of hair falling across his forehead. In fact, she couldn't resist getting her camera out and taking a snap of him.

After lunch, however, her camera lens found a very different subject.

The scene was so unreal to her that she felt unmoved. Sprawled on the road next to an open field and riddled with bullets was the freshly slain body of one of the prisoners who had passed them earlier. He was flat on his back, legs crossed delicately at the ankle, bare feet casually resting one on top of the other. His right arm reached out, and his light cotton shirt was drenched in blood. More blood pooled darkly at his forehead, cheek, and chin; it ran from his torso onto his sleeve, staining the dusty road. "Thirty shots fired—7 hits, and by the look of him, most of them in the face," she wrote home. "Not very pretty."

As bystanders, including shoeless children, stood gawking, Harkness climbed down off her *wha-gar* to join them. How could she have sobbed over a dead cat, yet stand here looking on impassively, she wondered. Her conclusion was that by now she had absorbed some of the Eastern belief in accepting the inevitable. Grisly as it was, this was the bandit's fate.

All around the corpse, there was a thrum of excited talk—not over the death but about the circumstances surrounding it. The small crowd relayed that the dead man was the leader of a massive horde of bandits—numbering as many as six hundred—who were rumored to be gathering for his rescue. Throughout the countryside, bandit gangs as large as armies did exist, and the soldiers, panicking at the report, shot him dead, running off before they could be overwhelmed by the lawless mob.

It was a sobering scenario. The members of the lightly armed and heavily laden Harkness expedition were now determined to stay close to one another for the rest of the journey into the city of Guanxian.

They made it to their night lodgings there without further incident, taking comfort in the friendly village. A covered bridge containing a thriving marketplace for entering travelers led to the city's magnificent gates, with a massive tower capped by two tiled roofs set wedding-cake style, one smaller pillared layer atop the first. When the caravan found accommodations, they discovered that their day of surprises wasn't over.

The dead bandit served as a warning to the Harkness expedition.
COURTESY MARY LOBISCO

Up a ladder, Harkness entered the two tiny chambers that would be home for the evening. As she perched on the edge of her cot holding a tiny ration of hot water with which to attempt something of a bath, she heard a familiar English-accented voice calling "Hello there" from the open courtyard below. It was Campbell, the League of Nations chap she had met at Cavaliere's. "What in Gods name the L of N is doing in this remote and wholly Chinese town I don't know," Harkness wrote home. Campbell, "a most nice man," was "looking British and blue eyed as hell." Harkness, peering over her bowl of now muddied bathing water, apologized for not even being able to offer him a cocktail.

Campbell volunteered to return her to her old world, out of the wilderness, figuring that two days of rough travel in this country would have been enough to send any Western woman scurrying back to city life. He asked her if she'd come to her senses and decided to retreat to civilization. Of course, she had not. Nothing could tempt her away from her odyssey.

The gates of Guanxian were a welcome sight. COURTESY MARY LOBISCO

Campbell accepted her decision, surrendering some mail he had brought along for her and kindly agreeing to post her outgoing letters.

Harkness and Campbell, likely the only westerners for miles around, did not dine together. Instead, she and Young slipped off for a quiet supper in town alone. They made it a bit of a feast: spiced pork, chicken with bamboo shoots, and cup after cup of hot wine that seemed infused with the flavor of peanuts. Warmed by the wine, and no doubt inspired by the sight of the bandit earlier, the two spoke philosophically about death. Young revealed that, should he die in the field, he would want Diana

Chen or, as Harkness referred to her, "the girl in the red sweater," to have a lock of his hair. The talk of mortality and other loves did not discourage their cozy mood. They returned to the inn at about 8 P.M., relaxing together on Harkness's tiny cot. Sitting at either end, they wrote letters by the light of an oil lamp. With a sense of timelessness suffusing everything, utter peace filled the lines of her letter home to Perkie. "My cot is under the eaves, looking down into the open courtyard . . . that is filled with soldiers who are singing and playing a 2 string violin—and above a slim hazy young moon just disappearing over the curling tip of the tile roof."

Tomorrow, she would press north for panda country.

CHAPTER FIVE

RIVALRY AND ROMANCE

A S HARKNESS TRAVELED, her movements were being noted, and the information eventually relayed to Shanghai. Gerry Russell, up-country himself, was able to track her whereabouts, reporting them to the by now quite sickly Smith back in the city. The American woman's progress was of considerable interest to the two men she had spurned, and checking up on her would be easy. The local people knew what Harkness was doing "almost from hour to hour," and the hunters "kept tabs on her movements from minute to minute," Smith would say later. Beyond field-intelligence gathering, though, there wasn't much Russell could do to thwart her except beat her to the punch, something Smith would have liked to have done himself—if he had been up to it. Smith, the collector who didn't think a woman could be equal to the job, was presently check-ing himself in to a sanitarium in Shanghai for a week's "rest," which would be followed by a month of more recuperation at home.

Unaware of any espionage, Harkness and Young had started their climb toward the mountain passes. Harkness was out in front in the *wha-gar* and Young was bringing up the rear, with about a mile of road between them. The only sound she heard was the soft, steady shuffling of marching feet. Suddenly, there was the sharp report of Young's revolver—three pops in quick succession—which prompted Harkness to command the coolies to halt. What could it be? A swarm of bandits? She waited in utter anxiety until Young came around the bend of the crooked path accompanied by a Chinese officer, Captain Chien, and a group of fourteen soldiers, all armed. Overjoyed that the signal hadn't been fired because of bandits, she then feared these men had come to suspend the expedition. Perhaps it was her nightmare come true—that she would have to return home, defeated as Bill had been.

The appearance of the soldiers, it turned out, was nothing more than a gesture of Cavaliere's protectiveness. Even in this time of great turmoil, they had been dispatched to ensure Harkness's safety. Cavaliere really would, she wrote, "turn the world upside down to help you."

Harkness felt an immediate fondness for the men, most of them barefoot and wearing weathered clothes in shades of faded blue. There would be two separate and equally congenial groups to accompany the team over the next several days. They shared cigarettes, swapped pleasant conversation, and drank tea the country way—a pinch of leaves at the bottom of a bowl, with boiling water poured over them. With Harkness, the men held an impromptu target practice, all laughing when she tumbled over backward from the recoil of a rifle.

She was touched when their leader made her a present, both practical and poetic, of two perfect eggs—a simple gesture, but one of great importance for the people here. Later, in a distant village, when the soldiers brought Harkness to meet their wives, she would sit with the tiny women drinking tea and eating sunflower seeds, delightedly spitting the husks onto the floor as the other women did.

The soldiers kept pace with the expedition as the week of travel after Guanxian marked a drastic change in the terrain, and in the bond between the American widow and her Chinese expedition partner. The ascent was beginning.

Harkness and Young rose each morning with the sun, stopped for three breaks a day, and turned in at about the time Harkness would have been headed out for early cocktails in Manhattan. They shared every-thing, including a battered washbasin. Evenings often saw them together on her cot, reading or writing letters.

As they climbed through higher elevations—up toward the eight-to-ten-thousand-foot zone where the pandas thrived—the world around them grew heavenly. There were deep gorges and tumbling streams, shrines and temples, Chinese girls carrying magnificent hundred-pound loads of tea, peasants bearing medicinal herbs on their backs and leav-ing fragrant trails behind them. At one point, Harkness and Young stum-bled upon a country funeral, complete with drums and cymbals, and large banners that cast their dancing shadows on the dusty village streets. Skittering along cliffs, Harkness could faintly hear the rushing waters of the Min far below. And early one morning, appearing like ghosts out of the fog, came a group of wild young men from the mountains. Wearing fur-trimmed leather coats and curled-toe shoes, they led a string of shaggy Tibetan ponies whose silver bells jangled with each step.

Harkness and Young were meeting their goal, covering twenty or thirty miles a day, most of it uphill, much of it rutted or rocky. It was a rougher life than Harkness had ever known. Yet she felt alive in a way she never had before. She walked and scrambled over miles of cliffs and forest and tumbled rock. Always petite, she now grew fit. The surround-ings were beautiful, the air was clear, the company ideal.

Everything seemed better to her here, even the simple food. Some-how a handful of dry grape nuts eaten while marching, she said, "tasted just as good to us as though they had been served in a china dish with bananas and cream." She feasted on local fare—corn cakes and turnips, cornmeal bread, cabbage, and peanut candy. She once used chopsticks to eat fried eggs in front of a crowd of two hundred. Sometimes she and Young dove into their own supplies, making breakfasts of English bis-cuits smothered in Tasmanian jam, or crabmeat and boiled eggs. In every village, they filled their enamel mugs with cup after cup of freshly brewed tea.

All things around her deepened and changed in her eyes—including her partner. The shy boy she had met in Shanghai seemed like a man now, and a very protective one. Every night, no matter what the accommodation, Young guarded Harkness, setting up his own bed close to hers. His impulse would prove sound one evening when he foiled a band of robbers as she slept.

Wherever they went, Young took care of everything. He dealt with the soldiers, he managed the porters, he kept the expedition on course and safe. He was also great company, and their intimacy grew, as they discussed the day's events, wrote letters, and reviewed plans and expenses together, almost always on the comfort of her cot.

LIKE SOMETHING out of a book of Chinese fairy tales, Harkness wrote, they came upon the old village of Wenchuan. It sat at the foot of great green mist-enshrouded mountains that looked like coiled jade dragons, complete with serrated spines and smoky breath. As symbols of good luck in China, the mythical beasts were forever appearing just as they did now—in the outlines of fog-bound mountains and hills.

The enchanted hamlet of stone and timber-and-mud houses, lighted at night only by the warm glow of candles and encircled by "crumbling, crenellated walls," seemed little changed since the fifteenth century, when foreign princes from Tibet, at the urging of the troubled Ming Dynasty, came to quell local rebellions. Their odd, semiautonomous empire-within-an-empire, Wassu, stretched over some twenty-eight villages, and when Harkness arrived it was still ruled by the princes' heirs, known as Wa-ssu tusi. The royal men and their descendants had built huge Tibetan-style fortresses and great stone watchtowers throughout the area.

Wenchuan, it turned out, this afternoon could offer no rooms to the travelers in the village proper, so Harkness and Young made their way to a fantastic, if ruined, Buddhist ghost temple at the outskirts. Soldiers, in a "revolutionary tornado," had come through the year before, dismantling it along with many other buildings in the town for firewood. Even so, what was left was remarkable. Blue life-size horses, one headless, stood at attention in a courtyard whose walls were painted with scenes of souls in purgatory. A barren loft, open to "three corners of the compass," was quickly converted into a comfortable camp with all the equipment and cots dragged up a wooden ladder.

Settling into the temple, Harkness installed a makeshift curtain for herself. After a sponge bath, she changed into her beautiful quilted Japanese dressing gown, an indulgence, perhaps, but at least it was warm.

The ghost temple in Wenchuan. COURTESY MARY LOBISCO

That night, Harkness and Young wandered into the village center for a hearty meal. The town—the last they would see before the mountains—would mark another pivotal point on the great journey. Over the next several days, emotionally and logistically, there was much to square away.

One evening here, as a bright moon filled the courtyard with a pearly light and a cold wind moaned, the soldiers argued with Quentin Young. Young wanted the recruits to part company with them so that he and Harkness could get on with the expedition into the mountains. But the military men were concerned about their culpability if something should happen to the American. The discussion unnerved Young as he began to think about the consequences he himself could face if Harkness were harmed.

He came to her, agitated and fretful, with a sense of rising panic she had never seen in him. She tried to convey her unshakable confidence that this expedition was blessed. She concluded, as did a character in a Chinese novel by a favorite writer of hers, that "when you yourself are right, nothing that ever happens to you can be wrong." She knew they could walk through an avalanche, emerging unscathed. "The utter impossibility of anything but the peace and beauty of the last few days of travel was so unthinkable to me that I believe I finally conveyed a little of it to Quentin," she wrote.

The soldiers were dismissed, but still, as a precaution, Young again issued strict orders for Harkness to carry the revolver with her at all times. She would never really comply. With a gun, she wrote, "I felt and looked so silly." And, "besides," she said, "the people were all gentle and friendly." The results of target-practice sessions had only reinforced her feeling that she should not be trusted with a weapon of any kind.

One morning, though, when Young was especially adamant, she acquiesced. Dressing in riding breeches and boots, strapping a big .38 Special police revolver to her thigh, she strutted out, feeling pleasantly ridiculous, and mock-saluted Young.

He was jubilant.

Saluting her back, he addressed her as "Colonel." She called him "Commander." The pet names stuck for the remainder of the journey.

AFTER YOUNG PAID off the old set of coolies from the city, he set about hiring a new staff of local hunters and porters. A man who was one of Smith's hunters came to the temple looking for work. What his motivation was would always be a mystery. Like Russell, he may have had in mind some spying on Harkness. He might have wanted to create a little mischief. Or he might simply have been looking for a way to double his salary—already being paid by Smith, he came for a share of the Harkness expedition's payroll. Whatever it was, Young and Harkness agreed that they wanted nothing to do with him.

It did ignite Harkness's resentment once again, reminding her of her strong conviction that she had been cheated. Back in Chengdu, some missionaries had told her that Smith channeled funds through them to keep hunters in the area working for him. She believed Bill's bank account was continuing to fuel Smith's operation. Now she felt that if she hired Smith's hunter, her poor dead husband would be paying the man a multiple salary: one from Bill via Smith, the second from Bill via Ruth.

She didn't linger long over the thought, though, because a very different character looking for employment presented himself at Wenchuan too. With two mountain dogs loping by his side, he seemed as old and wild as the great mountains he had emerged from. His name was Lao Tsang, though Lao was an honorific meaning "old," and Tsang could have simply been a variation on the word for "Tibetan." A member of the Tibetan-related Qiang people, he wore a leather coat with fur lining, tall leather boots held high by suspenders tied at his waist, and a garment of coarse, homespun cloth. His brown, weathered face was set off by a white turban, wispy strands of snowy hair straggling down from it, and a sparse goatee. He had a squinty expression, as if appraising everything before him. His gun, made of silver, turquoise, and coral, seemed more ancient artwork than formidable weapon.

He was the headman of his village, about a day's walk westward, deeper into the mountains. He had heard from what outsiders called the "bamboo telegraph"—some uncanny system of fast communication among mountain people—that they were hunting the giant panda. He told them matter-of-factly that he was the man to do it. He spoke of his hunting prowess, his knowledge of good panda habitat, and he informed them of what he would expect in the way of payment, which amounted to just a few dollars a month.

They hired him without hesitation, and the newly constituted group was soon on its way. Harkness, Young, Lao Tsang, and two porters were to travel fast and light to scout out the promised hunting area. Wang was

left behind with the heavy gear. On their departure, the entire town, including barking dogs and squealing pigs, saw them off.

At a tiny hamlet came evidence that they were on the right track—
not panda tracks or dung, but a pair of tweed trousers left behind by the
Sage expedition, which had traversed this very route the year before.

The small group would spend the first evening of its trek on the roof
of Lao Tsang's home, departing in the morning with the old hunter's
son-in-law, Yang. For two days they battled their way upward along cliffs
and through thick bamboo and beautiful spruce forest. The ancient Lao
Tsang was as talkative as he was agile, keeping up a constant dialogue
over the long miles. At sundown they camped outside, packed so tightly
together on a rock ledge that Harkness awoke during the night to find
Yang's head on her feet and Lao Tsang nestled against her stomach.

In the morning, she opened her eyes to a sunrise of spectacular
beauty, with fog lifting in ghostly wreaths from the valley below. Harkness would later write of coming into consciousness in that moment.
There was, she said, the "miracle of the sun coming over the mountains—and then it was time for that other miracle, trying to put on a pair
of pants in a sleeping bag."

The team was looking for fresh signs of giant panda, and, for effi-
ciency, it was decided that the foursome would split up into two teams—
Yang and Harkness, Young and Lao Tsang. The day was arduous for the
American as she lurched over fallen trees, struggling to advance through
the never-ending stands of bamboo, which can grow taller than a man,
and in patches are dense enough to shut out sunlight. It created what
Harkness described as "a perpetual twilight even when the sun is high
at noon." In addition, the altitude made it hard for her to catch her
breath. She took it all like a soldier, until she realized she had no matches
to light a cigarette, and then she nearly cried.

By the end of the day, the only reward was some panda dung Harkness had discovered. New droppings, which would indicate the recent
presence of an animal, would smell like fresh-mowed grass, but these
desiccated, nearly odorless specimens were too old to be of any use. The

team moved on, heading for new ground westward in the beautiful peaks and valleys of Chaopo, or what was then called Tsaopo-go.

Harkness was in for the roughest hiking yet. Her predecessor, Bill Sheldon of the Sage expedition, would maintain that his youth—he was in his early twenties—and his recent employment in a rain-soaked logging camp in Washington were the only reasons he had been able to cope with the terrain. Nevertheless, he often found himself crawling on hands and knees or falling thirty-five to fifty feet, feeling lucky he hadn't tumbled in areas where a misstep would have sent him crashing more than two thousand feet. Others in his party were not so fortunate. Sage's wife wrenched a knee early on, and another member had a mild heart attack. It was always a possibility that Harkness could die out here, but if she sustained even a relatively small injury it would halt the whole operation, and she might never get the chance to return to complete her mission.

Over the course of three hours of snaking around barriers, the team dropped twenty-five hundred feet, mainly down a boulder-strewn dry creek. It was here that the heavy hobnailed boots, which had seemed ridiculous in Shanghai, began proving their worth.

The party met a medicine digger of the Qiang people who was awestruck by Harkness, having never seen a foreigner before. Everyone had questions. Turbaned herb hunters, in their traditional brilliant blue gowns, knew these mountains in a way that no one else could. The diggers lived a reclusive existence, tapping into a fantastic side of nature, gathering such strange items as the "grass-worm"—a short amber-colored stalk made up of a predatory fungus and its prey, the captured caterpillar itself.

Most of the panda lore dispensed by the root digger's party was culled from evidence left behind: shredded bamboo stalks, pressed vegetation where they had lain, and scattered dung. Like many others from the area, these men claimed that pandas ate iron pots and pans. It was a popular tale, inspired, no doubt, by pandas chewing on food-encrusted cookware left out at camps. The hungry and strong-jawed animals would end up puncturing the thick iron as they gnawed.

The travelers enjoyed the talk, and after a lunch of hard-boiled eggs and sardines eaten near a tall stone watchtower in a tiny village, they went on, passing little shrines set out to the spirits of the mountains.

The terrain became even more difficult to negotiate, especially with temperatures nearing a hundred. By the afternoon, Harkness was unraveling. Her blue sweater had torn, and Bill's cut-down riding breeches began to fight her, simultaneously bunching up and tugging downward. Despite her efforts to hold them up with scarves tied about her thighs, at one point, the pants actually fell down to her ankles. As usual, Young looked neat, clean, and pressed, nimbly leaping from spot to spot.

Harkness, trying to keep up with the lanky athlete, could only watch as his red cap moved farther and farther away till she lost sight of it altogether. A long while later, at the bottom of an incline, perspiring and breathless, and with no Quentin Young in view, she gave up the pursuit, sitting down to light a cigarette with newly procured matches. Just then, Young popped out and teasingly claimed to have had time to take a nap as she descended. Harkness asked him how he had ever learned to negotiate the rough, rocky terrain with such fleetness. He replied that it

Harkness felt like a "sissy" in dealing with the log bridges that the porters crossed so nimbly. COURTESY MARY LOBISCO

was by observing blue mountain "sheeps." Whatever frustration she might have felt disappeared: Harkness found Young's occasional slips in plurals nothing short of charming. The two shared a smoke and a good laugh before setting off again.

There would be many more physical trials for Harkness before the day was done. Over and over again, the team crisscrossed the strong running mountain streams, which despite providing them with cold, clean drinking water also made travel so troublesome. The slippery "bridges" were merely knotty logs spanning the water. Harkness found herself growing more and more wary with each crossing, until she became, as she said, an absolute "sissy" about them.

By dusk, after having traveled thirty arduous miles, they reached their destination. Festooned with Tibetan prayer flags and ringed by lighted huts stood a crumbling castle, said to be five hundred years old. It was bleak and imposing, set high on a barren hillside. Its massive walls, ramparts, and towers were made of stone, giving foundation to a wooden structure three stories high, with whitewashed walls, dark wood beams, and a belt of balconies. Although truly Tibetan, having been constructed in the early days of the ancient Wassu kingdom, it looked like it had arrived straight from the Alps. At once stern and magical, the castle was a perfect setting for a Grimm story.

Exhausted, Harkness and Young made their way inside, past the flags whose every snap in the wind was believed to transmit a prayer heavenward. The vast fortress became a maze of dark passageways and uneven stone steps. The team lighted lamps, stumbling around until they found sizable rooms fit for encampment. Using just about every blanket and oil sheet she had, Harkness partitioned off a private space for herself, hauling out the well-used little basin to wash up. Cool soapy water washed away the sweat and dirt, especially from her blistered feet. For a fresh outfit, she was a bit stuck. All of the nicer things were by now soiled, so she would have to rely on her knack for making simple things elegant. As temperatures in the mountains descended quickly with the night, she fashioned an ensemble from Bill's long woolen underwear and the sheepskin coat that Su-Lin had given her.

Bathed and dressed, Harkness and Young made themselves a dinner on the portable stove: thick cornmeal bread and corned beef from a tin. As they sipped wine, Young kept Harkness spellbound with a saga of adventure from mysterious Tibet. He told her of a secret place, a spectacular, uncharted lake that he and his brother believed they had discovered. Harkness and Young vowed to map the lake as their next mission, and in that instant their hopes and their lives were entwined. The pact was impulsive. They laughed at themselves for planning a second venture before the first was finished. Harkness felt deliriously happy.

At some point, they decided to do a little exploring in the vast labyrinth of the stone castle. It was a sorry old hulk. Soldiers had harvested wood from its ancient walls. For countless years the elements had been punishing, wind and rain penetrating deep inside the ruin. Still, poignantly, there were great touches of life and art left intact. These were possessions of the lamas that had held no interest for the marauding army. The chants written on Tibetan prayer wheels and prayer flags silently endured. Serene Buddhas perched on lotus leaves in bright, colorful paintings kept company with many other gods.

The two adventurers came upon a hidden compartment. As they entered the chamber, their light brought to life an astonishing carnal scene. It was, to Western eyes, a playground of statues and paintings in which lusty gods romped in erotic abandon. The depictions were so graphic that they had shocked earlier Western visitors who had seen them. The botanist E. H. Wilson had described the "erotomania," in which "phallic worship holds unblushing sway," as "hideous and disgustingly obscene."

The deities seemed proud of their desires in this sect of Tibetan Buddhism, in which tantric sexual rituals were added to the menu of spiritual practices. Harkness, who loved the "frankness" of the East, was captivated. Something must have stirred in Young too, for in this secluded galaxy of lust, their intimacy became sensual, their bodies slipping into an embrace.

Taboos never mattered much to Harkness, except maybe to make things more desirable. She was living life to the fullest, with every sense heightened. Closing her eyes that night in a castle at the edge of panda country, she couldn't hope to find in sleep a fantasy any more beautiful than her waking life. "Time turned backward in a dream—or was it that other world of feverish activity that was illusion?" Harkness wrote.

ON THE FIRST MORNING there, while Harkness still slept, Young tenderly rigged a sheet to keep the sun out of her eyes. But the very next day, he was off early before she awoke. Engaged to one woman in Shanghai and sleeping with another in Sichuan, perhaps he felt the conflict of warring emotions.

Harkness was serene and sated. Contentedly puffing a classic yardlong Chinese pipe, its thimble-size bowl filled with rich native tobacco, she happily passed the three days of Young's absence. Having run out of cigarettes, her only crisis had been one of nicotine, a problem she found easy to solve with the purchase of a pipe from the villagers.

The solitude gave her time to reflect on their relationship, which of course was shockingly "mixed" for its time. But the issue had fascinated Harkness since her days on the *Tancred* when she met a beautiful Dutchman who was one-quarter Javanese. Clearly Chinese and Americans came together sometimes, Emily Hahn and the poet Zao Xinmei being a famous example. But there were other pairings of a less public nature. Harkness wrote home when she reached Shanghai about meeting sophisticated, well-traveled young "halfcaste" Chinese who would turn out to have names like Angus MacPherson. She made friends with an American woman who was married to a Chinese man. Harkness referred to her as "Mrs. Chun Tien Pao," reporting that she was fascinating but unhappy. There were rooms for ancestor worship in her large house, Harkness noted, "where she kowtows before the tablets with the rest of the family." Still, both whites and Chinese were horrified by such marriages. "Anglo-Saxons have rendered a signal service to civilisation, not only by maintaining the *prestige* of the white man all the world over, but by guarding the unmixed purity of their race," wrote the French poet Abel

Bonnard in a book about his travels, *In China,* published in 1926. A society of "half-breeds" is disgusting, he said, bringing with it a "debasement of the soul and confusion of the mind."

Harkness did not agree. Young was handsome and kind. People— native and foreign—respected him. He was capable and honorable and smart. She was a young widow far from the gossip mills of Shanghai, farther still from New York. Her husband had been dead for eight months, and away from her for two years. She had never felt so physically alive, so strong, so sure of herself. Her impulses must have felt as pure and potent as those tantric gods seemed to have ordained.

ON NOVEMBER 2, despite a cold rainstorm that carried the threat of snow, Quentin Young arrived full of good cheer from his scouting sortie, while luggage and mail were delivered from Wenchuan. Around the fire that night and into the next day, Young and Harkness ate pancakes and read letters. Dan Reib had sent an encouraging note and Harkness was delighted to hear from Cavaliere, who addressed her as "Dear Sweet Tender Lady." If she received news of the outside world, she didn't mention it, though, as they holed up in the castle, FDR was being reelected to a second term.

It was time to strategize for the final push. The expedition now counted twenty-three, which included, to Harkness's amusement, Ho, little Ho, and old Ho, as well as three Dzos, and many Wangs, Whangs, and Yangs. The staff was large enough that they could afford to dispatch a member once again to Guanxian, this time for material to make traps. They planned to send runners on a regular basis to Wenchuan for supplies and mail over the long months they expected to be in the field.

Young and Harkness hashed out their game plan. There would be three camps. Base camp would be one day's travel from the castle into the mountains. Wang, Yang, and Harkness would be stationed there. Camp Two was to be Quentin's, positioned one day from base camp. The third would be managed by Ho, who had been a member of the Sage expedition.

The travel coming next would sorely test the city girl. Sage had written extensively about the area they were about to enter. "The climbing we had hitherto done was nothing to what now confronted us," he wrote, "for the trail led up over ledges and crags whose abruptness was fairly staggering. . . . Up and up we struggled, inching a laborious way over slides and ledges and around precipitous slopes, with often a sheer drop from the narrow trail into the abyss of clouds below."

At 8 A.M. on November 4, Ruth Harkness's expedition headed into what she called "the lonely lost world of tumbled mountains." The morning sunshine in this province noted for its rains, she felt, was auspicious. Overall, the expedition had been experiencing great luck with clear weather. The team climbed and climbed. There were cliffs and bamboo forests, each turn providing a more stunning vista of snow-covered peaks. This "lonely, wild and unutterably beautiful place" made her wonder why anyone would choose to live in civilization. She continued to refer to the mountains as lonely, a complex sensation of many shadings that she and Bill knew well. Here, she embraced solitude, luxuriating in her reflective mood and continually comparing the life she had left behind to this glorious new one.

When she arrived, Harkness was thrilled. "New York has nothing like this," she said. Because Young sped on ahead to prepare the camp, the comforting smell of wood smoke hung in the air, and on one of the few level spots in the whole area stood a cooking lean-to and her lightweight tropical white tent. Her quarters contained a cot, a trunk, and a canvas case. Best of all, it provided privacy, something that had been in short supply throughout the journey.

Just before dusk, when all the porters were accounted for, Young organized a ceremony in which the American flag was raised in her honor.

Harkness enjoyed a meal in the warm lean-to with the men. And, later that night, bundled up in her silk sleeping bag on the cot, as rain and wind beat against the canvas of her tent, Harkness closed her eyes, listening to the reassuring murmur of the hunters in conversation nearby.

The next day, Young was off to settle his own camp, but not before expertly bringing down a goral—a husky and robust goat-antelope. It would provide a great deal of fresh meat, starting right away when they ate the liver for tiffin.

In Young's absence, Harkness sat in the field kitchen, banging out letters to friends on her portable typewriter and chatting with Wang in pidgin English. He was working his magic. Stripped to the waist in the steaming shed, he busied himself with the fire, making delicious scones for her while recounting his time as assistant to the cook of the French consul in Chongqing.

The next morning, a dispatch from Young arrived, along with a packet of mail he wanted sent off. The snowline, he said, descending further and farther down the mountain, had reached his camp. It was thirty degrees, foggy, and still snowing as he penned his note. At base camp, while a raw rain fell, Harkness stuck close to the fire, reading letters from Chengdu, Shanghai, and the United States, which arrived by runner just before nightfall. She relished the contact. Dan Reib cheered her on: "Hurry up and get your Panda and be back in Shanghai for Christmas," he wrote. Harkness laughed at the thought—wouldn't that be something? It was much more likely that she'd be right here for months to come.

Young strode down to her the next day, announcing his approach with two shots of a gun. He was full of energy and high spirits. And he carried with him a gift—two beautiful tragopan pheasants. All the plans were going forward at tremendous speed. His camp was completely ready for her stay, traps had been set, log bridges constructed. As soon as he checked on the third camp, run by Lao Ho and Lao Tsang, he would be back to base camp to pick her up.

Before he was off again, he found waiting for him a letter from Diana Chen. Tucked into the envelope was a newspaper clipping—a photograph of her in a recent triumph. She had won events in javelin throwing, shot put, and the broad jump. It was a strange circumstance for Young, reading the letter of his girlfriend in front of his lover. Harkness wrote that he was smiling as he told her that she herself looked like an athlete now too. In Harkness's New York set, a woman who could drive a standard shift might be considered athletic. Young's bar was quite a bit higher, and she was flattered. It was a sweet moment between them, and Harkness assured him that the pheasants would not be cooked until his return the next day.

Tethered to the small camp, Harkness, for the first time on the entire trip, grew impatient. While the panda hunt was so close, she wanted to be with Young.

She didn't have to wait long. On the afternoon of November 8, Quentin Young returned to guide her upward into panda country.

The terrain was as formidable as most adventurers would face in a lifetime. Not only were they climbing steeply at high altitude, but every step held another obstacle: dense stands of head-high bamboo, great dead logs covered in slippery moss, fields of knee-deep sphagnum moss engorged with icy water, and snow slipping off branches onto cheeks and down into coat collars. The constant fog kept everything wet, conspiring with the moss to make the footing as slippery as if it were oiled. They made their way through forest, over tumbled rock, and across icy churning streams. "Picture, if you can, a world of up and down," Harkness said. "Where the best refuge you may hope to find from icecold rain, chilling ghostly clouds and razor-edged wind is a space hardly bigger than a bridge table in the mountain crags under overhanging rocks. . . . Where you grope your way through thickly standing spruce, interwoven forests of rhododendrons, walls of bamboo that virtually grow stem to stem, with here and there a sprinkling of moss-covered rocks and clumps of ferns and other vegetation."

Harkness continued to struggle along in a reflective mood, particularly when she came upon what looked like nature's confirmation of yin and yang, the entwining of opposites. "A stranger thing I have never seen," she wrote, "than snow on green bamboo." It was proof that opposites coexisted, were part of each other, and gave each other life force. Evidence too, according to early philosopher Ko Hung, of the possibility of everlasting life—for bamboo showed that not all plants are bound to wither in winter. Scientists took note of the phenomenon as well. To them, the year-round life of bamboo, which provided a steady if not terribly nutritious food source, represented the twist in the road of giant-panda evolution.

In this foggy region, there were places where Harkness could see but a few yards ahead. She wrote, "Then suddenly, there would be a rift in the ghostly mass and, often as not, we would find ourselves clinging tooth and nail to a mountain-side with a dead fall of many thousand feet right below us."

Harkness and Young were drenched and tired when they reached Camp Two. Like Camp One, it consisted only of a cooking lean-to and a white tent in a cleared area, though this tent was Young's, and the flag flying above it was Chinese. Nonetheless, Harkness spent the night in that tent. Young, she wrote for public consumption in her book, slept with the hunters.

All along the route, they had seen "Panda signs. Droppings on the ground, claw marks on the trees, and bamboo stalks that had been ripped open and chewed." Ruth Harkness was finally in the realm of the giant panda.

THE BIG BEARS had lethal power in bulk and muscle, in their sharp claws and powerful bite. But what they wanted most was to be left alone to live a quiet life. And, strangely, it seemed they had accomplished that.

The giant panda, or *Mo* as it was often called, had been mentioned in ancient texts since before the birth of Christ, but not always in recognizable form. The *Shan Hai Ching*, or *Classic of Mountains and Seas*, a book on geography, and the *Er Ya*, or *Explanation of Words*, China's first dictionary, were just two that spoke of an animal that seemed very much like the giant panda. The *Shan Hai Ching* described the animal as living in what are now the Qionglai Mountains and having a taste for copper and iron. But the book could be confusing. Full of natural history data, it also delved into mythology and fiction, describing fantastic creatures like a horse with serrated teeth that ate tigers and leopards. In the various ancient references to the panda, it is often described as something like a white leopard.

Here in the mountains, of course, the local hunters knew of *beishung*, and they sometimes shot it for its wiry, coarse pelt, which was believed to ward off evil spirits in the night. In general, though, the hunters sought more valuable or useful game, and people in the area might live a lifetime without ever seeing the animal. Giant pandas hearing the approach of humans could disappear into the thick bamboo with amazing agility.

All around Harkness this chill night were those silent, vanishing pandas. Spread throughout this mountain chain, they were patiently enduring the late fall and facing the oncoming winter. Now, in the cold of November, they would be concentrating their consumption on old stems of arrow bamboo as well as some leaves.

For a male in the vicinity, this would be the rhythm of life—eating different parts of the bamboo seasonally, sticking to a home range of two to four square miles that overlapped with that of other pandas, posting claims and advertising his presence on trees by urinating and also rubbing secretions from a gland just under his short, broad tail. He would be eating and sleeping mainly, relieved of the mating pressure he would feel in spring. Then his masculinity would rally, his testes enlarging in preparation for the few days a female would be in heat. Precisely who she was and when she would be receptive would have been clear to him from the chemical signs she would be posting for him through her own scent marking.

On this night, not far from Camp Two, a female panda was nestled down in the hollow of an old tree with her two-month-old baby. He had been born, like most pandas here, in September, blind, nearly naked of fur, and utterly helpless. If he had had a twin, and there was a fifty-fifty chance he had, it was by now dead—an unbending rule of fate in the wild. Next to his mother, who was perhaps nearly two hundred pounds, he was truly tiny at birth, only the weight of a stick of butter. Small, slow-growing infants were just one of the consequences of the panda's low-energy diet. She suckled him as many as twelve times a day on her high-fat milk and dotingly licked at his belly and behind to stimulate him to relieve himself. For weeks, she had cradled him in her arms as she sat upright, delicately picking him up in her mouth when she needed to shift position. He would be gaining weight, growing hair, and beginning to show the telltale black-and-white markings of his species. Driven by the need to eat, the mother panda would start leaving the nest without him for increasingly longer periods to feed on bamboo. By this time, his coat was thick enough for him to stay warm during her temporary absences. To leave him in the nest alone for any length of time was to leave him vulnerable—to golden cats, to the big tree-climbing yellow-throated martens, and now, even, to humans.

That night, as Ruth Harkness drifted off to sleep in these darkened mountains, she couldn't possibly have dreamed just how close to her goal she was.

CHAPTER SIX

A GIFT FROM THE SPIRITS

WHEN HARKNESS FIRST AWOKE AT SIX, the dark and endless bamboo forest was just shrugging off its gloom and giving way to a luminous first light. It was Monday, November 9. The hunters, led by Lao Tsang, had already gathered around the fire in the field kitchen, preparing for another day of searching. Harkness had two luxuries here—the privacy of the tent for dressing, and a trunk full of clean clothes that included tailored riding trousers and sportsmen's wool shirts.

Once dressed, she made her way through the frigid, damp air into the smoky, warm lean-to, indulging fleetingly in the thought that she might wrap a great wool blanket about her and stay cocooned for the day. But she had come too far and bet too much on this mission for even a moment's hesitation. She ate a spartan breakfast, and when the men were ready, so was she.

At about eight, Harkness, Young, Lao Tsang, Yang, and two native hunters marched into the thick forest. Young led the way to a trap they had set—a wire noose tied to a bent sapling—but it remained empty. Harkness was told that the wire was strong enough to hold a thrashing panda but that it would not hurt the animal. Of course, that wasn't quite true.

The visibility was poor—less than three feet—and the hiking in this unmapped and trackless terrain was precarious and slick. Several times Harkness fell, sometimes sinking up to her waist in vegetation, leaving her soaked and shivering. Even the indomitable Lao Tsang was silenced by the struggle.

Harkness tried to light a comforting cigarette, but the wet matches would not strike. The small group continued, clambering into a bamboo thicket that rained water down on them as they bumped and jostled through. Again and again they were forced to crawl on hands and knees over piles of fallen bamboo.

In the dense fog of the ten- to eleven-thousand-foot elevation, Harkness was frustrated, hearing things she could not see. Over the next few moments, everything would happen in a blur. There was a shout from ahead, then the sound of a musket firing. Confusion. Young was yelling in Chinese when Harkness found her way to him. She gasped, "What is it?"

"*Beishung*," Young replied.

Then there was a gunshot.

Harkness feared the worst. Had the panda been killed? she asked. Though Young could not have known, he reassured her that he did not think so. Stumbling on, they heard from an old, rotting spruce a baby's whimper. Young rushed forward, thrusting his arms into the hollow of the great old tree. A three-pound black-and-white bundle of fur wriggled in his hands. When he quickly surrendered the kitten-size baby to Harkness, she felt her heart stand still. "No childhood fairy tale was more dreamlike, or more lost in a dim haze of make-believe," she wrote.

Speechless, Harkness and Young could only fumble a sort of hand clasp to mark the moment.

As the helpless creature nuzzled Harkness's breast, the two explorers realized they must race to base camp for the canned milk and baby bottles. Young, the fastest, tucked the panda into his shirt, to gallop ever downward. The trip up had taken five hours. The return would not come close. Harkness possessed a new athleticism that surprised her. She matched Young's pace in the scramble toward camp, darting over the slippery log bridges that had so intimidated her before. For both runners, hearts and thoughts were in high gear, while the little animal who had caused all the commotion was pressed next to Young's beating chest, sound asleep.

Entering camp along with Young, Harkness witnessed Wang's reaction to the panda. As Young pulled the dozing catch from his shirt, Wang broke into a smile that seemed to take up his whole being. "How got one piece baby *bei-shung*," he said, before turning calmly back to the cook shed to do his own job, preparing a meal.

At the bottom of Young's Tibetan trunk was a stout little cardboard container no bigger than a shoe box. Inside, wrapped carefully in paper and cushioned with cotton, was the fragile glass baby bottle.

It was the most important piece of equipment in their possession, prompting a rule set down then and there that only Young or Harkness could handle it.

Harkness would later recall, "In New York, Shanghai, Cheng-tu and points between, I had been told that my Giant Panda expedition was a million to one gamble. Well then, in the language of the gambler, that nursing bottle turned out to be the biggest ace in the hole that I could ever hope to have."

Harkness and Young were like nervous and inexperienced new parents. She held the little whimpering panda while he read the directions on the side of a tin of dried milk. Young anxiously prepared the formula and poured it into the bottle, suggesting to Harkness that she feed the animal on the fur lining of his coat, so it would feel more natural.

Sitting outside the tent, looking down into the upturned face of the tiny panda, who was sprawled across her lap sucking heartily on the formula, Harkness thought he was "a very small giant, indeed." She appreciated every detail. The creamy white fur, the silky black eye patches. The

pink smudge of a nose and the delicate pink line of his lips. The round-
ness of face and body. The little furred limbs that twitched and shook. So
beautiful, so helpless, so innocent.

Harkness would report later that she was amazed at how women,
especially mothers, would "take" to the animal. "There is something
about [the panda] that arouses the maternal instinct," she said. Intu-

*The baby panda drinking from the expedition's most crucial piece of
equipment—a baby bottle.* COURTESY MARY LOBISCO

itively, she saw what science would quantify many years later: even adult
pandas get to people. They possess exaggerated features that trigger a
nurturing response in human beings. Most of us are genetically dis-
posed to react emotionally to the sight of human babies, and pandas

have what they have but amplified: large heads, flat faces, chubby limbs, rounded bodies, small noses, and big eyes—in the panda's case, exaggerated by black patches. Pandas sit upright and can even hold food in what look like little hands. They have hardly any tail at all, and their genitals are hidden from view. They look clumsy and vulnerable and sweet.

This woolly little baby pulled at Harkness's heart with enormous strength. She would forever be referring to him not as "it" or "the panda," but "Baby." The panda "behaved like a baby and was treated as any human child would have been," Harkness wrote. He was, she said, "absurdly baby-like in everything" he did: "in the aimless way" he waved his paws, "or sprawled, feebly kicking the little hind legs that were not as strong as the front ones." Even his whimpering cry sounded so human. From that moment on, wherever she went, whatever she was doing, Harkness would either have the panda with her, touching her, or be compelled to steal herself away to where he was sleeping and gaze on his placid face. She would check on his safety, make sure he was breathing, and feel sweet relief in the simple rhythmic rise and fall of his warm, furry chest. He was, she believed, "the most precious thing I ever possessed."

No matter how closely held or examined this tiny creature was, however, Harkness and Young would make a couple of mistakes about him that many others—including veterinarians—would repeat not only in his case but in that of many others for years to come. Because there was no external scrotum in the young ones, and the penis was so tiny, many male baby pandas, including this one, were assumed to be female. The adventurers also, along with the experts of their time, believed the panda to be younger than he was—"a week or two old"—when he was actually about eight or nine weeks. With better-known mammals, their assessment of his stage of development would have been correct, but pandas are born nearly furless, weighing just a few ounces, and much less developed than anyone at the time imagined. While puppies start to open their eyes at ten or twelve days, for instance, panda babies keep theirs closed for about six weeks.

There was no doubt about the baby's hunger. He was so eager to nurse that Young enlarged the hole in the nipple so he could take more in. When the feeding was over and the panda dropped back into the hard slumber of a baby, Harkness and Young fashioned a comfortable cradle for him out of a canvas case. Over time, it would be lined with flannel shirts, a warm wool Hudson Bay blanket, or any scrap of clean, dry clothing they could find. They did everything to keep the animal snug—tearing up shirts, handkerchiefs, even underwear.

That first day, Baby was brought into the shaded safety of Harkness's tent to sleep. Then the two panda hunters sat outside in the morning sunshine. It had all gone to their heads like wine, Harkness said. They touched hands. She was teary. "The thing I most wanted in the world was mine," she wrote. She asked Young if he realized what had just happened. There was no way then to envision the full scope of it.

A part of Harkness didn't want to anyway. Life was so good here, it was hard to contemplate leaving for the world beyond this one. "I wanted to stay in our little camp, and watch the Baby grow up in that lovely valley," she wrote.

It was as though she had joined the Immortals of Daoist belief, the perfect beings who inhabit the mountains and walk among the stars and clouds. She was as close to heaven as a mortal can be, slipping into a sublime orbit straight out of the pages of a timeless text. As one Daoist-inspired poet wrote more than a thousand years earlier:

> *Heaven is my bed and earth my cushion,*
> *The thunder and lightning are my drum and fan,*
> *The sun and moon my candle and my torch,*
> *The Milky Way my moat, the stars my jewels.*
> *With nature am I conjoined*

In China, Harkness had finally found what she was searching for. If in a single moment there is eternity, then in this one she was experiencing a lifetime of bliss.

Out of this reverie, the practicality of survival took center stage when the men shouted that a wild boar was nearby. Young raced from camp in a chase that would keep him and the other hunters out for the balance of the day. When the group returned after dark, they were exhausted, disheveled, and dirty. There had been a close call with the wounded boar, apparently, but even then it had eluded them.

There was much to celebrate anyway. Dinner for ten that evening was as opulent as they could manage—roasted pheasants, native wine, a bottle of old brandy from Dan Reib, and a camp-concocted chocolate pudding for dessert.

Young had observed that Americans liked to be the first at everything. So the two decided that even the smallest panda-related moments would be memorialized as "firsts." Harkness was the first woman to sleep with a panda, and Young the first Chinese to feed one. It became a running joke.

After dinner, everyone, completely spent, turned in. Rain and sleet, gentle at first, soon became a deluge, which caused a kind of comical entanglement between Young and Harkness. The incident would be recounted later in Harkness's book, but no doubt in a sanitized version. She would write that because they had left Camp Two in such a hurry, they had forgotten bedding for Young, compelling them to drag an air mattress and heavy blanket for him to the very entrance to her tent. It's just as likely that he was in the tent to begin with. In any event, later, during the night, while she was trying to fix a bottle for the crying baby panda, Harkness tripped over something. As if in a scene from a screwball comedy, she landed on the sleeping Young and managed to tip the flagging above, sending rainwater in a torrent over both of them. The upshot was that Young was then "forced" to sleep inside the tent.

Whatever the details really were, Harkness and Young did spend the night of their great victory together, cozy and alone in her tent while a snowy rain pummeled the canvas from above. The panda was cuddled next to Harkness, sucking the lobe of her ear as he fell asleep. Waking later, the panda was fed by both his guardians, and in the dim circle of light inside the tent, Harkness glanced over at Young, thinking how "paternal" he looked with the baby on his lap.

THE NEXT NIGHT, carrying torches, Harkness, Young, and the hunters gathered by a massive rock near camp. The gentlest among them, Whang, held a great handsome red rooster. He chanted and lighted rods of incense, or "joss sticks," whose rising smoke would carry their prayers heavenward. He stamped his feet and lanced the neck of the rooster, all in rhythmic sets of three. Blood and then wine were poured over the earth, and using the warm, viscous blood, Whang pasted three feathers to a board. A pile of sacrificial paper money, which had no monetary value, only currency with the spirits, was ignited into a little bonfire. Firecrackers exploded in the still night, and Harkness, who normally hated handling guns, felt inspired to fire off three rounds into the air from Young's revolver.

The ceremony was to thank the gods of the mountains for their generosity in bestowing upon them the precious baby giant panda. The American was not patronizing the men, for she was a believer—not in religion or rules but in a larger mystery. She felt this from the Chinese themselves, who did not compartmentalize their spirituality but kept it close and intimate. They sometimes lived in temples, she noted, while "in America, no one would ever dream of camping or living in a church or cathedral even if it were partially ruined." Here, gods, spirits, belief, were not relegated to Sundays, she said—"The Chinese feel differently about religion. It is an everyday matter, and perhaps they think their gods are everyday people."

THE DEPARTURE PLAN was soon set. They couldn't afford to waste a bit of time in getting Baby out. Young would accompany Harkness as far as Chengdu, then trek back to the camps in pursuit of his own panda to shoot. There were, however, two pieces of important business to square away.

First, Harkness thought they should name their baby panda. Because he was curled up on Young's lap, cushioned by the sheepskin coat loaned by Jack Young's wife, she thought of "Su-Lin." One interpretation of the name—"a little bit of something very cute"—was perfect for the tiny baby.

The other task was much more solemn. The next morning, when Su-Lin's breakfast bottle was finished, Harkness and Young headed back up the mountain, knowing they had a window of about six hours free from panda feeding. (Wisely, Su-Lin had been allowed to establish his own schedule. "Since no one had ever brought up a baby of that kind before, we decided that she knew more about how much she should have and when she should have it than we did," Harkness said.) This expedition had been above all else a matter of honor. Now, climbing upward until mountain met cloud, Harkness placed the ashes of her dead husband in their permanent resting place. She couldn't bear lilies and conventional funeral parlors, so she laid Bill's remains beneath the twisted roots of a towering rhododendron, high in the cold, sacred mountains he had struggled toward but never reached.

When they were done, Harkness and Young left the site for nearby Camp Two, where they shared a cup of tea. Quickly, though, Young went on ahead to give Baby his next feeding. Alone with one of the porters, Harkness later took a tumble climbing down the mountain, wrenching her hip badly in the process.

She limped back to camp and, despite the injury, kept to the next day's schedule. Though it must have been grueling for her, the party reached the ruined castle that evening. Besides the panda, they carried with them bamboo from the capture site, which they hoped would help scientists in the United States distinguish which type Su-Lin should feed on.

It was a drizzly, miserable night. Harkness's sore hip, exacerbated by the hiking, ached, so at 3 A.M. she gave up trying to sleep and held Baby in her lap for a feeding. She felt comforted by the creature, and by the sight of Young, eyes closed, a few feet away.

With little rest, and her hip throbbing, Harkness nevertheless agreed the next morning to another long, hard march. Retracing the route to

Wenchuan, which had taken them five days out, they walked steadily, making it in ten hours. Stopping only for a tiffin of canned sardines, they were able to reach the swaying bamboo bridge that crossed the Min and led into the city just before sundown on Friday, November 13.

Nightfall again brought a drop in temperature. Inside the now-familiar ghost temple, before a great roaring fire, Young and Harkness bundled close together beneath a single wool blanket. After her days in the mountains, she said, the ghost temple now seemed "truly palatial." There was a mound of mail, retrieved from the local postmaster, which they read in the flickering light.

Their time together was coming to an end.

That evening, as usual, Harkness brought Su-Lin into her sleeping bag. She kept Baby close to her whenever possible, despite his sharp claws, which often cut her. A vigilant mother, constantly sterilizing in boiling water the things the panda would touch, she also had given up most of her remaining clothes to provide soft bedding. Harkness's efforts were working, for Su-Lin was thriving.

In the morning, everything was a little out of sorts, as often happens when separations are looming. Here in Wenchuan they had their first taste of the tremendous curiosity the rare animal would arouse around the world. Harkness had the protective urge that comes to most new mothers, yet she understood the interest. While she never minded crowds gathering to watch her eat, or brush her teeth, or type, or even bathe, she would not allow throngs of people to disturb the sleeping panda—though keeping them at bay was hard work.

Added to that, Young was cajoled into leaving her to attend a feast held by Smith's hired hunter, Wang. In Young's absence, Harkness grew anxious, even beginning to believe that Wang was plotting to detain them.

When Young returned, their departure was made all the more chaotic by two bungling porters who slowed them down over the course of the day and had to be fired by the evening. For the journey to Guanxian, it was Harkness, Young, four hunters, four porters, and one shaggy brown Tibetan pony. Over two cool, crisp days, they hiked hard and slept in smaller villages, avoiding the attention that would come in larger ones. To that end, they stopped just short of busy Guanxian, sending one of the men ahead with a message to be telephoned to Cavaliere asking that he send his car for them the next day at noon.

As rough as the travel was, and as uncomfortable and dirty as the inns could be, Harkness was melancholy as she watched the last moments of her happy expedition slip away. She would come back to China, she knew, but these had been the happiest days of her life and it was hard to let go. Her success in proving wrong all those patronizing people in Shanghai and New York would seem so much smaller a contentment than that of a hard march, of picking herself up when she thought she couldn't walk another mile and walking two more miles, of watching the sun burn away the fog from a snowy peak, of sharing a good laugh over a cup of hot wine. Life here had been the appreciation of a single perfect egg, of experiencing so completely the fullness of a moment that it left no room for longing.

It would be impossible to say goodbye to Quentin Young, on this, her last evening alone with him. Even if they had wanted it once they were back in Shanghai or New York, a relationship would be nearly impossible. That she had found "complete happiness" here with him, that this new world had so captivated her—how could she put these feelings into words? Nothing she said could convey things properly. Instead, Harkness pressed a gold ring into Young's hand. It was her own wedding band, the circle representing eternity; the gold, precious love. She said that it was for him to give to Diana Chen. And with it, she wished them great happiness. The gift was its own paradox, at once selfless and self-centered. It was a generous sacrifice, but it would always place her between the two.

At first light on November 16, they were up, dressed in clean clothes, and headed for Guanxian.

SHORTLY BEFORE NOON, in the center of Guanxian's marketplace, a missionary from Chicago named Miss Jephson was helping a visiting British aristocrat, Lady Dorothea Hosie, haggle over the price of a pair of blue-

and-white straw sandals. Lady Hosie was the daughter of a well-known China expert at Oxford and the widow of Sir Alexander Hosie, part of the diplomatic service in China, and her arrival in China had been much reported on.

Bumping smack into each other, the adventurer and the blue blood would have just the kind of high-profile meeting Harkness had been hoping to avoid, but as with everything else on this trip, it would turn out to be a stroke of luck. The chance encounter was recorded in a photograph which, when reproduced in the *North China Daily News,* later would provide evidence for an embattled Harkness.

The very British Lady Hosie, wearing a woman's fedora, button-down shirt, tie, and cardigan, was bowled over by what a romantic figure Harkness cut, and recounted the momentous meeting in her book, *Brave New China:*

> The crowd of tribespeople with their wide-open brown eyes and twisted blue turbans were pressing upon us, when a clear American voice called over their heads: "How do you do?"
> Through the crowd came a gallant figure, a young woman in grey flannel trousers, with shirt open at the neck and rolled-up sleeves, looking like a lithe boy. But a gay red scarf about her head proclaimed her sex, as did the lipstick, which, in bravura, she had put on even in those outlandish parts.

Harkness introduced herself to Lady Hosie, jokingly apologizing for having missed her recent lecture on Chinese art. Lady Hosie reported that the American consul had directed her to "keep a weather eye open" for the bold explorer, so she was glad to see Harkness safe.

Lady Hosie then noted Young standing behind Harkness in his khaki shorts and open shirt. He too carried a charged aura about him, seeming big and full of cheer. In her book she called him "Wong," and said incorrectly that he was from Hawaii. In the Western press, he would continue to be a character overlooked or carelessly and inaccurately portrayed, despite Harkness's efforts.

Young and Harkness asked Lady Hosie if she would like to be the first Englishwoman to see a baby panda. Delighted, Lady Hosie gathered up the missionary and another friend for the visit.

The women were brought to an inn, where Su-Lin was barricaded with the hunters. "We bent over the white-furred baby lying asleep at the bottom of a bushel-basket lined with Mrs. Harkness's sheepskin coat," Lady Hosie wrote. "But he had just had a drink of warm milk from a bottle and was disinclined to open his sleepy eyes with their circle of black fur."

As soon as the women left, the dashing Cavaliere blew into town with great fanfare. His caravan of two big motorcars, honking furiously, parted the startled crowd. Looking over at him, Harkness was amused to see that he had brought not one but two Chinese generals along for the ride.

When he came to a stop, Cavaliere took Harkness's hand in his own and kissed it. "Madame," he addressed her formally, "I know very little about exploration, but enough to know that only a woman would have taken care of that baby Panda as you have done."

She had to admit to herself that he might just be right. Perhaps she had succeeded not despite being a woman, but because of it. Once again, everything had gracefully and poetically been turned on its ear.

Back to her negotiating at the marketplace, Lady Hosie glanced up in time to see "Mrs. Harkness flash by in the postmaster's car. She waved her hand," the Englishwoman would recall, "and we knew the precious little animal from the wilds was in its basket at her feet."

Good luck again was riding with Harkness. Waiting back at Cavaliere's compound was the rangy, sandy-haired American pilot she had met before. He was spending the night and set to return to Shanghai the very next morning. James Ray McCleskey, or "Captain Mac," of the CNAC said he was eager to have Harkness and Su-Lin join him for the twelve-hour flight. There was a prohibition against passengers' bringing animals aboard, but Captain Mac assured Harkness it could be worked out. "Tell you what, I'll carry her as pidgin cargo in the control room," he said, using the local jargon for contraband.

Whatever trepidation Harkness had about leaving her mountain refuge was tossed aside that evening as Cavaliere uncorked his finest

sparkling burgundy and the gathered crowd offered one toast after another. Ruth Harkness felt it was all predestined—as a character out of a
Lin Yutang novel believed, "Men contrive, but the gods decide."

The next morning, November 17, Harkness and Su-Lin were aboard
a gleaming Douglas fourteen-passenger airplane, riding, she said, swift
wings over an ancient land. The panda traveled in the cockpit with the
all-American Captain Mac, while Harkness sat in the passenger section,
the lone woman and only westerner among all the Chinese men, some
in Western suits and others in traditional Chinese robes.

Because the planes of the CNAC often hugged the ground, snaking
their way between the cliffs that box in huge sections of the Yangtze,
Harkness was able to see the junks along the river—she could even
make out the straining forms of the coolies who at various points pulled
the boats from shore. Mile upon mile she watched this great land she
had come to love slip by beneath her. The lady explorer was reversing her
route by air, gliding over land and water, each inch of which had been
hard won on her way out. As much as she hadn't wanted to leave, she
now found herself willing the plane to go faster, back to the world she
had so joyfully left behind.

Harkness's restlessness only grew when foul conditions turned them
back near Hankou. November marked the start of bad flying weather in
China, and after being buffeted by turbulence, they had to put down to
wait out the front. She could only sit and ruminate as time ticked by.

Hours before, everything had been so rushed. Her goodbyes that
morning in Chengdu were fleeting, with barely enough time to gulp a
cup of coffee in Cavaliere's great dining room and ready the little panda
for the journey to Shanghai. Thoughtfully, Quentin Young had prepared
all the formula she would need for the long flight. In a flash then, she
had found herself at the muddy Chengdu airfield, at the first light of day,
waving farewell to Young and wondering when and under what circumstances she would see him again.

CHAPTER SEVEN

THE BATTLE ROYAL

THE SOUND OF DRONING ENGINES cut through the nighttime fog and pelting rain that had enveloped Shanghai, and in the skies over the rustic, muddy Lunghwa Airdrome, the lights of the Douglas plane emerged from cloud. Outside the CNAC passenger terminal, three people stood waiting for Ruth Harkness's arrival: Dan Reib, as expected, but also reporter Woo Kyatang, of the *China Press*, and his photographer.

When the plane touched down, Reib rushed up to his American friend, warning her of the media's presence. "Is the baby here?" he asked. According to Kyatang's account, Harkness looked at Reib, nodded, then pointed toward a wicker basket. Captain Mac, who had draped a raincoat over Su-Lin, was carrying him out toward Reib's car. Intercepting Harkness as she raced for the waiting room, the vigilant Kyatang asked her if, indeed, she had a giant panda in her possession. Harkness responded, "No. You must have made a mistake. Panda? What is a panda?"

She had taken such great pains to keep a low profile that she was now perplexed by the presence of the reporter. How could he have been tipped off? What Harkness didn't know was that as she flew eastward from Chengdu to Shanghai, an Associated Press report was being transmitted halfway around the world, tapped out on teletype machines in every newspaper office across the United States:

> CHENGTU, Szechwan Province, China, Nov. 17 (AP) The American woman explorer, Mrs. William H. Harkness Jr. of New York City arrived today from the Tibetan border with a live panda—a rare, bear-like animal.
>
> The animal is believed to be the first live panda captured in this part of Asia. A Chinese explorer accompanied Mrs. Harkness on her dangerous journey to the Tibetan border.

The flashed message was, *Time* magazine would note, "tantalizing to every zoologist in the world." As Harkness later realized, her friends in America heard the news of her success before those in Shanghai.

It was odd that the entire press corps of this city hadn't figured things out in time to come here, but still, the two representatives who had shown up were steadfast in their pursuit. Harkness was unsure what her status with the government would be now that she had a giant panda, and the last thing she wanted was publicity. Thinking quickly, she cut a deal with Kyatang. "After considerable persuasion," he wrote much later, "Mrs. Harkness finally consented to give some information regarding her trip and how she captured the only living panda in captivity." She would do this only on the night before she sailed back to the United States, and "on the condition that nothing was said in the papers about her arrival until that time." She wanted to make sure that she was safely plying the waters of the East China Sea when the story appeared.

Once the reporter agreed, Harkness collapsed into Reib's waiting car. Since the airport, surrounded by cabbage farms, stood at the far outskirts of the city, they had a long trip ahead. But there was much to discuss as Reib, Harkness, and Baby traveled the sodden, rutted paths, which eventually turned into the slick, nighttime streets of Shanghai proper. The return to the Palace Hotel felt like a homecoming. Warmed by the glow of a fire in the grate, Harkness shared supper and drinks with Reib.

Safe and cozy as she felt, Harkness knew she was in a jam—the fact that she had not applied for or received official scientific permissions for her outing would undermine her now that she intended to leave the country with this treasure. The two dear friends decided that the first priority must be secrecy. But, of course, this was Shanghai, the town in which it seemed every nationality in the world had convened for the purpose of gossip. It would have to be an open secret, with just the right people knowing. Against the odds, they pulled it off.

Shanghai was ruled by foreigners, particularly those in big business. As one of the heads of Standard Oil Company of New York, Reib had the connections in Shanghai to quietly secure Harkness the proper paperwork.

That first night back, Harkness and Reib picked up their easy intimacy where they had left off in September. For the rest of her stay in Shanghai, Reib would visit constantly, often settling himself in, drinking whiskey sodas, and cuddling tiny Su-Lin. He never seemed to mind when the baby panda inevitably wet on his expensive trousers. "She has personality, this Baby," he told Harkness.

Before he left that first night, Harkness could revel a bit in the fact that she had "broken all the rules" and admit that she was feeling like "a naughty child." With a glowing fire, a good drink, dinner, and the most adorable baby panda nestled and sleeping nearby, it was a small, closed, happy world.

But, of course, not for long.

The outsiders started coming in that very night. And as The New York Times would later point out, "her real troubles . . . were just beginning."

After feeding Su-Lin, Harkness fell into bed a little after eleven. Just after midnight, Baby woke her, whimpering with an urgency Harkness had not heard before. She comforted the agitated animal in her arms for an hour before giving up and frantically dialing Captain Mac's wife, Peggy, asking for a pediatrician. It simply didn't occur to her, she would report later, to call a veterinarian. At first, a puzzled Dr. Francis Nance, or "Frick" as he was known here, asked just what a baby "Pandor" was. Within a half hour, the young physician was at the Palace Hotel, seeing for himself.

Nance pressed a stethoscope to Baby's chest, listening to his heart, then took his temperature, having no way of knowing what normal should be for this rare species. Nonetheless, after a few gentle thumps of the belly, Nance diagnosed a simple case of colic, treating Su-Lin with a combination of peppermint drops in water and a warm-water enema. It seemed to do the trick. The panda grew stronger every day, with his weight rising shortly to four pounds, eight ounces. Nance went home that night to consult a number of references, dialing Harkness later with a new formula for the baby's feeding, which consisted of powdered milk, corn syrup, and cod liver oil.

The next day, Harkness sent a one-word telegram to her dear friend Hazel Perkins: "SUCCESS." She would shortly afterward also begin a cable communication with the Bronx Zoo.

Reib held a lunch that day for her and Su-Lin. And in the afternoon Peggy McCleskey, along with a gaggle of other friends, dropped in. Peggy, who had a new baby herself, provided some practical mothering advice for Harkness. Reib, of all people, would inadvertently stumble upon some too. At a regular checkup within days of the panda's arrival, Reib's doctor noted a rash on his legs formed in reaction to Su-Lin's urine. The doctor wasn't terribly worried about Reib, but felt that any urine that would cause such inflammation on contact was too acidic, so he recommended that Baby be bottle-fed water as well as formula.

This is the way it went for the next two weeks. That Harkness managed all the while to stay out of the press and under the radar was nothing short of miraculous. She was the hush-hush toast of the town, traipsing from one party to the next, always lugging the rarest animal in the world with her, causing a stir wherever she went. Decked out in her best clothes, throwing windows open for Baby's comfort as she strode through each room, she made quite a sight. In the mountains, she had worried about keeping Su-Lin warm; in Shanghai, she assumed that this high-elevation animal needed as much cold fresh air as was possible. In the town that lived to hobnob, the panda was invited to lunches, dinners, and even to tea. His popularity skyrocketed. "I don't suppose that any animal ever before had such a social career as Su Lin did in Shanghai," Harkness wrote.

Su-Lin's circle would not be wide enough, however, to include Floyd Tangier Smith, who had heard about Harkness's success from mutual friends at the Race Club. He and Elizabeth decided the explorer must be avoiding them, though they weren't sure why.

AS USUAL, MEN HOVERED around Harkness. Two chums she had made in Shanghai before her expedition, both young businessmen, were by her side constantly. They became Su-Lin's amahs, or nursemaids—Floyd James, or "Jimmy," an old pal of Bill Harkness's, and Jack Young's friend Fritz Hardenbrooke. Hardenbrooke, a Kodak employee, even abandoned his own Shanghai home for a time, renting a room on Harkness's floor

*Su-Lin's two "amahs," or nursemaids: the Shanghai businessmen
Fritz Hardenbrooke and Floyd James.* COURTESY MARY LOBISCO

to be closer at hand. He helped with panda-rearing chores and entertained Harkness with stories of his travels in Tibet.

Given Harkness's inner circle, it wasn't surprising when she observed that Su-Lin was especially partial to men. But some of the males coming by were unwelcome. One by one, starting on her first full day back in Shanghai, reporters from the many English-language newspapers in town, as well as correspondents for papers back home, began to nose around. In each case, Harkness would explain her predicament, asking for an embargo on stories until the day she was leaving. In return, she promised she would grant lengthy interviews and photo sessions on the day before her departure.

One correspondent, perhaps Hallett Abend of *The New York Times*, even arranged a meeting for Harkness with "an influential person ranking high in the affairs of China's government" so that she could find her way out of China despite the fact that she had no official permits. The powerful adviser who told her to continue with her current strategy of remaining under the radar was never named. But years later, Captain Mac's wife, Peggy, would remember that Ambassador Trusler himself had secretively stepped in to help.

The earliest liner Harkness could book was the *Empress of Russia*, set to sail on Saturday morning, November 28, at seven, meaning she would spend Thanksgiving in Shanghai. As the holiday approached, newspapers were filled with ads for turkeys, American potatoes, pork pies and cheeses, celery and "rutabagas from home."

For the successful explorer, all was humming along smoothly. But, of course, the worst wrecks occur when everything is in high gear. First, she came down with the flu, which she blamed on all those open windows but which was more likely due to her exhaustion and relentless partying. She was not only sick but desperately in need of sleep, having continuously stayed up round the clock socializing and then tending to Baby, who needed to be fed or comforted at all hours. Harkness was so sapped physically that she uncharacteristically burst into tears on a few occasions. Once, in a dark moment, when she was utterly alone, she revealed, "I had wished many times that the Commander had come on to Shanghai."

She also endured pangs of great guilt. She indulged the panda at every whimper. She gave up her time, her clothes, and her freedom for him, all the while worrying that the little innocent animal wanted something she had robbed him of, and that he was "lonesome" for his mother. Long afterward, she would still be consumed by the thought of the mother panda returning to find her baby gone. She became determined to somehow make up for that loss.

There was something smaller to feel sorry over too. A piece of film had stuck in the shutter of Harkness's Leica, and none of the seven hundred pictures from the mountains could be developed. There would be no photographs of Su-Lin's capture.

In the meantime, Harkness wanted to come clean with officials about Su-Lin, though without having to forfeit Baby. She was wrestling with that issue, when, on Thanksgiving Day, November 26, she went to the home of a staunch ally who would become one of the most influential figures in her life. Arthur de Carle Sowerby was the dean of foreign naturalists in Shanghai. A prolific writer and field zoologist, with an interest in art, literature, and politics, Sowerby owned, edited, and wrote a good deal of a well-respected monthly magazine called *The China Journal*. On this day, as his American wife oversaw a big holiday dinner, he must have been filled with joy to sit holding the most sought-after animal in the world.

The gray-haired naturalist came to know Harkness and the remarkable little animal she had brought to his doorstep. He thought it "eminently fitting" that Harkness had named the panda after Su-Lin Young. Not only was she considered the first and only Chinese woman explorer, but Sowerby knew her personally from her reporting work for his journal. He was thrilled to examine up close the mysterious little panda, who had begun opening his eyes. And, as accomplished as Sowerby was himself, he was very impressed with Harkness, referring to her as "the courageous lady explorer."

In the December issue of *The China Journal*, he would write a long article about her success. "The story of this attractive young American woman's 'great adventure' is a thrilling one. In fact, it is an epic in the history of travel and exploration, reflecting the greatest credit upon everybody concerned, including, of course, the heroine herself; her faithful and devoted assistant Quentin Young, youthful Chinese explorer and brother of Jack T. Young." The concern that was considered insurmountable, Sowerby wrote, was "the problem of feeding it and keeping it alive after it had been captured." For now, Su-Lin was thriving on Dr. Nance's baby-panda formula.

The next day was scheduled to be Harkness's last in Shanghai. She would send her luggage ahead during the daylight hours, then board the *Empress of Russia* at about midnight—settling in overnight for the 7 A.M. departure time on the 28th. There was much to be done, for this was the scheduled press payback day, when Harkness had to honor her pledge to all the patient reporters, and she had to manage it all without Dan Reib, who was suffering from the flu that she had been battling for days. With Reib out of commission, Hardenbrooke stepped in to assist.

As promised, all the reporters were invited to her hotel room for interviews and pictures. Harkness made a dramatic impression. When the door was thrown open, she stood, fit and slender, in good color from her expedition, wearing a striking purple, embroidered "mandarin gown," with Tibetan fur boots. As usual, there was the shiny black hair pulled straight back, the deep voice, and the irresistible charm. On this day, no little flu could keep her down. She held court with the flow of eager press, answering questions with aplomb. All the reporters were under her spell.

Of the expedition, the *North China Daily News* reporter asked, "Did it cost much?"

"Everything I had," the adventurer responded. "But I decided to have a final fling and back my last cent on the million to one chance that the expedition would be a success and that we'd either shoot or capture a panda."

She described the adventure as the reporters furiously scribbled down every last detail. The throng wanted to know about the baby panda, who was sleeping in his wicker basket in the corner. Soon enough, as one reporter said, "a queer noise" came from it. Harkness ordered hot

water from room service to heat the formula, then brought the squawk-
ing baby out. "When the bottle finally arrived, Su-Lin devoured the contents as rapidly as it could suck it out the nipple top," reported the *China
Press*. Harkness flopped the black-and-white bundle of fur onto her
shoulder, going through the motions of burping a baby. All the while
flashbulbs went off. She may have reveled in the cheery company of the
reporters, but Harkness never mugged for the cameras. She didn't seem
the least bit concerned about having an attractive picture taken of herself. Of all the thousands of shots that would be snapped over the next
months, very few show much of Harkness's face—that view seemed always reserved for Baby.

She told them that she owed her success to Quentin Young, and that
he had planned the whole trip, with her financing. Sowerby noted her
generosity in *The China Journal*: "Her praise for the way he carried out
his part of the programme was unstinted."

Later that evening, with the reporters gone and the luggage sent
ahead to the ship, Harkness sat down before the fire to a quiet meal with
Hardenbrooke.

At close to midnight, they headed out, taking rickshaws down the
Bund, then boarding a tender that would motor passengers to the anchored *Empress of Russia*. Baby rested in his wicker basket through it all.
Rocking gently in the little boat, Harkness felt relieved that she was finally on her way back to the United States.

But before the launch could depart, Chinese Maritime Customs officials suddenly appeared, asking her if she was Mrs. Harkness, and if she
had a panda. When she replied in the affirmative, one of the officials
said, "We are sorry to detain you, but you must come with us to the Customs shed. You must bring your panda, too."

She had pulled together an expedition in just a few months. She had
made it out of Shanghai, past Chongqing, through Chengdu, up a great
mountain chain, and back. She had kept the baby alive here in this teem-
ing city. Now, within sight of the great ship she was booked on, everything threatened to go bust.

Powerless, Harkness and Hardenbrooke lugged the wicker basket between them, following the officials to a two-story customs examination shed across the street from the Customs House. Temperatures in the unheated building dipped into the thirties, and icy gusts cut across the surface of the river. Harkness was stopped, she was told, because she did not have a permit to carry a live animal out of the country. Saturday's edition of *The New York Times* would explain, "The customs commissioner of Shanghai had issued special instructions to inspectors to be on the lookout for the tiny animal. They detained it on the grounds that certain necessary formalities had not been complied with." *The Times* called this "a technical charge."

Harkness was nearly hysterical with frustration. Her friends in Shanghai, she would write later, never knew that such a permit was necessary. They wondered now if the complaint was manufactured as a means of detaining her. Some influential people had gone to bat for her, dealing with government authorities behind the scenes. Everything should have been taken care of, and what this new wrinkle was, no one knew. Grabbing the shed's telephone, Hardenbrooke dialed Dan Reib.

As other calls went out, two influential American reporters appeared on the scene—Victor Keane and most likely Hallett Abend. Her flu raging, exhausted from lack of sleep and in a state of panic, Harkness began to cry. Things would not be squared in time for her to leave with the *Empress of Russia,* so her luggage was salvaged from it. Officials told the American they would write out a receipt for the panda, who would remain in the shed while she returned to the hotel. How preposterous. She wouldn't consider it. She said she would just have to spend the night, and using a borrowed pillow, she promptly stretched out on a cold countertop.

At the first light of day, having hardly slept, she drank a cup of steaming tea snagged from a street vendor, then spread open the local papers that had just hit the stands.

GIANT PANDA CAUGHT ALIVE, screamed the headline in the *North China Daily News.* "They said she couldn't do it. She wasn't an explorer. She was a woman. Her field was dress designing. Besides, who ever heard of a Panda being captured alive," the first paragraph read.

AMERICAN WOMAN LEAVES WITH ONLY GIANT PANDA IN CAPTIVITY: MRS.
HARKNESS CAUGHT BABY IN SZECHWAN, HAS NURSED RARE LITTLE BEAST IN
SHANGHAI UNTIL SHIP BOARDED LAST NIGHT, ran the front-page headline in
the *China Press*. The story was at the top of the page, front and center,
with two large photos taken in Harkness's hotel room. Its lead, written
by the enterprising Woo Kyatang, was no less momentous. "The futile
search conducted during the past half a century by scientists, and explorers for a live giant panda, reported to be the rarest, most elusive and
high-priced animal of the world, was being crowned with success in
Shanghai this morning when a five-week-old specimen, carrying the dis-
tinction of being the first of its kind ever to be held in captivity, left here
for the United States on board the Empress of Russia."

"This valuable find brought to a successful conclusion one of the
longest searches ever conducted by man for a rare animal," one awestruck reporter would write.

Harkness and Su-Lin were such big news that they had trumped a
front-page staple—the romance between the king of England and the
American divorcée Wallis Simpson.

The fame was cold comfort to Harkness that Saturday morning,
though. While she and all of Shanghai read of her departure aboard the
Empress of Russia, she was in fact stewing in the customs shed, her flu
worse than ever.

Floyd James made his way down to babysit Su-Lin, allowing Harkness to return to the hotel. Dan Reib, roused out of his own sickbed,
posted what *The New York Times* reported as the "heavy cash bond" the
commissioner required, then he and all of Harkness's other friends
swung into action. The people she knew were powerful enough that
within hours a tentative settlement had been brokered. But there would
be many more ups and downs, twists and turns ahead. Over the next few
days, the papers breathlessly recorded every detail they could uncover in
the ever-changing story, one that symbolized the chafing forces of Western power and the emerging Chinese national pride.

Before noon, Mrs. Sowerby came by in her car to pick up Harkness and the newly released panda, ferrying them over to the Palace, where a conference of Harkness supporters was convening.

By the afternoon, Harkness once again greeted the newsmen. The *China Press* would report that the panda was fine, despite his cod liver oil being misplaced. Harkness, however, was showing the effects of the harrowing ordeal at the customs shed, and seemed quite ill.

Ruth Harkness, surrounded by cigarettes, bottles, glasses, and crumpled handkerchiefs, ready to meet the press in her room at the Palace Hotel.
COURTESY MARY LOBISCO

Harkness's insistence on keeping the baby panda close to her at all times was crucial to his survival—later studies would show that panda mothers might not put the baby down for a moment during its first month—but now, in all the drama, something else became clear. Su-Lin had also stirred a fierce maternal love in the young widow. The thought of Baby being taken away had shaken her deeply.

On Sunday two New York papers—the *American* and *The Times*—were calling Saturday's alleged deal between Harkness supporters and

Chinese officials a victory: MRS. HARKNESS WINS FIGHT FOR BABY PANDA'S PASSPORT and MRS. HARKNESS TAKES RARE PANDA TO HOTEL; RELEASE OF ANIMAL BY CHINA IS HELD CERTAIN, ran the headlines. "High Customs officials," *The New York Times* reported now, were "adopting a helpful view."

In Shanghai, where the local newspapers still used carrier pigeons to send dispatches across town, every tidbit learned about Harkness was printed. The *North China Daily News* even ran an old photo of her meeting Lady Hosie and "Miss Jepshon" in Guanxian weeks before. The *China Press* was told by its sources inside the government that Harkness would be detained only about a week, and that she would be allowed to sail for the United States aboard the *President McKinley* on Wednesday, December 2. All she had to do was obtain a wellness certificate for Su-Lin and then pay a fee amounting to $7\frac{1}{2}$ percent of the value of the animal (judged to be two thousand dollars Mexican, the currency in use), which came to less than fifty dollars in American money.

In reality, the difficulty was not so settled. The clout of Harkness's friends was being well matched by large forces at work in the country. First, officials at the Academia Sinica, who had been ignored by Harkness previously, felt offended, with their fury feeding on something beyond any petty bureaucratic insult. There was a rising sense of indignation from those who were tired of watching their country being looted by westerners. They saw this latest affair as nothing more than scientific imperialism. These kinds of anti-Western feelings were becoming a "smouldering fury" in "Chinese hearts," according to Pearl Buck.

Westerners perceived the considerable, and more than justified, nationalistic pride as Chinese truculence: "The only danger of further delay," *The New York Times* wrote, "is seen in the possibility that certain organizations that object to foreign exploration in China and that attempt to prevent shipments abroad of unusual finds made in the country may oppose the panda's going abroad. Such organizations have previously hampered Roy Chapman Andrews and others. They prevented the late William Harkness from hunting the panda and held up his expedition for thirteen months until he died here."

Americans felt the Chinese weren't capable of taking care of their own treasures. *The New York Times* was one of many charging that "China lacks facilities and wild animal experts for keeping this rare specimen alive." There was no institution in China, Sowerby argued, "equipped to rear such a difficult animal to keep alive. The only hope of realizing the full results of the wonderful achievement of Mrs. Harkness is that the panda should reach New York alive and pass into the hands of those properly equipped and qualified to nurse it through infancy to maturity."

Though Americans used these justifications in Harkness's defense, she herself couldn't help seeing the Chinese point of view. While she never wanted to give up Su-Lin, she would always feel compelled to "repay" China for the loss of the rare animal.

She certainly felt that press reports of Su-Lin's skyrocketing value were not helping her cause. The *China Press* had placed a price tag of twenty-five thousand dollars on the panda, dubbing him "the most valuable animal in the world." Sowerby, her ally, refuted this figure publicly, saying that a more reasonable estimate would be five to ten thousand dollars. The *China Press* held fast to the figure no matter what Harkness or anyone else said, even gleefully reporting that the panda hunter was "indignant about" it. In fact, she hated any stories on her quest that focused on the financial angle. She had not launched the expedition to get rich, she said over and over again. She had sunk every penny into the venture with little hope of seeing any return. Her real wish now was that as a proven explorer, she would be able to attract funding for further expeditions to China as easily as some of her peers. She told the press that she wanted to conduct a thorough canvassing of the area in which Su-Lin had been captured to better understand the wildlife of the China/ Tibet border.

Back in her hotel room, with the storm still raging around her, Harkness figured that as long as she was stuck for a while, she might as well call Smith. She had been selective about whom she spoke with during her secretive weeks in Shanghai. But now that the panda was out of the bag, she rang up the old boy whom she probably considered neither friend nor foe, inviting him to visit. What harm could he do? Their meeting would be brief and cordial, and surrounded by other guests, she would lay out for him the details of the route she had traveled.

On Monday, November 30, what the *China Press* would come to call "the battle royal" was on again. The bumpy and bleak negotiations with customs resumed.

On Tuesday, Harkness was still front-page news, with the betting now going against her. SCIENCE BODY OFFICIAL DOUBTS PANDA CAN GO and PANDA MAY NOT BE ALLOWED TO SAIL, reported two of Shanghai's leading English-language newspapers. A world away, New Yorkers read in *The Times* that CHINA STILL HOLDS PANDA: MRS. HARKNESS MAY BE THWARTED IN EFFORT TO BRING ANIMAL HERE. As Harkness would later remember, "One day the papers said that I'd be allowed to leave; the next day, there was no hope. I didn't know myself."

The Times reported that without the consent of the Academia Sinica, the very agency Harkness had so gingerly skirted, Su-Lin would go nowhere. Its reporter heard that "Article XXII of China's hunting laws" was "likely" to be invoked. The paper explained that the rule "declares that if an animal is captured or killed without a proper permit it becomes the property of the national treasury." As the highest scientific research organization in the government, the Academia Sinica continued to take Harkness's affront quite seriously. A spokesman told the *China Press* that Harkness had still not applied for an export permit, and until that was granted, the customs officials would be required to prohibit the panda from leaving the country. There were persistent echoes of doubt from other high-placed sources inside the government too.

A breakthrough came by noon on Tuesday, when Harkness learned she would be able to sail on the *President McKinley* the very next day. *The New York Times* reported that against the objections of many Chinese organizations, "high government officials" insisted on granting the necessary permits. *Time* magazine said that "huffy officials consented to let her take her rare prize home." It's hard to know what happened exactly, since Harkness would always be vague about these few days in Shanghai. Much later she would tell an American reporter that a young aide to Chiang Kai-shek had been among the most instrumental in securing her permits.

The cheers from the Western corner went up immediately. Sowerby praised the relenting Chinese government. "We cannot help admiring the action of the authorities in adopting this wise course, for there can be no doubt whatever that, by getting the young panda alive to such a well-equipped institution for caring for and rearing it to adulthood as the Bronx Zoo, the interests of science will best have been served." Of course, this was the same Bronx Zoo that had trouble—as did all zoos— keeping some exotic animals such as gorillas alive for more than a few months at a stretch. It would know as little as anyone else about keeping giant pandas in captivity.

So far, Su-Lin's miraculous survival wasn't due to any scientific organization anyway, but rather to Harkness's instincts. In holding the baby close to her, in striking on a good formula, and in massaging Su-Lin's belly to aid in digestion, Harkness was often intuitively mimicking a mother giant panda, long before those secrets were known to zoologists.

Her friends had been powerful enough to button down the glowering Academia Sinica, but her success and its aftermath would bring her enemies. Overruled bureaucrats accustomed to having their way were now determined to regain face. The fastest route would be to bear down on other foreign explorers. *The New York Times* reported that although Harkness was getting out with the panda, it was expected that "the result will be a tightening of all the restrictions against scientific and exploring expeditions now in the field, and future expeditions will find it extremely difficult to obtain satisfactory permits or agreements." That outcome couldn't have done much to endear Harkness to the exploring community she had just thrashed so soundly.

But whatever crowing took place in the papers, it wasn't coming from the Harkness camp. Jittery over the roller coaster she had been on for the last several days, and not wanting to spoil the deal in any way, Harkness stopped the pipeline of information to reporters. While her journalist pals were shut out here, Harkness sent Perkie an unsigned cable telegram in Connecticut to put the lid on things there: KEEP ALL INFORMATION FROM PRESS. Shanghai's reporters were forced to piece things together by expending a little shoe leather in sleuthing around. The *China Press* discovered that Harkness had canceled her room at the Palace Hotel. The reporter also had heard but could not confirm that a compromise had been reached. Woo Kyatang recorded that Harkness was working in "the utmost secrecy," making "every attempt" to "throw local newsmen off her track."

With all the interested players coming to Harkness headquarters, it was said that the Palace had begun to look like "a Zoologist Association Conference" rather than "a Bundside hostelry." The staff was instructed not to reveal Harkness's whereabouts or any of her plans. Yet, on Tuesday night, a correspondent from the *Shanghai Times* made his way to her room. "Mrs. Harkness looked a trifle grim as she said: 'Still uncertain,' " the paper reported. Harkness was being so cautious that she even had her name deleted from the *McKinley*'s passenger list.

IT ALL WORKED. On Wednesday, December 2, Harkness boarded the waiting steamship with Su-Lin. All her export papers were in order, and she even had a voucher that read "One dog, $20.00."

Harkness, who had grown fond of the pack of reporters dogging her trail, allowed them into her first-class cabin. They found Su-Lin snuggled into the cozy wicker basket, sound asleep. Harkness, on the other hand, was still in a state of high anxiety, which worsened when they were interrupted by the appearance of a customs inspector. With just fifteen minutes left before the ship was to weigh anchor, he wanted to see a permit she had already handed to another official. There were several moments of sheer panic before a telephone message from shore straightened things out.

Just after 10:30 A.M., the express trans-Pacific liner, the *President McKinley*, pulled away from the lower buoys 12 and 13, heading for Kobe, Yokohama, and San Francisco, carrying, along with its passengers, the last batch of Christmas mail from Shanghai. It was a brisk, cloudy morning, and the feel of the boat thrumming its way to open sea came as bittersweet relief.

Harkness locked Baby safely away in the cabin and ran up on deck to wave farewell to her loyal friend "Jimmy," who had taken the last tender to see her off. She was saying goodbye too to China, where she had found a new peace. Where she had immersed herself in "the quiet, unheeded flow of Oriental life, immutable, impervious to the West, to the world, to everything but the great continuance of life." She experienced so sharply now the pull of this land. "China is generous," she wrote, "to those who give, she returns in brimming measure."

Harkness felt that her accomplishment was in keeping her precious panda alive. Su-Lin was, she said, "the only member of her clan who ever left her native haunt without being just a skin destined to be stuffed and stand in a habitat group for years in some museum hall."

When Harkness had first left this city in September, traveling deep into China, she had taken with her the ashes of her husband. Now, as she quit Shanghai's shores once more, she had in her arms a thriving, living creature and the bamboo that she hoped would nourish him.

AS HARKNESS WAS catching her last glimpses of China, there was someone on shore plotting against her, the man she had, as historians put it later, "pipped at the post." Floyd Tangier Smith would sit down with a reporter the very next day at his office in the French Concession. The big-game hunter was determined to dismantle her success, doing it with full awareness that when his accusations were printed, Harkness would be far out to sea, where she couldn't hit back.

CHAPTER EIGHT

ANIMAL OF THE CENTURY

The stages in darkness
Will light for Ruth Harkness.
The captor of Su Lin, the fair.

ONCE OUT ON THE OPEN SEAS, Ruth Harkness and the panda slept for what seemed like days. They were tucked away in their well-appointed cabin as the fatigue Harkness had been staving off through two wild weeks in Shanghai came crashing down. Because the explorer had kept her name off the passenger list, and now avoided the dining room by ordering meals delivered right to the door, it was easy at first for her to stay secluded. Since most on board were unaware of her presence, or that of Su-Lin, Harkness could take some time to regain her strength.

As she dozed aboard the *McKinley,* Floyd Tangier Smith, back in Shanghai, was striking, and striking hard, slapping Harkness's name back on the front pages yet again, this time under unsettling headlines: MRS. HARKNESS GOT HIS PANDA EXPLORER 'AJAX' SMITH CHARGES, blared the *China Press* version.

Smith claimed to a reporter from the *China Press* that his own hunters in Chaopo were about to capture Su-Lin when the panda's location was leaked to Harkness, who "went straight to the nest," snatching his prize.

It was a rich packet of gossip for the rumor-addicted town, but one that would prove rather unsatisfying. While Harkness's report of events would remain steadfast, Smith would begin a bizarre pattern of contradictions and embellishments. By revising his story with abandon, he would make it difficult or even impossible to believe anything he said.

After the revelations of the morning papers, the afternoon editions were, as one said itself, carrying a "slightly different version" of the story line. The following day, the picture changed once again, when Smith wrote a long letter to the editor of the *North China Daily News*, saying he had been widely misquoted. Later there would be even more renditions as varied as they were feverishly detailed. These would be among the first public signs that Smith was coming mentally unraveled over the fact that this woman, a dilettante, a dress designer, a laughable explorer, had done what he had been attempting to do for at least fifteen years.

Smith told reporters that without his knowledge his hunters had been monitoring a pregnant giant panda for a long time and had been aware that she gave birth. As they were waiting for the baby panda to be weaned before bundling him off to Smith, Harkness abducted him. Smith did not address how the hunters knew the panda was pregnant, and why they had waited so long to inform him. He said nothing of the improbability of men repeatedly visiting such a shy and sensitive animal without her feeling compelled to relocate.

No matter, because the facts would all change shortly. By the next day, in his letter to the editor, Smith professed that he had actually known of the panda for a long time. He wrote that when Harkness left Shanghai on her expedition, he received word from his hunters "that a giant panda had been 'marked down' and asking if I wanted it for double the price I had previously offered." It was a startling claim that he seems to have made only once.

In a dense eight-page letter written in the fall of 1937 and meant to set every detail straight, he would change things yet again. This time, he would say Su-Lin was brought to his "compradore," or business agent, in Chaopo, and that Harkness bought the panda there.

At the same time he would also write a magazine article in England asserting the impossible—that he had been in the Chaopo area just days before Harkness was.

His accusations were lobbed at every inch of Harkness's story, starting with the route she took. Smith told the reporter from the *China Press* when he launched his initial attack that Harkness had deceived him about the way she traveled. But right afterward, and for the most part forever onward, he would write that she had, in fact, told him the truth about her journey.

Somehow, with no recognition of the contradiction in his argument, even when he was giving her credit for "very frankly" telling him the truth of her trajectory, and verifying her story in this regard, he would say that her account of having traveled ten days north of Chengdu was "impossible." Not only did Harkness's tally for distance and time make perfect sense, it was verified by the Sage expedition, which also traveled from Chengdu to Chaopo in the same amount of time, making stops, as did Harkness, for several days in places like Wenchuan.

Smith could have been caught in other lies too, if anyone had been paying close attention to his statements. He once denied having ever said that Harkness stole his panda. Yet he did write that any money she received for the panda was "so much hard cash transferred directly out of my pocket and into her hand-bag." He said that she was "morally, if not legally, a thief."

Simultaneously, Smith struggled to promote a high-minded, magnanimous public image of himself. He had wanted to give Harkness a "sporting chance to succeed," after their tenuous and never-cemented partnership dissolved, he said, so he continued to provide invaluable strategic advice, giving "her every 'tip' that I could as to the best localities and the best methods to be followed to help her get a panda 'on her own.' "

After the partnership was "quite amicably terminated," Smith said,

Harkness had agreed to his fiat that she steer clear of "any part of the territory in which my trained organization was carrying on operations." It was a demand he had made of no other panda hunter.

The bottom line, as Smith's wife, Elizabeth, put it, was that "Mrs. Harkness has bagged the prize Floyd had set his heart on getting." Years before, Smith had predicted to his beloved sister Ruth that she would "very probably be the first white woman to set eyes on this curious creature," the giant panda.

Underlying much of his fury was the fact that Harkness had found her success with a strategy that he had been certain would fail. Now he was the one left empty-handed, sputtering, and telling the press what he still wanted to believe himself: "the only way to catch animals is to move slowly," he said. "One must spend time in training people to set traps, and then to watch these traps. It takes months and years."

He held tight to his belief in the face of evidence against it: either he had been wrong all this time about how to catch a panda, or Harkness had swindled him. He chose the latter. He had staked everything—his finances, his life's work, his reputation—on its being so. He couldn't believe that what he saw as Harkness's haste and naïveté could possibly have yielded the most sought-after animal on the planet, the thing he wanted most in the world. It just wasn't fair. The giant panda belonged to him. By rights, it should be his.

In his agony, he would grant Harkness nothing. Her achievement was meaningless, he wrote. "Any ten year old school girl with the necessary money could have done as much." Later on, he would go even further in his interpretation of events, claiming publicly to have had a hand in capturing Su-Lin.

Counting against Harkness was the fact that her camera did not record the actual capture of Su-Lin. The lapse, which she said was due to a length of broken film stuck in the shutter, was unfortunate. But had she truly been a cheat perpetrating a hoax, it would have been easy to stage the moment of discovery. She could have put the newly purchased baby panda into the hollow of any big tree and snapped away.

And then there were the "eyewitnesses." A handful of people would step forward over time to claim they had seen Harkness purchase the panda. She had allegedly simultaneously bought the panda in Chaopo, in Chengdu, and in Guanxian. The stories always conflicted with one another, and in a way helped her cause by canceling one another out. Often the witnesses were anonymous. The easiest to dismiss would be those who said Harkness never left Chengdu, that she had bought the tiny panda right there in the city, for there is proof—in pictures and letters—that she was in the field. Others claimed to be the actual hunters who sold the animal to her out in the wilds. No evidence existed that Harkness had done anything but what she said. Yet the notion occasionally floated from the start—that Quentin Young had paid off the hunters, staging the discovery without her knowledge—would be impossible to disprove, and would remain a question forever after.

Over the coming weeks, Smith's mental anguish would prove to be clinical. He was "terribly cut up," his wife said, her own indignation egging him on, as she obsessed with him over events, writing her own wrathful letters.

By the magic of the wireless, the news of Smith's charges hit *The New York Times* on the same day it was reported in the Shanghai papers. A small story just a few paragraphs long, it was soon forgotten. The few American papers that mentioned the trouble gave no details. On the rare occasions she was asked about it, Harkness would simply say the accusations were "perfectly ridiculous."

Without Harkness present to defend herself in the early stories in the Shanghai papers, though, Smith's accusations went unchallenged except by reporters' own skepticism. "Whether the baby panda that Mrs. William Harkness is now taking to America was a planted panda, a bought-and-paid-for panda, an escaped panda, a stolen panda or a genuine discovered panda was agitating local exploring circles," the *Shanghai Evening Post and Mercury* reported.

Very soon, no less a person than Arthur de Carle Sowerby would stand in for Harkness, talking to the press, writing letters to the editor, and landing several body blows to Smith's claims.

Smith would be reeling anyway. Within a short time of Harkness's departure, he was a shattered man in complete breakdown. Although his thinking would be muddled, he was always clear on one point: Ruth Harkness was the enemy. "I knew her at last for a Judas, Annanias and Munchausen all rolled into one," he would write.

Smith's humiliation was compounded by the predicament he found himself in. He was stuck fast in Shanghai, unable to scrape together, from any source, the funding needed to get back in the field and prove himself.

All of it fueled a rage that would first lead him to a mental and physical collapse and later drive him to a ruthless pursuit of giant pandas that would result in the deaths of perhaps dozens of them.

HOW DIFFERENT THINGS were for Ruth Harkness. On board the *President McKinley*, she had characteristically shaken off her lethargy to find a "second wind." For her, that meant socializing. She made a small circle of friends with whom she involved herself in all kinds of parties and late-night pranks. Once, after the usual reverie, Harkness, in a formal white lace dress with train, busted into the galley with her drunken mates to fry chickens in the middle of the night.

She could afford to be euphoric. Far from Smith's dark cloud, she was entering the bright light of celebrity and acclaim. Even before she landed, *Time* magazine was honoring her success as "a scientific prize of first magnitude." Like most other American publications, *Time* glorified her achievement, never even mentioning Smith.

While she was sailing, Quentin Young would find success with stunning speed, shooting two giant pandas and returning to Shanghai within a fortnight of her departure. On his arrival, he would meet up with and marry Diana Chen.

Aside from a patch of bad weather that had the American explorer trading staterooms for a few days, and despite the scratches and claw marks the robust Su-Lin was etching on her arms and neck, life was very good for Ruth Harkness. She could build her strength now, ensuring she was both fit and composed for the moment the boat docked, bringing her face-to-face with her own fame.

IT WAS THE GREATEST press reception San Francisco "lavished upon any celebrity since the coming of George Bernard Shaw," according to the *Examiner*. On a crisp morning, in San Francisco Bay, Harkness, with a turbanlike cloth binding her hair and a large gold brooch at her throat, sat down to bottle-feed Su-Lin before an army of reporters, photographers, cameramen, and sound-reel technicians. They nearly swamped the *McKinley*, jostling one another for better positions. Flashbulbs popped, scribes shouted questions, cameras clicked and whirred. A wall of newshounds surrounded her, all wanting pictures, all demanding a story.

Harkness and the panda were a welcome Christmas gift to a country still on the skids. "America was like a boxer," John Steinbeck wrote of the period, "driven to the floor by left-hand jabs for a seven count, who struggles to his feet to catch a right-hand haymaker on the point of his chin."

Everything seemed out of balance, even nature itself. Through unprecedented drought and misuse of the land, "black blizzards," massive dust storms, turned the midwestern and southern plains into the Dust Bowl. Millions of tons of topsoil blew away, sending two and a half million once proud "Okies" and "Arkies" and other plains folks scrambling in the largest migration in U.S. history, mostly to California, where they were often rebuffed by unwelcoming police squads—the "bum brigade," which didn't want its public-welfare rolls to swell.

Eighty-five million people a week, on the other hand, headed for movie theaters across the country to the blissful escape that Hollywood provided. FDR and his "Brain Trust" were battling economic woes with an alphabet soup of social programs, but even he couldn't do what the studios did—make the Depression disappear, if only for ninety minutes or so. Then it was back out into the real world of cutting cardboard soles for worn-out shoes, sleeping four to a bed, and hearing the sound of horse hooves in the middle of the night as someone avoided another month's rent with a midnight move.

Americans were hungry for stories of the little guy triumphing over adversity; they craved a drama like Ruth Harkness's. On that bright morning in San Francisco, the adventurer possessed the makings of a hero. With just a hint of movie-star glamour and a dash of high class, she was a can-do girl who had beaten the odds. She was plucky and clever and brave. Like some fairy-tale figure, she strode home, carrying in her arms a mythical, magical creature captured from a distant land.

Harkness was the darling of the media, enjoying a welcome that could not have been more boisterously positive, fevered, or widespread. "That was fame," *The New York Times* observed of her high-profile entrance, and it would keep coming as she made her way east.

The Times had already started lauding her achievement before she landed, saying that Harkness "would not accept discouragement nor defeat where many men had failed." She had faced a rugged and alien terrain, with dangers at every corner, and emerged with what *The Times* described as "the rarest quadruped in the world." It was "the most important single achievement in collecting animals in modern times," according to the Brookfield Zoo in Chicago.

The American public adored stories of women getting into a man's game. There were a number of dashing aviatrixes who were breaking records one after another. Beryl Markham and Jacqueline Cochran, and, of course, Amelia Earhart. The American Gertrude Caroline Ederle was the first woman to swim the English Channel in 1926. In 1932 Hattie Caraway was the first woman elected to the U.S. Senate. And, now, here was Ruth Harkness, American Explorer. She would soon appear on best-dressed lists and in an ad for Quaker Oats. Her expedition was the stuff of lusty, bright-colored comic strips.

As grand as it all could be, in San Francisco Harkness found the American press much more unruly than the polite gang in Shanghai. She longed for the days when Dan Reib could "control publicity." She bristled at some of the questions, such as how it was that she "happened" to find this creature. And she hated the presentation of the page-one story in the *Examiner*, which did not mention Quentin Young at all, and referred in its headline to the panda capture—without intending any connection to the Smith flap—as a "kidnap."

AFTER THE MORNING's media assault, then some haggling with customs over the bamboo she had brought (the dirt on the roots was washed off in compromise), Harkness, Baby, and a few of their friends from the ship battled their way over to the Saint Francis Hotel. There, railroad and airline companies vied for the high-profile opportunity of transporting the world's only captive baby giant panda. A few days later, on December 22, she pulled in to a cold, wintry Chicago aboard the *Overland Limited*, dealing with a new throng of eager reporters. At the Palmer House hotel, Harkness conferred with Edward Bean, director of Chicago's Brookfield Zoo, sometimes called the Chicago Zoological Park. Bean made his desire explicit about "the most important and valuable animal in captivity." He wanted Su-Lin. The Associated Press reported that the Bronx Zoo, the London Zoo, and any number of circuses were in on the bidding too.

All the newspapers had said what Harkness herself had probably assumed—that Su-Lin would be headed for the Bronx, where Bill's other catch—the Komodo dragons—had gone. Harkness was careful, however, not to shut the door to Chicago. DON'T CLOSE NEGOTIATIONS WITH ANYONE, she had cabled Perkie. She didn't know what she'd find back in New York, and once again, her instincts would prove to be valid. She made clear to Bean that she wanted Baby in a place that could care for him properly, and that she would choose the institution that would finance her next expedition. With that, Harkness and Su-Lin were on their way, that afternoon, aboard the sleek, futuristically streamlined *Commodore Vanderbilt*, hurtling toward Manhattan.

At 9:47 A.M., on December 23, 1936, a svelte Ruth Harkness, wearing a thick Chinese otter-fur coat, carrying her "baby girl," and trailed by hordes of reporters, stepped up to the registration desk at New York City's Biltmore Hotel to secure a room that could accommodate her and the wildest media frenzy yet. "All that seemed lacking," *The New York Times* would note later, "was a ticker-tape parade and a reception at City Hall."

Along with excited friends and relatives, Harkness had been greeted earlier at Grand Central Terminal by a wall of shouting reporters and cameramen setting off their flashes as she emerged from the train. De-

Ruth shows off Su-Lin to the United States. COURTESY MARY LOBISCO

spite now being experienced with the media, Harkness was bewildered by the size and fury of this onslaught. The panda too grew irritated by the lights. Harkness was determined to get Su-Lin away from the railway station, which she considered too dangerously filled with baby-threatening germs. It would be easier to deal with the platoon of media people in a hotel than in her own apartment, which she hadn't seen in months.

In a large room on the eighth floor of the Biltmore, Harkness called for all windows to be opened to the fresh winter air, in order to simulate "the native Tibetan climate of the panda." "I keep the radiators off and all the windows opened, regardless of temperature," she would say. The chain-smoker-turned-worried-mother then requested that all cigarettes be extinguished.

She settled herself and Baby onto the bed's nubby pink spread. A tray with pots of hot water to warm the formula was delivered, while a throng of "shivering newshawks" circled around her. As flashbulbs popped, she fed Su-Lin, answering questions she already "knew by heart."

There were the basics—How did it happen? Where?—but also some comical ones like, was Su-Lin housebroken?

With Harkness's great sense of humor, they all had a few laughs. To the question of whether Su-Lin was intelligent, she responded confidently that Su-Lin was "the smartest panda that's ever been in captivity."

At one point in her press briefings, she would be asked about being the only woman with all those Chinese men, to which she replied, "I was accepted by those men with less comment probably than a woman who rides in a smoking car from New York to Philadelphia."

To questions about Smith's charges, she protested, "There's not a word of truth to it!"

When another reporter asked, "Why does anybody want one anyway?" Harkness said, "Oh, because it's a completely new species. We want it for scientific study."

Would she be giving the panda to a zoo? they wanted to know. "I think we'll both wind up together in a cage in some zoo," she responded.

During the rapid-fire questioning and all the frivolity, the baby panda bit the nipple off his bottle, or as the papers reported, "misbehaved," right "under the guns of the press," spilling milk onto the bed. With affection, Harkness said that Su-Lin was "a spoiled little beggar."

The panda was so adorable that writers found it hard to do him justice. He was compared to a Scottish terrier and a teddy bear. The *New*

York Herald Tribune reporter was struck by how much like a human baby the panda seemed, as he woke, yawned, stretched, and waved his arms "in an aimless fashion."

His eye patches were invariably called black "spectacles." His "unearthly voice" sounded like "an off-key violin note." The *Sun* said Su-Lin was "rare and priceless as a maharajah's jewel." *Time* magazine called him the "Animal of the Year." Much later, with the perspective of history, a noted zoologist would jack up the designation a hundredfold, calling Su-Lin "the most famous animal of the twentieth century."

All the reporters were struck by the emotional bond between Harkness and this little infant. The baby panda, *The New York Times* said, "seems to have a real affection for her mistress" and "to delight in the warmth of human contact" as he sucked "greedily" on the lobe of Harkness's ear. The *Herald Tribune* wrote that Su-Lin obviously was "something more than just an animal infant to its captor." The *Sun* reported that Harkness referred to Su-Lin "merely as 'the child.' "

She would tell the press that she understood the meanings of his various yips and squawks, which, she said, indicated contentment, hunger, irritation, and fright.

During that chaotic first day in New York, several visitors arrived at the Biltmore. Charles Appleton, a friend of Harkness's, shyly presented a poem. It celebrated Harkness's capture of "what no man has caught up to now," and predicted another race—the one for movie rights.

A few big guns of natural history came too—the famed Raymond Ditmars, curator of reptiles and mammals at the Bronx Zoo, and Donald Carter of the American Museum of Natural History. The sight of the little panda electrified them, especially Ditmars. The *Herald Tribune* reported that grinning like a boy, the august scientist said, "I just want to be able to say that I touched a live panda."

Throughout the day, and in every meeting with the press, it was of vital importance to Harkness to credit all the Youngs. "Jack and Su-Lin Young did countless things for me," she said, "but my biggest stroke of luck was obtaining the cooperation of Quentin. His forehand knowledge of the conditions we were to encounter, plus his keen mind, tireless energy and thorough understanding of the people with whom we had to deal in our journeys up-country really paved the way for my success. Without Quentin Young, I should have failed."

Of herself and her own capabilities, she said, she was a very fortunate person. "That it should be my luck to be the first human being to bring a Giant Panda—especially a baby one—out alive seems so unbelievable that there are times when I can hardly realize that it is true."

Though she may have downplayed her determination, she now vowed that she would dedicate the "remainder of her life to adventure." She made clear to the press that any reputable zoo that would finance her next expedition would get Su-Lin. She felt complete happiness while abroad, telling the scribbling journalists, "I loved the Chinese people and the country and can hardly wait to get back."

Once the press had finally cleared, Harkness, along with her entourage, made her way to her apartment at 333 West Eighteenth Street. She would have an enormous amount of catching up to do with everybody.

The next night, Christmas Eve, Harkness found herself alone for what would turn out to be a few surprisingly dark hours. As radio stations played jolly and wistful tunes, candles and Christmas lights burned in the windows along the New York streets, and cheerful families rushed up the sidewalks with bright packages under their arms, a wave of melancholy came over the solitary explorer. She had felt such contentment in the lonely mountains in a lost part of the world, but now in the heart of one of the most crowded cities on earth, the place she had lived for her entire adult life, she was lonely. Though not the only Christmas she had spent without Bill, it was the first since his death. The sense of homecoming she had experienced so intensely in China would leave her feeling oddly out of place here. Surrounded by the familiar, she seemed not to belong.

Thankfully, a friend dropped in. They had cocktails, then went out, toting Baby down chilled Manhattan avenues in his wicker basket. As they indulged in a fine dinner in a favorite restaurant, Harkness declared that charging an extravagant meal on credit was always a reliable anti-dote to feeling broke.

Right after Christmas everything started to hum again. There were some increasingly sour talks with the Bronx Zoo as the lofty zoological institution balked about taking the panda. Never expressed openly, it was almost certainly Harkness's demand for expedition money that put them off. Harkness wanted the same amount she had spent on her first expedition, which *Time* and *Life* magazines gauged to be twenty thousand dollars. She had said as much herself at one point, appraising her four-pound panda at five thousand dollars a pound.

It was a whopper of an asking price, way out of line with standard invoices for zoo purchases. Monkeys could be had by the dozen at $12 each, scarlet ibises for $15, and Malayan sun bears for $250 per pair. Besides, no matter what the price, the Bronx preferred and often expected catches brought in by well-mannered gentlemen to be donated.

That wasn't going to be the case with this woman. The director, W. Reid Blair, saw the newspaper stories in which Su-Lin was said to be worth anywhere from $10,000 to $150,000. So the zoo started its grumbling early. Blair complained to the papers that the explorer had been lax about staying in touch, asserting that "aside from a cable to the effect that Mrs. Harkness was on her way, the institution had had no word from her since she left China." But more to the point, he said of her and the panda, "she'll probably want to sell it." The zoo would be willing to acquire it only if the price were "reasonable."

Furthermore, Blair told the *New York Herald Tribune* that "no zoological park desires to pay from $2,000 to $10,000 for a live animal unless there is a fair chance it can live a reasonable time in captivity." Since a sick panda could be a colossal waste of money, some zoo officials began to wonder aloud if Su-Lin's perfectly natural bowed back legs meant he was suffering from rickets.

The Bronx, apparently, wouldn't budge above $2,000, and terms could not be agreed on. So Baby continued to live the life of a modern city panda—riding around Manhattan in taxicabs with all the windows rolled down, living in a nice flat, and attending cocktail parties.

Oddly, no other zoo was coming forward with a check for the most sought-after animal in the world, scared off no doubt by the price tag as well as the liability of caring for such a vulnerable baby. Harkness was surprised and discouraged. She had a "heavenly" fantasy of scraping together enough money to return to her lost world with Baby in tow. She also considered the possibility of bringing Quentin Young to the States. She wondered if he had, in fact, married the girl in the red sweater.

One sunny day in January, Harkness strolled around the streets of Manhattan, thinking of Young. As she watched the skaters at Rockefeller Plaza and looked up at the soaring skyscrapers, she decided to send her field companion his reward money, despite the fact that she still had no deal with any zoo. Her bank account was so close to empty anyway, she thought in true Harkness style, what would it matter if it drained out a little faster? She cabled Young the cash, musing about whether he would spend it on a ticket to America.

Harkness may have been downhearted about the zoo situation, but she had plenty to distract her. "The world came to my door by mail, by telephone and in person," she recounted. Among others, there were author, critic, and radio personality Alexander Woollcott, whose promotion had been instrumental in the success of *Lost Horizon;* the great wildlife artist Charles Knight, coming daily to sketch Su-Lin; and the daughter of the Chinese ambassador to the United States.

Also, perhaps surprisingly, there were the men who had made names for themselves by killing pandas: the Roosevelts, Brooke Dolan, and Dean Sage.

Theodore Roosevelt, Jr., arrived with his son Quentin and brother Kermit. The colonel was sitting with the woolly baby panda on his lap when a friend said that should something happen to Su-Lin, he could be stuffed and placed with the grouping of specimens that the Roosevelts had provided to the Field Museum. Roosevelt replied, "I'd just as soon think of stuffing Quentin and putting him in a habitat group."

Sage had a similar reaction. "Do you know," he said to Harkness, "I shall never shoot another Panda!"

"And this," Harkness said, "from a man whose highest ambition three short years ago was to collect a Giant Panda Group in China for the American Museum of Natural History. . . . But I have since wondered if the American Museum would have had the wonderful Panda specimens Mr. and Mrs. Sage brought back, if Su Lin had seen the Sages first." The baby panda's ability to convert hunters into peaceable admirers was not lost on the lady explorer. "I hope something will be done," she wrote, "to prevent more of these rare and interesting animals from being killed. Science I believe has learned all that can be gained from dead specimens; it remains now to learn something about the live one." As one Harvard mammalogist said of collecting specimens for museums, what was observed of an animal could be summed up by saying, "When we found it, it ran like hell, whereupon we shot it!"

Waging her soft campaign to disarm big-game hunters, she got the chance to address a slew of them. On Saturday evening, January 16, Ruth Harkness was the first woman to attend the annual banquet of the prestigious and all-male Explorers Club. Members had included President Theodore Roosevelt, Sir Ernest Shackleton, both Frederick Cook and Robert Peary, and Richard Byrd.

The club would not tolerate naming a woman the guest of honor—that glory went to the panda himself. But, as Harkness dryly pointed out, "They couldn't very well ask Su Lin without me." Though they were forced to invite her, they made clear she was not being commended: *The New York Times* reported that Su-Lin was "ceremoniously announced as the one and only guest of honor."

Wearing her gray Chinese otter coat over a peach gown, Harkness swept into the chandeliered lounge of the Plaza at 7:15 P.M., and parted the sea of hundreds who were milling about in formal jackets with their cocktails and cigars. Horrified by the billowing smoke, she dashed out just as quickly. Harkness, Su-Lin, a hotel employee, and a maid Harkness brought along, Frances Horn, hurried through the gathering once more, this time on their way to suite 363, rented for the evening, so windows could be opened to the fresh air for Baby. Harkness's anxiety and the brief appearance of the panda caused enough of a stir among the gentlemen for *The New York Times* to note it.

During dinner, Harkness and Su-Lin were seated next to club president Walter Granger. At ten-thirty toastmaster Lowell Thomas signaled to Harkness. She wrapped Baby in a bath towel, and carried him to a microphone for a live broadcast. Granger asked a series of questions, to which Harkness responded for the panda. "What's your name?" he inquired, and Harkness answered, "Su-Lin."

"Where do you come from?"

"I came from the border of Tibet."

Before the broadcast ended, the annoyed animal did his own talking, which, *The Times* said, "was exactly like a baby crying." Although there were a number of speakers, the paper asserted, "It was Su-Lin's show"—as it would be for some time to come.

Newspapers couldn't get enough of the panda and the panda hunter. Among others, the *New York American* told the tale in sizable and splashy spreads over four Sundays in February. For the series, Harkness's byline was accompanied by the legend "First woman to lead her own expedition into Chinese Tibet and the only explorer who ever caught a living specimen of the rare and elusive Giant Panda."

THROUGHOUT JANUARY, HARKNESS began to worry about Baby's care. She knew that her apartment was not adequate for his needs. It was also increasingly difficult to keep up with the growing animal's hunger. "Day by day, she grew bigger and stronger," Harkness told a reporter. "Her appetite, always healthy grew by leaps and bounds." The eight-ounce bottle was quickly replaced by a twelve-ounce, and four feedings a day had to be supplemented, but by what? Su-Lin seemed unaware that carrots, lettuce, asparagus, or celery were anything more than toys. A single stalk of bamboo that Harkness had saved because of the giant panda-tooth marks on it became a favorite possession. Though ragged, cracked, and dry, it held some magic for the little panda, who chewed on it endlessly.

Since this growing baby was obviously going to need solid food soon, Harkness was determined to get him into the hands of experts who could puzzle out a decent diet.

Edward Bean at the Brookfield Zoo had treated her well, so she negotiated with him to take Su-Lin on loan until matters could be sorted out. Late in the afternoon of February 6 Harkness once again boarded the *Commodore Vanderbilt,* this time heading west. Her friends saw her off from Grand Central Terminal, bringing roses and violets for the bittersweet farewell. She would stay one week, making sure little Su-Lin settled in properly.

Two days later the panda was welcomed at the zoo, where he would not be put on display for months. He was kept in the first-aid station, after zoo officials realized that the planned space in the Australian House was too hot for the woolly baby, and too frightening with the yips of the dingo dogs echoing through the halls. The director's daughter, Mary Bean, a registered nurse, would care for the baby by day; her brother, Robert Bean, the curator of mammals, took the night shift. Lloyd's of London insured the animal that Pathé News considered the most valuable in the world.

Clearly, Harkness wasn't the only one who saw the panda as nearly human. Kept in a large room, he was given a bright green Chinese grass rug, a cradle, a playpen, and a football. Harkness was pleased to see that her Su-Lin would receive "the sort of care and attention that have gone into the upbringing of the Dionne quintuplets"—then the most famous babies in North America.

Mary Bean would correspond with Harkness over time, providing details of Su-Lin's regimen. He would be fed on a regular schedule:

7:30 A.M.	one and a half ounces of prune or orange juice
8:00	Seven ounces milk (Klim) with one teaspoon codliver oil
11:45	two-thirds cup Pablum or oatmeal
12 Noon	Milk (Klim) with half teaspoon of Haliver Malt
1:45	four ounces Gerber's vegetable soup

4:15   Milk with H.M. (7 oz.)

10:00   same

Carrots, celery, lettuce, and spinach leaves were provided for chewing, and the doting nurse said Su-Lin enjoyed "a little warm water two or three times a day."

HARKNESS WAS ALL smiles about the transfer, but it was with a great deal of emotion that she relinquished the panda into the Beans' care. Since the morning of November 9 she had hardly let Baby out of her sight. Now he would be gone for good.

That night, alone in her room, she woke sobbing. Tellingly, she wrote, "but for whom or what, I do not know." She may never have been able to properly express her despair over Bill's death in her writing, but here was a glimpse of her pain. Su-Lin was Bill, his cause, the life the young couple should have had, the children they would never have. When she gave the animal away, all the other sorrows were laid bare.

HARKNESS RETURNED to New York, eager to accomplish her objectives. She wanted to produce a book about her adventure, receive enough money to underwrite her next expedition, and get back to China and Tibet.

Her story was big enough, and she had enough connections to the publishing world—among others, Perkie had befriended author Faith Baldwin, and Harkness's in-laws had lived near a successful literary agent—that she landed a contract with a new publishing house, Carrick & Evans, for two books: one for adults and another for children. She could start right away, using as notes the stockpile of letters she had written home to Perkie during her expedition.

Gnawing at her at all times, though, was the impermanence of Su-Lin's situation. She met with various zoo officials and contacted others. All with little result. In frustration, she wondered aloud in the pages of the popular *New York Herald Tribune* if she should just take the panda out of the zoo to return him to his native home. "There are times," she said, "when I feel that the best thing to do would be to take Su-Lin back to her ancestral jungle, set her free and let her live her life the way Mother Nature intended."

When the article hit, the public reacted. Letters poured in begging Harkness not to take Su-Lin away. In Chicago, zoo-goers were clamoring to see the famous captive, who was still being kept off exhibit until Harkness and the zoo could come to terms.

What else could Brookfield do? It quickly brokered a deal with Harkness in order to keep its star attraction—an animal that had managed to mesmerize the public before even being displayed. It would pay Harkness $8,750, for her next expedition. Not quite what she had been looking for, but enough. She was so mad to get back to that life of adventure, she figured that somehow she'd make do on the small investment. The book contract would help buttress her finances. Most of all, she now felt she knew how to live in China cheaply. She had learned "that to travel simply was to know and enjoy a country and its people."

So, in mid-April, Harkness returned to Chicago to close the deal and have a much longed-for visit with Baby. On the way west, she was anxious about the sting she would feel if Su-Lin did not remember her.

Her fears were groundless. As soon as Su-Lin saw her, the now thirty-one-pound panda lumbered into her arms, nuzzling her hair just like in old times. It was more than satisfying to see how much he had grown. The reunion, of course, would have to be followed by another separation, which was hard to face. Even as the rowdy panda clawed and bit her, Harkness could only hug him tighter.

That day, April 20, the public adoration of Su-Lin began. He went on display for the first time, for only two hours a day in the available space in the monkey house. The zoo was overrun by eager fans. Tens of thousands of them came in the first few days; 325,000 in the first three months. In that short period alone, Su-Lin drew 87,000 more spectators than would that year's five World Series games played in New York. Over time the panda even entertained such celebrities as Shirley Temple, Helen Keller, and Sophie Tucker.

The Bronx Zoo, which had so haughtily rejected Su-Lin, saw what was happening and began making quiet inquiries about the animal—How was his health? What effect was he having on attendance? They must have felt sorry for themselves when they learned that Su-Lin was healthy, eating solid food, and quite effortlessly had become the most popular animal in the country.

BACK IN SHANGHAI that spring, Gerald Russell, fresh from months in the field, and Floyd Tangier Smith, broken and confined to the hospital, arranged a reunion. With Harkness's success, Smith's collapse, and Russell's tales from up-country, there was much to discuss.

Looking skeletal in loose bedclothes, the old man was quite a sight to the young adventurer. Bitterness had eaten Smith to the bone, bringing his weight down to just 118 pounds. Even more alarming was his behavior. Russell found that he "juxtaposed various ideas and events with phantasy," and his mind "was at times clouded."

Smith had been in a complete tailspin in the wake of Harkness's departure from Shanghai. As she traveled farther and farther away from him, her image loomed ever larger in his fevered mind. Just before Christmas he had turned to his wife, saying, "Do you know, I think I am slowly dying." He told her that he could see no way out of his "present condition."

Though able to pull himself together for the holiday, just two days later he was thrown back into utter despair.

He was broke, "financially embarrassed," his wife said. And his nerves had "all gone phut." Smith confided to his sister that he was "feeling all broken up in nerves." In this state, he had been "ready to lay down and pass up everything without a hope or interest in the future." Instead of continued life, he would write her much later, he had been facing "a possible blotting out altogether." From winter into spring, battling physical ailments, including pleurisy and an infected throat, as well as psychological demons, Smith fell apart, experiencing, as he said, a real "knock down."

What both he and Elizabeth continued to focus on through it all was Ruth Harkness. She was a treacherous woman who had played a "dirty trick." Tracking details of her progress from press accounts—amounts offered for the panda, books she might write, plans to return to China— they thought all her ideas were "crazy."

Closer to home, word was getting back to Smith that Harkness had been privately critical of him to certain people in the city. As if it hadn't been humiliating enough for him, he began to hear from friends "slanderous statements" made by Harkness while she had been in Shanghai. These rumors only served to stoke his vendetta. After this Smith said, "I could no longer ignore the fact that she had been making a complete 'sucker' out of me and had been crooked through and through from start to finish."

The talk had the ring of truth to it—that Harkness said she had been paying him a salary, and that she found his work "unsatisfactory." In fact, she did believe he was still operating on Bill's money, and almost from the start Harkness had suspected Smith was not up to the task. The irony was that all the time Smith had been so dismissive of Harkness's abilities, he had never considered that she might just be measuring his competence too. "She knew about as much about my work in China as I would know about designing ladies' dresses in New York," he sputtered.

Although many years later Russell would assert, unbelievably, to "know of no ill-feeling between Ruth and Floyd," it is highly unlikely the two men didn't go over it all in great detail that day in the hospital. After all, it was Smith's obsession at the time. Further, Russell said that he had met one of the many hunters who would claim over time to have sold Harkness the panda. It is almost certain he would have shared with Smith this news, which would have been so welcome.

But Russell had another significant tale to recount from his adventure, a shameful story that even made it into the pages of *The China Jour-*

nal. While in "Wassu country," near the Tibetan border, Russell had come across a farmer who was in possession of a quite tame juvenile giant panda. The young animal was so docile that it was free to roam the farm on its own. He was apparently in good health, being fed a diet of grass as well as a variety of vegetables. It was a moment of enormous good fortune for the adventurer. To procure another live panda would have been a great feat. "But," the *Journal* wrote, "Mr. Russell is reported to have considered it better to shoot the animal and bring it out of the country as a skin-specimen." Transporting voracious giant pandas out of the country with enough bamboo to keep them alive was always the great concern of those who hoped to bring them west. It was enough to daunt Russell. So, it appears that, quite cold-bloodedly, the great hunter walked right up to this tethered, trusting creature and pulled the trigger, or at least ordered that it be done for him. With a single bullet, a hard-to-manage animal would become a transportable pelt.

As for Smith, sometime in March he began to experience what he would describe as a "miraculous recovery." It would, in reality, be a long road. By the end of April he was only well enough to "sit up indoors," occasionally going for rides with his wife. His appetite had returned—he was as hungry as a wolf—he told his sister, and he hoped to put on several pounds. To his great relief, there was, he said, "no sign of any return of the distressing mental affliction I had up to the beginning of March and that was worse than all the purely physical ills I can imagine combined."

One of the most important elements in his recuperation was financial. From America, his sister bailed him out, for which he was extremely grateful. Through this influx of cash, he could foresee the possibility of "wealth for the future." He would no longer consider "running away under fire"; instead he was "all for fighting it out." He was once again the optimist—the man who, Harkness had said, was always certain that his fortune was just around the corner.

Harkness and Smith were now set on another collision course: the very same week that she was pocketing her expedition check from Brookfield, Smith was laying his plans to get back into the field to prove himself. If the competition between the two had been keen before, now it was on fire.

THE RACE TO snare the next live panda was not just for these two rivals. Others still wanted a chance. Captain Brocklehurst, for one, whose name was already on the short list of panda killers, was just returning emptyhanded to Shanghai from the interior. Several missionaries were in the game too. Perfectly situated for the task in western China, they would act as agents for Western zoos.

In New York, Harkness was wildly busy. Even with an expedition to plan, she was blazing through writing her books, *The Lady and the Panda* and *The Baby Giant Panda*. With financial backing in hand from Brookfield, she could end *The Lady and the Panda* with what to her was the most pleasing thought imaginable: "I shall return to China," she wrote, "to the country that gave me so much of its kindness, its friendliness, its hospitality; to the country whose generosity allowed a blundering foreigner to leave with a baby Giant Panda."

She could close her eyes, serenely imagining her return—"Again there were visions of blue seas, high mountains and the beauty of far lonely country," she wrote as she contemplated recapturing the joy of her first quest. But Tibetan Buddhism would have cautioned her that everything changes.

CHAPTER NINE

BOMBS RAIN FROM THE HEAVENS

RUTH HARKNESS ENTERED a sweltering, seething Shanghai on Wednesday, August 11, 1937. Under thick cloud and dense heat, the combustible city was filled with the threat of war. Harkness knew of the danger ahead even as her ship, the Dollar luxury liner SS *President Hoover,* rounded the sharp left turn of the Huangpu River, plowing toward the banks of the International Settlement. A fellow passenger, a young Chinese army general named Lea Tsing Yao, had warned her about the escalating rage between China and Japan, painting an unsettling picture of the great tumult building in the city. He told her that in these dicey days, she would never get her ammunition through customs on her own. So she was grateful one humid night when he offered to go down to the airless baggage room with her to put his name on her trunk of matériel.

Now, crowded up on deck, the *Hoover* passengers witnessed a distressing validation of all they had heard: staring down the shipping traffic, and glowering within sight of the Palace Hotel, was the big, graceless Japanese flagship *Idzumo*. It had backup too—a fleet of twenty Japanese destroyers and light cruisers that had made its way to Shanghai on this very day.

Yet all around these ships of war were the comforting, familiar scenes of Harkness's beloved Shanghai—beautiful, tattered-sail junks bobbing on the chocolate waves, the skyline of the Bund, and the parade of humanity along the shore's walkway. As her ship drew in to the S&H Pootung Wharf, there was another heartening sight in store for her. Her steadfast friend Dan Reib was waiting, having planted himself among the throngs gathered dockside.

As soon as the two Americans connected in the middle of the chaos, Reib bundled Harkness up and whisked her away. In the short distance from the quay to the Palace, Reib could outline the city's dire predicament. Japan and China were amassing troops around Shanghai, the Japanese making a great show that day of unloading piles of ammunition while bringing ashore troops in full marching kit. Outside the International Settlement, sandbag-and-barbed-wire barricades were being erected and trenches dug. The excuse for the brinkmanship was an incident the month before outside Beijing, at the eight-hundred-year-old Marco Polo Bridge, with its thirty arches and its rows of carved marble lions. During Japanese night maneuvers there, right after Chinese soldiers fired some shells, a Japanese soldier had gone missing. Though he would later turn up safe and happy in a brothel, it didn't matter; the two sides were spoiling for a fight anyway. The clash that resulted is considered to be the first battle of World War II.

Now Chiang Kai-shek had moved his elite German-trained divisions to the periphery of Shanghai, where they would outnumber the Japanese ten to one. It looked to observers as though he was at last serious about facing the Japanese, something many of his countrymen had been impatient to see happen. Just that past December one of his own generals kidnapped him for a time in an effort to induce him to drop the civil war and link forces with the Communists against the intruders. But Chiang had continued to believe that others would combat the Japanese. By deflecting the action toward a treaty port filled with foreigners and, just as important, foreign investments, he may have been hoping to precipitate just such an engagement.

Overall, war strategists such as General Stilwell couldn't be very optimistic about what was to come. China had "numbers, hate and a big country," the military attaché wrote, but not "leaders, morale, cohesion, munitions nor coordinated training." No one knew what was going to happen, though the buildup of men and guns on both sides was no bluff.

There was a lot for a new arrival to take in. As Harkness settled into her quarters in the sturdy old Palace, she had a little time to herself before Reib would pick her up for lunch. She dashed a note home to friends, writing half in longhand, the rest on her typewriter. She scrawled "China again" with some of the old sweeping satisfaction across the top. But the body of the letter was sober: "I have an idea that this trip will present even more difficulties in some ways than the first one."

HER LANDING MADE manifest that this was a complicated homecoming, the trouble in the city acting as a harbinger of the strife that would mark this journey. Still, neither Harkness nor the tawdry old city was deflated easily. At the hotel two cases of twelve-year-old Scotch aged in wood were delivered, compliments of Reib. It was apparent from the social invitations stacked up and waiting that it was party time. Her old pals were hovering like incoming planes at a crowded airfield: It was Reib for lunch, then Fritz Hardenbrooke for her first night's dinner. The next day, Arthur de Carle Sowerby and his wife had planned a tea in her honor at their home on Lucerne Road.

If anyone in Shanghai hadn't known Harkness was coming, they found out fast enough from the papers. Despite the city's anxiety, word of her arrival was splashed all over the news, sometimes on front pages. She was greeted like a celebrity for two days with headlines like MODERN DIANA RETURNS and PRES. HOOVER BRINGS NOTABLES FROM AMERICA. It couldn't help but amuse the wry American, who had to share a laugh about it with Perkie. "What a reputation for a quiet little dressmaker," she wrote.

THE PROBLEMS STARTED right away, beginning with a jolt—Quentin Young was nowhere to be found. Through her correspondence with him,

Harkness had believed they were set to join up in Shanghai before heading into the field together. Among all the cards and phone calls waiting for her when she hit town, however, there was nothing from her old expedition partner. No one seemed to know where he was. "I can't find Quentin although I have tried everything I can think of," Harkness wrote home. She was in the dark, unable even to track Quentin's brother Jack, who was said to be in Beijing.

In his dealing with Harkness, Quentin Young would often appear racked by conflict, by turns attentive, then remote. The emotional push and pull would never resolve itself. Many years later, he would still harbor paradoxical feelings about her, dismissing their romance in one breath, but in another asserting that he had considered leaving everything behind in China to chase after her—all the way back to America.

The high tide of sentiment in which he had corresponded with Harkness over the past few months receded now. As Harkness stepped ashore, Young, it was reported a little later in the press, was in "the Netherland Indies" on a collecting trip, though he was in fact in Macao with his already pregnant wife, working for a Hong Kong bank.

What could his relationship with Harkness possibly be now? Most likely the two adventurers didn't even know themselves. They probably had never had a frank conversation about it before parting, and wouldn't have broached it in the pages of their correspondence, since Harkness was always reluctant to write about anything sensitive in letters that could end up in the wrong hands.

Neither one likely had a clear sense of what would happen between them when they next met. They might not even have known themselves what they wanted, though it's doubtful Harkness would have carried on an affair with a married man.

Young, for whom the emotional stakes were much higher, dealt with it immaturely. He vacillated. He dodged. He disappeared.

The newlywed had clearly led Harkness to believe that he would be ready for a second expedition with her. But when it came time to act, he simply didn't show. In fact, in his youthful confusion, he couldn't manage to send a note of explanation to the Palace, where he knew Harkness would be staying, or even to Reib, who could have passed along the information to her.

Harkness was truly on her own, even dealing with this emotional twist by herself, unable to discuss it with anyone. The expedition itself, which she would have to handle solo, would clearly be a far bigger trial. She didn't hesitate. Nothing was going to stop her; after all, as she told the *China Press*, returning to China for a panda was a mission she held sacred.

First, though, she had to wrangle with Floyd Tangier Smith. He wasn't actually in town at the moment, but distance did not dim the rivalry between them; if anything, it was glowing hotter. They were each quite intent on being the one to bring the next giant panda to the West.

For a few weeks Smith had pulled well ahead. Months before, from the infusion of funds his sister had sent, he had jump-started his hunting operation. He reconnected with local trackers he had trained years before.

In June, hunters, though they very well may not have been his own men, captured two giant pandas and sold them to Smith. Once in Smith's custody, the young male died of an infected foot while being transported out of western China. The young adult female, Jennie, who was being fed a diet of bread, rice, and fruit, made it all the way to Shanghai, where she boarded the *Andre Lebon* at the end of July. There were rumors that Smith had shaved the panda and dyed her fur in an effort to smuggle her out of the country as a brown bear. He would admit to shaving the animal, but only to keep her cool.

Smith always said that Harkness had gone sneaking around Shanghai in an effort to smuggle Su-Lin out. Yet he behaved in exactly the same manner during the two weeks he spent in the city with his giant panda, keeping the animal at the far reaches of town, and only bringing her to the dock at "the last possible moment." He sailed eventually with what the *Shanghai Sunday Times* described as "a mysterious box," the contents having been a well-guarded "deep secret." The poor panda wouldn't even make Singapore. She died in her wood-and-iron crate in the unbearable tropical heat. Harkness would hear of the sad news within about a week of her arrival in Shanghai.

Pandaless, Smith continued on to England, where he chased after new sources of revenue, while crowing to the press that he planned the following year to branch out into unexplored areas of China, certain that he would find not just new species but whole new genuses.

Even in his absence, his bitterness lingered in Shanghai. Almost as soon as she had stepped ashore, Harkness learned that Smith had "kept alive the story that I stole Su Lin from his hunters in the Press, and made a nasty mess of things," she wrote home. "I would feel very badly about it, but anyone who has ever known Ajax of course does not believe him. There has been a constant bunch of publicity ever since I left."

Sowerby had amassed a small mountain of clippings on the subject, which he shared with her over tea at his house on her second day in town. Reading the details and grasping the extent of Smith's attack for the first time triggered a fresh fury. "Such slander and vituperation I have never seen before," she wrote. "And Ajax paints himself as being so honorable in the Press; that I made arrangements that he should hunt Pandas while I stayed in civilization and we were to share the profits; that I have double crossed him in every way; never a mention that his hunters are still working upcountry on Bill's money, and that these Pandas he got were bought with money that should be mine. . . . It is all unbelievable."

She also read Sowerby's thoughts on the matter. He had repeatedly championed her cause, getting his licks in where Smith was concerned. An inveterate writer of letters to the editor, the old naturalist sent notes about the feud to the *North China Daily News* on July 26 and August 4. With a tone of calm authority, he said that by gathering "independent evidence offered by foreigners" who had been in western China, he found that Harkness's story held up. He pointed out that Smith's laying claim to any territory or hunters in western China was ludicrous. He also taunted Smith, as he would again and again, with the point that cut the deepest. "That Mrs. Harkness, a mere woman, succeeded where many men had failed was a feat greatly to her credit, but it must have been a rather bitter pill for some of the male hunters."

Smith, in England, wouldn't see the paper for months, but when he did, he would draft a furious letter, quoting those lines, as he responded to what he said was a personal attack. He was filled with "righteous indignation" over being portrayed as "a sneaking skunk." He wanted to make obvious that "I have not failed, and that Mrs. Harkness has not yet succeeded." As Smith saw it, he was trying to clear his own name, which Sowerby had "rather dragged in the mud."

He shouldn't have used the past tense, for Sowerby had just begun. In the July issue of *The China Journal,* he reported on Smith's pandas, burying the news low in a story that focused on Ruth Harkness's panda. Even though the writer-naturalist had already covered her victory extensively by that time, he again took another opportunity to call it "an epic in the annals of zoological exploration in China—and in the history of world exploration." In the August issue, as he updated the news on Smith's pandas, he also mentioned Harkness's "first." Long after Harkness had left Shanghai again, the campaign would continue. In September Sowerby would begin an item on pandas with a briefing on Harkness and Su-Lin, followed by a report on the death of both Smith's pandas.

By October, the editor would publicly dispute Smith's explanation of Jennie's death, dismissing the notion that she had died because of the tricky issue of feeding a panda anything but bamboo. He would point out that Su-Lin was thriving on a varied diet provided by the Brookfield Zoo. "We are [inclined] to disagree with Mr. Smith's diagnosis of the cause of death of his giant panda, suggesting, rather, that it was the excessive heat of the tropics which killed the animal." Sowerby, who thought Smith a fool, didn't bother to conceal his disdain. "To attempt to transport such an animal through the tropics in the middle of summer seems to us to be courting disaster. . . . It is a very great pity that some other route, preferably that by way of Canada was not chosen, for the loss of so valuable and rare an animal is a great blow to science."

Adding a little salt on the wound, Sowerby would choose that issue to run three full pages of photos of Harkness and Su-Lin.

As grateful as Harkness must have been for Sowerby's staunch defense, she naturally wanted to stand up for herself before the people of Shanghai. "The whole story told by Ajax is ridiculous," she told reporter James Hammond. "It simply doesn't hold water. . . . Does he think that the whole West China belongs to him? It certainly does not." She underscored the very salient fact that several other panda hunters had entered that same area without riling Smith.

Harkness began her interview by answering Smith's charges, then quickly went on the offense. This was an all-out brawl. Unconcerned with appearing ladylike, she struck out at Smith, portraying the old boy as a touch artist who had pressured her for cash the previous summer, and who had surreptitiously socked away plenty of her dead husband's money before she had ever had a chance to inquire about it. In fact, she told the reporter, she suspected that it was Bill's money paying for the two pandas Smith had recently acquired.

She disliked having to descend to "the level of Ajax" in the disagreement, she said, but felt forced to. Frankly, Harkness said, "I want to forget this whole sordid, vindictive business. I am as fed up with it as I imagine a good portion of the public is." Putting it all behind her, however, would not be easy—both her ex-partners would remain in the picture for some time. Her fortunes would eerily continue to inversely mirror Smith's many times afterward. And she actually corresponded with Russell, though he never seemed to have told her what she was now hearing about him in Shanghai. It would appear, she wrote home, that the story about his tethering a perfectly tame young giant panda and blasting him were true. "Can you believe such a thing?" she wrote her friends. "The missionary boy who was with him told friends of mine. Two fine men, Ajax and Jerry [sic]."

All of the personal problems Harkness faced, however, were about to fade into insignificance. On Friday morning, August 13, hearing the sounds of a skirmish across Soochow Creek, Harkness headed over to see what was going on. By the time she got to the site, the fighting had ended. She witnessed, instead, something even more astonishing. In torrents, through the awful summer heat, thousands of Chinese poured into the International Settlement seeking safety from what everyone feared was the coming battle. "Wide thoroughfares and bridges were literally jammed tight with suffering, sweating humanity as the exodus to the foreign-controlled areas continued during the day and well into the night," the *North China Herald* reported. The frantic refugees carried everything they owned in wheelbarrows, carts, and on their backs, camping out wherever they could find space. Many could stake out just enough room for a simple straw mat on the Bund's foreshore, or in the alleys of the northern section.

Everything in Shanghai started going haywire. All entrances to the Settlement save one were sealed. Train, bus, and boat traffic was disrupted or shut down. The big North Station train terminal became a Chinese fortress. Settlement authorities projected mobilization orders for members of the volunteer corps on the screens of movie houses across the city, and audiences applauded as the men rose from their seats.

"A fine little war brewing," Harkness wrote home ominously. Shanghailanders were buzzing with speculation.

By Saturday morning, it seemed the wind had been knocked out of the city. In the still summer heat, fear simmered under a tight cover of cloud. In her hotel, Harkness received a call from Dan Reib. Relying on information from well-placed sources, he told her that under no circumstances was she to leave the safety of the hotel that day. Something big was about to happen.

Sure enough, trouble came in spades. Over the next few hours, under Chiang Kai-shek's orders, Chinese biplanes itching to sink the *Idzumo* swooped in and out of clouds, drawing antiaircraft fire. After each raid, rings of smoke hovered in the air. "Half-thrilled, half-fearful" elite foreigners couldn't resist standing out on rooftops to watch the action, while below, on the crowded streets, falling shell fragments killed and injured several homeless Chinese who were unable to find cover.

In the late afternoon all hell broke loose in what became the worst day in the history of the Settlement. Chinese planes battling it out with the *Idzumo* accidentally dropped two bombs on the Bund. One landed directly on Harkness's hotel, slamming down three floors; the other detonated just outside on Nanking Road, between the hotel and the Cathay.

Scene of utter devastation outside the Palace Hotel on Nanking Road on "Bloody Saturday," August 14, 1937. COURTESY TALESOFOLDCHINA.COM

The explosions were deafening and deadly, shattering glass and smashing masonry. When the smoke lifted, "a scene of dreadful death was uncovered." The pavement ran slick with blood. Severed limbs and heads lay among the shards of glass and rubble. In burned-out cars, charred occupants remained upright in their seats. The smell of blood and burning flesh mingled with the acrid bomb fumes. As the hundreds of dazed and dying came to, they writhed in pain on the debris-strewn street, filling the air with their sobs.

Minutes later, another two bombs exploded nearby in the French Concession outside the Great World Amusement Center, where Chinese refugees were packed tight to receive a handout of rice and tea. The devastation here was even worse. In a flash, the corpses of these desperate people were piled high, the remnants of their once-precious boxes, bundles, and birdcages strewn all about them.

"Death from little bombs rained from the heavens in the International Settlement and French Concession . . . to bring a screaming hell to hundreds of Chinese and foreign civilians such as has not been seen nor scarcely imagined in this city," James Hammond wrote in *The China Press*. "All told," according to historian Stella Dong, "it was the worst civilian carnage in a single day anywhere in the world up to that moment." The tally for what was quickly dubbed "Bloody Saturday" was 1,740 dead, 1,431 injured.

Friends and relatives across the Settlement were frantic to locate loved ones near the bomb scene. Harkness's gang must have been distraught—particularly Reib, whose orders had put her directly in harm's way. But Harkness was unhurt. In fact, she hadn't been anywhere near the hotel when the bombs fell. Ignoring Reib's dire instructions, she had gone off to have lunch in what was considered a more dangerous part of the city—the Japanese section. "I naturally disobeyed orders," she would later write of her decision.

Unscathed physically, she was not spared the horrible sight of the disaster. She had returned to the hotel minutes after the attack, finding a picture beyond imagination. "I hope never to see anything like it again," she said.

If Reib hadn't realized it before, by now he knew how little Harkness needed coddling. When friends from the States wrote to him, worried about her, he replied, "Do not worry about Ruth, as she is fully capable of looking out for herself and has very devoted friends scattered over the country that will assist her in every respect. Besides this, she is a most resourceful person, and as you well know fully capable of looking after herself, if need be."

That night, Shanghai, the flashy nocturnal city, went dark. A lights-out curfew was instituted, with most restaurants, cinemas, and clubs closing and locking their doors.

The day, which had been rougher than anyone would have guessed, prompted an immediate race to reach safety. While hundreds of thousands of Chinese continued to pour into the International Settlement, the foreigners began to flee from it. By Tuesday, the first wave of British women and children were evacuated to Hong Kong aboard the P&O *Rajputana*. On Wednesday hundreds more left, but by now no traffic along the river was believed safe. With heavy Japanese fire directed at Chinese planes overhead, British men-o'-war, instead of tugs, ferried the evacuees to the ship as a precaution. American women and children began their exodus aboard the SS *President McKinley*, bound for Manila. It carried away the heaviest load of passengers it had ever borne, with desperate refugees "stuffed into remaining nooks and crannies." Thousands would be moved over the coming days. Harkness was not interested in joining the women being evacuated, though she did ride one of the tenders out to the *McKinley* to ensure that her mail bound for the States made it aboard.

Ever more determined to follow through with her expedition, she stayed in Shanghai, where the smell of death still lingered. The "incessant bombing, shelling, and the horrible chatter of machine guns and anti aircraft" did, she had to admit, "get under my skin a bit." And, yes, Shanghai was "a pretty nerve wracking place to be in," particularly because she found she had a knack for being out in the open along the Bund during big raids, but the words of a psychic in New York had bolstered her already strong conviction that she would be safe. "I know that this War will not be my finish. So with perfect confidence I can go to the Bund during the heaviest bombardment and know that it is not for me. A rather cozy feeling, although one does feel sorry for the other poor devils."

In all the commotion of the next few days, she somehow managed to collar her young Chinese general again, learning that her trunk was locked up in the vaults of the Central Bank of China. By the time she decided that she wanted to get at it, though, she had lost track of him all over again. Doing without the ammunition was of little consequence to her, since she had never liked guns anyway. The problem was that there were other things more precious to the designer in the same trunk. "My beautiful new boots and pants are there too," she lamented.

The China Journal reported that Harkness continued to hope for a reunion with Quentin Young somehow in southern China. But weeks later she still would have no idea what had become of him.

She proceeded anyway—sans partner, team, or even supplies. She had a job to do.

And so it was on Saturday, August 21, that Harkness waved goodbye to Dan Reib and a burning and battered Shanghai. The launch of her second major campaign may have been even more preposterous than the first, for she left the city alone as a refugee, carrying with her only two small leather satchels and a typewriter.

Through the next desperate few months, Chinese forces would fight heroically at Shanghai in a death stand against the heavy Japanese artillery. The cost in casualties would be staggering, with roughly 250,000 Chinese troops killed or wounded, and more than half of Chiang's elite division annihilated. The horror would play out under the noses of those left in the International Settlement, including journalists who would transmit images and stories from it around the world.

Harkness was scrambling to settle her plans. She couldn't rely now on her tactical knowledge from the first expedition—with traffic limited up the Yangtze, she was forced to chart a wholly unfamiliar route. Aboard the coast-hugging French MM *Aramis* out on the China Sea, she wrote home to brief her friends on her seat-of-the-pants scheme. In the face of all the adversity, she put on some good cheer. "You'd better get out your maps children," she wrote. "I've changed my course. . . . I am on my way to Hong Kong, Saigon in French Indo China (for a picnic) Yunnan-fu, Chungking, Chengtu and Pandas."

While she had never complained during the days in war-torn Shanghai, she did now aboard the plush *Aramis*, with its stone-pillared pool and fancy kiddie playroom. "The coffee on this boat is vile and the cocktails are worse," she groused. But there was a deeper and darker mood creeping over her, and it would not dissipate for quite some time.

CHAPTER TEN

SAIGON TO CHENGDU

Inscribe on your heart
Every inch of the time at sunset

—JUAN CHI, THIRD CENTURY

FTER A BRIEF STOP in Hong Kong, Harkness parted ways with the Marseilles-bound *Aramis* in Saigon. She would spend a few days here before making her way overland, heading north to Hanoi, then across the border into China. From Kunming, formerly Yunnanfu, the capital of Yunnan Province, she hoped to catch one of the unscheduled planes that sometimes touched down on their way to Chongqing and Chengdu.

Once at her hotel, she received a cable from Jack Young offering to join forces with her. Certainly there were many reasons to have said yes, chief among them the simple fact that she was so alone in this strange land. Yet she turned him down, her rationale being that she sensed they would not be successful together, and that she was not afraid to go it on her own.

Of course, she was rarely by herself for very long, as there were always people who wanted to spend time with her. She had several letters of introduction from Standard Oil friends to various contacts along her route. Right away in Saigon she hooked up with an interesting man who was a radio engineer, a big-game hunter, and a little bit of a bad boy. Under his "tutelage," she smoked opium, probably something of an antidote to all the carnage of Shanghai.

She was drawn also to visit a place that would add a shiver of mysticism to the wistfulness that was overtaking her: the otherworldly jungle

Harkness spent a day wandering the temples of Angkor Wat.

temple complex of Angkor Wat, just a few hours by automobile from the city, in Cambodia. The great place had been abandoned, lost for centuries in a creeping mausoleum of jungle greenery until a Frenchman rediscovered it in the 1860s. It was a stunning find that captivated all who came near it, with its five great stone towers rising up above the tops of the palms in the dense forest. Spreading out from their bases, in a labyrinthine complex the size of Rome, was a tapestry of fantastic carvings, statues, temples, passages, stairways, and bridges—a delirium of delicate, intricate, endless patterns and pictures chiseled into the stone.

As ancient as it was magical, with beginnings stretching a thousand years back; great stone Hindu and Buddhist temples, part of the Khmer kingdom, had taken centuries to complete. The site was overwhelming in beauty and scope. Here was the result of centuries of labor—and of neglect; of artistry, passion, and a moldering stagnation. The stone was known to come alive at sunset in orange and pink hues, and then as the shadows of the forest spread, spirals of bats would pour like funnels of smoke out of the darkening towers.

Harkness wandered about the temples snapping photos. As she pressed on toward the Tibetan border, images of Angkor Wat would continue to tint everything. She saw eternity in each dawn, the divine in every vista. The great scenes around her seemed to reflect the deep, unquenchable feelings stirring inside. Her return to the East. The great tragedy she had witnessed. Her lonely passage through an unfamiliar land. During the entire trip, she would be immersed in a deep spiritual reverie.

She returned to Saigon with her driver, leaving that very night for a trek of more than a thousand miles to Kunming, in a second-class compartment of a "funny little train" that, she said, "screams and snorts and hurtles along." From her berth, she watched the terrain flash by. Described in glowing terms by Western travel writers as "an oasis of peace and beauty," French Indochina was noted for its rubber plantations and its prosperity. But the passing scenes only made Harkness long for what she called "my China." The country was pretty, Harkness mused, but it was missing something for her. A "quality" she had no name for. She was bothered by the fact that the inhabitants did not rule their own land. "The white races certainly mess things up," she said.

At night, as the train jolted through dense, pitch-black jungle, Harkness began to experience nightmares about Su-Lin. She would wake to the darkness and the swaying of the compartment, unable to rid herself of a horrible fear. The dreams were so insistent, coming every evening, that she began to despair, thinking they were a sign. Perhaps on the other side of the world, the innocent little animal was dying or already dead.

Her feelings of general foreboding and doom could only have been heightened when her train was wrecked by a nighttime mudslide in the pouring rain near the border town of Lao Kay, now Lao Cai. In the aftermath, Harkness sat hungry in her quiet compartment for nearly ten hours. She was tapping away on the portable typewriter when a Frenchman came by to deliver the good news—a local train from the north was about to arrive, and they would be able to transfer.

Harkness spent Saturday night in a local hotel, "a night which I shall never think of without remembering Somerset Maugham's 'Rain,' " she said. The place was comfortable—she had a spacious if rather bare bedroom dominated by a mosquito-netted bed. "But the rain, rain, rain," she wrote, came down in a wall of gray in the "swift tropic dusk." It was as steady as it was heavy, shredding banana leaves with its force. Below her window trudged "a Tonkinese funeral wailing its way thru the rain to deposit its dead in a watery grave."

A certain blackness was taking hold inside her, one that was revealed in her dispatch when she wrote of the hotel clerk who played two love songs over and over in rotation on the phonograph. "There was something a little sinister," Harkness said, "about the relentlessness of both, the phonograph grinding out its sobbing misery and the gray clouds pouring their steady deluge on the little hotel, the few huts, and the jungle. Even after I had closed my door and crept between damp sheets, the sound of both drummed in my ears."

She was rescued the next day by a fancy Michelin train, with a cabinet full of pâté and crackers and whiskey free for the taking, chugging through tunnel after tunnel (her tourist folder claimed there were 172), climbing for twelve hours to the high, cool city of Kunming.

SHE ARRIVED AT THE HOTEL DU COMMERCE in the grip of an aching depression, mystified by her own mood. "There has been a vague unrest that I can't explain," she wrote home, ignoring the number of valid reasons to feel that way. She was alone with no idea where exactly she was going or how she would get there, since planes were not scheduled; she might have to endure forty-two days of rugged overland travel by chair, not speaking any of the languages she would confront; everyone now in Kunming was telling her flatly she would never reach Chongqing; she was tight on money until she could reach Chengdu; and her second wedding anniversary was approaching on September 9.

Smoking and drinking, no doubt, she typed a letter to Hazel Perkins that was so morose she would apologize for it more than once later. Traveling could be "hellishly lonely," she wrote. "Sometimes I could die of it." She brooded in her hotel room, staring at the unfamiliar walls, wondering just why she felt compelled to wander the world. It all looked so bleak to her now that death seemed welcome. The American who believed so strongly in reincarnation wrote to her friend, "I'll be rather glad when this particular life is over."

All her distress was channeled into a sickening anxiety over the fate of Su-Lin. She was desperate to have her morbid question answered—so desperate that she cursed the fact that she didn't have the money to send a swift cable. She wanted to know, and as quickly as possible, how Baby was. "For about a week now, I've been worried about Su Lin," she wrote. "I've had funny dreams about her. I wake and tell myself that it isn't true." She wanted her friend Perkie to cable her at Cavaliere's as soon as she received the letter. Just say, she wrote starkly, "Sulin well or Sulin dead." It must have been a bitter moment for her to even type the words. Yet Harkness remained resolute: "I'm not weakening, I assure you," she wrote. "The chin is still up."

As it turned out, good luck was just around the corner—there would be a plane north after all.

At dawn she boarded a bus for the airport. As she would do so often through this journey, she found herself in a reflective state, with the land and all the life about it mirroring the stirrings of her soul. "Early rising gods and coolies scattered before the furiously honking horn," she wrote.

From the plane, Harkness gazed out through the mud-streaked window, at the colors of the sunrise on the lake below, at groups of moun-

The everyday scenes of the Chinese countryside were like poetry to Harkness.
COURTESY MARY LOBISCO

tains that "came sliding toward us out of the future," and at the land she loved. "China from the air is like watered silk," she wrote dreamily. The tilled land of Chinese farms was not squared off American-style, rather it "conformed to the moods of the hills," the shapes following, instead of fighting, the ancient decree of nature. The people here followed "their own particular pattern—the pattern of life, which is reflected in the patterns of their fields," she wrote. She saw beneath her "a slow gentle way of life that has time to consider the plan of Eternity." The plane ride lifted her up out of her despair. It was just what she needed.

Once she landed in Chongqing, her task was to book passage to Chengdu. The only planes flying there were nimble little Stinsons, which, with room for only four or five passengers at a time, were booked for several days. In need of someplace to stay, Harkness headed for the SOCONY office, looking for a man named Jones, who was yet another friend of Dan Reib's.

"How in God's name did you get here?" he bellowed when she appeared at his office doorway. He explained that Chongqing was so unsafe that Standard Oil was making plans to evacuate wives and children. Things were jumbled enough at this point that Western Union in the States required some customers who wanted to transmit telegrams here to include the phrase "sent at our own risk." In fact, matters weren't very good anywhere else either. Word was that a presidential order had come through days before requiring all American citizens to abandon Peiping.

While Jones gladly pledged any help he could give her, the consular service, Harkness knew, would be "cursing me out for coming up here." In fact, while she thought she had dodged all U.S. officials as she went, she would be shocked later to learn that no less an official than secretary of state Cordell Hull had sent the concerned McCombs family a telegram outlining Harkness's exact route to Chengdu—including her departure date from Shanghai.

After tiffin with Jones and the Chinese staff in the Standard Oil offices, Harkness was packed away in a regal and luxurious sedan chair that was done up in bamboo, white slipcovered cushions, and brass lamps, and sent to Jones's home. The trip would take half an hour. Coolies lugged her down the riverbank, across to the residential side of the city, and up the stone stairs of the sheer cliff to the Joneses' beautiful, low, rambling home, complete with wide-screened verandahs overlooking the river.

Harkness liked Jones's wife, Doris, and daughter, Peggy. If she had to be marooned somewhere for nearly a week, this peaceful house, removed from the chaos of the city, was a rather deluxe way to go. She would enjoy long nights of good sleep, mornings with breakfast in bed, and lazy days spent chatting with her hosts. It was so cozy that she rarely had any desire to go out.

Things couldn't have been better, especially because on her second day there, her mind was finally put at ease about Su-Lin. Hazel Perkins had wired the zoo about Harkness's concerns, and now Harkness received Perkie's cable along with one that was routed from zoo director Edward Bean: SULIN NOW IN NEW HOME IS FINE WEIGHS 59 POUNDS, it read. If there had been room in a telegram for more, he might have sent details, for by now, Su-Lin was not only gaining strength and weight, he was soaring in popularity. Each day, children would throng to his exhibit, shrieking with joy and leaving only when they were dragged away from the animal described by one Chicago paper as "the roly-poly clown who waddled about among her toys." Any cry from him during play would beckon Mary Bean, his constant attendant. She found that he was doing quite well without bamboo, eating apples, rice, cornstalks, grass, and grapes—anything he was given.

The good news made Harkness giddy. She immediately wrote home that she had read the telegram at two o'clock Friday in China, which would be one o'clock Thursday in America. "I really got it before you sent it," she joked. She typed away, relating her immense relief, and apologizing for her "crazy depressed letter" from Kunming.

"For the first time in months I am relaxed, and contented," she wrote. She said her roundabout route would all be terribly funny if the war that had caused it weren't so "ghastly." Later to the Beans in Chicago she would report that "aside from having run into a war two days after I arrived with bombs through the roof of my hotel, everything is going splendidly."

On Sunday, the day before Harkness's departure, a caravan of sedan chairs brought her and the Joneses to the customs commissioner's house for a "delicious tiffin buffet." It was to bid farewell to the departing wives, who had received word that evacuation plans had been finalized, and to provide a poker game for the husbands. It seemed to Harkness that the whole foreign population turned out, "gossiping about the few people who were not present." The foreigners made up a community not unlike a village in Kansas or Nebraska, Harkness said, complete with the "old dame" who snooped on everyone with her telescope.

Late in the afternoon, in a "solemn line" of three chairs, they trooped home. Harkness didn't feel much affinity with her fellow westerners at the party, but her heart was full of love for China as she looked out at the passing countryside. In what she called "the deepening dusk," as Chinese peasants were busy with cooking, washing, basket making, and harvesting the rice, as "great gray buffalo" trudged slowly through the paddies, followed by a "plowman thigh deep in the ooze," Harkness absorbed every element.

CHENGDU WAS YET another homecoming. As soon as the light plane touched down, Harkness bundled her few things into a rickshaw, perched on the carriage seat, and gave instructions to head straight for the post office. Looking over the shoulder of the trotting coolie at the wide, bustling streets of the city that held so few foreigners, and anticipating her imminent reunion, she could feel happy.

The silver-haired Cavaliere was "barking orders," in Italian-accented Chinese, as she entered. Turning to face her, he said, "Well, well, dear lady, here you are again after another panda." Immediately, he sent her in his own rickshaw to settle in at the house.

As before, she was provided with a beautiful room off the magnificent palm-filled courtyard. It contained a massive bed that was pragmatically, yet romantically, draped in mosquito netting. Ching Yu, "the No. 1 boy," served her lunch, and Harkness found him so dear that she was unembarrassed to use her halting and meager Chinese with him. She had been trying to learn the daunting language, in which just a slight variation in tone would completely change the meaning of what was being said.

As wonderful as it was to be back, she saw how different things were from last year. Since the big planes weren't flying into Chengdu, all the frothy fun had been drained from the great estate. Even after Cavaliere came home that evening, his house remained strangely still. Empty and quiet now, the huge tile-roofed pavilion was nearly swallowed by the night. The countless guest rooms, aside from Harkness's, remained dim and silent. It seemed the whole place was muted by melancholy. Even Kay was morose, and it wasn't just because of the absence of parties. His lively, fun-loving White Russian mistress, Genia, a dental student, had gone, sent off by the missionaries who employed her at seventy dollars a month. If it were possible, Harkness noted, it made Cavaliere even more resentful toward them. He would have happily matched that slim salary to keep her in Chengdu, but she wouldn't stay. "Kay God dams the missionaries up and down," Harkness wrote. And the feeling was mutual. "The situation is impossible. The dear missionaries think that Kay is a depraved soul (I'm sure they think I am too which makes less than no difference to me)." She never had any patience for anyone with an attitude of superiority, particularly the missionaries. Harkness's own earthiness was diametrically opposed to their sense of propriety. She felt that they were missing out on life—removed from what really mattered, and desiccated in their devotion.

On her first day in Chengdu the explorer arose with nothing but empty hours stretching before her. In the wake of having lost Quentin Young, as well as having had to exit Shanghai without equipment or plans, she had been unable to secure any arrangements at all. It was a miracle that she had made it this far. She would have to put together a team from here, and plot her course. There was no urgency, since Harkness, who knew that panda young were probably born toward the end of September, was after a baby again.

Besides, the idleness was rather seductive. She and Cavaliere quickly fell into an easy pattern of companionship, developing the cozy rhythms of a couple. Kay would come home midday from work for lunch and a glass of wine. Dozily, he would then sit out in the courtyard for a spell, "sun helmet in hand, blue eyes twinkling, or perhaps squinting in the pale autumn sunshine." After a bit, he would make a big show of his departure, saying dejectedly, "Well, dear girl, I must go to work." Harkness enjoyed the daily ritual. He would sigh deeply for good measure, then flash his engaging smile to reveal it was all an act.

In the afternoon Harkness might leaf through stale copies of *Esquire* or other American magazines that could be found lying around the house, or she would slip back to bed for a nap. Often, she would wander about Chengdu, sometimes shopping.

She and Kay passed the evenings having long dinners, then sitting together in the living room. They might read by lamplight, or Cavaliere, who loved to fiddle with his radio, would tune in the news of the world. There was also the Victrola and the library of opera recordings that could, with the flick of a switch, turn the Chinese pavilion into a hissing and crackling Teatro Alla Scala.

"I find myself sunk in a beautiful lethargy here," Harkness wrote home. The tranquil time was uncharacteristic for both her and Cavaliere, yet they embraced it. A contented Kay suggested that should she not find her panda this season, the American adventuress might like to ride out the winter here with him, trying again the following year. She said she thought she would.

She had her very best evening dress here at the pavilion, and for her thirty-seventh birthday, on September 21, Cavaliere uncorked a bottle of sparkling burgundy. As if to underscore how different this trip would be from the last, though, Harkness reported home that "it didn't sparkle."

Perhaps it was this reminder of the passage of time that prompted her to shake off the indolence. In part too, it was sparked by a reunion with her cook, Wang Whai Hsin. He had been so kind and loyal to her that despite all the reasons against it, she decided to launch the expedition with him alone. He was neither a hunter nor an explorer, and they had very little language in common. Still, by muddling through together, he could serve as interpreter, and by their mutual trust, they would direct the campaign. Her first expedition had been modest; this would be far smaller—just Harkness and Wang, hiring porters and hunters as needed. The paucity of her expedition gear—it would be whatever she could scrape together from the previous year's leftovers—had one benefit: they wouldn't require as many hired hands.

Under the heading of essential items in a Harkness expedition, though, would come something others might consider a rather low priority—the wardrobe. Wang understood his boss only too well, immediately securing her a sophisticated, Shanghai-trained tailor. Harkness so indulged herself in the task of designing, sketching, and modifying her new apparel that some days she would have to lie down for naps in between fittings.

"I have two new Chinese costumes you'll like," she wrote to Perkie, "the sort of house lounging things that I love in the evening. One Chinese coat is regulation with embroidery—pale blue and one is a very old one, a black purple very heavy with gold and silk embroidery." For about forty-five cents each, she also had two pairs of silk pants sewn—one red and one purple. She ordered up a sheepskin coat lined with cotton; Chinese cotton shirts; and, most outrageous, a yak-hair coat lined in green silk, "a camp tea gown thing," she called it, for the cold nights she would be spending in the mountains.

The next step was to survey the stored gear. It was a fright. Many items were ruined and unusable. Two old coats, one army-issue, the other sheepskin, were writhing with worms; boots were moldy; a half block of cheese had grown a thick fur coat. Much worse than that was the troubling fact that critical pieces were missing. Her tent, silk-stuffed sleeping bag, wool socks, wool shirts, and raincoat, to name just a few, had simply vanished. "The devil of it is," she wrote home, "that all the evidence turns toward Jack Young." Ching Yu and others on staff swore that when he came through on a trip through the area, Jack had helped himself to her stash. She resisted believing it, but, damningly, in among her stored things she discovered a notebook of Jack's that must have fallen out of his pocket.

For Cavaliere, there was no hesitation. He trusted the word of his top servant. Incensed, he said he would never allow Jack Young to stay with him again. Harkness felt tremendously unhappy about the whole affair, not so much about the goods themselves, but she hated deceit, especially from someone she was so fond of.

There was too much work to be done now anyway to stew. She set about cleaning guns, something she never imagined herself doing. Mulling over how haphazard this trip was compared with the last, she thought her chances for getting another panda were just as favorable.

When she wasn't sorting and packing, she was writing. She had been able to produce two books before she left the States, and with the help and encouragement of her agent, George Havell, she hoped to make a living as a writer. The two of them thought she might be able to earn money steadily as she traveled. So, she typed away, sending regular dispatches—travelogues, war reports, stories—back to New York. She had no idea what was publishable, or even if the letters were making their way out of the country, since she wasn't hearing back from anyone. To be a writer, supporting herself through labor that came so naturally to her, was something she desperately wanted. But as weeks passed without a response from Havell, she faced the uncertainty with humor. "I have gone on with the letters that George Havell said he thought he could publish," she wrote to Perkie in Connecticut, "and I should so like to know if they are useable—otherwise I am wasting my genius and my very precious time (I slept all afternoon). High-ho my dear."

Time was precious. It was something she had raced against and even transcended in the past. Now, on her second expedition, out of sorts with life, she would feel tortured by it over the long, cold, lonely months ahead.

CHAPTER ELEVEN

HIGH-ALTITUDE HELL

The Face of the autumn moon freezes.
Old and homeless, will and force are spent.
The drip of the chill dew breaks off my dream,
The cold wind harshly combs my bones.
On the mat, the print of a sickly contour:
Writhing cares twist in my belly.
Doubtful thoughts find nothing to lean on:
I listen at the least stir, and am disappointed . . .

—MENG CHIAO

A MISERABLE, DRENCHING RAIN christened the launch of Ruth Harkness's second Asiatic expedition on October 9, 1937. She and Wang and at least a dozen porters trudged through mile upon mile of slick, oozing mud as they headed for the mountains. Conceding nothing to the weather, they soldiered on for hours. By the end of the day, reaching the first inn, Harkness was in a foul mood. The rustic little place, no different from the year before, was intolerable to her this time around. Particularly when in the nighttime darkness she made her way out to the toilet, a communal pit built over a pigsty. Through the maggot-covered slats of the floor, she looked down at the animals, which greedily consumed human waste, grunting at her with anticipation. The year before, the "ter-lets" had been funny; now they disgusted her. Back in her room, it didn't take her long to abandon efforts to type a letter home. Everything she put on the page was "so dam depressed" she tore it all up, and tucked in for the night.

Waking to clear skies the next morning, she stiffened her resolve for the long march, which under dry conditions turned out to be a much more pleasant endeavor. By that evening, in a better frame of mind, she reached fairly cheerful lodgings, where she could rest comfortably, in-dulging in a cup of hot tea mixed with wine. She unpacked the type-writer, and as she was tapping out a newsy letter home, the fact that she was truly on her own began to sink in. Pulling the page from the carriage to look it over, she added an impassioned note longhand, set off urgently across the top: "I miss Quentin terribly. I hadn't realized what priceless companionship it was."

She probably missed him even more when she and Wang were back in their familiar old ghost temple in Wenchuan.

Many friends called upon her over the next several days, allowing her once again to laugh with people even when there was no shared lan-guage. It seemed that everywhere she went, she ran into old friends. She and Wang had already begun to attract their former employees as they traveled. One night, a familiar hunter appeared like some apparition out of the gentle rain, placing a handful of dark walnuts in Harkness's palms as a gesture of good faith. By the time they reached Chaopo Valley, she and Wang had reconnected with every comrade from the first expedition, and had enlisted more men as well.

As a staging area for many panda seekers, where native hunters and trackers could be hired for about $3.50 a month, Wenchuan was an im-portant stop. Here Harkness and Wang happily reunited with their old crew leader. Whang Tsai Hsin, a holy man who Harkness said measured "no bigger than a boy," had led the expedition's sacrificial ceremony the previous year. Seeing him now, she was struck once again by his "beau-tiful calm and gentle face."

It was vital to be as clear as possible with all the men about the decisions Harkness had made. Through Wang, she informed them that she wanted not just one panda this year, but two: a male and female. She even had their names picked out: Yang for the male, and Yin for the female.

In order to accomplish such a thing, she had made another crucial determination—that she would forgo hunting in the mountains herself, instead holing up in the old castle at the entrance to the kingdom of the giant panda, two days' journey from here. She would sit tight in a central location while as many as one hundred hunters radiated out and scoured the forests. Though tactically astute, this decision would wreak havoc on her personally. Abstaining from what had given her great pleasure last year—the hard marches and rough travel—she would instead force herself into the kind of isolation she always feared.

Before leaving the cheery confines of Wenchuan, Harkness, with Wang's help, made *joss* for the coming journey. In the shadow of the great green mountains that rose up behind the old village, she bowed to all the gods, burned the paper money, and lighted candles. She summoned her dreams, sending prayers upward in the smoke of fragrant incense to mingle with the low-hanging mist.

With that sacred duty done, on the morning of October 19, she and Wang and a group of porters began their short journey to Chaopo.

NO HOMECOMING was ever so like an exile. Early in the afternoon of October 20, Harkness, sick with a stubborn flu that would last weeks, Wang, and the porters reached the grim walls of the castle. Though familiar, it remained imposing as ever with its high stone ramparts and bulky wooden top stories. Set against a stubbled, nearly barren slope, and crowded by other desolate hillsides, it was flanked by the ruins of two watchtowers. They scrambled up the steep, crumbling stone stairs, picking their way through deserted rooms filled with the neglected artifacts of the old monks who had long since fled. There were battered prayer wheels, boards used to print prayer strips, and thousands of the strips themselves. Though its days as a lamasery were long gone, the "ancient, spicy odor of incense" still lingered in the air. Inside, there was no escaping the wind that howled down the mountains, plowing through the gaps in the walls and racing in frigid streams through the rooms.

The adventurer and the cook staked out a corner of the castle high in the upper reaches: Harkness would have one large room, the least blighted, as her living quarters, and Wang the one adjacent. A small ter-

The ruined castle was Harkness's uncomfortable home during the cold months of 1937. COURTESY MARY LOBISCO

race overlooked the disintegrating wall and staircase below, allowing a view of the stark countryside. Containing a small, shrinelike enclosure in the corner, the balcony would make a perfect kitchen for Wang, who began unpacking his pot and frying pan, chopsticks and other utensils, producing much of it from underneath his coat. His little oven, complete with tiny door and rack, was made from a ten-gallon Standard Oil tin. In a niche high up in the little shrine, Harkness noted something protruding and questioned Wang. "Tiger bones, goodee *joss*, Master," he replied.

Harkness rummaged through her bags for the several sets of oil sheets, which she began stringing across doorways and windows for some semblance of privacy and perhaps a bit of insulation. She would decorate as best she could with what little she had, tacking up the picture postcards of Su-Lin she had gotten from the Brookfield Zoo.

As night fell, Harkness, sniffling, and blowing her raw, red nose, tried to make her camp cot snug with heavy wool blankets. She and Wang fought against the chill every way they could. A shallow plate in a little cookstove held one of the fires they kept going in the rooms, while Wang wore padded pants with several coats.

It wasn't just the intensifying cold but the desolation that would seep into Harkness's veins over the coming months. She steadfastly warded off the inevitable for the first few weeks by setting tasks to keep herself busy. Some days Tibetan or Qiang villagers stopped by with their wares: rings, paintings of strange-looking gods, old prayer wheels caked in grime. Often they came to sell food. "A Jarung man would put his hand into his homespun robe and proudly produce a packet of wild honey wrapped in leaves," she reported. Industrious local women, with children hauled in slings on their backs, would spin wool as they walked up to the castle—"A little basket of raw wool hung from their belts, and deftly they shredded and twisted it into yarn, which, with the flip of the wrist, wound itself on the spindle that hung dangling and swinging rhythmically." They would bring vegetables, the likes of which Americans had never seen before. Harkness would always purchase something—stock for the larder, or a few gadgets, as she said, for friends back home.

Sometimes people would hike in for medical attention, imploring the castle-bound explorer to do whatever she could with the few supplies in her medicine chest. Through it all, a surprising number came from a nearby circle of huts, too small to be called a village, just to look at her. "They come, lift up the curtain, which partially covers my door, talk, giggle, spit on the floor, blow their noses on the floor, snuffle in your ears, etc. etc. etc.," she said. The people were achingly poor, and no doubt they appreciated Harkness's hospitality—"In our kitchen in the lamasery shrine there was always tea," she wrote.

Closer by was another neighbor, an aristocratic old man, the resident mandarin, or official, who lived in another section of the castle. He kept to himself, mostly, venturing out to sit in the sun on clear days, allowing a villager to pick lice from his hair. An opium addict, he would look to Harkness once in a while for money to keep himself supplied.

Harkness spent time wandering the castle sorting through the thousands of prayer cards, or Tibetan *tsakli*, heaped about, collecting them to send to friends. Lying among the countless common versions bearing

Harkness collected beautiful tsakli, *or Tibetan prayer cards, including this one with a painted Buddha.*
COURTESY LINDA ASH

only written prayers were a few strikingly artful ones featuring Buddhas on lotus leaves, and beautiful painted gods she could not identify, all depicted in "tempera of exquisite color." The thick, rough squares of sepia paper had fantastical scenes bordered in red on one side, with several lines of prayer handwritten on the back. There might be a serene, half-smiling Buddha in flowing red robes, or, because Buddhism had mixed with the indigenous Bon religion in Tibet, there might be another god from a diverse cast of dramatic figures. Harkness loved these. A green god full of fury intrigued her the most. His hair was the color and shape of a flame, and his eyes—even the third one at the center of his forehead—flashed. In his right hand, a sword, itself ablaze, seemed poised to slash.

Unfortunately, with no real work to do, Harkness was soon bored. Sometimes she would just hang around, lazily watching Wang, who squatted before the stove by the hour, "his long blue gown tucked up under his knees, stirring some delicious mess with a pair of chopsticks." The meals he turned out, she thought, were "nothing short of genius." Since the team had not brought any preserved goods beyond dried milk, they would be living on the country. That meant eggs, bamboo shoots, chestnuts, black walnuts, squash, Chinese turnips, cabbage soup, pheasant, and a few times a week, chicken. Wang dried pieces of meat on a line strung across his room. And he cooked the ever-present cornmeal many different ways, sometimes into pancakes, occasionally as a dessert with eggs, walnut meats, and dried milk. Wang called native dishes "Chinee speakin' chow," and Western selections "Englis' speakin' chow."

Wang was so playful and creative with words that Harkness invariably adopted his freshly coined phrases. If something was lost inside the castle, he would murmur as he hunted, "What city that thing?" Farther-off locations were "bungalows." Any meat was ham or "porky." The old mandarin at the castle was, to Wang, the "manderman." Wang, who was married to two women, once asked Harkness for one piece of paper for his two piece wives.

Her funniest exchange with Wang, though, had come on her very first night at the castle, when she realized that with her raging cold, she was running low on clean handkerchiefs. She asked Wang if he would be willing to launder them. Yes, he could, he said. But then he began to speak to her in his idiosyncratic slang, referring quite insistently to something he called "sheeties." Harkness was perplexed. There were no bed linens on this pared-down trek, so she was "quite befogged." Wang kept trying to get through to her, then finally, exasperated by her dullness, he took her across the castle to the opposite wall, pointing to a small flying balcony. At its center was a square hole with a long drop to the court below. While pantomiming "intestinal evacuation," Harkness said, he triumphantly announced, "Sheety house." Harkness wrote home, "Thus was I shown the 'Ladies Room.' "

If pidgin English had a tendency to make Chinese speakers appear simpleminded in the eyes of westerners, it had to have cut both ways, for Wang never seemed confident in Harkness's abilities. As he would go off to the village, wearing all his coats and carrying his black cotton umbrella, he would leave Harkness with stern instructions, as though she didn't know enough to come in from the cold. "Master, sun go down; you go inside; catchee cough."

For most daily needs, Wang and Harkness were able to communicate. The kindness and loyalty of this man who was, as Harkness put it, "true to his salt," meant the world to her. Pidgin English, though, just didn't allow for deep, complex conversations. There would be no one here in these cold mountains for her to pour her heart out to. Inexorably, Harkness found herself being pulled into a dark vortex of loneliness. There were outside signs of it from the beginning, as the American, once the toast of Manhattan, lost any interest in dress or hygiene. It was the first step in her slide downward, even though she made light of it. "My appearance at the moment should be a guide to all lady 'explorers' in the matter of the smart thing to wear when hunting pandas," she wrote home. "I have on a pair of violent green wool socks; a pair of very soiled flanellate pajamas that my sister made me some years ago, a pair of Chinese cloth shoes that are many sizes too large, and my best Tibetan woolly coat lined with a different but equally violent shade of green; this garment is designed to make one look like a grizzly bear—or a panda— in all directions is girded about my loins with a really beautiful handwoven blue-green Jarung belt with much fringe that trails a few odds and ends of cornstocks. In the absence of hairdressers I brush my hair as well as possible; it is getting to look quite Chinese; I have a small cold so my nose is red. But otherwise I am quite as lovely looking as ever." She also didn't bathe very often, and her clothes got dirtier by the day. She would bundle up in a grimy outfit and do nothing.

Her typewriter was her liberation—her tenuous tie to the outside world—and she wondered with mock horror what would become of her if the ribbon ever gave out. Even though mail was spotty at best, she could talk and talk by typing, sending batches of mail off by runner to Wenchuan to be posted. Her first words to Hazel Perkins on October 24 were, "It is a most discouraging fact that I have had only one letter from you since I left America; I do hope that you have written and someday I can sit down and spend hours reading about things; I want to know what you are doing and why." Though the days were uneventful, she wrote like mad anyway, sometimes typing up prank letters. In one packet, she presented a business proposal, in playful legalese, to Perkins and her friend Anne Pierce, for opening a health spa at the castle. She said the renovated complex would be good for the soul, with a bungalow available on the "yang," or sunny side, of the mountain, and one on the "yin," or shady side. "The one great point concerning this project which should have great publicity appeal in America is the fact that from the standpoint of health, the trip alone here, will kill or cure."

Over the first few weeks she learned with some effort how to pass the days. And by night she could lie on her cot under wool blankets reading by the dim glow of candlelight. She had with her Dickens's *Pickwick Papers*. Comic and crowded with characters, it was a perfect escape. She also pored over and scribbled in the margins of an odd volume, dense and pessimistic, called *Man, the Unknown,* by scientist Alexis Carroll. The work suggested that society should keep an open mind where mysticism and the paranormal were concerned—a perspective that, of course, interested Harkness—but Carroll also advocated eugenics, something Harkness didn't have much patience for. If she was lucky, she would nod off after reading and sleep until dawn.

Mornings were dreary, with little sunlight, just thick cloud and gauzy veils of mist and fog. Standing out on the balcony, she could see the passage of the seasons simply by looking across the valley during clear moments, to monitor the fall colors—reds and oranges and yellows—creeping down the mountains, descending lower and lower, being chased right on their heels by snow and the icy grip of winter.

Each day passed with no news of pandas. Wang remained optimistic:

"Oh yes, Master, can catch," he told Harkness, predicting that a panda would be in hand by November 10. Periodically, the hunters checked in with her. Combing the ridges and valleys, they were capturing all kinds of game, bringing her flying squirrels, gray squirrels, foxes, grouse, pheasants, and even a takin—none of which she wanted. Occasionally, though, the catches were so cute, she couldn't help keeping them for a while. Once, she suffered a nasty laceration from a squirrel, who gave her a bad bite on what she said was one of her most important typewriting fingers.

Along with the live animals, the hunters would also bring welcome meat—wild boar, venison, goral, partridge, and pheasant. Years later, Harkness would write for *Gourmet* magazine about how she unwittingly ate ten thousand dollars' worth of rare pheasants presented by the men—orange and gold tragopans, impeyans, Lady Amhersts. The hunters carried them in bamboo baskets, or, if alive, tied in cornmeal sacks, though eventually Harkness would ask that the birds not be brought in breathing, for she couldn't bear to see them proud and beautiful one day, then lying dead the next. However they arrived, Wang would cook them in rice wine, soy sauce, and a red pepper seasoning, till the skin was a delicate lacquered crisp.

The men came and left many times, never staying long. After the drop-off, they would set right back out again, stoic and spartan. "In the preparations for the long trips which they made for me high into the snows of the mountains, sometimes to be gone for a week or ten days," Harkness wrote, "they took with them as their only rations a homespun bag containing perhaps eight or nine pounds of corn meal, a lump of grey rock salt, perhaps a few bunches of *bei-tsai*, which is a Chinese green like a cross between romaine and cabbage, a *lobo* or two—reminiscent of both radish and turnip—and, if they could get it, a piece of fat salt pork." They traveled lightly, Harkness said, carrying no blankets, "sleeping close to the fire on snowy nights. Not one had a pair of socks, only straw sandals and thin blue cotton trousers and jackets."

Aside from the visits of the men from the field, the only other break in her monotonous agenda came when there was a rare mail drop. One evening, Dzo, a hired hand from the first expedition, arrived from Wenchuan carrying a bundle. Harkness was overjoyed. "Letters in that remote place were thrilling things," she said. "With no companionship of any sort, mail is the breath of life." She tore into the cache, smoking cigarettes and drinking corn wine as she discovered what her friends and family were doing, reading, thinking. The letters were dated—many had been written at the height of summer—"but gosh it was good to have them," she said. There was a clipping from Chicago of Su-Lin sitting atop a pyramid of logs, which Harkness propped up by her typewriter. With the rush of remote companionship, she had gotten carried away with the wine, and by the time she finished reading and rereading, she was drunk.

It was late at night, but with her spirits reeling, she couldn't bear the thought of going to bed. She wanted more. In New York or Shanghai, the night would be young. Here, far out in the country, skies went black early and the long, cold, silent nights would begin. This evening, she wanted to stave off the gloom for a change. There weren't many options. Finally, descending the crooked, darkened hallways and stairs with the light of a candle or kerosene lamp, she went looking for company. She clambered through the maze of rooms and passageways, searching out the dignified old mandarin. Her dancing light found him in his rustic chambers, where the air was filled with the sweet, acrid scent of opium. In the silence he sat like a wise god, serenely puffing on a filthy old pipe. They couldn't talk to each other, but when he offered for her to join him in a smoke, she sat down gamely, taking a good pull on the pipe. At the farthest reaches of civilization, in the middle of the night, she had found a little vice, after all, and she lingered long enough to finish off a couple of bowls. She reported feeling nothing from the narcotic, but when she left the old man to head back upstairs, she was still drunk. Collapsing into bed, she broke a canvas strap on the cot, nearly sinking to the floor. In the morning, as light poured into the big room and she sobered up, she thought about how she had spent the night, wondering what she "might have collected in the way of germs from the ancient pipe."

It would be her last after-dark blowout. From here on out, the nights would become increasingly difficult. On her previous expedition, she had marched and hiked and pushed herself physically every day. She had bathed in icy mountain streams. And when she had curled up just past sundown, she invariably had been pulled into a deep, contented sleep. This year, slumber escaped her. Days of laziness, in which she sat "like a hermit on his mountain top waiting for all things to come to me," stoked nights of anxiety, restlessness, and despair.

This would be a tougher test for Harkness than all the danger of last year's trials. But she dug in, determined to see it through. She knew she needed some sort of release, and obviously, opium wasn't the answer. So she embarked on a journey involving something infinitely more reliable than drugs—her imagination. Harkness now would dwell in a shaded and mysterious world, one full of spells and passion; a place where nature sheltered those who honored it; where animals and people could communicate. Alone in her room, she would sit at her typewriter, transforming this lonely valley into a place filled with exciting characters and intrigue. She resumed writing a story she had begun the year before, set in a beautiful forest, just like the one that rioted beyond her. It held the great themes of her life, and the dichotomies that she struggled to balance. In it, a half-breed woman was torn by her two different worlds—East and West—and by the love of two men, one a sophisticated American, the other, a handsome, brave young villager muscling his way over the edge into manhood. The forest was a primitive idyll. Modern civilization beckoned with physical comfort, medicine; but it also threatened with greed and intolerance. The story allowed Harkness to simplify some of her most complicated emotions about life and love, about home, and mysticism, and harmony with nature.

In reality, nature was now a trial. The beginning of November felt like deep winter. The days were gray and raw, with only rare breaks of sunshine. The drizzly nights were plunged into the bone-chilling cold of high mountains. By this time, Harkness cursed her decision to remain in the castle rather than join the hunters in the field. Marking time while hired men did the legwork was a strategy Smith had advocated the previous year, one that she had rejected outright. Now she was doing just that. Not in the comfort of Shanghai, of course, but in the discomfort of the castle, and achingly within sight of the forest and the life she should have been immersed in. Why hadn't she gone? It wasn't the hardships of the field that had halted her. She craved intense sensation, which a good hard trek granted. Her only explanation was that she would have been a liability to the endeavor. She was no good at pitching tents or tying knots; she certainly couldn't shoot game.

Other things must have weighed heavily on her. Quentin Young wasn't there, and the personal and practical considerations of entering the wild without him may have been too much. She was under tremendous pressure to succeed—ironically, much more than last time. In her first expedition, hardly anyone even knew what she was up to, and among those who did, there was little expectation. This time the world was aware of where she was and what she was doing. There were high hopes. And the Brookfield Zoo had staked money on this trip. There were also Smith's charges that she wasn't a real explorer. And her own desire to make a life for herself doing this work—the need to prove to herself before anyone else that she, in fact, could. Then too there was the debt of honor in reinforcing to the great white hunters that animal capture could be kind, and soft, and feminine. Of Smith's two pandas that died, Harkness said, "I believe the spirits of Ajax's pandas were completely broken." She felt there was a viable alternative to all the rough work of traditional hunters. There was a lot riding on this trip, and Harkness had to stick with the tactic that had the best chance of success.

At this point, it probably seemed too late and foolish, even too selfish, to change plans in order to go hunting herself. But she was at such loose ends, perceiving herself as so useless, she felt compelled to do whatever was in her power to hurry things along. For Harkness, that meant one thing—another ceremony to the gods of the mountains. She ordered the purchase from town of a large red cock for sacrifice.

Several days later, at dusk, the runners returned from Guanxian with the animal and all the ceremonial provisions. Wang arranged with the hunters that they would carry the rooster, incense, candles, and wine to the same spot that had been used for Harkness's big *joss* service last year.

She lobbied to travel with the men, if not for hunting, then at least for the rites, but Wang preferred the comforts, such as they were, of the castle. His reluctance only added to Harkness's suspicion that he was tethered by a romance in the village. Wang sometimes dressed up and disappeared for hours somewhere in the vicinity of those huts beyond the castle. One day, when he had vanished for a long time—an afternoon and into the evening—Harkness sent for him. In his embarrassment, she reported, "he came rushing back puffing and dithering up the castle stairs." She thought he was guilty about something.

As for a trip into the forest, Wang wouldn't budge. He told Harkness that they could time things so that the night the hunters reached the ceremonial rock, the two of them could "make joss" simultaneously, close to their own protective roof.

With all the preparations in place, a few nights later, near a little peach tree, Harkness and Wang lighted their candles, burning sacrificial money in obeisance to the Tibetan gods. Staying put was a small concession to her dear Wang. He had been so good to her that she couldn't have pressured him about it.

By mid-November, the seclusion was truly taking its toll on Harkness. In letters home, she didn't even try to hide it anymore. "Slowly but inevitably I am losing my mind," she wrote. Her distractions weren't distracting enough. She was even coming to the end of her meager reading selection, having almost completed the Dickens. She said that when she turned the last page of the book, her last vestige "of sanity will have fled." When she wrote, she still threw in a witty line or two, but invariably her predicament would become apparent. "Patience is, I am told, a great virtue. Mine I fear is wearing thin. Not for me the years on lonely mountain tops in contemplation; I have too much to do in this world."

Her humor blackened while inch by inch her confidence eroded. Dirty, bedraggled, and without a single in-depth conversation to steady her in reality, she began to think for the first time that she might just fail. She feared she would never see another giant panda. With every passing day, each night that closed to total blackness, it got worse. Deep inside the lonely castle, she might hear only the rushing wind, the sounds of her own footsteps in the echoing dim halls, the sputtering of an oil lamp, or the crackle of a precious campfire. She caught the sound of her own language only inside her own thoughts.

If she took stock of her life, she would see no safety net below. She was a thirty-seven-year-old widow with a lust for adventure and a nebulous hold on underwriting it. When she lost her husband, she sidestepped a family fortune. If she failed on this trip, she would have trouble supporting herself. She would have to find a way to earn her keep. Furthermore, she wasn't even sure which side of the world she wanted to call home. At times it could seem that her life was at stake: "This year I'm afraid will end in failure . . . and what will I do if I fail?" she wrote. Too easily, she would seek solace in corn wine. It took some of the sting out of the tortured hours, which always worsened at sundown.

Some nights she abandoned any effort to sleep, and when Wang would hear her moving about, or coughing with the cold she had trouble shaking, he would rouse himself to boil her a bowl of pale tea. He would give her tiger balm and stoke the fire in her chilled room.

But that didn't always bring her peace. In this wild, desolate place, she began to have strange dreams of Bill. Sometimes it was comforting to sense his presence and to feel protected by his spirit, but she was also distressed by a recurring nightmare: horrible images of Bill in terrible condition, "ill and penniless." He must have been reproaching her in some way, because over and over, in the nightmare, she would have to defend herself, laying out the whole story of Su-Lin to him, explaining why she had to leave to bring the panda back a mate. In this castle where she had first made love to Quentin Young, and with nothing to occupy her mind, she began to drown in despair.

It opened the door even wider to the mysticism and spirituality she had always craved. She felt that she was in the presence not only of Bill's spirit but of "other forces too." The previous year, she had ascended these mountains into the realm of the gods. Now, paradoxically, from this great height, she seemed to be descending, ever downward, into perdition, fueled by local corn wine and dark thoughts, into a netherworld where dreams would become portents, and opium and mysticism would call to her.

The mountains seemed to erupt with mystical signs. Their silhouettes, blacker than the night they were enveloped in, would sometimes emit mysterious twinkling lights. They came from areas where no people could possibly be. It seemed so far-fetched that when she wrote of the sight to friends back home, she assured them that she "wasn't tight." What she saw was real, and would be observed by a man of science many years later, who would attribute the phenomenon to something more prosaic than sprites—phosphorescent fungi or the like.

To Harkness, she was seeing the unexplained. And she was hearing it too. An almost indescribable sound seemed to lift right off the slopes. It wasn't the wind, or the cries of wild animals. One night, the rhythms were particularly strong. "Their cadences of three tones were endless," she wrote home. "It is a very difficult thing to explain but it's like silent music, if that makes sense. Sometimes it's like a harp, the zing, zing, zing of fine drawn strings; then it's a bell and then it's a drum—deep toned like the Ghost Temple's drum-bell." Out here, she had faith in a way she never had been capable of in a church. "I'm not fooling," she wrote. "I believe in the spirits of these mountains."

In this mood, she could mull over the pages of her fantasy story of the forest girl. Her agent would end up calling the work "tripe," and in fact its premise was as clichéd and simplistic as its author was original and complicated. But it did seem to allow her to distill her roiling emotions. Her fictional world mirrored her own dilemmas. Did she belong in the United States or China? Could she, in fact, love a man like Quentin Young, or would it always be Bill? "Jungle Magic" was no roman à clef, but bits of Harkness and the people around her were woven all through the characters and plot.

BY THE MIDDLE of November, there was suddenly hope—good news had come in from the field. The hunters had sent back carefully wrapped packages of panda dung. It was fresh, and judging from the size of the droppings, the men believed the animal to be a good-size young adult. Overjoyed, Harkness reaffirmed her trust in the gods, and in Whang, the holy man who was leading the trackers. He came to see her a short time later to deliver his assessment. Sitting down for a cigarette and a cup of tea, Whang communicated his belief that within a week they would have a panda.

On November 19, late in the afternoon, the hunters arrived at the castle, summoning Harkness downstairs. In a dark corner of a lower room she saw a wretched and frightened black-and-white bear, about seventy-five pounds. It was tethered and trussed from nose to tail. The animal, which they presumed to be female, could not move, and cried out in little panicked laments. With a bamboo muzzle fashioned over her nose, she would have been unable to take food or water during the trek here. Tears stung Harkness's eyes. Though custom dictated a slow and methodical haggling with the men over price, she couldn't stand to see the animal remain this way for even another minute. She stared at the pitiful panda as the hunters conveyed the story that eighty men and several dogs had participated in the capture. They would all have to be compensated. Harkness didn't ask questions; she merely shelled out the cash. She "paid through the nose," she said, because she just wanted to have "Yin" carried immediately up to her room, without taking the time to quibble.

Harkness ordered a cage be built so the animal could be free of her shackles, and in the meantime, she had as many of them removed as possible. The sorry state of the captive made her sick. "For the night and day," Harkness wrote, "the poor baby crouched in a corner and sobbed. I practically did the same." She was tortured by the animal's suffering. "This is all a miserable business," she wrote, "and if I ever accomplish this, God help me I'll never be responsible for capturing another animal of any kind."

Harkness, whose experience with pandas had been from the gentle Su-Lin, tried to comfort the wild animal. But Yin wanted none of it. "I tried to approach her and she'd rear and strike and hiss rather like a cat," Harkness wrote. "My hands are still a mass of scratches bites and are badly swollen from my attempts at pacification." She must have thought yet again about how things had been the year before. Of Su-Lin's serene face tipped up toward her own as he greedily gulped his formula. Of the comfort of Quentin Young's body next to her own. Of the tenderness and physical exhilaration she had then.

Now, as she sat helplessly watching the poor panda, she must have had a thousand thoughts. She had finally received word from Quentin Young—he was in Macao, the Portuguese colony outside Hong Kong. She had written him back immediately, asking him to join her in her quest for a male panda, and to help her transport the animals to the States. But that was not to be. Another letter from Young would say that he and Diana had had a baby girl on November 19—the very same day Harkness got her panda. He told her that since he didn't have the good fortune to have a male, he thought Harkness would get a male panda. He also told her that he and his wife would name the baby after her, Harkness reported, though in fact, they did not.

It was clear that for this trip, Harkness would remain on her own. At least she had one panda in hand. If she could get the animal out alive, it would be the second panda to come to the West, and that would mean she had trumped Smith again. But the impending victory seemed less than hollow. Even though Harkness had her prize, she felt so disheartened that for two weeks she couldn't even bring herself to write letters.

"Really I can't describe the days," she would write when the black spell had partially lifted. "Just endless waiting, waiting waiting with not a thing in the world to do." It had gotten so cold that she wouldn't even tolerate stripping down for a sponge bath. "Haven't had my clothes off for about ten days now," she wrote. "I confine my ablutions to hands face and teeth, and hate to do that, I did wash my feet yesterday and was a little appalled when I got a whiff of them." Her hair had gone unwashed since the start of October.

As miserable as she felt, though, she wasn't quitting. She could easily have headed out with Yin, but she was still bent on getting another panda, and she resigned herself to the fact that she might just finish out the winter here, spending months more in this unhappy state.

At least poor Yin finally had a cage, which allowed her to be released from her restraints. With some freedom of movement, the animal began to settle down. "She is sweet now," Harkness reported, "and inflicts no intentional injury but she every now and then gives me a nip." Fresh bamboo was brought in for her, while simultaneously, Harkness tried to interest her in vegetables so that she could survive far from these forests. The bamboo-obsessed bear would not touch them. And, though giant pandas must eat almost constantly, the disoriented animal slept most of the day through, eating pounds and pounds of tough bamboo in the still of the night. "How I'm ever going to shift her diet God only knows," Harkness wrote. She was distraught about it because in no time at all, she had become very attached to the poor creature. "I love her dearly," Harkness wrote; "she is particularly entrancing when she stands on her head," she said, describing a common giant panda behavior.

Since she couldn't go inside the cage with the panda, Harkness would clean the area with long fire tongs. "It's great sport," Harkness said, "because she takes them in her paws and then we have a battle to see who'll keep them. She uses her paws exactly like hands and is she strong."

Harkness soon felt that the cage was too small for the animal, so she decamped to a draftier portion of the castle, sacrificing her own comfort to that of the bear. The new, loftlike quarters were not only larger but had a dirt floor, which would be cozier for Yin than the stone one. Eventually, Harkness would give up the room entirely to the bear, fearing that building a fire for herself would make Yin too warm. So she moved in with Wang next door, where she could have heat but still be close enough to hear the comforting sounds of Yin munching bamboo through the night.

Through experimentation, Harkness discovered that the panda would accept a mixture of milk with thin cornmeal gruel. She was elated, even though she had to share her only bowl with the animal in order to feed her. "She has her milk from it," Harkness wrote, and "at dinner I have soup in it and later I use it to brush my teeth." Feeding time was as much fun as cleaning. As Harkness would attempt to pour the gruel through the bars of the cage, the panda would alternately place a paw and muzzle in the rapidly filling pan on the floor, and then try to bite at the bottle it was all coming out of.

WITH FEWER COMFORTS, and the prospect of unending months of this life, Harkness made all kinds of plans and determinations in her head, while having no idea, really, how things would come out. If she failed to get a second panda, she figured she would leave Yin in Chengdu with Wang, then offer her services to the Chinese government, though what she could do, she wasn't sure. "It's a dream I've been dreaming ever since I've been here to do something for China," she said. "I've been plotting and planning some way to help my beloved China!"

Cavaliere had begun sending her a little newsletter, compiled from radio reports and published by the missionaries. What she was hearing of the war between Japan and China horrified her. On November 11 Chinese troops had begun their retreat out of Shanghai and toward the capital of Nanking. But within no time, the government itself would be fleeing from that city to Hankou, which for eight months would become the capital of unoccupied China. Harkness was desperate for America to care, to help. But at home the mood was resolutely isolationist, with millions signing petitions to "Keep America Out of War." She promised herself that at the very least, she would do what she could. Bagging pandas from China, she thought, would be senseless if China couldn't reap some reward from it. She would find a way for the animals—assuming she would get two—to aid the Chinese people. In the meantime, she had sent a war-relief contribution and received Chinese Liberty bonds in the mail. She hoped somehow to rally her fellow Americans to do the same.

If the panda or pandas were to be of any help, though, Harkness had to get them to civilization alive. Smith's fiasco with his two loomed like a nightmare, and the escalating war with Japan was threatening to block her way out. She had managed to fly a good distance of her trip in, but she figured the airline would not allow a large panda or two on board, so heading home through French Indochina was not an option. The Yangtze? She wondered if she could somehow swing that. But the thought of arriving in Chongqing and asking to be evacuated on a U.S.

gunboat with two giant pandas seemed far-fetched—she already felt like a renegade with American officials there. Though there was no easy solution, the effort of strategizing was helping to pull her out of her fog.

On the first day of December, she forced herself to lighten up, writing home once again. As local villagers peered in through her windows, nearly obliterating her light, she set herself up as close to her fire as she could get, placing her typewriter on a suitcase, and sitting on the floor. Try as she might to hide it, her first letter out carried the residue of her funk, and it frightened her friends back home. She mentioned the capture of Yin casually, as though they would have known about it somehow already. Harkness didn't seem to be thinking clearly.

Within weeks, even the false cheer she labored to exude was gone. And on an overcast, forlorn day she wrote home again. "This is getting to be a miserable lonely business." Her letters were peppered once more with despair. "It is much harder to achieve contentment in the midst of solitude, with not a thing in the world to do," she wrote. With the holidays approaching, she was writing, she told her friends, from a place where "there are no Sundays or Christmases."

As gray as things were for Harkness, the image of the explorer was being treated to a Technicolor blast in the United States. Her story was emerging once again, this time in the color-saturated comics pages of American papers. The Quaker Oats company had paid Harkness two hundred dollars to feature her exploits in a splashy comic-strip advertisement. "A Great American Explorer tells what a Quaker Oats breakfast means to folks who lead lives of adventure," it read in papers across the country. Seven panels, in bright red, yellow, blue, and green, portrayed a beautiful and sophisticated Ruth Harkness intent on capturing a panda.

Su-Lin was also front and center in books, articles, toys, and ads.

Two American women produced a small fifty-cent children's book for Rand McNally called *Su-Lin*. Newspapers everywhere grabbed any excuse—"Su Lin Doesn't Mind Winter at All"—to report on the panda and run his photo.

Giant pandas were so irresistible that even the unlikeliest products used them for promotion. A clothing company featured a giant panda holding a dress and carried the legend "Panda-ring to Your Desire for Cool Cute Wash Togs." Calvert whiskey employed the likeness of a foxy-looking giant panda to accompany the poem

The panda is a choosy beast,
On bamboo shoots alone he'll feast;
You too, if wise, will choose with care,
And call for CALVERT everywhere!

Both Marshall Field's and Carson Pirie Scott & Company produced dueling plush-toy Su-Lins. There was a jointed thirteen-and-a-half-inch toy panda for $2.50 and a more conventional panda version of the teddy bear. By Christmastime, Su-Lin toys would be all the rage, clutched by some of the most famous chubby hands in North America, including those of the Dionne quintuplets in Ontario.

None of the profits for the toys were earmarked for Harkness, though she did make money selling her manuscripts. Harkness's agent wrote to her that her children's book had been accepted by the Literary Guild, and she would receive seven hundred dollars at publication. Adding in the money due her for *The Lady and the Panda*, she wrote with happy disbelief, "My books will have brought me $1,500.00 before being published."

ASIDE FROM THE GRUEL, "Yin baby" would accept nothing but bamboo, making the prospect of keeping her alive outside the bamboo zone seem impossible. Compounding the somber situation, some unsettling news arrived. Harkness heard over the bamboo telegraph that Smith was back in the field, hunting pandas. He might show up anywhere, even spoiling things with all those hunters she was employing. She had seen enough of his tricks to know that with him, anything could happen. He might just put as much energy into foiling her as he would into trapping.

In letters home she would refer to him for the first time as her "rival." But Harkness was always game, and the new challenge revved her up. She gauged the competition, preparing to meet it head-on. Of Smith's sudden reemergence, she said, "That doesn't worry me, because if I can't do it successfully, he can't."

Although Smith had not, in fact, made it back into the action by then, having spent the fall in England, Harkness had been very much on his mind. His indignation seemed to energize him as he partnered with the British Museum and the London Zoo. In order to cement his newly forged alliances, the American so proud of his patriotic ancestors filed an application for British citizenship.

With his latest associations, and the money from his sister, he planned to get right back into the field to bag "bigger and better Pandas." He was even feeling upbeat enough to write magazine articles in England, taking credit for the capture of Su-Lin. "During my recent spell of four years in Western China," he wrote, "I have succeeded in securing at my collecting headquarters a baby and an adult male and a female of the giant panda. . . . Only the baby is still in captivity." And in another article: "It has been my great good fortune," he said, "to have been the active agent in effecting the capture of the only three Giant Pandas that have ever been taken alive." "The first specimen thus secured," he went on, "the baby Panda recently sold in Chicago—it was not my privilege to take home myself."

He happily laid out his thoughts on many aspects of panda hunting. He said the giant panda was lazy, comparing it in size to "a good-sized hog" and in personality to "a contented, well fed brood sow." He bragged that he had perfected a system of foolproof lures for capturing giant pandas. He could not, unfortunately, share them with the readers, however, for they were "trade secrets" and his "sole property." He also told this whole new audience about the hazards of facing bandits, and of the difficulties of dealing with what he described as astoundingly stupid native hunters.

————

THINGS BEGAN to look up a bit for Yin. Strained vegetables were added to her gruel, and whenever Harkness approached the cage now with the basin and the bottle, the panda trotted over like a dog. Even better, in Harkness's mind, was the fact that Yin had flown into a rage one day. "She stormed around and swore at me in Chinese," Harkness wrote. Not only did Harkness believe that the passion of the animal was a good sign, but in the throes of her fury, Yin thrashed, then ate some cornstalks that were in the cage. Harkness was so delighted that it didn't matter that the strong animal had also raked her thumb, causing it to blow up to twice its normal size. That Yin was eating something other than bamboo was solace enough. The development may have even been enough for a little celebration. In the cold castle, Harkness finally relented, taking a bath in a washbasin, scrubbing her hair for the first time in two months.

Despite the mood-lifting powers of a good shampoo, Harkness had had enough of her isolation. She began making plans to start back to Chengdu on Christmas Day.

Wang suggested that they cover ground by the dark of night to avoid curious crowds along the way. She thought it might be worth a try, but travel was treacherous enough as it was in sunlight; at night it would be hair-raising.

She still believed she would leave Yin with Wang in the city, going off to make herself useful in Hankou, while the hunters continued their work. She had received a clipping from the papers saying that passports were being invalidated, so leaving China was now even less of an option. Not that she had the money to sail to the United States and return any-way.

Once she had made up her mind about what to do, some of her anxiety lifted. "Nothing is quite as disturbing to me as uncertainty," she wrote home, "not knowing the definite—I'm happier now than I've been in weeks, even tho' I have failed for the time being, because I've decided upon a definite course of action." She had always felt that nothing in life worked out precisely the way it was planned but that something else always grew out of it. The point was to at least try, and then another, un-expected door would open.

As it turned out, Harkness was right. On December 31, 1937, Hazel Perkins, in far-away wintry New England, received a telegram from Ruth Harkness, who was already in Chengdu. It read, exuberantly: HAPPY YEAR SMALL FEMALE.

.

CHAPTER TWELVE

ONE GRAND THRILL

RUTH HARKNESS'S DAYS of isolation ended in a blaze of exploding flashbulbs and detonating rockets on January 6, 1938.

Resplendent in a turban and leopard-trimmed fur coat, she was carrying a magnificent little baby panda in her arms when she appeared before the ecstatic press gathered at Hankou, the temporary capital, just as a Japanese air raid hit.

A sortie of pursuit planes and heavy bombers pummeled the area around the airfield, killing about a dozen people, while antiaircraft fire dotted the sky with shell bursts.

As Harkness emerged from the chaos with Diana, the thirteen-pound baby, headlines around the world beamed the news that Ruth Harkness had triumphed once again, ushering the rarest and most adorable of animals out of one of the remotest corners of the globe. The big wire services, United Press and the Associated Press, with electronic tentacles reaching into every newsroom in America, couldn't bat out the story fast enough.

The bloodshed that gripped the city only made already hot copy sizzle for the newsmen who wrote of Harkness's success and of the cub who slept through all the action. PANDA IS BORED BY JAP AIR RAID, screamed one headline.

As much fun as the reporters had with the incident, the attack was serious and deadly. The Japanese were swarming over much of China now, and their swaggering brutality was reaching its lowest depths at that very moment with the "Rape of Nanking." Having won the battle of Shanghai, Japanese forces moved on to the nearby city. Beginning on December 13, 1937, and continuing over the course of about seven weeks, Japanese troops would rape and murder tens of thousands—perhaps hundreds of thousands—in a tempest of savagery that would have in horror and scale few equals in history. Women died from repeated brutal sexual assaults and were sometimes disemboweled or nailed to walls. Prisoners were killed in horrifying ways—buried alive, decapitated, doused in gasoline and set on fire, or used for bayonet practice. About fifty thousand soldiers hacked their way by hand through the city's population, leaving piles of bodies stacked in the streets.

For Harkness, the grim assault on China would cast a pall over her moment of victory. There was simply no pure joy allowed on this trip, from start to finish.

Facing the press, though, she had a job to do, one that she always pulled off with aplomb. She would, over the course of several stops in China and the States, tell the story of her second expedition in the breeziest fashion. As best she could understand, she said, the discovery of the little panda had been a lucky surprise for the hunters. On December 18, when they were out scouring the forest, one of their dogs suddenly dashed into a thicket after what turned out to be a hidden adult panda. As the animal fled, a roly-poly baby was revealed barreling through the open nearby. The men easily caught the little creature, who refused food and water during the six-day trek back to Chaopo. The hunters reached the castle on the morning of Christmas Eve, waking Harkness up with the gift of the baby panda, who was much bigger than Su-Lin had been at capture.

The days without nourishment had taken their toll on the baby, who was then near death. "It's a wonder she survived at all," Harkness said. Distraught, Harkness scrambled to get some warm formula into the panda but was rebuffed again and again. "Diana was a sickly child when I got her," Harkness said. "I tried every way to make her eat. I tried put-

The baby panda Diana, who would become known as Mei-Mei.
COURTESY MARY LOBISCO

ting furs around the bottle, but she just simply refused to touch it." The struggle with the traumatized animal would go on for more than forty-eight anxious hours. Then there was a break. "I was ready to give up hope when on the third day Diana finally showed signs that she was interested in life."

Once the baby was taking the milk, Harkness packed up, mustered the troops, and got to Chengdu as quickly as possible.

By December 31, her months of deprivation were over. In the big city, she indulged in every gratification she could. "I reveled in the luxury of a hot bath, coffee, and buttered toast for breakfast, and a clean dress instead of dirty, ragged trousers," she said. Bringing fifty rare pheasants, which required three separate porters, back to the city, she celebrated with friends. There was an extravagant, elegant dinner party in which guests wore formal dinner clothes and gathered around a gleaming table set with white linen, polished silver, delicate wine goblets, and decorated with pink camellias. This new panda would be fêted in high style just as Su-Lin had been.

At one point, Associated Press correspondent James A. Mills stopped by to snap pictures. He caught Harkness and her crowd frolicking with the world's latest wonder. The weather was chilly enough for topcoats, but the revelers slipped them off for the session out on a wool blanket spread across the garden lawn. Mills's black-and-white shots would be a rarity—for in them, the American didn't play the society matron. Instead, he captured a happy, more natural Harkness, wearing a ribbed-wool boatneck sweater, cuffed wide-leg pants, and dress shoes whose laces crisscrossed up past her bare ankles. Her hair was pulled back simply. There was a slight puffiness under her eyes—a hint, perhaps, of the long months of loneliness up-country. But nonetheless, without turban and fur coat, she appeared fresh and young. She looked directly into the camera and smiled.

The photographs showed Wang joining in the fun. Sitting on the blanket, wearing a cherished winter helmet with earflaps pulled down over his head, he cuddled the little panda against the great padding of his coat and pants.

For the public, everything would be smiles. No one would have to know about the complete melancholy Harkness had experienced over the months beforehand. Few would ever hear of the death of the nearly adult panda Yin. That was bleached out of the public telling, either by Harkness herself or by her friends in the press. *The China Journal* was one of the few publications, perhaps the only one, to refer to the incident, and then only in the vaguest terms.

It appears that Yin must have already been dead by the time the Harkness expedition hightailed it out of Wassu-land and to Chengdu, for the American covered that journey as quickly as she had the year before with Quentin Young. She simply couldn't have kept that pace if the team had been burdened by the transportation problems a large panda would have presented. How Yin died was addressed only obliquely later in a letter from Harkness to the Beans in Brookfield. She was convinced, she said, that the animal had sustained internal injuries from the hunting dogs, and that she had never truly recovered from them in captivity. Whatever the details of Yin's end, it must have been devastating to Harkness. In her code of honor, the death of a panda in her care was a paramount sin.

HARKNESS HAD COME to Hankou—"the bunghole of creation," according to Joseph Stilwell—to obtain travel permits from the upper reaches of government. There was a long road between this city and the Brookfield Zoo, with much to overcome. Even when she got to Chicago, she knew there might be a very big problem to deal with. It was a male panda she had promised, and now it appeared she had another female. Later, this one too, like Su-Lin, would be revealed to be yang, not yin.

If she were able to book a plane to Hong Kong, she could grab a boat to Shanghai, then sail back to America. Things went better than expected. Officials in Hankou not only gave her the paperwork she needed, they secured her free transit aboard a passenger plane bound for Hong Kong, where she planned to meet up with Quentin Young.

At 8 A.M. on Saturday, January 8, Harkness flew out of Hankou. Less than five hours later, "the queerest passenger ever to arrive in Hongkong by air landed" in a Eurasia plane, according to the *South China Morning Post*. The pair was a sensation.

Surrounded by eager reporters and photographers through the few hours before her boat sailed, the successful collector wouldn't have had much of a chance to speak seriously with Young, who was now the father of a baby girl. They at least made arrangements to work together once again.

By Thursday, January 13, Harkness was in Shanghai, once again the object of a fresh yet familiar media frenzy, speaking with such newspaper pals as Woo Kyatang of the *China Press* from her room at the Palace.

Ruth Harkness and her baby panda emerge from the wilds in high style. COURTESY MARY LOBISCO

Done up like a movie star in an elegant mandarin coat, which some thought brought out "the dark, sharp features of her American Indian ancestry," she charmed them all with talk of the expedition. Understanding just what they were after, the old pro depicted the whole trek as "one grand thrill."

The city was still under the threat of hostilities, though the Japanese ruled over only the Chinese section. The International Settlement itself was breathing again, with many of the big luxury ships resuming service, the nightclubs back open for business, and the Palace Hotel having replaced the plate glass in its front windows. Ernie Kaai's Swing Orchestra played the newly decorated Metropole Ballroom, known for its moving scenery. And the movies *The Good Earth* and *Lost Horizon* were beginning their runs here.

Everything wasn't normal, of course. Fireworks, for instance, would be banned for the upcoming Chinese New Year celebrations, and there was still an outrageous 11:30 P.M. curfew. Fights broke out anywhere, with dance-hall girls sometimes refusing to oblige Japanese customers. Arguments all too easily erupted between Western and Japanese patrons.

The Japanese were beginning to assert their authority, censoring and shuttering some Chinese newspapers. A few telegraph offices were closed. And before the month was out, the papers would report that unknown terrorists had lobbed hand grenades out of car windows in both the International Settlement and Frenchtown.

EVEN IF THIS was just a shadow of the old Shanghai, Harkness was the toast of it once again. To cope with the hectic schedule she had the help of Floyd James, and, as much would be made of it in the press, she hired an amah to care for the panda. Photographs of the woman, dressed in high-collar tunic and silk pants, bottle-feeding Diana appeared in the *Shanghai Times*.

Harkness, like many mothers, found herself more relaxed the second time around. The *China Press* reported that she and James had jumped at every cry of Su-Lin's. But with Diana, who was three times the size Su-Lin had been on arrival, the paper said, "there is less anxiety. Su Lin was the first panda ever held in captivity, and there was no precedent as to the manner in which it should be fed and otherwise attended to. But with the bouncing Diana it is different."

Harkness's celebrity only escalated as reviews of her book, *The Lady and the Panda,* which was excerpted in *The Christian Science Monitor,* began pouring in from the States.

The travelogue's style was in keeping with the genre of the day—light and witty, vague on personal details. Yet Harkness couldn't fail to shine through—her story was a rollicking good read, often poetic, and always respectful of Chinese culture. Her affair with Young nearly lifted right up from between the lines in her descriptions of him.

With the publication, her glory was burnished at nearly every turn. *Time* magazine, *The New York Times,* the *New York World Telegram,* and countless others seemed besotted. "The book amply testifies the romantic courage of Mrs. Harkness—a city bred woman who ventured into a foreign wilderness with no preparation beyond the reading of adventure stories," *Time* noted. *The New York Times Book Review* said the "story of achievement" had been told "with enthusiasm and charm," "with disarming frankness" and "descriptive skill" and was "one of the sprightliest travel books of recent months."

For better or worse, to most, the Ruth Harkness story centered on gender. The reviewer in the daily *New York Times* reported that *The Lady and the Panda* truly deflated some of the macho posturing of he-men explorers. "It beautifully debunks quite a lot of the big-game-and-a-book-to-come explorer's art." And *The Christian Science Monitor* likened her bravery to "the insouciance of ladies who go bargain hunting."

Yet some wondered why this woman couldn't be more like a man. *Time* grumbled that *The Lady and the Panda* was "a woman's book, full of distaff concern with clothes, medicines, the handsomeness of hunters." Because she didn't write in the very male style of other explorers, one *New York Times* review accused her of verging on "baby talk in her account of Su Lin's troubles and travels on her way to America."

What no one could miss, in any of the reviews, was Harkness's love for China and the Chinese. *The New York Times* said the "grace" of the Chinese people was prominent in the book. And its Sunday *Book Review* said that in China Harkness had "kept her eyes and heart wide open."

WHILE A WINTER CHILL settled on Shanghai, up in Harkness's hotel room life was quite cozy, with cocktails before a small fire. Yet, sipping a whiskey, smoking a cigarette, and looking out across the open waters of the Huangpu from her hotel at dusk, she wouldn't have been able to keep darker thoughts at bay. For her, twilight always brought reflection and longing, and now there was more reason than ever for a rush of intense, bittersweet feeling. What had she accomplished? Who was she? Where was her life going? Would she always be alone?

The upending of everything fit only too well with Buddhist teachings about the temporary nature of life: "So you should view all of the fleeting world: A star at dawn, a bubble in the stream; A flash of lightning in a summer cloud; A flickering lamp, a phantom, and a dream." There was always a lesson to be learned, with life giving instruction each second of the day, but in the aftermath of this trip, Harkness would have to struggle for comprehension.

There were other, more practical matters to worry over too. She would have to deal with Brookfield now.

While the press was kicking up its heels over this panda, Harkness knew the zoo was not so pleased. In fact, it had retained the right to refuse a female panda. When she first wired them with the news, she made the situation clear, addressing the cable to Su-Lin and writing HAPPY NEW YEAR SMALL SISTER NO HUSBAND. "Su-Lin" had wired back, CONGRATULATIONS HAPPY NEW YEAR DO TRY GET ME HUSBAND ALSO AM WELL AND HOPEFUL.

The *Chicago Times* had then published an open letter to Su-Lin saying, "You needn't start a hope chest, Su-Lin, and there's no use sewing those little things. It's a girl. . . . Sorry, Su-Lin, but it was the best we could do." Harkness would just have to keep her fingers crossed and hope that by the time she and the new panda baby arrived in Chicago, riding a wave of fame, they would be welcome. But even as she enchanted Shanghai, the officers of the Chicago Zoological Society were meeting at the Palmer House, declaring that a male panda for Su-Lin would be the top priority for the year. The *Chicago American* speculated that a male specimen would fetch anywhere from ten to fifteen thousand dollars.

Harkness had craved companionship over the last months, and now with two weeks in Shanghai, she could get her fill. Even without Dan Reib, who left China for good that year, Harkness and Diana would do up the town. Sowerby showed the panda off to the gentlemen at the all-male Shanghai Club, trotting her out at the longest bar in the world, and Floyd James, who had just returned from seeing Su-Lin in the United States, brought the newest panda to the American Club, giving time to both the men's bar and the ladies' lounge.

With all the clamoring interest over the animal, Harkness lived up to a promise she had made herself—she would put the captured panda to use in helping the Chinese people. A big fund-raiser, featuring a personal appearance by Diana, was arranged. Newspapers were saturated with the plans, running both stories and ads in the days leading up to the event.

Under the sponsorship of the Rotary Club, Diana would make her debut at the Sky Terrace of the Park Hotel. Admission for the event was one dollar, and since the hotel had offered the space for free, all the proceeds could go to the Refugee Children's Hospital. From 5 to 7 P.M., on a day when temperatures dipped below freezing, Harkness and Sowerby presented the panda before a crowd of eight hundred. Diana alternately sprawled on the dais and drank from a bottle. The audience was packed with children who oohed and ahhed over every move, as Sowerby filled them in on everything there was to know about pandas. It was all a great success, with front-page coverage and eight hundred dollars raised.

With her pledge fulfilled, Harkness could now be on her way. This time her visit to Hankou had ensured that her getaway would be clean, and she happily allowed the *China Press* to run a large, detailed photograph of what it called "Diana's Passport." Thinking of Smith's fiasco off Singapore, she had chosen a ship taking a more northerly route, booking herself on the *Empress of Russia,* due to depart on January 28, for Vancouver.

At 5 P.M. on Friday, January 28, under heavy, slate-gray skies, Harkness, surrounded by Shanghai friends, was handed a huge bouquet of flowers, and then, with Diana snuggled down in a custom-made wicker basket, she left the customs jetty for the *Empress of Russia*. It went off without a hitch. Within minutes, she was safely aboard in her first-class cabin on the trans-Pacific luxury liner, which would weigh anchor in the morning.

Out on the Huangpu, the ship afforded an expansive view of Shanghai as large snowflakes began to float down in silence, coating the streets of the city known for sin in a mantle of pure white. It was "*Hsu hsueh,*" the fortunate snow, an auspicious event coming as it did just before the start of the lunar new year. It would be good for the earth, and good for the soul of the country, which would be entering the Year of the Tiger the next month. For those who believed, this snow was good *joss*.

The press was certain Harkness would return to catch more pandas, but she herself was sure of nothing. A beautiful night like this was enough. It would have to be. If she had learned anything, it was to embrace beauty as it materialized. When she had come to Shanghai months ago, bombs fell on the city. How could she not feel peace and happiness now, when in the dark of night it looked as though millions of angels were descending?

HELLO, I MUST BE GOING

THE RETURN TO AMERICA was a relatively brief and unsatisfying interval in the life of Ruth Harkness. It seemed she just couldn't shake the nagging bits of bad luck that had dogged her throughout this expedition.

After she docked in Victoria, British Columbia, on February 12, 1938, her planned flights every leg of the way were delayed because of deteriorating flying conditions. Seeking refuge in New Mexico, Harkness kept her cool and her sense of humor. LOST IN A CITY WHOSE NAME WE CAN'T EVEN SPELL, she wired from Albuquerque before boarding the *California Limited,* bound for Chicago.

At every stop, scheduled or not, Harkness and the panda had roused gangs of newsmen and photographers. Nowhere would that be more true than in Chicago, where the ownership of two giant pandas was something to boast about. The travel delays may have even added to the anticipation when Harkness and the panda pulled in on Friday, February 18.

As the two sat tight in a parlor car at the Dearborn Street Station, an excited committee of local VIPs—"a delegation of dignitaries, radio workers, numerous uniformed policemen, and newspaper and news reel cameramen," according to the *Chicago Tribune*—came aboard to welcome them.

Harkness and the panda arrive in Chicago.

When the contingent was ready, they posed on the train's rear platform behind a railing that carried the *California Limited* logo. Before the assembled crowd, Harkness, in her leopard-skin coat, gave zoo director Edward Bean a kiss on the cheek as she juggled microphones, panda baby, and a big wreath of flowers sporting a satin ribbon that read FROM SU-LIN TO MY NEW PLAYMATE. The president of the board of county commissioners made a speech for radio.

During the course of the media event, the panda popped Harkness on the nose hard enough that she had to retire to her drawing room for a moment. Harkness told the press, "Su-Lin did scratch me up when I

Su-Lin and Mei-Mei meet at the Brookfield Zoo.

brought her back, but she was gentle and demure compared to this little hoyden. I'm a mass of bruises and scratches."

The reporters asked her how she could have succeeded twice where so many others had failed. "I'm part Indian," she told them, "one thirty-second American Indian." That bound her to the Chinese, and the people of the mountains, she explained. "That's why I can get pandas."

The group was soon whisked away in an open-air car, accompanied by a police escort, to the Brookfield Zoo. The newsreels covered every second of it, while two national radio broadcasts set up for the panda's arrival.

At Brookfield, Harkness shed her sophisticated ensemble, slipping into zoo-issue striped overalls and wool workman's jacket. Appearing with staff members before a rapt crowd of children, the little twenty-four-pound panda cub and the 126-pound Su-Lin were introduced. At first, Su-Lin ignored the new arrival, and Edward Bean, walking over to herd the big panda toward the smaller one held by Harkness, grumbled, "Look at your baby sister, you mutt." In closer proximity, Su-Lin batted at the little panda, and when keeper Sam Parratt intervened, he got a swat too. Harkness dabbed at his scratched face with a handkerchief.

Finally, the throng got what it was waiting for when Su-Lin delicately touched noses with the little panda in a moment captured on Universal Newsreel footage. Harkness, concerned about both pandas, could be seen on film smiling at them and saying, "Oh! Oh!" each time they made contact. Su-Lin, known to those who cared for him as such a gentle animal—even standing on hind legs to listen to Mary Bean's baby talk—once again proved himself.

By now Diana, who had been named after Quentin Young's wife, was being called Mei-Mei, or "little sister," a nickname that would eventually win out entirely.

Taking a suite at the Stevens Hotel, overlooking Lake Michigan, Harkness spent a few days in Chicago to settle the panda in and meet with officials. Zoo life seemed to agree with the littlest panda, and Harkness found him "in the pink of condition—seemingly happy and contented." Su-Lin was too. In light of his continuing good health, Brookfield decided to cancel a five-thousand-dollar life insurance policy it had out on him.

Mei-Mei's status was still a bit up in the air. Harkness owned him, and purchasing the animal who was thought to be another female would be up to the committee and board members from the zoo, which had not met yet.

It apparently was a foregone conclusion to Harkness. When she swept into New York on Saturday, booking herself into the Algonquin Hotel and toting a two-foot-tall stuffed panda toy that she described as "a grand bedfellow," she told *The New York Times* with certainty that the zoo would be sponsoring her next endeavor. The paper reported that "despite the natural obstacles of war, illness and economic reverses experienced by exploration in war-torn territory," the panda hunter was planning to return to the Tibetan border for a male by the middle of summer. She felt duty-bound to provide a breeding pair of the animals because she was concerned about preserving the species in captivity. After this trip, she revealed, she would not go after pandas anymore.

The loneliness of the last trip, and the behavior of zealous trappers desperate to yank these animals from the wild, was profoundly shaking Harkness's thoughts about her own future. She was no animal dealer, she told a reporter, and she would not persist in this work. If she was successful on this upcoming trek, she would put an end to her career in exploration, though not her life in China. She was vague about what exactly she would be doing, knowing only that she must return east, to the land she so loved.

In taking stock of her life, she realized there was something she had to face up to. Harkness had always been a two-fisted drinker, able to keep pace with the hollow-legged sophisticates of the day. After the endless nights of corn wine up-country and cocktail marathons in Shanghai, she had decided to dry out aboard the *Empress of Russia*. Now she was keeping company with her hard-drinking brother, Jim, in New York, while being pampered by the Algonquin staff. She had no book project to occupy her, and was still pursued by the demons that had haunted her in the mountains of the borderlands.

Booze was getting the best of her. Once, she invited Hazel Perkins from Connecticut for a visit, then went on an all-consuming bender for the entire stay. Perkie was no teetotaler, but Harkness had gone too far. That Tuesday, when the explorer came back to a sober, if throbbing, consciousness, her guest was gone, and she was repentant.

She asked for a chance to make up for her behavior, pledging to stop drinking again. "Jimmy and I went on the wagon and I haven't had a drink since," she wrote. "As a matter of fact I had been on most of the time since I left Shanghai with periods of falling off, but I'm on again now."

Her patient friend Perkie forgave her, returning to New York while Harkness had moved into an apartment for a very brief stay. As a host, Harkness toed the line, making up a clean bed, mixing her guest's favorite rye and ginger ale, and even serving duck—the simple things that blind drunk she had been unable to do. The two women could now indulge in a heart-to-heart, something Harkness was in need of.

She managed to hide the melancholy from a public that still couldn't get enough of her. In March she made famed Hollywood gossip columnist Hedda Hopper's column, along with Dolores Del Rio, Kitty Carlisle, and Ginger Rogers, when she was named one of America's best-dressed women by the Fashion Academy in Rockefeller Center.

The New York Times ran a splashy photo spread of her expedition in its "Rotogravure Picture Section" with the headline LONE WOMAN EXPLORER ON THE TRAIL OF THE PANDA, RAREST OF QUADRUPEDS. Alongside several exotic photos of Harkness in the field, a block of text chronicled her adventures "into a mountainous wilderness seldom penetrated by white men."

She gave lectures on her expeditions, one of the most memorable coming at the end of March when she shared the podium, before a crowd of four hundred, with Sinclair Lewis, the distinguished American novelist, for a book-and-author luncheon held at the Essex House by the American Booksellers Association. The next day, her book for children, *The Baby Giant Panda*, which would be praised by *The Washington Post* as "a touching yarn," was published.

HARKNESS WAS SKATING along in this rather undemanding life when, on Friday, April 1, news came that would send her staggering—Su-Lin was dead.

The illness appeared to have begun the previous Monday when the night watchman noted on his report that the panda, who normally had a robust appetite, refused to eat his 5:45 A.M. breakfast. Curator Robert Bean assessed the animal that morning and detected some slight frothing at his lips, and some reluctance or inability to open his mouth. Suspecting distemper, he called in two veterinarians. The first, Dr. Kuehn, examined Su-Lin thoroughly, including inspection of his mouth, ruling out distemper. The veterinarian was not alarmed, thinking that the foaming would subside by evening. Su-Lin was able to consume milk and cereal over the course of the day. But at nine that night his condition took a turn for the worse—more frothing, and his jaw had become rigid. The Beans—Edward, Robert, and Mary—and keeper George Speidel conducted their own physical. Mary Bean found a two-and-a-half-inch-long piece of twig lodged at the base Su-Lin's tongue, which was removed. It had not been there on earlier examinations, but a rumor would leak out later that the splinter of wood had done Su-Lin in. That evening through the next day, the panda continued to refuse food, taking only some milk and water. His health deteriorated to the point that on Wednesday he had to be fed through a tube. Distraught zoo officials vainly placed an oxygen tent around the gravely ill animal. On Friday the Beans, Sam Parratt—as one of Su-Lin's devoted keepers—and the zoo veterinarian were with the panda when he died at 1:17 P.M. "She was so sweet in her illness," Edward Bean would say of Su Lin, "that it was pitiful. Up to the last three hours it was impossible to impress the doctors that she was really so sick."

Across the country hundreds of thousands of Americans mourned the animal's death. Telegrams of condolence poured in to the zoo and to Chicago newspaper offices. The *Chicago Tribune* ran a previously unpublished color photograph of Su-Lin and sold framed copies for one dollar each. *Life* magazine called Su-Lin America's favorite animal, and the *Tribune* reported that he was the most photographed. As his popularity had been stunning—with about two million people coming to the zoo just to see the panda—so too was the grief over his death. But "of her countless mourners," *Life* noted, "none wept more bitterly than Mrs. Harkness." Reached with the news, Harkness burst into tears. "This is terrible," she cried. "I never expected anything like it to happen. She was the sweetest, best natured little animal I had ever seen." Heartbroken, Harkness said she "could not feel much worse if Su-Lin had been a child."

The Beans assured her that everything that could have been done for Su-Lin had been done.

A distinguished panel of pathologists from both the University of Chicago and Northwestern University was assembled. The cursory postmortem revealed nothing, so an edgy Edward Bean ordered Mei-Mei to be kept in a separate area until a close examination of Su-Lin's quarters could be completed. The body of the beloved panda was sent off to the Field Museum of Natural History where a team of medical experts, led by Dr. Wilfred H. Osgood, curator of zoology, and Robert Bean could perform a thorough check.

The necropsy revealed several things. The heart was "grossly perfectly normal." That meant that the altitude change had not harmed Su-Lin— good news to the zoo, which was keeping Mei-Mei and shopping for another panda. The lungs were a different story. Analyzed sections showed that Su-Lin had died of pneumonia.

The press was agitating for answers, but a tight-lipped Robert Bean said only, "We shall neither confirm nor deny the findings until the Chicago Zoological Society's physician can make a complete examination. Until that time no official of the park will speculate as to what caused Su-Lin's death." In fact, it would take more than a year for the discovery that Su-Lin was a male to come to light.

EVEN IN DEATH, the animal was valuable to naturalists, this time to those at the Field Museum. A taxidermist there made a death mask of the beloved panda, then, using glue, burlap, and plaster, took his hide to create a mounted figure in a glassed-in exhibit. The effect was one of incredible pathos as the beautiful bear's face was forever set in an expression of deep sadness, his posture upright but slumped like that of a person with the weight of the world on his shoulders.

In the meantime, the horrible news was now twisted for Harkness.

Word came from Chengdu that Smith had scored a remarkable triumph, collecting four giant pandas—three of them reported to be male cubs. Elizabeth Smith was telling the press that her husband planned to charter a plane to Hong Kong, bringing the animals west as quickly as possible. Papers everywhere carried the provocative bulletin, often combining it with stories about Su-Lin's death. *Time* magazine placed both items under the headline PANDAS GALORE. The *Chicago Tribune* said that "the bottom fell out of the baby giant panda market yesterday." And *The New York Times* reported on his "record catch," noting that Smith's were the only males believed to be in captivity.

It was welcome news in Chicago. "Oh boy—wonderful!" exclaimed Robert Bean. It made sense the zoo would want to acquire a male, since they thought they still had a female. A member of the Chicago Zoological Society's animal committee not only told the press that the zoo would be very interested in a purchase, he also implied that Mei-Mei might just get the boot. Francis E. Manierre mentioned that while Mei-Mei was on exhibition, the panda had not actually been purchased yet—the implication being that there was still time to drop Harkness and pick up Smith. He was accurate in his description of the panda's status. The zoo had, in fact, retained the right to refuse a female panda, since it was assumed at the time that Su-Lin was also a female. And the zoo had not yet laid out the cash for Harkness's next venture. But with Su-Lin dead, getting rid of Mei-Mei to buy a lone male would make no sense—one panda, male or female, could not reproduce. Besides, the zoo hadn't heard a thing from Smith himself.

Mei-Mei was proving to be quite an attraction even without Su-Lin. The first day the panda was exhibited, forty-two thousand people showed up—many lining up before opening time, several carrying stepladders in anticipation of the frenzy. A poll conducted in Chicago placed the panda's popularity equal to that of Chicago Cubs pitching ace Dizzy Dean. Not surprisingly, the zoo didn't go forward with the plan to throw Mei-Mei over for a Smith panda. The zoo's slight, public as it was, was only momentary, and it was clear it wanted a male in addition to Mei-Mei, not as a substitute.

Privately, Harkness was livid over the public disloyalty, telling friends that Brookfield had "turned cold on my contract with them after news of Ajax's captures." She had to have felt marginalized by the very people she had come through for.

Enough had transpired for Harkness to speak up about a few things. She was no scientist, she freely admitted, but she began to realize that her basic common sense, which had resulted in successful panda captures in the first place, might just be valuable in determining the way the animals were kept.

The zoo's insistence on feeding Mei-Mei cooked vegetables seemed preposterous to her. On previous occasions she had suggested that Su-Lin receive cornstalks and sugarcane to chew on. Now she became much more outspoken about the issue of a proper panda menu. "I realize that since I have turned Mei Mei over to the Chicago Zoological Society, I have no jurisdiction whatsoever in the matter of her diet or her care," Harkness wrote to Edward Bean. "Nevertheless, that does not prevent my feeling about her or my interest in her welfare.

"I am strongly convinced that she should have something—some hard substance—on which she could help to cut her teeth. In spite of what some doctors say, I should think that a million years of rough—and exceedingly rough—diet warrants continuance of same. In spite of the fact that doctors say that all vegetables should be cooked, I would like to put myself on record as disagreeing with them." The fact was, Harkness wrote, "the very nature of pandas is to eat hard, flinty substances (I speak from first-hand experience), and I don't think Mei Mei, for her own health and well-being, should be deprived of these." She was right, of course.

She also felt compelled to return to China, for Mei-Mei's sake. The zoo had at this point paid eighty-five hundred dollars toward her next expedition, prompting her to immediately plan "a third expedition to save Mei-Mei from loneliness."

At a luncheon lecture she gave before New York City's Town Hall Club in April, she revealed that perhaps Quentin Young would be available for the next campaign. She was playing her cards close to the vest, for she was already corresponding with Young, and within weeks he would be in the field on her behalf.

The Bronx Zoo, meanwhile, made headlines with news of its own baby giant panda. The animal, named Pandora, was purchased from hunters by Frank Dickinson, a professor at the West China Union University in Chengdu. After all the wrangling and bitterness between Harkness and the zoo over the price of Su-Lin, Dean Sage, who was a trustee at the New York Zoological Society, could now gloat over the fact that the panda they were getting would cost only three hundred dollars—even factoring in transportation costs. It was a bargain-basement price, and one that set Harkness's friends buzzing. Simultaneously, the zoo entered negotiations with Smith to purchase one of his animals.

Just then Quentin Young cabled Harkness with incredible news. Though there would be some confusion about it later, it appeared he had secured two pandas—one male and one female—and they were in Chengdu.

Harkness's plan for a leisurely trip via Europe, India, Burma, and Yunnan was scrapped. Now she needed wings, for she couldn't waste a moment. Her pandas were ready to go, and Smith still had not gotten a single panda out despite all the press reports. She would speed for China, taking planes the whole way. She would fly from New York to San Francisco, board a trans-Pacific Clipper to Manila, then continue on to Hong Kong and Chengdu.

Once aboard the ultramodern Pan Am Flying Clipper, high above the Pacific, she jotted a note to her friends. Even her spirits seemed to be taking flight. "Be good—you angels," she wrote with the utter contentment that only the journey to the East could bring.

CHAPTER FOURTEEN

THE BACK OF BEYOND

IT WAS EARLY JUNE. Chengdu, though warm and humid, had not entered the worst of its summer heat. From behind the great walls of what had been until recently Cavaliere's estate, the air was filled with birdsong and "the music of the wind in the bamboos." On the open terrace of one of the grand but crumbling pavilions, Ruth Harkness, still in pajamas at lunchtime, sat comfortably, sipping hot tea, as she composed her thoughts before a typewriter. A tame goose paraded around the lush, green grounds importantly, while miracle of miracles, a mischievous young panda, her belly taut from a recent feeding, was casually sprawled nearby.

Harkness was like a satisfied cat luxuriating in a pool of sunlight. Once again immersed in the East, she felt good and strong and sure of herself. Though Quentin Young had left early the previous morning to go up-country, they had just spent several days together.

She could take a sip of that good pale tea, then sit back, listening to the cadences of Chinese life buzzing in the busy city around her. "Outside the high walls are the never ending street cries," she typed, "rickshaw bells, crying babies, street hawkers, calls and creaking wheel bar-rows." From the theater across the street came occasional bursts from cymbals and drums. She was back in the ancient frontier city, savoring the world that she loved so much and craved so terribly when away from it. She reveled in "a certain peace" in this place of delicate Asian charm.

China was still in great turmoil, though the worst of it hadn't reached this far west. The generalissimo had just taken the drastic step of blow-ing up the dikes of the Yellow River near the railroad junction at Cheng-chow in north-central China. The flooding did stall the Japanese, but at a huge cost, destroying four thousand villages, displacing two million people, and killing untold numbers of peasants.

Harkness had arrived at the beginning of June. Quentin Young—whom she had not seen or spoken directly to in months—was waiting. He had promised her in a cable that he had a male and a female panda, and though the story was confused in various reports, it appears the lit-tle male died in an accident.

There was a mountain for the two to hash out between them now that they were reunited, and experiencing an extended privacy for the first time since their romantic interlude in the fall of 1936. So much had changed, yet here they were with each other again.

They made a comfortable camp of one of the old buildings at Cava-liere's, living more outside than in, eating wonderful meals that Wang cooked for them on a rear balcony. Together they cared for a baby panda. All of it reminiscent of the life they had shared in the wilds two years before.

Now that Cavaliere was gone—apparently back to Italy as the drum-beats of political upheaval grew louder—there was a new administrator in residence. He was the "high and mighty officialdom type," Harkness said, granting them only squatter's rights. It was better than staying with the missionaries, Harkness thought, so they denned in the abandoned buildings.

The emotions that had swept over Harkness in the first expedition had either changed or matured. They were just as deep, but now she seemed fond of Young without the urgency of lust or love. Her letters home during this time carried a strong, centered tone—serene with a sensual trace of world-weariness. Harkness wasn't past her prime; she was settling into it. She certainly had not finished with romance. What she wanted, she told her friend Anne Pierce, was "the sort of companionship that every normal woman craves. I think what I really want more than anything else just now is to fall deeply in love and be married." That companionship would not be with Quentin Young. It wasn't the difference in their races that would stop her—she had never played by society's rules. But she did possess a code of personal integrity that would have made it unlikely for her to carry on an affair with the handsome hunter. As a widow in the wilds of Tibet two years ago, she might have eagerly bedded a college boy who was tied to a youthful school courtship. A married man was another story.

Bill had been her one true love. He would figure in her thoughts, dreams, and writing for the rest of her life. When Harkness had slipped her wedding band into Young's hand that night in Chengdu, perhaps she had simply hoped to pass along a little of the amazing happiness she had experienced.

Quentin Young's heart was another story. Whether it was their accommodation, his emotions, the fact that he had betrayed Diana Chen with this woman, or some craving in his own life, his feelings for Harkness remained impassioned and confused. Years later, he would speak about her with a jealous intensity. He still bristled when recounting an incident in which Harkness visited his parents with a male companion. He would never speak of her with emotional distance.

When word came through that there might be another panda available from the hunters up in the mountains, Young began to indulge in the oscillating tender-then-remote routine that had by now become familiar. After days shared so closely with the spirited American widow, he rose in darkness, leaving before the sun came up, while she remained in the pavilion with Wang and the panda, who by now had been named Mei-Ling, in honor of Madame Chiang Kai-shek.

Harkness had originally intended to stay in Chengdu only long enough to gather up the pair of pandas Young had secured. She thought

Over their
two previous
expeditions,
Ruth Harkness
and Wang Whai
Hsin had
become quite
comfortable
caring for young
pandas.

COURTESY
MARY LOBISCO

she would be on her way home within a week or two. Now she would remain in the city at least until Young's return.

In the meantime, she was never bored. There were still enough foreigners around for her to socialize from time to time. She attended a dinner party where she met Alexandra David-Neel, the stout French matron celebrated for her daring studies of the forbidden inner reaches of Tibet. She was there with her equally famous adopted Tibetan son. But Harkness did not care for the woman who had once dyed her hair and darkened her face to enter Tibet disguised as a beggar. "Did she rub my fur the wrong way!" Harkness wrote home.

What occupied the bulk of her time was, of course, the panda. At fifty pounds, she was already an animal of the wilderness, a big girl, not a baby anymore. When Harkness would pick her up in play, the formidable little panda might, without warning, suddenly fight to be left alone. "Everything I owned was in ribbons," Harkness said, "including the skin on my hands and arms."

It sliced up her emotions too, for she sensed that Mei-Ling had experienced some terrible trauma during capture. "This baby will always remember that she was hunted and will never I believe quite trust people." She was a pistol, always "casting a tentative eye about," Harkness said, "to see what she can get into." What she got into, generally, was a walnut tree in the courtyard. The panda would shinny high up into the branches, leaving a nervous Harkness to pace down below, a cigarette her only comfort.

"The vixen," Harkness wrote, was always "raising hell." "No matter where I put her she can manage to get out, and usually can succeed in half choking herself about it. She is a darling, but not the sweet gentle little lady that Su Lin, or Mei Mei was." The robust animal also loved to spend the day in the upper branches of a small pear tree. Unable to tempt her down to the ground, Harkness, the ever-indulgent panda mother, would inch up the trunk to deliver food. "I dam [sic] near break my neck taking her lunches up to her," she reported. Sometimes as night fell, the panda wouldn't budge. Then Harkness would once again hoist herself up along the limbs to lug the animal down to safety. The effort whipped her, as well as her wardrobe. "My trousers are about to drop off of just plain exhaustion," she said.

On rainy days, the "little hellion" was kept indoors on a leash, which would only get her more ginned up. Then Harkness would capitulate and let her out. "I wish you could see the baby now," she wrote home once. "Perfectly happy in the drizzling rain, sound asleep in the top of her pear tree; one hand limply hanging on to a branch and two silly little black legs just hanging in space."

Strolling around the grounds of the estate, Harkness could feel the passage of time. The lovely moon doors, ornate gateways, and rock gardens still held fast their accustomed grace, yet everything was so changed without Cavaliere. The houses, shaded by overgrown walnut trees, pomegranate shrubs, palms, and bamboo, were falling into decay and at times seemed sinister. It felt as though the very life of the pavilion had been siphoned out through the front gates as the doors had closed behind Kay for the last time. The atmosphere that had risen up in the old Italian's absence was strange and warring, with a dark spookiness that lingered in the nighttime shadows.

Harkness and Young became convinced the place was haunted by the ghost of a dead army general who had been buried there without his head. They were told that he roamed the gardens, walking the camel-backed bridges within these walls searching for it. None of the talk was quite enough to unnerve Harkness, who happily chose the chamber rumored to be the ghost's "nocturnal headquarters" as her own bedroom.

THIS EXPEDITION was presumed to be one of reckoning. With yards of newsprint dedicated to their feud, and months of acrimony having raged between them, Harkness and Ajax met face-to-face one day in Chengdu.

It was no showdown. Direct confrontation was not Smith's style, and Harkness, as usual, took the high road. Neither was in a fighting mood—she was feeling the full measure of herself; he was finally within striking distance of getting what he wanted. American newspapers had been reporting for months that Smith was on the verge of heading out of China with several pandas, but in reality, the goal was continually inching away from him. Without much luck, he was just then in the midst of trying desperately to charter a Douglas airplane.

As soon as Harkness encountered the old collector, she saw how bad off he was. He was so broken down and pathetic, so near the grave, she was tempted to pity him. Suffering from tuberculosis, he confided in her that he was headed for the hospital to have a lung collapsed, a common therapy in which the diseased organ was shut down and given a chance to heal. But to Harkness, even with her hair-trigger compassion, his condition couldn't mitigate what he had been up to professionally. "I can't feel sorry for him," she said with some certainty. What he was doing to pandas, the way he treated his captives, was "a disgrace to humanity. And so is he."

Pandas were dying in the gold-rush-like fever that capturing them had become. A legion of hunters using guns, snares, and vicious dogs were unleashed on the once-tranquil hills. "It's just a crime what that man has done," Harkness wrote. "He sent agents to the mountains telling the natives that he wanted 20 pandas and they have gone haywire."

Inevitably pandas meant to be captured alive were killed in the process. Some died on the way to Chengdu. Once delivered to Smith, who was working out of a compound in the city, even more succumbed in captivity. "He is simply collecting wholesale and letting them die," she reported. She heard that on this trip alone six big pandas that had been delivered to him had died. "He keeps them in tiny dirty cages in hot sunshine; no shade, no freedom. Naturally they die."

Smith's response to the high mortality rate was to intensify the hunting in order to constantly replenish his stock. He had such a reputation for losing pandas that when *The China Journal* reported that he had a shipment of five pandas due in London, it cautioned, "if they survived."

It wasn't just Smith behaving this way. The missionary-zoo connection was in high gear. As the Bronx Zoo learned, it was much cheaper to send money to a missionary who could hire hunters to capture a panda than to launch an expedition of its own. It didn't matter that no one was on the scene to ensure ethical or moderate behavior. There were several men who could carry this out, but best known among them was Dr. David Crockett Graham at the West China Union University. Graham never killed a panda himself, but he would finish up his animal-export career having provided fifteen giant-panda hides and skeletons and four live pandas to the United States over thirteen years.

Young had told Harkness that his impression from being up-country was that two valleys northwest of Chengdu seemed to have been hunted clean of giant pandas. *The China Journal* would report a few months later, based on accounts from travelers including Harkness, that the panda-hunting situation was dire. "Other reports indicate that many pandas, old and young, brought alive to Cheng-tu by native hunters, have died there before they could be shipped out of the country; while many more skins of dead ones have been offered for sale in this city, showing that an intensive hunting of giant pandas is going on. A rare and not too plentiful animal at best, the giant panda can not long survive such persecution." Sowerby said steps needed to be taken to protect the panda from what he called "wholesale commercial exploitation." "The collecting and exporting of so many of these rare animals from China can hardly be justified on scientific grounds," Sowerby continued, "especially when it is taken into consideration the number that have already died since being captured. We, therefore, appeal to the Chinese Government to intervene to save the giant panda from extermination before it is too late." By April 1939, the government would, in fact, place a partial ban on panda hunting.

Harkness, disgusted by what was happening, had to have been considering her own role in the mess. In the middle of it all, she faced a separate controversy. The mercurial Madame Chiang Kai-shek had gotten wind of Harkness's naming a panda after her and was feeling miffed instead of honored. "I hadn't been here a week, before a rumor came to me that Madame was much offended," Harkness wrote. "A missionary here whom she knows received a long letter from her secretary on the subject, and asked him to communicate with me, which he did. I swear, Anne, I didn't know whether to laugh or cry or have hysterics." What she did was rechristen Mei-Ling as O Lin. Within days, though, she changed her name once more to the more appropriate Su-Sen, or "little tomboy."

Rather than roll her eyes over the whole affair, though, Harkness felt sorry about the culture clash. "I can understand how she would feel," Harkness reasoned, "just another crazy American, capitalizing on something from China; and China is so hurt. Her people are being butchered by the thousands and America doesn't even stop war supplies to Japan— the America that has professed such undying friendship for China."

The United States was, in fact, continuing to sell scrap to Japan, dragging its feet on any trade embargoes and basically standing by as the tiny island nation ripped through China. Yet it was clear that American sympathies, from top to bottom, were with China. Generalissimo and Madame Chiang Kai-shek had landed the coveted *Time* magazine cover as "Man and Wife of the Year" for 1937. Polls reflected that only 2 percent of the population was pro-Japan. And church groups, fired up by their missionaries and lay organizations, tried to bring aid to the suffering country. Ultimately, though, the only measure that would help the Chinese would have been American military involvement, which was not forthcoming.

The Nationalist government in China wasn't doing much to help itself either. Chiang believed that no matter what devastation the Japanese inflicted, his great country could endure it—at least until the Western allies charged in to save them. And so he waited. It was a notion he clung to despite the continued pattern of Western lip service and impotence.

In Chengdu, there was a new development. Young was back, with a magnificent, one-hundred-pound male giant panda in tow. To Harkness, the animal was as sweet as Rex—a harlequin Great Dane from home.

Su-Sen, on the other hand, continued to rampage around the walled compound. Wrestling her down from dangerous perches was frequently a two-person job, from which Young and Harkness would emerge skinned, bruised, or missing a hank of hair. One day, high in a tree, Su-Sen stepped on a branch that couldn't hold her. At the first sound of the cracking limb, Young leaped into action. "Quentin made one of the quickest moves I've ever seen and caught her as she fell," Harkness reported. With him on an expedition, everything was taken care of.

In the evenings, the two would sit together in the warm summer darkness "making and unmaking plans getting no nearer to anything."

As for the practical matter of how Harkness would get out of the country with two pandas, she wasn't sure. China was torn apart, with bridges and roads bombed out or intentionally flooded. Japan controlled most ports, railroads, and cities. Waves of fleeing refugees packed railway cars and thoroughfares. Air travel had become so difficult that even powerful men like Stilwell couldn't get a plane ticket. Seats had to be booked a month in advance, and even then nothing was certain.

It was driving Ajax to distraction. Here he finally had his pandas, but he couldn't get his hands on a plane. Worse, the Chinese government was making noises about allowing him to leave with only two of the animals. Harkness wondered if she had stirred up government scrutiny herself with the Mei-Ling misstep.

She and Young decided that with the big male they should try to go downriver as far as Hankou and catch a train from there. But then they realized they wouldn't be able to stake out enough space for a full-grown giant panda. With all the chaos of war, the trains would be jammed tight with refugees.

In the purgatory of the pavilion, unable to establish a good plan, disturbed by Smith's antics, and perhaps experiencing some emotional strain with Quentin Young, Ruth Harkness had a lot to think over.

The uncertainty would come to a shattering end on one of the last nights in June. That evening there was a mild, misting rain coming down as Harkness left for a dinner party. The affair was pleasant enough, though a fierce storm had begun to kick up as everyone sat socializing. By the time Harkness headed back home, the rain was falling in stinging sheets, which ricocheted up from the dark streets. Here at the outskirts of the great Sichuan plain, thunder cracked, and the black skies were split by a chain of lightning strikes. Despite the tempest, the streets of Chengdu were still crowded with people, and a soaking-wet Harkness pressed her way through them to the gates of Cavaliere's old place. Entering, Harkness felt a chill. In the flashes of searing light, the pavilions and grounds seemed positively ghostly. The thrashing palm trees and bamboos played tricks on the eyes, and darkness obliterated familiar scenes in the garden. "There seemed to be something evil about it," Harkness wrote.

She was caught up short then by the frightening vision of a drenched and distraught Quentin Young emerging from the shadows, revolver in hand.

By the thin beam of flashlight and a flickering candle, Young quickly laid out the nightmare that was unfolding. The big male panda was going berserk, making splinters of both cages that had been built to hold him, lunging and lashing at anything within his reach. Possessing a powerful bite and raking claws that could kill a man, the dangerous animal and the innocent people on the streets outside were separated by nothing but one thin rope and the stone walls, which could easily be scaled. Within minutes, he would be loose. Young insisted on a horrifying solution—the panda had to be shot.

The torrential rain drowned their candle flame, and by the weak light of the remaining flashlight, they approached the panicked animal. "We made no sacrifice to the gods of the mountains for this panda," Young said to Harkness, with some bitterness. He raised the pistol.

The sound of the three shots was lost in the ear-splitting crashes of thunder. In the quick flares of lightning, a young black-and-white bear lay crumpled, his blood seeping into the wet earth. Harkness stood sobbing in the pouring rain.

If there really were ghosts, an echo of the great crying voice of Caruso must have rung out this night from the sorrowful garden. Such a broken world. "You must not feel too badly," Young said to her as the rain continued to pummel them. "In this life all these things are fixed."

"I shall never forget the look on Quentin's face as he did it," Harkness wrote home. "As we did it," she corrected herself. It would be the last, terrible thing they would share. Claiming illness, Quentin Young abruptly left for Hong Kong.

They would never be together again.

HARKNESS'S FAVORITE PSYCHIC in New York City, consulted just before her departure, had warned that things would not unfold as expected. Her chances of success on this trip, the clairvoyant warned, were only "60–40." She also foretold that the answer to the question on this trip would be a question.

And here it was. If the American explorer solved all the logistical puzzles about how to get a panda out of a war-ravaged country, she would still be left asking this: What was it all for?

Just days earlier, *The Washington Post* had written of her exploits, crediting her with "making the world panda conscious." If that was what it was for—so that people could learn about these incredible animals and care about protecting them—then it was all worthwhile. But it seemed to Harkness that it was becoming a profane circus without concern for the welfare of the animals. She saw pandas pulled from every corner of Wassu-land. And while the Bronx was exultant over its inexpensive panda, it and other zoos were just helping to cheapen the lives of these animals. Pandas were dying in untold numbers—during zealous hunts up-country, in inhumane cages in Chengdu, and even in caring surroundings like that of the Brookfield Zoo.

Harkness's intent was to bring mated pairs of pandas over to increase their numbers, to ensure their futures. But from what she could see, all the swashbuckling, including her own, was having the opposite effect. The disenchantment wasn't new—she had already begun mulling this over on her last trip—but now there was clarity. Dispirited, she wrote, "Somehow, I think this sort of thing is over for me."

There wasn't much she could do to save the world from itself, but she could right her own path.

While watching over the independent-minded Su-Sen as the animal conquered every tree and hazard in the estate, Harkness recognized a kindred spirit—a tough little wild thing, willing to stand up to anyone but hemmed in by walls and restrictions she didn't understand. The comparison was easy. "She too gets herself in the damndest situations," Harkness wrote. "She is utterly fearless—nonchalant and doesn't give a damn about anything."

The animal, she knew, would never be happy in captivity.

Word came to Chengdu just then that the Chinese government was clamping down on panda exports, requiring stringent permissions from the Ministry of Education.

Harkness was not worried. In fact, she felt relieved. First, she hoped that it meant the government was becoming serious about protecting pandas. But more than that, the change was to her a lodestar. A bright, buzzing neon sign that lighted the way toward a direction she had already decided to aim for. This trip wasn't about a reckoning, after all. It was about redemption.

With deep conviction, Harkness saw that the liberty of this wild animal outweighed any of the morally bankrupt reasons to haul her away. More headlines? Another best-dressed list? That wasn't glory. "Publicity," Harkness would write, "if people only realized what a very empty thing that is."

She was experiencing an epiphany as strong as the one that had led her to bring a baby bottle on her first trip. She had one big campaign left in her. She would go back to the magnificent Qionglai Shan, back to the mountains of the immortals, and return Su-Sen. If people had thought her mad for attempting her very first expedition, this time they would be certain of it.

Harkness was making one of the most important journeys of her life. She was on her own, doing something that brought no prestige, and— scratched, bitten, and hissed at—not even gratitude from the recipient.

With bundles of incense and candles and paper money to match the size of her desire, Harkness lighted a bonfire to the mountain gods. Basking in the lighted glow of the flames, breathing in the pungent smoke, she prayed for Su-Sen's protection.

On the Fourth of July, in preparation for the upcoming journey, Harkness sent Wang out to cash her traveler's checks. There were torrential downpours again that day, and the American sat inside the summer pavilion watching Su-Sen, who refused to leave her high perch in one of the trees. Hours went by. The continuous bursts of fireworks exploding at the neighboring residence kept Harkness on edge.

Finally, "Wang came wandering thru the dripping bamboo toward dark," Harkness wrote, "very drunk." He had spent the day right next door enjoying the fireworks, which were not to celebrate American independence, but to drive away the evil spirits that had infested a local woman. With the liquor, the cook had become tearfully sentimental. He had returned as always, making it clear they would reach the mountains together after all.

There was little to scrape together in the way of gear. About all that was left of the old supplies in Chengdu was "one lonely tin" of corned-beef hash.

Within days, Harkness and Wang set off with their hired porters. Since they were in the thick of the wet season, they should have faced long days of pouring rain and splashing mud. But they had good fortune with the weather, enjoying a few stretches of warm sunshine, followed by cool, dry nights.

The long, flat road out of Chengdu, the gates of Guanxian, the little towns and villages, were all so familiar. Harkness knew the way, knew how to keep up a good pace, and could march in a rhythm that would propel her for hours. She was well acquainted with the smoky and dirty inns where she settled after sundown, and she enjoyed the simple peasant food that was offered.

She was an old hand now. On her first expedition she felt certain that she couldn't have managed the porters without Quentin Young. But by this time she knew the ropes and had no trouble at all with the poor coolies. The places, the people, the sensations, were well known to her. But she was on a mission, not stopping to dally with old friends. In no time, Harkness's team had made it to the main trail deep in the Min Valley, where they would await new coolies who could trek into the mountains.

Summer was the easiest time of year for pandas, the season of plenty when an abundance of juicy bamboo leaves filled them up, granting more time for rest. It would be a perfect time for a young panda's return. The mountains were alive too with birches in leaf, fir, and wild cherry. The expedition made its way up and around rushing streams, waterfalls, and breathtaking ravines. The ascent was beautiful yet punishing.

Harkness and Wang had to claw their way along the slick, perpendicular slopes. There was, at one point, eight full hours of straight-up climbing on trails that were only a foot wide at best. Harkness found that the native grass sandals were better than boots but still not reliably secure: "One slip and you'd land either in a tree, a waterfall, or at the bottom of a cliff," she wrote. She was back in the grand-but-deadly terrain that other explorers had written of with awe. She kept going, heaving herself upward, getting tangled in vines, slipping in the mud, and fighting the thick bamboo. By the tenth of July, at an altitude of about nine thousand feet, she had reached the area from which she believed the panda had been captured. She had gone to great lengths to determine the exact spot Su-Sen hailed from, which, given panda notions of home range and dispersal, might make the difference between life and death to a newly released animal.

Arriving "at the back of beyond," as Harkness put it, the team threw all the cargo down on a precariously staked-out ten-by-four-foot ledge, the only flat ground to be found in this vertical realm. The campsite was just big enough to set up a small pup tent. With the porters departing, it would be only Harkness and Wang clinging to this little space, shrouded in low-hanging clouds and now awash in the torrents of rain that had been expected all along, until the men returned for them. Right above them was a cave; below, if they dared peer over the edge of their rock balcony, they would see a dizzying drop of hundreds of feet to a waterfall underneath.

Only with great effort could Wang keep a fire burning around the clock in the pouring rain. Their entire stay would be one long torrential downpour, with streams running off the mountain and through the middle of their tiny camp. Everything stayed soaked. "My one quilt is so wet it could be almost wrung out," Harkness wrote. "And it is full of fleas—all my clothing is clammy and my feet are never dry." In addition, Harkness wasn't well. She thought it was due to eating unrefrigerated food in the summer heat of the plains on the way to the mountains. She had lost her sense of smell, and her digestive tract was in an uproar. Some mornings they were reduced to eating fried cucumbers and coagulated chicken blood for breakfast.

But that of course wasn't her main worry. It was Su-Sen who occupied her mind. Harkness had no idea what would happen when she released the panda. She might stay right in the trees nearby, as she had done for the past month in Cavaliere's old garden. She might not go at all. Inexperienced, she could skitter off a cliff or slip into a deep gorge.

Nevertheless, Harkness did not delay the big moment. Unable to deprive the panda another second of freedom, she immediately set her loose. Su-Sen didn't hesitate either. The instant she was released, she took her emancipation in galloping strides. This was not the landscaped garden in Chengdu; this was her home. She plunged back into it with abandon, her furry black hindquarters visible for just moments as the green world swayed and closed around her. "She wandered off without a backward glance," Harkness would recall with a bittersweet pride. As the curtain of vegetation shut tight behind Su-Sen, Harkness hoped that she would become "once more the gay-hearted comrade of all the lusty mountain gods."

It was a rare moment—watching such a wild spirit untethered, set free. But the real test wasn't whether Su-Sen would go away, it was whether she would stay away. In the miserable rain, Harkness was determined to sit vigil. "There we lived in a cave for a week," she would recall, "to see if she would come back for the food to which we had accustomed her."

She watched for the beloved Su-Sen constantly, and hoped she would never see her again.

Each evening, in the dark, cold wetness, she and Wang made their offerings to the gods. Incense and candles were lighted, and piles of sacrificial money burned. The tiny camp would be bathed in the bright warm light of the flames as the stacks of bills ignited. Harkness believed her prayers lifted skyward with the smoke of the paper money and the fragrant incense. She had protected the panda in the dangerous world of man; now she wanted the gods to take over in the natural one.

She would close her eyes, curled up in her wet quilt, and picture the little animal alone in the forest. She would wake in the still of the night to listen for her. But the sounds of a frightened panda never came.

Day after day of pouring rain nearly washed them right off the map. In her misery, she sought help from an old friend, one of the few left in the country—booze. Over dinner one night she commandeered Wang's supply of native wine, downing enough of it to make herself sick. She had to rush from their living area to throw up her dinner. Stumbling back into camp, she collapsed into a deep sleep until a torrent of icy water on her face woke her at midnight. The mountainside had shifted, redirecting a fast-running stream that spilled all over the camp ledge, spoiling food, swamping Wang's bed, carrying off loose items, and drowning the fire. There wasn't an inch of space free of the runnel. The two campers, in danger of being carried off too, had to search out footholds in the pitch black, battling their way up the sheer slope against the surprisingly strong current. Harkness thought she'd never make it, but she and Wang—and her quilt—reached the cave just above.

As they stood shivering in the night, Wang began to curse their miserable condition, "swearing a blue streak in Chinese," Harkness said. The jolly cook was a man transformed in the storm—screaming, yelling, and jumping up and down, while balancing his little cotton umbrella over his head. Harkness watched his performance and then couldn't help herself. She started to laugh. She was probably near hysteria, but whatever the reason, it infuriated Wang. He ratcheted up his tirade, even cursing Harkness, blaming her for all that had befallen them.

Stunned, she did something equally uncharacteristic, something she would regret all her life. She slapped him across the face. She hadn't been standing close enough to him, she said, for it to carry much of a wallop, but the disrespect was deep.

Given the circumstances, she realized it was dangerous too. If he'd been angry enough, he could have simply pitched her over the cliff, she wrote later. Instead, he turned his back on her, seeking out a corner of the cave to silently stew in. Harkness wrapped herself in her sodden quilt and sat on a rock. The two friends spent the miserable remaining hours of the night in silence.

In the morning, Harkness said, "Wang still had his mad on." She apologized to him, but it did no good. He was grim anyway over the fact that the team of porters, which included his son, had not shown up when they were due. The rain had made the mountains so treacherous that he worried some disaster had befallen Dze Wha. He was determined to set off in search of his son; Harkness was aghast. She did not want to be left alone waiting on the mountain, not knowing if anyone would return. It took some effort, but she persuaded Wang to sit tight.

With that settled, she trudged back into the cave, out of the rain, to sit by the fire. Watching the flames, she was lost in thought when she heard a noise outside. Looking up, she saw the upside-down, black-and-white face of Su-Sen, who was clinging to the bushy slope above the cave's mouth. Harkness thought a thousand things at once—she was happy to see the animal but crushed she had come back. She was also horrified by the sudden prospect of now having to spend months here, acclimating the panda to the wild.

In the instant Harkness's mind was reeling, however, so was the panda's. Whatever had driven her here, it wasn't a desire to be comforted. Upon seeing her old captors, the panda, Harkness said, "ran as fast as her short little legs could carry her back to her own safe bamboo jungles." She kept running too, "as though all the demons of hell were at her heels." Su-Sen was a wild creature once more.

Less than an hour later, Wang's son and all the porters fell into camp. With fresh supplies, and plenty of backs to haul gear, they could put the expedition into reverse. And down they all came.

As tough as the trip up was, the descent was even worse. It was unlike anything Harkness had ever experienced before. The treacherous journey, nearly straight down, brought them over moss, mud, and stones, all slick from the downpour. Since a stumble could launch a skidding, frantic traveler into oblivion, Harkness negotiated much of it on the seat of her pants. With miles to go, she could only inch along. Streams were so swollen that the dreaded old log bridges were submerged or gone and, as it turned out, sorely missed, for she often had to walk through icy rushing water that was thigh-deep. She desperately worked to stay upright through the torrents that could make legs go numb, steadying herself as best she could with a walking stick.

The long days and nights of driving rain had scrubbed clean all traces of the familiar. Old trails—ghostlike at best before—had now been washed out completely, and with no footsteps to follow in, she would have to forge the path home herself.

Of course, it was fitting.

In this, her holiest hour, the circle of yin and yang was closing. Her career as a panda hunter, which had pulled in opposite directions, would end as it had begun. Once again, Ruth Harkness would make her own way. She would choose her own course of action, and she would hew to it. It was not easy, but it was right.

SONG OF THE SOUL

I N THE FALL OF 2002, a small band of travelers—Ruth Harkness's niece Mary Lobisco, Mary's daughter Nicole, Hazel Perkins's granddaughter Robin Perkins Ugurlu, Jack and Su-Lin Young's daughter Jialing "Jolly" Young, and I—retraced Ruth Harkness's steps from Hong Kong to Shanghai, down the Yangtze, toward the still-wild Tibetan border. We hoped to rediscover as much of the explorer's world as possible, and to help one of our members complete a mission.

Among Mary's possessions as we headed deep into the Chinese interior was a small container of ashes and soil that had been exhumed from her aunt's grave site in Titusville. She planned to return them to the land where Harkness had experienced her greatest joy.

Sixty-six years is a long time—time enough for a trail to grow cold, particularly in China, where war has ravaged the land, and a zealously repressive Cultural Revolution attempted to sweep the country clean of all vestiges of Chinese culture, everything from books to temples. It was unlikely, I was warned by every expert I consulted, that anything would be left of these sites as Harkness knew them.

We were very happily surprised. We visited the beach at Repulse Bay in Hong Kong where Harkness had enjoyed a refreshing swim with her ship's captain in the summer of 1936; we walked the creaking halls and skimmed a hand along the polished mahogany banisters of the Palace Hotel in Shanghai; we listened to a jazz band, made up of elderly musicians who had played in the 1930s and '40s, at the old bar at the Cathay (now the Peace Hotel) on the well-preserved Bund. And we were dwarfed by the great soaring cliffs of the famous and famously doomed Three Gorges of the Yangtze, just before they were forever altered by a giant dam.

In Chengdu, we visited the lush, green campus of the West China Union University, now the West China University of Medical Sciences, and we took pictures of the only remnant of the city's once massive and protective wall. In the bar of the ultramodern Sheraton Chengdu Lido Hotel, as we sat munching peanuts and drinking Tsingtao beer, our guide, Steven Chen, talked to us about where we wanted to go next—Old Wenchuan certainly was not a typical destination for tourists. That might be troublesome, yes, but we figured that it actually boded well for our mission. The more the place had been left alone, the better. Outside Chengdu, where the border between China and Tibet constantly tacks back on itself, there are, in fact, villages tucked away in the shade of the great mountains that have been forgotten by time.

In a caravan of three Jeeps, we drove northwest along the big, smooth Chengdu-Guanxian Expressway, covering in less than an hour the distance that took the Harkness expedition two days by foot. We were headed for the Qionglai Shan, the mountains of Ruth Harkness's great adventure, the place she called "that lost triangle of the world."

Following the curves of the mighty boulder-strewn Min River, we eventually found our way to the old stone village of Wenchuan, which had, in the intervening years, been eclipsed by a second, more modern city nearby with the same name. We entered what was left of the old perimeter walls, walking down the streets that Harkness had traveled so many years before. Some tall concrete towers were wedged in between older buildings now, and telephone poles jutted from the wet pavement.

But still remaining were the warm, handsome old stone houses with tiled roofs and massive, yellow-painted double doors. The street was as alive as ever with industrious people cleaning, shopping, and trading news. The magic lived on in this mountain village.

We made our way down twisting lanes and back in time to a stone courtyard piled high with baskets and wood and bushy brown animal pelts and bones, and then to a fence separating it from another courtyard. Through its slats, we could see the curly-tipped tiled roof and open loft of what looked like Harkness's "ruined Buddhist Ghost Temple." Scattering dozens of brown chickens in wide arcs around our steps, we approached, holding up Harkness's photo against the great building. It was a perfect match: the magnificent black-tiled roof, the sturdy round pillars, the carving in the wood that separated the two floors.

This was where, sixty-six years before, a makeshift curtain was set up in the second story for a road-weary Harkness to take a sponge bath. This was the place in which she slipped out of expedition clothes, then into a beautiful padded silk dressing gown for a little touch of well-earned luxury. Where she gratefully sipped hot tea after a long day of marching, and where she and Quentin Young had christened each other "Colonel" and "Commander."

It was hard to leave, but we finally tore ourselves away, with the most sacred part of our mission still ahead of us.

THERE WAS NO question that Ruth Harkness would have wanted to be buried in China. Bill was there, of course, and the last nine years of her young life were testimony to the fact that away from her beloved Asia, she could not be happy.

After releasing Su-Sen in July 1938, she took up residence at the Palace Hotel in Shanghai once again, contemplating her life. She knew that as long as she stayed in the East, there was a chance of contentment. Yet her choices were being narrowed by world events and her own finances. Within months, all of eastern China would be firmly in the hands of the Japanese—ports, railroads, and big cities included. The whole world now, not just Shanghai, was changing, jerked along in a tor-rent of violence.

Harkness watched as waves of desperate Jewish refugees poured in from Germany. She entered the hospital, probably to have an ovary re-moved. Then with nothing to do and nowhere to go, she slipped into a "degenerate frame of mind." Toying with the idea of setting up a home in Shanghai, she had lunch with *New Yorker* writer Emily Hahn and her little gibbon, Mr. Mills, to discuss sharing an apartment. She had an in-tense affair with Fredi Guthmann, a mysterious Jewish gem merchant from Argentina with "a face like Christ" and the soul of a poet. But noth-ing worked out. "I've simply got to find myself again," she wrote.

Harkness headed for India, not really knowing why.

Darjeeling, in northeast India, was the lush, green summer retreat of the British at the foothills of the 28,000-foot Kanchenjunga, or "great five-peaked fortress of snow," the third-highest mountain in the world. A place of mist-shrouded tea plantations, it soothed Harkness's troubled soul.

"It is beautiful here—I wish you could have some of it," she wrote home. From this safe distance, she could sit in the sunshine and watch the plumes of snow shooting high in the air from avalanches that crashed down the mountains. "For the first time in the last four years I believe I am approaching the state of being a normal human being," she wrote. In her hotel room, Harkness nestled by the coal grate or some-times sat outside in the sunshine, sipping hot tea and reading *Gone with the Wind*. Forgoing both meat and cocktails, she had begun to feel "mar-vellously well."

Restless by the middle of December, she hired porters and a pony, starting off on what she called "a ramble," during which she would stay in "dak bungalows," Hindi terminology for traveler's rest houses, set along well-worn post roads. Carrying her own food and bedding and sup-plying her own servants, she stayed at a few of these furnished cabins. She followed the Lhasa trade route toward Natu La, the 14,200-foot pass on the border between Tibet and the Himalayan state of Sikkim. "We passed caravan after caravan of mules and tiny donkeys no bigger than big dogs bringing down Tibetan wool to Kalimpong in Northern India whence it is shipped to America and England for rugs," she wrote.

On Christmas Eve, she was settled in just the way she liked it—"at the end of the world," cozy in a bungalow, and sitting before a roaring fire with a ten-year-old copy of *The China Journal* to read. A sharp wind howling down the pass outside only added to her satisfaction.

On her return from the border, she spent two days with the British political officer in Sikkim, Basil Gould, and his family at the British residency in Gangtok. Gould, one of the rare westerners who had traveled deep into Tibet, showed her his pictures from Lhasa. "You can imagine the utter fantasticness of the country and the architecture of the monasteries—for once in 'Lost Horizon' Hollywood did not 'go Hollywood' enough," Harkness said.

She was soon back in the saddle, off again by horseback through the rugged, lush hills, her mind now filled with those snapshot images. "This trip is the very best thing I could have done," she wrote to Perkie; "it has settled me and made me know what I want to do—1939 at home—the Spring of '40 to Lhasa!"

With renewed vigor, she continued her travels, landing near Darjeeling just after New Year's Day, then making her way to Calcutta, Allahabad, Bombay, and finally, on February 16, 1939, Liverpool.

HARKNESS WOULD REACH England in the wake of Floyd Tangier Smith's triumphant tour there with an astonishing cargo of five giant pandas, which had arrived just before Christmas. It had been harrowing for him, placing him closer to death than to life just as he was accomplishing what he had always dreamed of.

When he had finally gotten his healthy giant-panda count in Chengdu up to six in the fall, he found himself scrambling for a way to get them, and the other wildlife he had collected, out of the country. Unable to secure air transportation for the menagerie, and too ill to take them on the grueling and dangerous overland route from Chengdu to the coast near Hong Kong, he had his wife, Elizabeth, step in. She survived a month of hardship overseeing the caravan of trucks, while he flew to Hong Kong to convalesce in a hospital. Minus one panda killed in an accident, Elizabeth got the other five safely to Hong Kong, where they all boarded the SS *Antenor* with her husband on November 16.

After being fêted in London, Smith, free of his cargo, would head to New York, where Harkness would already be living. In mid-July, when they once again were just miles from each other, Floyd Tangier Smith died at the age of fifty-eight.

THE QUICK YEAR Harkness had planned to spend in America preparing for an expedition to Lhasa turned out instead to be a plodding and "futile" one. The world at large was becoming ever more chaotic—Hitler had already taken Austria and then brazenly overrun Czechoslovakia; Mussolini invaded Albania. In May, when the seasonal fog lifted over Chongqing, the Japanese began their terror-bombing campaign. Germany and Russia shocked observers by signing a nonaggression pact. And when the Führer took Poland in September, England and France declared war. The United States, clinging steadfastly to neutrality, began to wrestle with its conscience, soul, and sense of safety.

The adventuring game was on hold for just about everyone, including Harkness. The benched explorer, virtually bankrupt from her last expedition and uninspired by life, seemed unable to make a career of writing. For the "humpteenth time," she said, she found herself back in New York trying to "start life over again."

In the early fall, Harkness participated in a benefit for Chinese relief, then began a long-anticipated lecture tour of the Midwest. Using "The Alton Railroad" stationery, on November 4, 1939, she summed up her experience: "The Social season in Missouri has been unexcelledly brilliant but slightly wearing—the friends of Mrs. Harkness—'that rare exotic individual, the turbaned, hair-parted-in-the-middle sort of person who wears leopard coats and jade earrings without looking startled' have all slept peacefully through her most intellectual efforts."

Back home, she again felt aimless and broke. "If there is anything in the world a little more useless than another, it is an unemployed explorer," Harkness would write. "Sometimes," she said, explorers "even get to the point where they aren't quite sure what there is left to discover. Then indeed is the world a bleak and unromantic sphere."

In that frame of mind one gray January day in 1940, she went out to lunch with her literary agent, Jane Hardy, at the Algonquin Hotel, where the two concocted an expedition to South America.

ON FEBRUARY 23, 1940, at five o'clock in the afternoon, Ruth Harkness set sail for Peru on the Grace liner *Santa Elena,* in order to, according to *The New York Times,* "study the descendants of the Incas for comparison with the inhabitants of Tibet."

In Lima, however, ensconced in an elite pension run by American Hope Morris, who was said to be a cousin of Wallis Simpson, Harkness, the ultimate urbanite, found herself caught up in "a rather elaborate nothing," which, she pointed out with some humor, often kept her up late at night.

Eventually, she joined forces with a handsome, reserved entomologist, whom Harkness would call Sandoval in a later book, *Pangoan Diary,* but Noriega in letters home. They would travel far inland in search of what would turn out to be a nonexistent "Peruvian panda."

Noriega was something of a mature, South American version of Quentin Young: gallant, intelligent, and patient. With his help Harkness set up house in his tiny, poor home village—renting, for less than a dollar a month, her own thatched-roof "chalet," which had, like most others in the town, no doors or windows. She learned to cook tortillas, beans, rice, and *fideos,* a kind of pasta; she got involved in local intrigues, many surrounding Noriega's malevolent sister-in-law; and she drank whatever locally brewed booze was available. Days were taken up with the tasks of procuring groceries and cleaning. Evenings were spent playing rummy, talking, and drinking. Harkness would write of her time here in *Pangoan Diary,* which contained none of the intensity and joy she had brought to *The Lady and the Panda.*

Frequent bouts of malaria and heavy drinking took their toll. Toward the end of 1940 she wrote home to Perkie with a confession, punctuated by frequent ellipses, which probably reflected the galloping nature of her thoughts: "My mind never stops and the pressure sometimes is bad; then that's when I drink and my God Perkie it worries me . . . I drink for oblivion . . . and I drink alone as you do and it worries me like hell; it wouldn't be so bad if I didn't go over the edge at times and then I am filled with remorse and say never again . . . but I do. In fact, I am having a drink right now . . ."

She was falling into a forlorn mood, writing in reflection: "Sometimes an intense sense of the deep and ultimate loneliness of every human being suddenly grips me, and I am sad."

Since Bill's death, she had spent her life, she said, "wandering the lonely world. Searching sometimes one thing, sometimes another. Often it seems to me that I have lost my destiny and am hunting to find it again."

Perhaps, deep inside, she knew she never would. For those who have experienced a fleeting moment of "illumination," her favorite mystic had written, there could be an awful aftermath in its wake. "This feeling exists only for a moment," wrote the author, under the name Yogi Ramacharaka, "and leaves one at first in agony of regret over what he has seen and lost." This "is the song of the Soul, which once heard is never forgotten."

By the time Harkness returned home in January 1942, she was physically broken. Admitted to the hospital almost on arrival, she was prepared—eager at times—to shed this body, this life, without a backward glance. Within months, *Pangoan Diary* was published, receiving positive, if not rave, reviews. Over the next three years, Harkness would wander around, to Mexico and New Mexico, then back to New York.

Her health had not rebounded and never would, while her drinking had only intensified. The deterioration would begin to show in some of her magazine writing. She sold a few strange articles to *True*, a men's magazine whose stories were sometimes literary and very often lurid.

One, on her history of panda hunting, was full of inaccuracies, even re-porting that Quentin Young had given her Su-Lin in a provision basket. From these perplexing pieces, the wild explorer settled into a tamer ven-ture, making a small living writing two ten-part series for the very civi-lized *Gourmet* magazine. Focusing on recipes and often high farce, Harkness wrote "Saludos" on life in Peru, beginning in 1944, and "Mex-ican Mornings," from her time in Tamazunchale, in the east-central state of San Luis Potosí, starting in February 1947.

The two series are similar—often to a discomfiting degree. Anec-dotes, sayings, even characters first presented in "Saludos" were at times transplanted to Mexico for a barely veiled retelling in the second series. Bending reality was part of keeping the wolf from the door, for though the Depression was over for the country, Harkness's own financial posi-tion was more precarious than ever.

On the Fourth of July, 1946, the out-of-work explorer found refuge with an old friend who had been married to Hendrik Willem van Loon, the best-selling and award-winning author who had died two years be-fore. Chunky and strong, with close-cropped gray hair, Helen "Jimmie" Criswell van Loon had possession of a big, handsome, three-story Dutch colonial, Nieuw Veere, which overlooked a beautiful cove in Old Green-wich, Connecticut. The van Loons had known everyone in politics and publishing, and Nieuw Veere had in its prime hosted a long parade of celebrities. Even President Roosevelt was counted as a friend.

Jimmie ran a cheery household that included a Swiss couple, William and Elsie Spiess, working as chauffeur/handyman and housekeeper, and their teenage daughter, Sieglinde. As soon as Harkness moved in, she felt very much a part of the Nieuw Veere family.

Young "Sig," now Linda Spiess Ash, idolized Harkness, recalling decades later how the former explorer could, even then in her broken-down state, still dress with panache, lighting up a room just by entering it. Harkness took Sig under her wing, telling her stories and making presents of the little souvenirs she still had among her ever-dwindling personal possessions.

Nieuw Veere held the promise of a comfortable and intellectually stimulating life. Harkness was given as her bedroom Hendrik's great handsome study, with its cases painted Chinese red and filled with books. During quiet days at home, she could collaborate with Jimmie, a Bryn Mawr graduate who had earned a reputation as a fine editor, having labored over her husband's works for years. Ready to pitch in for the cause, she often typed up Harkness's various manuscripts.

Problems, however, crept into the country idyll. Harkness, beset by medical problems, made frequent visits to the doctor and dentist. Sometimes, as recorded in Jimmie's diary, the former explorer would spend entire days in bed "feeling lousy." Through it all, Harkness's writing stalled out. Night after night she was, as she had once put it, drinking for oblivion. The problem was extreme, casting a shadow over the household and only compounding her increasingly awkward predicament of not being able to scrape together the funds to cover her rent.

When the tension inevitably reached a critical point, Harkness was asked to leave. In the face of the devastating banishment, on Saturday, May 3, 1947, she attempted suicide, falling unconscious from an overdose of sleeping pills. While she spent the following day in bed, immobile, her belongings were packed for her, and on Monday, when she was on her feet, she moved out as ordered. Harkness ended up in the famously bohemian Chelsea Hotel in New York, a luxury she likely could not afford.

On Friday, July 18, 1947, just weeks after her suicide attempt, Harkness traveled alone to Pittsburgh. At almost midnight on this warm and humid evening, with thunderstorms rippling across the region, she checked in to the William Penn Hotel.

Trouble may have come as early as that very night, for all day Saturday the service maid was unable to enter the room. In alarm, she notified assistant manager James Greer. When by midnight Harkness had not responded to repeated telephone calls, Greer used his master key to enter her room.

The bedcovers had been pulled down, and Harkness's nightgown had been laid out. A half-empty bottle of wine stood on the dresser.

Everything was quiet. Greer walked toward the bathroom, where, in a partially filled tub, her head above the water, lay the lifeless body of Ruth Harkness.

An emergency call was placed, and police officers and a coroner were summoned in Sunday's early darkness. They investigated the scene, noting that the deceased had been smoking in the bath. In the opinion of medical authorities, Harkness had been dead "a number of hours," though the date and time of her death would be listed as the moment of discovery—12:20 A.M., July 20, 1947.

The officers searched her luggage, finding copies of *The Lady and the Panda* and the address of her next of kin, her sister, Harriet Fay, in Titusville.

Harkness's relative youth, coupled with the strange circumstances of her death, led authorities initially to suspect foul play, but the autopsy, performed by T. R. Helmbold of the Allegheny County morgue, reported "acute alcoholic gastro-enteritis" as the cause.

It is unclear just what happened in that anonymous room, where, as the *Pittsburgh Post-Gazette* reported, "in the luxury of a hotel bathtubful of tepid water, death came obscurely . . . to a woman who had spent a life of high adventure."

She was cremated on July 21, and her ashes were buried on July 24 at the Union Cemetery, which bordered the McCombs family property. The simple services, arranged by the Tracy Home of Funerals, cost $248. The family, who could not afford a headstone, paid the debt off in three installments.

QUENTIN YOUNG would not learn of Harkness's death until 1962. He was widowed and living in Indonesia at the time. The news, he would write to Harkness's sister years later, came as "a heavy loss" to him.

Unlike his resilient brother Jack, who would attain the rank of colonel in the U.S. Army, ending a long career with two Silver Stars and three Bronzes, and who could thrive no matter what came his way, Quentin Young was, according to his biographer, Michael Kiefer, "melancholy, a black hole of misfortune, sucking bad luck into the void from every corner of the universe." The common Chinese expression *chi ku*, "to eat bitterness," seems only too aptly to fit the aged adventurer.

After some exploring stints, Young had lived in the Dutch East Indies, now Indonesia, where he, his wife, Diana, and their daughter, Jenny, survived the Japanese occupation. Over the coming years, he would sometimes say that he had worked as a spy. He and Diana, who soon added a son to their family, struggled through years of political tur-

Ruth Harkness in Shanghai, 1937. Despite her continued sorrow in not being able to return to China later in life, she carried herself with panache.

COURTESY MARY LOBISCO

moil. In 1960 Diana died of cancer, and six years later Young married a fellow employee at the bank in Indonesia, moving with her to Taiwan in 1968. There he began to work for RCA and became a Jehovah's Witness.

Meanwhile, Jack retired in Missouri, having finished off his military career with stints in Korea and Vietnam. He had been so absorbed by his globe-hopping work that his daughters would claim they saw more of him in Movietone newsreels than they did at home. He remarried, and, belatedly, family members would discover that he had fathered a son, Jack junior, in Hong Kong.

Kiefer would write that the Young brothers "were forever secretive, glossing over details as they edited their words, mistrusting even each other, and I was never certain at what point the embellishments, if any, became indistinguishable from the truth—even in their own minds."

In 1974 Jack arranged for Quentin to move to the United States. Just before leaving Taiwan, Young began a correspondence with Ruth Harkness's surviving sister, Harriet McCombs Fay Anderson, that would continue for years. He told Anderson that he had lost almost everything—pictures, field notes, even the wedding ring Harkness had given him—so he asked for and received photographs and archival material Harkness's family had kept, for a book he said he was working on. From his home in St. Louis, his letters to Anderson were full of high hope that the book project would become a movie deal. In fact, he told Anderson he was moving to California in order to be closer to the production company. Ruth Harkness's sister was pulled into the dealings, selling the film and television rights to Harkness's book *The Lady and the Panda* for ten thousand dollars to the producer with whom Quentin Young was associated.

In December 1983—a crucial time for Quentin Young, as he had seen his dreams of a Hollywood biopic recede again and again—an article about Harkness's expedition appeared in *Smithsonian* magazine. Young complained in a letter to the editor that the story had diminished his role in the affair. He not only presented himself as the single most important person in the mission; he dismissed entirely Harkness's contribution. "In fact," he wrote to the editor, "all that entourage and the Western woman were an encumbrance." Reading the letter, Harkness's sister was stunned.

As time went on without Quentin Young's projects panning out, his blighted feelings about everything appear even to have poisoned his memories of Ruth Harkness. In his first letter to Anderson, in 1974, when he was looking for historical material from her, he had written, "Your sister was such a fine woman and I could never forget those limited days I spent with her in panda country." Over the course of years of interviews with journalist Kiefer, starting in 1988, however, Quentin Young would portray Harkness in a much darker light.

The rising tide of Young's unhappiness soon swamped family members and even Kiefer, who through writing several articles and the 2002 book, *Chasing the Panda,* had developed a friendship with the elderly man. The two would be estranged before the work was published. Unwilling to discuss his past, Young has turned away journalists, including this author, and filmmakers who have contacted him. At this writing, Quentin Young is ninety years old and still living with his wife, Swan, in California.

His older brother, Jack, who continued to live his life with high energy and intrigue, worked on his memoirs until his death in St. Louis at the age of eighty-nine in 2000. At ninety-two, Su-Lin, Jack's first wife and the woman immortalized by Harkness's giant panda, now resides in California. Working for the Social Security Administration in New York and California, she raised three daughters on her own. When I met the still-exuberant and kind Su-Lin in 2001, it was, so many decades after the fact, quite clear why Ruth Harkness chose to name the panda after her.

DURING OUR EASTERN travels in 2002, it felt as though a curtain on Harkness's world had truly parted for our group. Milton was right, time is a thief. But like a crass and harried burglar, it often steals what doesn't matter, leaving behind what is most precious. That is what we discovered in China. For here we could still find what deeply moved one American explorer: the grand, sweeping beauty of the land, the spell of the magnificent giant panda, and, perhaps most of all, the warmth and wisdom of the Chinese people.

No smile ever went unreturned, Harkness had written of her interactions. And this was the truest signpost we would encounter. We may have been seeking old buildings, but it was always the smiling faces of these rural people—who helped us find what we were looking for, or told us of their history—that lingered in our minds.

Down roads established in Harkness's time, now paved, if poorly so, it seemed we were four-wheeling through classical Chinese landscape paintings as we made our way to the Chaopo Valley where Harkness had found Su-Lin. On October 29, our SUVs were grinding and tearing, even sliding crashingly into one another, up rutted mud roads till they could go no farther. We emerged from the vehicles into the cool mountain air to begin a treacherous climb on foot, up a thousand-foot bluff that seemed to lead straight into the sky. The trail often had us panting and scrambling on all fours, up just the kind of slick, mossy vertical ground that Harkness had known so well. With little time before sunset, we paused, taking in the expansive view of the valley—the raging yellows, reds, and oranges of autumn below. It was here, before a magnificent old Chinese elm bearing characters that someone had artfully carved in the trunk, that Mary Lobisco unpacked a small ceramic container with the image of giant pandas on the top. Inside were the ashes and soil from Ruth Harkness's grave site in Titusville.

Mary recited a short prayer, then returned Harkness's remains to the country she so loved, to the mountains where she had laid Bill to rest and where she herself had contemplated with deep joy the thought of spending eternity. It was the valley, she had always said, of "her complete happiness." We knew it was the perfect spot—high up, serene, and exactly where Harkness had roamed so long ago.

Just miles away, appropriately, was China's most famous—and, at 785 square miles, largest—panda reserve, Wolong. The preserve is on the front lines in the battle to save the giant panda, at the center of worldwide efforts to ensure that there will always be a place for them.

There are still great problems in the fight to save giant pandas. Logging and human encroachment have gobbled up much of the animal's range. In Sichuan Province alone, between 1974 and 1989, panda habitat was reduced by 50 percent. Some of the threats are long-standing ones, having been around since Harkness's time: the animals are so popular, and displaying them so lucrative, that the motives and methods of those who do so must be closely monitored.

Today China is struggling to protect the giant panda and to preserve its home. While dozens of reserves in six mountain ranges have been established in western China, the world of the giant panda is fragmented. More restricted than that of any other bear, panda populations have become isolated from one another. Inbreeding in circumstances like this can lead to many physical problems, including an inability to fight disease.

Throughout the world, Harkness's gift can be seen in the care and concern given to the preservation of the giant panda. But here in this wild corner of China, which folds forever into Tibet, we saw what we hoped was her legacy in the flesh.

Our little group was able to see dozens of giant pandas here, and even to cuddle a young one, laying our hands gently on his wiry, deep-pile coat.

Scientists today say that Harkness's Su-Sen might very well have survived after her release in 1938 and could have lived long enough to reproduce, right here in the mountain range we were visiting. As we met one magnificent giant panda after another at Wolong, we hoped that a few were her descendants.

Even if we hadn't actually met them, we could content ourselves with a sweet dream—that somewhere in these green, fog-bound slopes before us, there might just live the great-great-grandchildren of one little panda whom Ruth Harkness had, against all odds, and in a moment of pure bliss, set free.

ACKNOWLEDGMENTS

PERHAPS SURPRISINGLY, writing a book is a terrifically humbling experience—not least because an author of nonfiction arrives at the finish line on the strong shoulders of friends and strangers alike who have amply given of their time and expertise. *The Lady and the Panda*, it seems, has been particularly blessed by this kind generosity.

So much of the spirit and substance of this book can be traced to the kindness of two families.

Ruth Harkness's niece, Mary Lobisco, along with her husband, Vincent, and their daughter, Nicole, opened the family photo albums, archives, and history to me, and, of course, so much more. Mary, who is enviably intuitive and pragmatic, provided insights and sometimes even lodging as I traveled and conducted research. Always patient with inquiries and eager to do some sleuthing herself, Mary plunged into wild excursions to cities as different as Chicago and Chengdu for the cause.

Equally important was the contribution of the Perkins family, descendants of Ruth's best friend, Hazel Perkins. Robin Perkins Ugurlu, Hazel's globe-trotting granddaughter, was always on call, ready to roll up her sleeves or pack her bags, to do the dusty work of archival sifting, or to secure us entry to the world of exclusive clubs, such as the one at the

Ritz-Carlton in Shanghai (in the name of inquiry). She has kept Ruth Harkness's story close to her heart her whole life, and I am touched by how much she shared with me. Robin's parents, Bruce and Alice Perkins, opened their astonishing collection of the correspondence between Ruth and her "dear friend Perkie," which turned out to be the master key that unlocked so many of the mysteries of this complicated adventurer. Three generations of Perkinses now have remained loyal to Ruth Harkness, and her memory lives on with vividness and clarity because of them.

While this book has provided me with immeasurable gifts, highest among them has been the chance to know these deeply good people. The families of Ruth Harkness and Hazel Perkins embody the American ideals of honesty, integrity, kindness, strength, and spirit. I am honored to count them as friends, and hope this work at least in some small way reflects their virtues.

Although Quentin Young chose not to be interviewed for this book, members of his family and his biographer, Michael Kiefer, author of *Chasing the Panda*, helped unstintingly. By any logic, Michael should be something of a rival, yet he has always offered information, advice, and friendship. I couldn't ask for a better or more principled colleague. And through his insightful book, I have come to know Quentin Young. Quentin Young's sister-in-law, Su-Lin Young, an explorer herself, and the woman for whom Ruth Harkness named America's first panda, graciously presented her memories of the book's main characters. Her daughter Jialing "Jolly" Young, who has carefully chronicled the family's storied past, particularly that of her dashing father, Jack Young, has provided me again and again with information and understanding, and more than that, a raucous friendship. In helping with this book, both she and her brother, Jack Young, Jr., have drawn me a modern portrait of the swashbuckling their father was famous for.

I am indebted to Linda Ash and the late Peggy McCleskey, who knew Ruth Harkness at very different stages of her life. Over the telephone and in many conversations, they offered stories about Harkness in heart-stirring detail. Linda also—without hesitation—offered to share her store of mementos (including photos and Tibetan prayer cards) saved from her friendship with Harkness.

Dan Reib's daughter, Jane Pollock, kept me spellbound one evening with wonderful stories about her larger-than-life father. And Reib's grandson Edward Reib has been of enormous help with information and my first glimpse of a photograph of Harkness's great and steadfast friend.

I continue to feel happily stunned by the caliber of those willing to read this manuscript and lend their expertise: George Schaller, director of science, Wildlife Conservation Society, who is simply and unarguably the greatest naturalist of our time; Stella Dong, author of the wonderful, wise, and rollicking *Shanghai: The Rise and Fall of a Decadent City 1842–1949;* playwright Yin-Yin Zeng and her husband, Tony Saich, the Daewoo Professor of International Affairs and faculty chair of Asia Programs and the China Public Policy Program, Harvard University.

Thanks especially to my friend Sarah Queen, professor of Chinese history at Connecticut College, who not only read the final manuscript but helped shape it through many probing discussions over meals, around crying babies, and during hikes with dogs. It was only because of Sarah and her canny reading of a Chinese map that I was able to reach the old village of Wenchuan and find Harkness's lost ghost temple. I will forever be grateful for her intellectual drive and her knack for asking simple questions that launched weeklong ruminations.

In this same regard, I thank two of my dearest friends, both talented writers and editors—Louise Kennedy and Jan Freeman. Despite being immersed in their own work and lives, they have unfailingly reported for duty as muses, witty scolds, experts, Scotch-sipping companions, and twenty-four-hour emergency copy doctors. During the polishing phase of this project Jan helped me find light at the end of some kinked and collapsed sentences. Every chapter bears the graceful touch of these punctuation-toting guardian angels.

Thanks, also, to Tess Johnson, an American resident of Shanghai who has written extensively about its history. Tess has more than a dash of Ruth Harkness's salty panache and was generous in lending books and spending an evening over an edifying, fun-filled dinner in the territory that was, in Harkness's time, the French Concession.

I am beholden to an army of kind and brilliant librarians at Cornell University, Harvard University (particularly Yenching and Widener), and the Shanghai municipal library. To Raymond Lum at Yenching, Armand Esai at the archives of the Field Museum in Chicago; Christel Schmidt and Janet W. McKee of the Library of Congress; Julia Innes, former archivist at the Brookfield Zoo; Steven Johnson at the Wildlife Conservation Society's library at the Bronx Zoo; the library staff at the American Museum of Natural History; and David Dressing and Erika Hosselkus of the Latin American Library at Tulane University.

I am grateful to A. J. Joyce, whose skilled computer searching revealed the pathway to the details of Harkness's last years. To documentary filmmaker Jessica Louchheim for both her charity and proficiency in helping with research in Washington, D.C. To Richard J. Reynolds III for sharing his illuminating correspondence with Gerald Russell from the 1960s. And to Devin Hollands for generously providing key Harkness family documents.

Specialists who weighed in on issues large and small include panda expert Devra Klein; Tibetologist Per Kvaerne; *Port of Last Resort* author Marcia Reynders Ristaino; and Asia chronicler Harry Rolnick.

Thanks also to *Washington Post Magazine* editor David Rowell and *Gourmet* magazine editors John Willoughby and Barry Estabrook, for material used here that originally appeared in those publications. I am appreciative of their fine work.

I will never be able to thank editor Jonathan Karp properly. His vision, spirit, and skill have been as singular as they are sure. I am most indebted for his ability to banish the reams of nonessential details and anecdotes that threatened to weigh down the vitality of this adventure story. It is through his stewardship that this galloping work came up to speed and stayed on track. He is also the kindest champion a writer could hope for.

Working closely with Jon has been another remarkable editor—Jonathan Jao. Jonathan is as kind in his manner as he is exacting in his expectations. The pages have become lean and clean from Jonathan running them hard and taking a good stiff-bristled brush to them.

None of this would even have come into existence without the drive of my extraordinary agent, Laura Blake Peterson. Laura understood Ruth Harkness from the start, and she believed in the story when not everyone did. This project has been elevated by Laura's own elegance and conviction.

I thank my talented and resolute nephew John Biando for his help in researching archival material from Standard Oil's days in Shanghai, and for his Herculean effort to organize the unruly endnotes. I look forward to reading his first book, whenever that comes (and I only hope I won't have to help with his endnotes).

My parents too, as usual, did all they could. In this case, that included loading me and their standard poodle, Portia, into the backseat of the Lincoln for a ten-hour drive up from Florida to meet Su-Lin Young.

I am indebted to a cast of characters who have walked wolfhounds for me, made me laugh, been patient with my obsessions, or even been willing to leave me alone so I could keep working: Kathleen Shinnick, Amy Macdonald, Mary Crowley, Ellen Maggio, Michael and Marissa Barrile, Linda Carmichael, Brian Kilcommons, Sarah Wilson, Richard Buell, Boyd Estus, Edith McBean, Paula Abend, Alice Turner, and Jennifer Clifford.

Although, as Ruth Harkness would say, this journey has been one grand thrill, sadly, three close friends, who all led large, joyful lives in the Harkness style, could not finish it with me. How I wish I were invoking the lives and not the memories of Dorothy Greelis, John Castagnetti, and Franklin Loew. Dorothy, my old pal, I will definitely drink one for you.

Finally, with all my heart, too many thanks to count for my love, Scott Beckman.

NOTES

A NOTE ON SOURCES

Dominating the citations in these endnotes are the hundreds of letters written from Ruth Harkness to her best friend, Hazel Perkins, mainly from 1936 to 1939, often typed out on Harkness's portable. Access to the correspondence was generously provided by the Perkins family—Bruce and Alice, and their daughter, Robin Perkins Ugurlu. In the text, I have cleaned up obvious typographical errors contained in the letters, which were often rushed and written under less-than-optimal field conditions, but I have not altered them in any other way.

Some newspaper and magazine clippings taken from Ruth Harkness's family's archives, the files at the Brookfield Zoo, the papers of Floyd Tangier Smith from the Library of Congress, and some others contained no identification of the publication and/or the date. Occasionally, I could puzzle out the date or rough time period from information within the text or from the stories on the reverse. Sometimes I could identify the headline fonts as that of a particular paper. And often enough I found the articles themselves during microfilm research. But not always, and in those cases where clippings remain as orphans, endnotes appear with incomplete information.

Along with the citations, I have also included some rather lengthy informational notes. There just wasn't enough room in the main story itself for background details on a number of topics (Ruth's relationship to Bill Harkness's family, for instance), but because so much of it has never been published anywhere else, I have provided it here in note form.

PREFACE

xv   *Something one newspaperman*   Ruth Harkness, travel club speech, 1939.

xv   *No animal in history*   *Field Museum News* 9, no. 7 (July 1938), Field Museum archives.

xvi   *"making the world panda conscious"*   *Washington Post*, 26 June 1938; *Field Museum News* 9, no. 7 (July 1938), Field Museum archives.

xvii   *getting baby-panda formula right*   "Improved Nutrition and Infant Survival," "Panda 2000 Conservation Priorities for the New Millennium," workshop at the San Diego Zoo, Oct. 2000, http://www.sandiegozoo.org/conservation/fieldproject_panda2000.html.

xvii   *"little was known"*   World Wildlife Fund website: http://www.wwfchina.org.

xviii   *"a very important nail"*   Ramona and Desmond Morris, *Men and Pandas* (New York: McGraw-Hill, 1966), p. 83.

xix   *Su-Lin "was virtually changing"*   Ibid., p. 82.

xix   *"In a few brief moments"*   Chris Catton, *Pandas* (New York: Facts on File, 1990), p. 17.

xix   *"evoke universal sympathy"*   "Giant Pandas in the Wild," World Wide Fund for Nature website, http://www.panda.org, printed 11 July 2001.

xix   *"part in giving the animal world"*   Ruth Harkness to Hazel Perkins, likely 13 Sept. 1940.

CHAPTER ONE: DEATH IN SHANGHAI

3   *It was a bitter winter night*   "Explorer Harkness Dies of a Cancer," *Shanghai Evening Post and Mercury*, 20 Feb. 1936; "Harkness Dies of a Throat Cancer," *Shanghai Times*, 21 Feb. 1936, p. 7; "W. H. Harkness Jr. Is Dead in Shanghai," *New York Times* 20 Feb. 1936, which describes the Shanghai sanitarium as a "Seventh Day Adventist institution."

3   *sunny notes*   Ruth Harkness, *The Lady and the Panda: An Adventure* (New York: Carrick & Evans, 1938), p. 20.

3   *But, finally*   Floyd Tangier Smith to Keith Spalding, 5 Mar. 1936, Field Museum archives.

4   *A world away*   "Cold to Continue Over Week-end," *New York Times*, 1 Feb. 1936.

4   *Late in the afternoon*   Harkness, *Lady and the Panda*, p. 19.

4   *along icy sidewalks*   "Near-Zero Cold Returns to City; 33 on Ship Saved," *New York Times*, 19 Feb. 1936, p. 1; letter to the editor, dated 13 Feb. 1936, from "taxpayer," complains about snowy, icy sidewalks in New York City, *New York Times*, 15 Feb. 1936.

4   *"pretty little mulatto maid"*   Harkness, *Lady and the Panda*, p. 19.

4   *The devastation of that loss*   Siglinde Ash, conversation with author, interview, 12 Sept. 2002.

4   *"Do you have that"*   Harkness to Perkins, 20 May 1936.

5   *Handsome, short, and wiry*   Lawrence Griswold, *Tombs, Trouble and Travel*, Resnick's Library of Worldwide Adventure (1937; reprint, Alexander, N.C.: Alexander Books, 1999), p. 167.

5   *He was not a member*   *Wall Street Journal*, 10 Feb. 1915; "Mrs. Harkness Aids College," giving $150,000 to Connecticut College for Women, 14 Dec. 1933.

5   *But Bill had graduated from Harvard*   "Harvard Graduates Its Largest Class," *New York Times*, 20 June 1924. Bill Harkness listed under Bachelor of Arts (also in next year's list under "Bachelors of Law"). See also "Florence Rhein Picks Bridal Party," 3 Oct. 1928.

5   *scion of a wealthy New York family*   *Shanghai Times*, 21 Feb. 1936, p. 7.

5   *The Harknesses were powerfully connected*   Bill Harkness's records from Harvard indicate connections to government officials and the FAO Schwarz family, as well as a sense of entitlement.

5   *Never arrogant*   Bill Harkness always let his companions do the talking to the press when he was on expedition; he didn't care about being given credit or seeing his name in print, as is clear from treks with Griswold and Smith.

6   *She could fill a room*   "Su Lin, Panda Baby, Checks in at Biltmore," *New York Herald Tribune*, 24 Dec. 1936.

6   *She had, according*   Adelaide Hawley, editor of "The Woman's Page," MGM Newsreels Chairman, Town Hall Round Table Luncheon Club, as quoted in Ruth Harkness lecture brochure from William B. Freakins, Inc.

6   *Born on September 21, 1900*   "Mrs. Harkness Dies Suddenly in Pittsburgh," *Titusville (Penn.) Herald*, 21 July 1947.

7   *temporary move to nearby Erie*   "Woman Explorer, Former Ericite, Is Found Dead," *Erie Daily Times*, 21 July 1947.

7   *After a semester*   Greg Swenson, news office, University of Colorado, e-mail correspondence with author. Ruth McCombs is listed as a freshman in the College of Liberal Arts for the 1920–1921 academic year.

7   *twenty-five dollars as her war chest*   Ruth Harkness to family, Jan. 1939, from Bombay.

7   *Powdered and dressed up*   Jill Carey, professor of fashion history, LaSalle College, Newton, Mass., conversation with author.

7   *as quintessential a flapper*   "Appreciating the Flapper," *New York Times*, 13 June 1999.

8   *her face was not her fortune*   Ruth Harkness to family, Jan. 1939, from Bombay.

8   *"had to work like the devil"*   Harkness to Perkins, 12 Aug. 1936.

9   *"a bare derriere"*   Harkness to Perkins, 12 July 1936.

10   *slugging back bootleg booze*   Mary Lobisco, conversation with author, 12 April 2003. Ruth Harkness's niece, Lobisco recalls a story of her mother's. When

Harriet McCombs came to visit Ruth, she took up smoking just to keep her
hands busy while socializing with Bill and Ruth and their friends, who were
always drinking.

10 *Sitting together in the haze*   Harkness, *Lady and the Panda,* p. 56.

10 *"game trails in remote corners"*   Ruth Harkness, as told to Hans Christian
Adamson, "How I Caught the Rare Giant Panda," part 2, "Mrs. Harkness'
Thrilling Story of Her Hunt in Asian Wilds," *New York American,* 14 Feb.
1937.

10 *college-entrance examinations*   Undergraduate Registrar's Office, Harvard
University.

10 *author*   U.S. Bureau of the Census, 1930, Washington, D.C.

10 *a man of letters*   Harvard College Class of 1924 Sexennial Report, 1930,
p. 95.

10 *"Big Medicine" .405 rifle*   Griswold, *Tombs, Travel,* pp. 180, 194.

10 *at his family's estate in Connecticut*   William senior, a widower, thought his
son was a bit reckless, but the two men were close, and soon enough Ruth
was folded into the Harkness family. She and Bill served as bridesmaid and
best man at William senior's wedding, to a much younger woman in 1928.
From then on, weekends were a time for the foursome at the family estate in
Danbury, a handsome manor enviably outfitted with an in-ground swimming
pool (it would later be purchased by contralto Marian Anderson). Despite
finding the country life of swimming and tennis a bit of a bore, Ruth went
along with it all, even trying to befriend Bill's stepmother, Jane Green-
Penfold, who was close to her own age but nothing like Ruth in outlook or
philosophy. Jane always seemed to squelch Ruth's exuberance and naturalness, sometimes exploding in anger over petty matters such as the time Ruth
arrived late to the farm. At least Ruth had a confidante and ally in Danbury—
someone close to the family who felt the same exasperation over Jane's
dampening ways. Hazel Perkins, an industrious and ambitious woman raising two boys alone, had worked in the real estate office handling matters for
the Harkness estate. She would become Ruth's closest friend forever after.

Throughout the years of Danbury visits, Jane and William senior eroded
Ruth's confidence, always implying, she said, that she had no common sense
and lacked good judgment. They had the same concerns about Bill, which
was made clear in the patriarch's will. William senior had designated that
upon his death, all his worldly goods and fortune would be left to his new
wife to use as she pleased. Should she predecease him, the estate would go
to Bill, but with the proviso that it would be managed by a trust, administered
by overseers presumably with more sober perspectives.

Even after the stock market crash of 1929, Bill's family-fed bank account
proved Depression-proof, and he continued to live as he pleased. See "Jane
Green-Penfold Weds W. H. Harkness," *New York Times,* 27 June 1928, p. 25;
Bill's *New York Times* obituary, 20 Feb. 1936; "William H. Harkness to

Marry," *New York Times*, 19 June 1928; Bruce Perkins, son of Hazel Perkins, conversation with; Ruth Harkness to Hazel Perkins, 22 Aug. 1936; Last Will and Testament of William H. Harkness, of Danbury, Fairfield County, Conn., 21 Dec. 1931, From files of Probate Court, District of Danbury, District no. 034.

10   *tropical romantic getaways*   Ruth Harkness to family, postcard from Virgin Islands, 1925.

10   *"A dash of absinthe"*   Harkness to Perkins, 28 May 1936.

11   *Each of them was haunted*   Griswold says this in *Tombs, Travel*, and Ruth's personal correspondence is filled with ruminations on loneliness.

11   *Her intuition*   Harkness to Perkins, 8 July 1936.

11   *"He had a divine faith"*   Harkness to Perkins, 8 July 1936.

11   *She felt in a fog*   Harkness to Perkins, 1 June 1936.

12   *She was to receive about $20,000*   This is what she said she spent on the first expedition, and it had to have come from Bill.

12   *not enough to last much more than a year*   Paul A. Samuelson, *Economics* (1948; New York: McGraw-Hill, 1997), p. 64.

12   *She left it*   Harkness to Perkins, 16 June and 22 Aug. 1936.

12   *his mother's jewelry*   Harkness to Perkins, misdated 12 July 1936, should be 12 Aug. 1936.

12   *Over many chilly days*   "I was drinking because I felt that I needed it," Harkness said in a letter to Perkins, 6 Aug. 1936.

13   *As she sent instructions*   *Shanghai Times*, 21 Feb. 1936, p. 7.

13   *"brown lean men"*   Theodore and Kermit Roosevelt, *Trailing the Giant Panda*, (New York: Charles Scribner's Sons, 1929), p. 1.

14   *"Whenever one arrives"*   From the 1931 fifty-cent *Popular Official Guide* to the New York Zoological Park, by William T. Hornaday.

14   *Demand for animals was strong*   Arthur de Carle Sowerby, "The Lure of the Giant Panda," *China Journal*, May 1938, p. 251.

15   *Adult elephants*   Vicki Constantine Croke, *The Modern Ark: The Story of Zoos: Past, Present, and Future* (New York: Charles Scribner's Sons, 1997).

15   *Over the course of his career*   Ibid.

15   *Since Bill was the obvious*   Griswold, *Tombs, Travel*.

15   *"was fortunately furnished"*   Ibid.

16   *Ruth Harkness wasn't impressed*   Harkness to Perkins, 27 Aug. 1936. In another letter to Perkins, 17 Oct. 1936, Harkness calls assertions of Griswold's in an article he wrote, or was in, a "pack of lies," and she wonders what he is doing, "besides being supported by his actress wife."

16   *a scientific paper the decade before*   Mark Cheater, "Chasing the Magic Dragon," *National Wildlife Magazine*, Aug./Sept. 2003.

16   *"Bill's own invention"*   Griswold, *Tombs, Travel*.

17   *"a yearning desire"*   Harkness, "How I Caught the Rare Giant Panda," part 1, 14 Feb. 1937.

17 *It was a living mystery*   *National Geographic* devoted pages and pages to articles on China from the late 1920s throughout the '30s.

17 *When he noticed*   George Bishop, *Travels in Imperial China: The Intrepid Explorations and Discoveries of Père Armand David* (London: Cassell, 1996), pp. 158–59.

18 *He wrote in his diary*   George Schaller, *The Last Panda* (Chicago: University of Chicago Press, 1994), p. 135.

18 *"easily the prettiest kind"*   Morris and Morris, *Men and Pandas*, pp. 37–46.

18 *"the most challenging animal trophy"*   Ibid.

18 *"This animal is not common"*   E. H. Wilson, *A Naturalist in Western China*, vol. 2 (New York: Doubleday, Page, 1914), p. 183.

18 *Wilson himself never*   Schaller, *Last Panda*, p. 46.

18 *There were natural calamities*   "Tibetan Guides Get Lost on 'Roof of the World,' " *Christian Science Monitor*, 11 Jan. 1936, p. 2.

19 *Injured and shocked*   Schaller, *Last Panda*, p. 145.

19 *So elusive*   *Journal of the West China Border Research Society* 8 (1936).

19 *British military attaché*   Peter Hopkirk, *Trespassers on the Roof of the World: The Secret Exploration of Tibet* (Los Angeles: J. P. Tarcher, 1982), p. 231.

19 *J. Huston Edgar*   Arthur de Carle Sowerby, *China Journal*, p. 337. Sowerby in Dec. 1936 and May 1938 says the two men were together in 1914. Morris and Morris, *Men and Pandas*, says two separate incidents in 1916. Catton, *Pandas*, p. 10, says 1916; Catton spells Huston "Houston."

19 *Spotting something*   Morris and Morris, *Men and Pandas*, p. 47.

19 *"Waiting for the Panda"*   *Journal of the West China Border Research Society* 8 (1936).

19 *Considering how many people*   Morris and Morris, *Men and Pandas*, p. 49.

19 *"like the unicorn"*   Hallett Abend, "Rare 4-Pound 'Giant' Panda to Arrive in New York Soon," *New York Times*, 20 Dec. 1936.

19 *sea serpent*   Robert F. Whitney, "New Road to Riches and Fame: Be First to Catch Giant Panda," *Washington Post*, 30 Mar. 1934, p. 10.

19 *By the time Teddy Roosevelt's*   *China Journal*, May 1938, p. 252.

19 *returning from a central Asian expedition*   Roosevelt and Roosevelt, *Trailing the Giant Panda*; and Karl E. Meyer and Shareen Blair Brysac, *Tournament of Shadows: The Great Game and the Race for Empire in Central Asia* (Washington, D.C.: Counterpoint, 1999), p. 492.

19 *Funded by a generous patron*   "Mrs. Harkness Kidnaps Panda," *San Francisco Examiner*, 19 Dec. 1936; *New York Times*, 20 Dec. 1936, just says "more than $10,000." See also "Two Live Pandas Captured," *North China Daily News*, 7 July 1937.

20 *pine for their own pelts*   Morris and Morris, *Men and Pandas*, p. 54.

20 *"the imaginations of the younger generation"*   *China Journal*, May 1938, p. 252.

20 *"panda country along the Tibetan"*   Ibid., Dec. 1936, p. 336. American Brooke Dolan's effort was sponsored by the Philadelphia Academy of Natural Sci-

ences. And in May 1931 a young German on his team, Ernst Schaefer, shot a baby giant panda in Weigold's "Wassu-land," the region around the Qionglai Shan in Western Sichuan. It was the second giant panda to fall to a Western gun.

20 *Nab a giant panda*   Robert F. Whitney, "New Road to Riches and Fame," *The Washington Post*, 30 March, 1934, p. 10.

20 *In a civil service*   Titusville (*Penn.*) *Herald*, 13 Sept. 1934.

21 *Heading up*   Harkness, "How I Caught the Rare Giant Panda," part 2.

21 *After a few wild adventures*   On 27 Dec. 1934, *The New York Times* carried the headline "Four Adrift 5 Days with Water Gone: Griswold Party Finally Reaches Borneo After Struggling with Disabled Motor." Harkness's group had left a small island at the southern tip of the Philippines aboard the *Faraon*, a small launch carrying several Chinese passengers. The motor died in a swift current leading to the Celebes Sea, and it was soon discovered that little drinking water had been stowed. For the thirty-two desperate people, there was only sixty-two ounces of muddy water in a rusted tank.

The Griswold-Harkness gang took possession of the ship. First, four men were sent out in a launch to get help but returned in failure. Next, the men made a sail from a tent, simply to fight the drift, as they tried to repair the motor. Water was rationed, though Griswold would draw off and hide a quart in what he described as an emergency precaution. The thirst became unbearable over days of brutal heat. The biggest worry, Griswold reported, were the twenty-two "hysterical Chinese" passengers. "Never let anyone tell you that the Chinese are calm in emergencies," Griswold carped. He and Bill declared martial law, using guns as a threat and staking out a "white side of the deck." Ultimately, Griswold reasoned, "if it came to a question of one race or the other surviving, we had a good idea which it would be."

The ante was upped when Griswold spied the dorsal fins of sharks, cutting the surface of the sea silently as the sharks trailed the boat. He had to subdue his own rising sense of panic, grappling with his emotions in private, for, he said, "a white man can't afford the luxury of hysteria in such circumstances."

There wasn't much evidence of the white nobility Griswold claimed. A member of their own party, dubbed "Scotty" in Griswold's veiled account, did something dirty that none of the Chinese whom Griswold held in contempt had done. Dehydrated and desperate, Scotty stole and guzzled a pint of precious water. And Bill Harkness happened to catch him. Griswold witnessed the scene: "Bill was standing in the narrow alley, and he was fighting for control of himself. His pistol was in his hand and his light blue eyes were menacing in a face white with fury. . . . Fortunately for Scotty, Bill's pistol had been unloaded for cleaning. The interval had been enough to save his life. Slowest of us all to anger, I don't believe Bill ever forgave Scotty for that."

Finally, after all the setbacks, the men were able to repair a cylinder and get the engine sputtering back to life. Griswold, who had seriously thought there might be executions to maintain order, reported in a book he would write later, "There would be no massacre today!" Five days after the disaster began, they reached safety.

The two principals, Griswold and Harkness, took the disaster in stride and simply headed off for a little hunting in Bali, where, with some logistical help from a local rajah, they killed two of the island's soon-to-be-extinct tigers. In Borneo, they plugged a rhino.

When they weren't blasting animals, they were getting blasted. Wherever they went, there were always parties. They even shared cocktails and bawdy limericks in Indonesia with Hollywood leading man Ronald Colman.

In the town of Bima, on an island near Bali, a fat and cheery Dutchman driving a Model A Ford whisked them off to a cottage, where a bottle of Scotch was set out on the porch. Soon a steady stream of locals began to fill the lawn. The party-minded adventurers felt compelled to entertain. It was Bill who recalled that, in the mountains of gear, they had stowed a portable phonograph.

The men unpacked the player along with a number of shiny albums, some by Josephine Baker. Out through the acoustic horn came voices from a world away. And surrounded by the dense, dripping tropical vegetation, the crowd chose Baker's tinny but infectious "La Petite Tonkinoise" as their favorite. Sources: *New York Times*, 27 Dec. 1934; Griswold, *Tombs, Travel*; and *China Journal*, May 1938, p. 252.

21 *finally reached Shanghai* Harkness, *Lady and the Panda; China Journal*, Feb. 1935, p. 70; and Harkness, "How I Caught the Rare Giant Panda," part 1.

21 *Within weeks* Less than two months into the venture, Bill learned that his father had died in a single-car crash in Arizona. "W. H. Harkness Dies in Crash in West: Former New York Lawyer's Wife Is Hurt in Auto Upset on Way to Los Angeles," *New York Times*, 16 Nov. 1934.

21 *His advancement was opposed* Abend, "Rare 4-Pound 'Giant' Panda"

21 *Early on, Bill met up* According to Smith's letter to Keith Spalding, 5 Mar. 1936, Bill's first disappearance came just after the two had entered an agreement.

22 *Smith signed on* Elizabeth Smith to Ruth Woodhull Tangier Smith, 23 Dec. 1936, Floyd Tangier Smith Papers, Library of Congress.

22 *Bearing a draft for five thousand dollars* *Shanghai Evening Post and Mercury*, 20 Feb. 1936, says he went missing on March 14, and was found at the Palace on March 20.

22 *United Press carried a dispatch* United Press, dateline Shanghai, 18 Mar. 1935.

22 *just fine at the Palace Hotel* Ibid., 19 Mar. 1935; and "American Citizen Not Missing," *Shanghai Times*, 20 Mar. 1935.

22 *"William Harkness Hunted in China"* Associated Press, dateline Shanghai, 4 Apr. 1935.

22   *Bill was found holed up*   Hanson, according to *Shanghai Evening Post and Mercury,* 20 Feb. 1936, and Hansen, according to Smith to Spalding, 5 Mar. 1936.

22   *The fourth panda to fall*   Catton, *Pandas,* p. 13.

23   *tally of giant pandas*   Morris and Morris, *Men and Pandas,* p. 60.

23   *"As a result"*   Ibid., p. 54.

23   *He was ordered to report*   "Baby Giant," *Time,* 7 Dec. 1936.

23   *A dejected Bill Harkness*   *New York Times,* 5 Apr. 1935.

23   *"stir the imagination"*   Harkness, *Lady and the Panda,* p. 16.

23   *Just weeks before*   Gerald Russell to R. J. Reynolds III, 1 Apr. 1965. Russell came aboard in the early summer of 1935. This jibes with Smith's account, (letter 19 Dec. 1935).

23   *Cambridge-educated Englishman*   Information from R. J. Reynolds, and his correspondence with Ivan Sanderson, who went to school with Russell. Sanderson letter, 16 Dec. 1964.

24   *began the journey to Chengdu*   Smith to Spalding, 5 Mar. 1936. Russell to Reynolds, 1 Apr. 1965, disagrees, saying they went by steamer. But Russell's memory is faulty on many matters, and Smith wrote the letter with details in 1936.

24   *Despite the uncertainty*   Oddly, at the same time Bill's China expedition was finally going forward, Griswold, back in New York, was announcing to the press that he and Bill planned to leave for Brazil in September. Their venture, he said, would focus on proving that humans evolved in many separate places: *New York Herald Tribune,* 23 July 1935.

24   *In July 1935*   *China Journal,* July 1935, p. 39.

24   *near Leshan, in Sichuan*   Harkness, *Lady and the Panda,* p. 17. "Kiating" or Jiading is modern-day Leshan in Sichuan, according to Peter Valder, *Garden Plants of China* (Portland, Oreg., Timber Press, 1999) and http://www.encyclopedia.com.

24   *unresolved permit problems*   Russell to Reynolds, 1 Apr. 1965.

24   *By September 30*   Smith to Spalding, 5 Mar. 1936.

24   *There was no mention of failure*   *China Press,* 9 Oct. 1935.

24   *Later Smith would even say*   Smith to Spalding, 5 Mar. 1936.

24   *Instead, Harkness and Smith*   Harkness, *Lady and the Panda,* p. 18.

CHAPTER TWO: INHERITING AN EXPEDITION

25   *Out of the blue*   Catton, *Pandas,* p. 14, says Russell recently graduated from Cambridge in 1935.

25   *unaware of Bill's death*   Russell to Reynolds III, 1 May 1965.

25   *333 West Eighteenth Street*   *New York Herald Tribune,* 24 Dec. 1936; and Harkness, *Lady and the Panda,* p. 19.

25   *"tough and determined"*   Russell to Reynolds, 1 May 1965.

25 *"someone bearing his name"* Ibid.

26 *Ruth had already* In *Lady and the Panda*, p. 20. Harkness says within days of Bill's death she was thinking of taking over for him.

26 *She had the will* "Mrs. Harkness Got His Panda, Explorer 'Ajax' Smith Charges," *China Press*, 4 Dec. 1936.

26 *"upset all calculations"* Smith to Spalding, 5 Mar. 1936, Field Museum archives.

27 *For when he next revealed* Harkness to Perkins, 12 Oct. 1936.

27 *They would meet in Europe* Russell to Reynolds, 1 May 1965, says it was France. Harkness to Perkins, 12 Oct. 1936, says London. They may have met in both places.

27 *then get an expedition together* Russell to Reynolds, 1 May 1965.

27 *"She's as mad as a hatter"* Herschell Brickell, "How a Dress Designer Became the World's Best Panda-Catcher," "Books on Our Table," no date or publication on clip, but Brickell wrote for *New York Herald Tribune, New York Evening Post,* and *Saturday Review of Literature*.

28 *"I'd probably"* Harkness, *Lady and the Panda*, p. 13.

28 *She was among a throng* Harkness describes a scene like this of watching the Statue of Liberty in her fantasy work of unpublished fiction, "Jungle Magic."

28 *The crossings to Europe* Harkness to Perkins, 30 April and 29 June 1936.

28 *Russell met her in London* Harkness to Perkins, 28 May 1936. She said the martinis in England tasted like dishwater, and the Manhattans even worse. An ice cube for a highball was apparently, she grumbled, a luxury. Worse, the British sense of superiority staggered her. While making her way through a book titled *The English—Are They Human?* by G. T. Renier, she wrote home, "I haven't finished it, but I'm sure they're not." It was a bit of a love/hate relationship, for she reported that she couldn't tell anymore if she was "an Anglomaniac or an Anglophobiac."

28 *the two left for France* Harkness to Perkins, 30 Apr., 1 May (Hotel du Louvre stationery) 1936.

28 *"More than ever"* Harkness to Perkins, 1 May 1936.

28 *She was, by the time* Harkness to Perkins, 1 June 1936.

28 *"Sometimes I think"* Harkness to Perkins, May 1936.

29 *From Suez on . . . "all life"* Harkness to Perkins, 16 June 1936.

29 *A whiskey soda* Harkness to Perkins, 15 July 1936.

30 *Past oil-supply* W. Robert Moore, "Cosmopolitan Shanghai, Key Seaport of China," *National Geographic*, Sept. 1932, p. 316.

30 *Harkness took in* Ibid., pp. 316–32.

31 *Concrete rafts* Amanda Boyden, "Changing Shanghai," *National Geographic*, Oct. 1937, p. 494.

32 *It was thick and heavy* "The Shanghai Boom," *Fortune*, Jan. 1935. Boyden, "Changing Shanghai," mentions the smell too.

32 *Shanghai possessed*   Harriet Sergeant, *Shanghai: Collision Point of Cultures 1918/1939* (London: Jonathan Cape, 1991), p. 2. Professor Sarah Queen changes Sergeant's *"jenao"* to *"rinao."*

32 *It was a test of character*   Stella Dong, *Shanghai 1842–1949: The Rise and Fall of a Decadent City* (New York: William Morrow, 2000), p. 75. This is the best, most rollicking history of Shanghai ever. It is as exacting in its historical detail as it is vibrant in its storytelling.

32 *At least Harkness could*   Harkness to Perkins, 16 June 1936.

32 *refugees*   Marcia Reynders Ristaino, *Port of Last Resort: The Diaspora of Shanghai* (Stanford, Calif.: Stanford University Press, 2001). In an e-mail to author from author Ristaino: "The first German refugees came in 1933 and included professionals who were able to integrate into Shanghai and other parts of China. They were not a large group, but they were aware of what was happening in Germany. The real flow began after Kristallnacht. . . . The largest group arrived in 1939, having read the signs of what was to come."

32 *fifty nationalities*   Moore, "Cosmopolitan Shanghai," p. 325.

32 *He wasn't averse*   Floyd Tangier Smith to Ruth Woodhull Tangier Smith, 22 Apr. 1937, Smith Papers.

33 *The conservative old Palace*   Boyden, "Changing Shanghai," pp. 490–91.

33 *Harkness was on a budget*   *All About Shanghai: A Standard Guide Book*, with an introduction by H. J. Lethbridge (Oxford: Oxford University Press, 1935; reprinted 1983), p. 86.

34 *a German Jew*   Harkness to Perkins, 22 Aug. 1936.

34 *Speaking of her youngest suitor*   Harkness to Perkins, misdated 12 July 1936, should be 12 Aug. 1936.

34 *Among her many new pals*   Harkness, *Lady and the Panda*, p. 242.

34 *"WHOOPEE!"*   *All About Shanghai*, p. 73.

34 *great verandah of the Race Club*   Harkness to Perkins, 25 Aug. 1936.

34 *a lush, green twelve-acre*   Dong, *Shanghai*, p. 30; Boyden, "Changing Shanghai," p. 507.

34 *candy-colored neon signs*   Vicki Baum, *Shanghai '37* (1939; Hong Kong: Oxford University Press, 1986), p. 359: "lighted up with white, red, green, and blue lights."

34 *At the Chinese clubs*   Boyden, "Changing Shanghai," p. 491.

34 *"closed up Shanghai"*   Harkness to Perkins, August 1937.

35 *Cocktail hour*   *All About Shanghai*, p. 75.

35 *"a really entrancing"*   Harkness to Perkins, August, 1937.

35 *When he had to make trips*   Ristaino, *Port of Last Resort*, p. 15; *All About Shanghai*, p. 76; and Pearl S. Buck, *My Several Worlds* (1954; New York, Cardinal Giant Pocket Books, 1956), p. 207. White Russians—czarist loyalists— had started pouring into Shanghai in 1919, defeated in their campaign against the Bolsheviks, or "Reds." They took advantage of Shanghai's status as an open port, providing sanctuary to stateless people. The downside was

that they received no protections under their nation's extraterritoriality and were, therefore, subject to harsh Chinese law. Without legal privilege, and not speaking English, the language used for business, they were in a tragic situation. Destitute and degraded, they embarrassed fellow westerners by how low they sank in order to survive—the men working shoulder to shoulder with Chinese laborers, or as bodyguards for rich Chinese businessmen and warlords; the women—many famously beautiful blue-eyed blondes—singing or dancing in cabarets, or just as likely turning tricks on the street. Still, most claimed to be descended from royalty, and Keane's girlfriend possessed the legendary transcendent Russian haughtiness. Pearl Buck wrote that the White Russians were arrogant even while begging. Given a handout, they might complain, "Have you no better shoes than this?"

35 *"an outlaw's haven"* Dong, *Shanghai*, p. 117.

35 *In her letters home* Harkness to Perkins, 25 July 1936.

35 *He may very well have been* "War Lords and Dope in Szechuen: Danish Journalist on Life in the Provinces," *North China Herald*, 7 July 1937.

35 *The two explored* Ristaino, *Port of Last Resort*, p. 19.

35 *"All of China"* Harkness to Perkins, 25 July 1936.

36 *Through such wanderings* Dong, *Shanghai*, p. 13.

36 *Once only the drug* Ibid., pp. 6–8.

36 *feeding frenzy* Sherman Cochran, ed., *Inventing Nanjing Road: Commercial Culture in Shanghai, 1900–1945* (Ithaca, N.Y.: Cornell East Asia Series, 1999), p. 4.

37 *It called itself Zhongguo* In conversation with author, Sarah Queen, professor of Chinese history, Connecticut College, 10 Apr. 2003 and 24 Jan. 2004.

37 *All strangers were barbarians* Barbara W. Tuchman, *Stilwell and the American Experience in China, 1911–1945* (New York: Grove Press, 1971), p. 26.

37 *"to make money"* *North China Herald*, 9 Sept. 1936, p. 466; and Richard Pyke, "Why Shanghai Is Not China," *Listener*, 12 Aug. 1936.

38 *In the drenching, one-hundred-degree heat* Harkness to Perkins, 12 Aug. 1936.

38 *Some days she would pinch* Harkness to Perkins, 27 Aug. 1936.

38 *"ZIANG TAI"* Harkness to Perkins, 27 Aug. 1936.

38 *"There is really"* Ibid.

38 *"advertising sales"* Moore, "Cosmopolitan Shanghai," p. 330; and Boyden, "Changing Shanghai," p. 507.

38 *"a great sprawling rambling"* Harkness to Perkins, 25 July 1936.

39 *Just down the street* Although many sources talk about the banners on Nanking Road, Boyden, "Changing Shanghai," says they had mostly disappeared (p. 492).

40 *Several blocks west* Boyden, "Changing Shanghai," p. 493.

40 *pidgin English* Dong, *Shanghai*, pp. 32–33. Pidgin English "never allowed for sophisticated discourse," Dong says.

40 *According to the guidebooks* *All About Shanghai*, pp. 120–21; and Rev. C. E.

Darwent, M.A., *Shanghai: A Handbook for Travellers and Residents* (Shanghai: Kelly & Walsh, 1920; reprint, Taipei: Ch'Eng Wen, 1973), p. i.

40 *Kidnappings too* Ristaino, *Port of Last Resort*, p. 86.

40 *Within days of her arrival* North China Herald, 29 July 1936 (Lt. Col. Orville M. Johnson jumped on 21 July 1936); *North China Herald*, 22 July 1936; and *China Press*, 12 Aug. 1936.

41 *He and his associate* "Madame Chiang, 105, Chinese Leader's Widow, Dies," *New York Times*, 24 Oct. 2003.

41 *When Chiang Kai-shek's* Jonathan D. Spence, *The Search for Modern China* (New York: W. W. Norton, 1990, reprint 1999), pp. 333–34; and Dong, *Shanghai*, p. 182.

41 *And by 1930* Dong, *Shanghai*, p. 45.

41 *One particularly twisted* Tuchman, *Stilwell*, pp. 107–8.

41 *and he once sodomized* Dong, *Shanghai*, p. 125.

41 *She wanted to keep fit* Harkness to Perkins, 27 Aug. 1936.

41 *"I think I am"* Harkness to Perkins and Anne Pierce, 25 July 1936.

42 *"jealous as hell"* Harkness to Perkins, 19 Sept. 1936.

42 *Sometimes tucked away* China Press, 9 Oct. 1935.

43 *He was all too eager* Floyd Tangier Smith to Field Museum, 26 July 1936, Field Museum archives.

43 *"He has been here"* Harkness to Perkins, 25 July 1936.

43 *Smith was a practiced storyteller* "Zoologist Tells of Perils in Remote Sections of China: Returns After Consorting with Half-Civilized Tribes and Bandit Hordes for Two Years While Collecting Specimens" ran one headline above an Associated Press story in 1932.

43 *"It was a long job"* Floyd Tangier Smith, "Collecting a Zoo in China: The Search for the Giant Panda," *Home and Empire*, Nov. 1937, Smith Papers.

44 *"little pile of coppers"* Harkness, *Lady and the Panda*, p. 28.

44 *"I divide the whites"* Harkness to Perkins, 30 Sept. 1936.

44 *The notion of* This is revealed in all his correspondence about her after her success.

44 *"Those who think that the animals"* Smith, "Collecting a Zoo in China," p. 6.

44 *"I don't know how you"* Ruth Harkness, travel club speech, 1939.

45 *Even now* Russell to Reynolds, 1 Apr. 1965.

45 *Born in Japan in 1882* Catton, *Pandas*, p. 13.

45 *Here he wore suits* Smith's résumé, Smith Papers.

46 *From 1930 to 1932* Smith's letters to sister.

46 *mammals, reptiles, birds* William G. Sheldon, *The Wilderness Home of the Giant Panda* (Amherst: University of Massachusetts Press, 1975), p. 73. In 1935 the Sage expedition to west China collected 1,150 animals in just six weeks.

46 *his desire for a panda* Clipped article came from Smith Papers, with a handwritten note: *China Herald & Examiner*, Dec. 20, '32. Smith to Ruth Woodhull Tangier Smith, 25 June 1931, and 3 Feb. 1932; and 6 Mar. 1932, "I am

highly expectant over what may have been accomplished while I have been away," he writes, "and even dare to hope that a live panda or takin or two may be eating out of hand when I reach the various present headquarters," Smith Papers.

46 *But the exhausting work*   Details of Smith's life in the field from his correspondence with Field Museum, 17 Jan. 1931; Mar., June 23, 1931; 9 Oct. 1931; 27 Nov. 1930; and 6 Mar. 1936, Field Museum archives.

47 *In the words*   Russell to Reynolds, 1 Apr. 1965.

47 *The haggard and luckless*   *China Journal*, Oct. 1934, p. 171.

48 *"always just around the corner"*   Harkness to Perkins, 25 July 1936.

48 *In fact, Smith*   Smith correspondence with Field Museum, 6 May and 30 June 1936, Field Museum archives.

48 *Smith had faced*   Elizabeth Smith to Ruth Woodhull Tangier Smith, 23 Dec. 1936.

48 *"I think Ajax is out"*   Harkness to Perkins, 25 July 1936; sentiment echoed in letter of 6 Aug. 1936.

48 *the diplomatic corps was*   Tuchman, *Stilwell*, p. 145.

48 *From high in the air*   Harkness to Perkins, 27 July 1936.

49 *The moment Harkness presented*   Information from Harkness to Perkins and Pierce, 25 July 1936, and from Political Graveyard website: http://www.politicalgraveyard.com: Nelson Trusler Johnson (1887–1954), Ambassador to China starting 1935.

49 *Ambassador Nelson Trusler Johnson*   Details about Johnson from Tuchman, *Stilwell*, p. 148.

50 *"Now be sure"*   Foreign embassies were already beginning to move down to Nanking: "British Envoy to Quit Peiping for Nanking," *Christian Science Monitor*, 3 Aug. 1936.

50 *She must have smiled*   Tuchman, *Stilwell*, p. 120.

50 *Sunlight and the dust*   NASA photographs of the phenomenon on 25 Apr. 2001; Associated Press report (6 April 2000) that a million tons of Gobi Desert dust hit Beijing. Also Tuchman, *Stilwell*, p. 65.

50 *"A sudden feeling"*   Harkness, *Lady and the Panda*, pp. 37–38.

50 *"horse, guide, and mentor"*   Harkness to Perkins, 6 Aug. 1936.

50 *There were the dazzling*   Picture in *National Geographic*, Dec. 1936, plate 15.

CHAPTER THREE: GAINING THE WHIP HAND

53 *Gerry Russell finally arrived*   Harkness to Perkins and Anne Pierce, 25 July 1936.

53 *Initially Harkness*   Harkness to Perkins, 25 Aug. 1936.

53 *A case of dysentery*   Harkness to Perkins, 6 Aug. 1936.

53 *The illness was*   Tuchman, *Stilwell*, p. 192, mentions that the French attaché died of it in the late 1930s.

53   *Doubled over*   Harkness to Perkins, 6 Aug. 1936. Undated letter from Perkins to Harkness refers to a possible operation. The letter clearly was written after Harkness's Beijing trip. Perkins's return letter from Aug. 1936 refers to the recommendation of "an operation." See also World Health Organization's fact sheet on dysentery; and *Columbia Encyclopedia,* 6th edition (New York: Columbia University Press, 2003).

53   *"out of the question"*   Harkness to Perkins, 6 Aug. 1936.

54   *"a minor repair job"*   Harkness to Perkins, 17 Aug. 1936.

54   *However gently*   Harkness to Perkins, 27 Sept. 1936.

54   *Russell, Harkness*   Russell to Reynolds, 1 Apr. 1965.

54   *Too broke*   Elizabeth Smith to Ruth Woodhull Tangier Smith, 8 Dec. 1936, Smith Papers. It is clear that Smith was broke in December, and likely that he was in the same or a similar state in September.

54   *"Ajax is being"*   Harkness to Perkins, misdated 12 July 1936, should be 12 Aug. 1936.

54   *There had been seven . . . for another surgery*   Smith to Spalding, 5 Mar. 1936, Field Museum archives. Though Smith doesn't say clearly what the operation was, he reports later that further growths appeared on Bill's neck, so they must have prompted the first hospitalization.

55   *the tumors were malignant*   Details of Bill's illness: Smith to Spalding, 5 Mar. 1936.

56   *Apparently it was lonely*   "Explorer Harkness Dies of Cancer," *Shanghai Evening Post and Mercury,* 20 Feb. 1936.

56   *There was a rumor*   Michael Kiefer, *Chasing the Panda: How an Unlikely Pair of Adventurers Won the Race to Capture the Mythical White Bear* (New York: Four Walls Eight Windows, 2002).

56   *Smith not only rebuffed*   Floyd Tangier Smith, document/letter, 12 Mar. 1937, House Papers.

56   *But Smith also contended*   Smith, letter/document, 12 Oct. 1937, Smith Papers.

57   *Although she joked*   Harkness to Perkins, 8 July 1936.

57   *"My God, Perkie"*   Harkness to Perkins, 30 Aug. 1936.

57   *"The messed up"*   Harkness to Perkins, 27 Aug. 1936.

57   *But years later*   Russell to Reynolds, 1 Apr. 1965.

57   *Just as Harkness*   Harkness, *Lady and the Panda,* p. 51.

57   *He was so dashing*   Jialing Young (Jack's daughter), conversation with author. All other information from Su-Lin Young, interview by author, Spruce Pines, N.C., Dec. 2001.

57   *Only twenty-five years old*   Jolly Young, e-mail to author, Jan. 2003, gives her father's birthdate: 13 Nov. 1910.

58   *Gongga Shan, in Sichuan*   Jon Krakauer, *Eiger Dreams: Ventures Among Men and Mountains* (New York: Anchor Books, 1990), p. 120.

58   *Americans Richard Burdsall and Terris Moore*   *China Journal,* Mar. 1936, p. 172.

58   *With his beautiful*   The prestigious *China Journal* was quite impressed with the Youngs, "who for several years have been carrying out hazardous expeditions into the wilds of the Chinese-Tibetan border lands to collect zoological specimens." *China Journal*, Mar. 1936, p. 172.

59   *Despite his urbane look*   Harkness to Perkins, 25 Aug. 1936.

59   *Quentin was startled*   Su-Lin Young interview.

59   *"If much of young China"*   Harkness to Perkins, 13 Oct. 1936.

60   *The notion of finally*   Harkness, *Lady and the Panda*, p. 56.

60   *Shortly, a plan was in place*   Harkness to Perkins, 7 Sept. 1936.

61   *"barbarian"*   Harkness, *Lady and the Panda*, p. 69.

61   *Considering the constant*   "Mrs. Edward S. Harkness gives $150,000 to Conn. College," *Wall Street Journal*, 14 Dec. 1933.

61   *"a poor working girl"*   Harkness to Perkins, 19 Sept. 1936.

62   *He was only*   Jane Reib Pollock (Reib's daughter), telephone conversation with author, 2 Dec. 2003.

62   *he was a "cyclone"*   Harkness to Perkins, 12 Sept. 1936; and Harkness, *Lady and the Panda*, p. 69.

62   *He had black*   Jane Reib Pollock, telephone conversation.

62   *Most of all*   Harkness to Perkins, 19 Sept. 1936.

62   *He had even been captured*   Harkness to Perkins, 12 Sept. 1936.

62   *He adored women*   Jane Reib Pollock conversation; Edward Charles Reib, (Reib's grandson), e-mail correspondence with author, 30 Nov. 2003.

62   *The second time he came*   Harkness to Perkins, 12 and 19 Sept. 1936.

62   *As an executive*   Harkness to Perkins, 9 Sept. 1936.

63   *It was an enormous gift*   Sherman Cochran, *Encountering Chinese Networks* (Berkeley: University of California Press, 2000), p. 39.

63   *In fact, Fortune*   "The Shanghai Boom," *Fortune*, Jan. 1935.

63   *"everything from maps to brandy"*   Harkness to Perkins, 30 Sept. 1936.

63   *Reib, Harkness wrote home*   Harkness to Perkins, 27 Sept. 1936.

63   *"One gains sometimes"*   Harkness to Perkins, 19 Sept. 1936.

63   *Reib liked strong women*   Jane Reib Pollock conversation; and Edward Charles Reib e-mail correspondence. Case is *Grigsby* v. *Reib*, Texas Supreme Court, 1913.

63   *"a marvelous companionship"*   Harkness to Perkins, 12 and 27 Sept. 1936.

64   *Of course, the funny thing*   Harkness to Perkins, n.d. but clearly late summer or fall 1936.

64   *He was a divorced man*   Harkness to Perkins, 19 Sept. 1936.

64   *"The speed"*   Baum, *Shanghai '37*, p. 364.

64   *"Shanghai gossip"*   Emily Hahn, *China to Me* (1944; E-Reads, 1999), p. 5.

64   *"The most intimate"*   Harkness to Perkins, n.d. but written before 24 Aug. 1936.

64   *"I am becoming"*   Harkness to Perkins, 19 Sept. 1936.

64 *met with Reib at any hour*   Ibid.

64 *sukiyaki dinners*   Harkness to Perkins, 30 Aug. 1936.

64 *"It is rather uninteresting"*   Harkness to Perkins, 17 Aug. 1936.

64 *There was so much to do*   Harkness to Perkins, 19 Sept. 1936.

65 *In the lingering summer*   According to Harkness to Perkins, 3 Sept. 1936, she started the process that morning.

65 *Bill was to have enjoyed*   Harkness to Perkins, 3 Sept. 1936.

65 *rifles, shotguns, pistols, and bayonets*   Harkness to Perkins, 30 Aug. 1936.

66 *shrunk by a resourceful Chinese shoemaker*   North China Daily News, 28 Nov. 1936, describes clothes cut down, even "Tibetan boots."

Their expedition was to be a leaner proposition than others, Harkness declared. She would not be including the linens, silver, and "facilities for iced champagne" that some had been known to carry. In fact, she wouldn't even pack a fork.

The majority of Bill Harkness's possessions would be sold. Almost two whole groups of items were jettisoned—the arsenal of guns and the enormous stock of sophisticated medical supplies, which contained anesthetics, surgical instruments, and suture silk. Harkness was petrified she would end up killing someone with articles from either group, so only the essentials of each were sorted and retained. Dan Reib would take over from here, arranging the auctioning off of the equipment that she couldn't use and turning it into cash, which she could.

66 *recurring nightmare*   Harkness, Lady and the Panda, p. 56.

66 *"When Quentin Young consented"*   Harkness as told to Adamson, "How I Caught the Rare Giant Panda," part 3, "How Mrs. Harkness Kept the Baby Panda Alive," New York American, 28 Feb. 1937.

67 *"much hooted-at expedition"*   Charles Poore, "Books of the Times," New York Times, 15 Jan. 1938.

67 *interest these gentlemen took*   Telegram, 26 July 1934, from the files of the Wildlife Conservation Society, Bronx Zoo archives.

67 *"an innate dignity"*   Harkness to Perkins, 19 Sept. 1936.

67 *"Quentin says"*   Harkness to Perkins, 30 Aug. 1936.

67 *Ha Gansi*   Translation worked out by Professor Sarah Queen, Connecticut College.

67 *It was Reib's version*   Harkness, Lady and the Panda, p. 85.

68 *first Chinese woman explorer*   China Journal, Dec. 1936, p. 338.

68 *"glamorous"*   Hahn, China to Me.

69 *Once they were in the snowy*   Su-Lin Young interview.

69 *She could meditate*   Harkness to Perkins, n.d. but from the early 1940s.

69 *"I am looking for . . . the madness of the East"*   Harkness to Perkins, 9 Sept. 1936.

69 *"China has given me"*   Harkness to Perkins, 6 Aug. 1936.

69 *"After mature thought"* Harkness to Perkins, 25 Aug. 1936.

70 *Some of the old issues* Ruth Harkness to Hazel Perkins, 27 Aug. 1936.

70 *While complaining* Floyd Tangier Smith to Field Museum, 19 Dec. 1935, Field Museum archives.

70 *As Russell raised* Harkness to Perkins, 27 Aug. 1936.

70 *But the problems* In Harkness to Perkins, 12 Sept. 1936, she says the Russell situation had been bothering her for nearly three weeks.

70 *"a day of Chinese rain"* Harkness to Perkins, 9 Sept. 1936.

71 *The fact was that the more* Harkness to Perkins, 12 Sept. 1936.

71 *Before she ever got to China* Ruth Harkness to Hazel Perkins and others, 17 Oct. 1936.

71 *She didn't want anything* Harkness to Perkins, 9 Sept. 1936.

71 *Over and over* Smith, document/letter 12 Mar. 1937.

71 *Their differences had* Harkness to Perkins, 12 Sept. 1936.

71 *"The VRYENGLISH GENTLEMAN"* Harkness to Perkins, 7 Sept. 1936.

72 *Her dealings with Smith* Harkness to Perkins, misdated 12 July 1936, should be 12 Aug. 1936.

72 *for his return ticket* Harkness to Perkins, 12 Oct. 1936.

72 *She thought he loathed her* Harkness to Perkins, 19 Sept. 1936. He did retaliate in some way, for she would write home mysteriously that she was shocked that Russell did "things that no 'crude' American would dream of." Elizabeth Smith would later say that in the wake of it, Harkness had "dished Gerry." What exactly it was didn't seem to bother her for long, and went unrecorded.

72 *"Jerry [sic] I think behaved rather badly"* Harkness to Perkins, 27 Sept. 1936.

72 *Russell was about* Harkness to Perkins, 12 Oct. 1936. The Yangtze flows eastward from Tibet to Shanghai.

73 *"That was sheer, unadulterated"* Harkness as told to Adamson, "How Mrs. Harkness Kept the Baby Panda Alive," part 3 of 3-part series *New York American,* 28 Feb. 1938.

73 *She was a bear* Diet is 98 percent bamboo in the wild; "Improved Nutrition and Infant Survival," "Panda 2000, Conservation Priorities for the New Millennium," workshop at the San Diego Zoo, Oct. 2000, http://www.sandiegozoo.org/conservation/fieldproject_panda2000.html.

73 *It looked to one zoologist* Quote from Robert Bean of Brookfield Zoo, in "Baby Panda Here, Enjoys Its Bottle," *New York Times,* 24 Dec. 1936.

74 *"They had lived"* Harkness, *Lady and the Panda,* p. 268.

74 *Late at night* Tess Johnston and Deke Erh, *A Last Look: Western Architecture in Old Shanghai* (Hong Kong: Old China Hand Press, 1993).

74 *cool swimming pool* *All About Shanghai,* p. 88.

75 *mountains on this hot dreamy night* Peggy McCleskey, interview by author, 29 Aug. 2002.

75 *"Collapse of Revolt"* *North China Herald,* 22 July 1936.

75 *"Keeping the Reds"*   Ibid., 19 Aug. 1936.

75 *"Mrs. Ogden's"*   Ibid., 29 July 1936.

75 *Thousands of Communist*   Buck, *My Several Worlds*, p. 168.

75 *"roaming bandits"*   Spence, *Search for Modern China*, p. 386. And, in fact, during the Long March, Mao had joined forces with two bandit chiefs. But when Chiang Kai-shek dubbed his anti-Communist efforts the "bandit suppression" campaign, it really was some good old-fashioned Chinese name-calling. Throughout history, warlords had always claimed their rivals were "bandit chiefs."

76 *But there was no getting*   Buck, *My Several Worlds*, p. 42.

76 *The adherents of the cause*   Tuchman, *Stilwell*, p. 32. J. A. G. Roberts, *A Concise History of China* (Cambridge: Harvard University Press, 1999), p. 201.

76 *subjugation to the Manchus*   Henrietta Harrison, *The Making of the Republican Citizen* (Oxford: Oxford University Press, 2000), p. 31.

76 *In the eyes*   Spence, *Search for Modern China*, p. 143.

77 *imploded within five years*   Roberts, *Concise History*, p. 213; and Spence, *Search for Modern China*, p. 263. But there was much confusion and separatism. Sun became the president of the provisional Republic but quickly yielded power to a military powerhouse named Yuan Shih-kai.

77 *"to fill the void"*   Tuchman, *Stilwell*, p. 9.

77 *Without a unified government . . . his own government*   Ibid., pp. 40–105.

77 *The generalissimo*   Jonathan Spence, review of Jonathan Fenby's *Chiang Kai-shek*, *New York Times*, 29 Feb. 2004.

77 *Making Chiang even more attractive*   Tuchman, *Stilwell*, p. 116.

78 *Whatever his religious leanings*   Ibid., p. 86.

78 *To critics*   Roberts, *Concise History*, p. 239.

78 *Independent provincial leaders*   Tuchman, *Stilwell*, p. 121.

78 *spawning discord and bloodshed*   Roberts, *Concise History*, pp. 234, 235.

78 *Students could gather*   Tuchman, *Stilwell*, pp. 146, 151.

78 *burying people alive*   Boye Lafayette De Mente, *The Chinese Have a Word for It* (Chicago: NTC, 1996), p. 118.

78 *or beheading them*   photo of severed heads of outlaws posted on Nanking billboard, *National Geographic*, June 1927, p. 709.

78 *One of the most important events*   Spence, *Search for Modern China*, p. A58.

78 *"in a very short time"*   Roberts, *Concise History*, p. 226.

79 *"I was told"*   Harkness, "How I Caught the Rare Giant Panda," part 2.

CHAPTER FOUR: WEST TO CHENGDU

81 *Well after midnight*   Harkness to Perkins, 30 Sept. 1936.

81 *Taking a drag*   Dong, *Shanghai 1842–1949*, p. 10.

81 *It was September 27*   *North China Daily News*, 27 Sept. 36, "Passengers."

81 *The steamer* Whangpu   Deidre Chetham, *Before the Deluge: The Vanishing World of the Yangtze's Three Gorges* (New York: Palgrave MacMillan, 2002).

82 *"dear, dear Perkie"*   Harkness, *Lady and the Panda*, p. 238. Harkness expresses the sentiment in very similar terms in a letter to Perkins, 19 Sept. 1936.

82 *The transformation startled*   Harkness to Perkins, 7 Sept. 1936.

82 *including Gerry Russell*   Harkness to Perkins and others, 17 Oct. 1936.

82 *Elizabeth and Floyd Tangier Smith*   Elizabeth Smith to Ruth Woodhull Tangier Smith, 8 Dec. 1936, Smith Papers, Library of Congress.

82 *In Shanghai, the trendsetting*   Boyden, "Changing Shanghai," *National Geographic*, Oct. 1937, p. 491.

82 *Undoubtedly, Chen's powerful parents*   Kiefer, *Chasing the Panda*, p. 67.

83 *"First class accommodations"*   Details of boat trip from Harkness to Perkins, 30 Sept. 1936.

84 *"Shop after shop"*   Harkness to Perkins, 30 Sept. 1936.

85 *One of the panda hunters*   Dean Sage, Jr., "In Quest of the Giant Panda: An Account Describing the Work of the Sage West China Expedition in the Highlands of Szechwan Province, Near the Borders of Tibet," *Natural History*, Apr. 1935.

85 *Here, in the half-light*   Harkness to Perkins, 19 Sept. 1936.

85 *"I wonder when"*   Harkness to Perkins, 27 Sept. 1936.

86 *The 150-mile*   Sage, "In Quest."

86 *"He seems to have"*   Ruth Harkness, *The Baby Giant Panda* (New York: Carrick & Evans, 1938), p. 19.

86 *expedition's finances*   Harkness, *Lady and the Panda*, p. 83.

87 *He had taken this expedition*   North China Daily News, 28 Nov. 1936.

87 *She never could have fit in*   Sheldon, *Wilderness Home*, pp. 147–49.

87 *Young was managing*   Tuchman, *Stilwell*, p. 197.

87 *Aggressively jostling . . . "of the open sewage"*   Harkness to Perkins and others, 12 Oct. 1936.

88 *Half the people in China*   Tuchman, *Stilwell*, p. 147.

88 *"When I see"*   Harkness to Perkins, 13 Oct. 1936; and Tuchman, *Stilwell*, p. 144, corroborates the impression.

88 *Then word came in*   Harkness, *Lady and the Panda*, p. 93.

88 *Rather than sailing to America*   Floyd Tangier Smith, letter to the editor, *North China Daily News*, 7 Dec. 1936. In this letter, Smith says Russell left one day after Harkness, even though he has her departure date as 23 Sept., when it was actually the 27th; still, Harkness confirms in her letters that Russell left the day after.

88 *"He is trying" . . . "wring his redheaded neck"*   Harkness to Perkins and others, 12 and 17 Oct. 1936.

89 *The more she thought about it*   Harkness to Perkins, 17 Oct. 1936.

89 *What she didn't know*   China Journal, Apr. 1937.

89　*Reib had arranged*　Harkness as told to Adamson, "How I Caught the Rare Giant Panda," part 1, "Led by Tibetan, Mrs. Harkness Finds Prize in Frigid Wilds," *New York American*, 14 Feb. 1937; and Tuchman, *Stilwell*, p. 77. Tuchman verifies "the habitual Chinese failure to keep roads in repair."

89　*Completely protected*　Ross Terrill, "Sichuan: Where China Changes Course," *National Geographic*, Sept. 1985, says 40 feet wide, p. 287.

89　*At the very frontier*　Chengdu history from *Nagel's Encyclopedia Guide: China* (Geneva: Nagel, 1979), p. 1262; Jeannette L. Faurot, *Ancient Chengdu* (San Francisco: Chinese Materials Center Publications, 1992), pp. 4, 118. Once nearly destroyed by Mongol hordes under the rule of Kublai Khan, Chengdu received the great Marco Polo, who walked streets that even in the thirteenth century were covered in paving stones.

89　*It was a sprawling walled*　Harkness, *Baby Giant Panda*, p. 44.

90　*Behind the grand front gate*　Details about Cavaliere from Harkness to Perkins, 17 Oct. 1936; and Harkness, *Lady and the Panda*, p. 136.

90　*At seven o'clock*　Harkness to Perkins, 17 Oct. 1936.

91　*Pilots, explorers*　*North China Herald*, 29 July 1936.

91　*In this wilderness outpost*　Harkness to Perkins, 17 Oct. 1936.

91　*Harkness discovered*　Harkness to Perkins and others, 17 Oct. 1936.

91　*the CNAC kept him*　W. Langhorne Bond, *Wings for an Embattled China*, ed. James E. Ellis (Bethlehem, Penn.: Lehigh University Press, 2001).

91　*Kay had settled*　Harkness to Perkins and others, 17 Oct. 1936. Her chambers included an opulent bathroom, though this being Chengdu, the taps on the tub were purely ornamental, with hot water having to be carted in by the servants.

91　*He provided*　Harkness to Perkins, 17 Oct. 1936.

92　*The mountain chain*　Abend, "Rare 4-Pound 'Giant' Panda." Also this is what botanist Wilson says, as well as *China Journal*, Apr. 1937, which simply calls them a "mass of high mountains, by no means all of which have been explored," p. 189.

92　*The mountains of Tibet*　Hopkirk, *Trespassers*, p. 5.

92　*The Chinese had marveled*　Terrill, "Sichuan," p. 302.

92　*Even where the mountains*　Hopkirk, *Trespassers*, pp. 6, 232.

92　*A no-man's-land*　Simon Winchester, *The River at the Center of the World* (New York: Henry Holt, 1996), p. 363.

92　*beyond the reach of law*　Faurot, *Ancient Chengdu*. In his double-volume set, *A Naturalist in Western China*, botanist E. H. Wilson reported that the entire region was "practically uncharted and unsurveyed." It was impossible to delineate "with any approach to accuracy, the political boundary between Szechuan and Thibet," he said. "Indeed, no actual frontier has ever been agreed upon." The only fair description, Wilson concluded, was to call it the "Chino-Thibetan Borderland."

92 *Panda hunter Dean Sage*   Sage, Jr., "In Quest," pp. 312–17.

93 *Even Western climbers*   Orville Schell, *Virtual Tibet: Searching for Shangri-La from the Himalayas to Hollywood* (New York: Metropolitan Books, 2000), pp. 238–39, 190, 235–36.

93 *While in this state*   Joseph F. Rock, "Sungmas, the Living Oracles of the Tibetan Church," *National Geographic*, Oct. 1935, pp. 475–85; and Melvyn C. Goldstein, *A History of Modern Tibet, 1913–1951* (Berkeley and Los Angeles: University of California Press, 1989), pp. 140–41, fn. 8.

94 *"a beautiful forgotten world"*   Abend, "Rare 4-Pound 'Giant' Panda."

94 *Wang Whai Hsin*   Full name from the back of a photograph from the Ruth Harkness family archives. Shows Wang at the end of the second expedition and reads: "Wang Whai Hsin my one servant."

94 *He agreed with*   Schaller, *Last Panda*, pp. 130, 132; Harkness, *Lady and the Panda*, pp. 55, 56; and Roosevelt and Roosevelt, *Trailing the Giant Panda*, endmap.

94 *The only road*   Harkness to Perkins, 17 Oct. 1936.

94 *That was where Floyd Tangier Smith*   Sheldon, *Wilderness Home*, p. 32.

95 *Throughout this time, Cavaliere threw*   Harkness to Perkins, n.d., Oct. 1936.

95 *This one included*   Harkness to Perkins, 21 Oct. 1936, and second letter marked "later same evening."

95 *The* China Press *had reported*   "Lolo Chiefs Interested in Gen. Chiang: Jack Young Says Tribe Heads Believe Generalissimo Old, Wise," *China Press*, 18 Aug. 1936.

95 *Wearily, Cavaliere*   Harkness, "How I Caught the Rare Giant Panda," part 1.

96 *a ragtag caravan*   Ibid.

96 *blue cotton expedition suit*   Harkness, *Lady and the Panda*, p. 113.

96 *densest rural populations*   *Lonely Planet: China* (Australia: Lonely Planet, 1994), p. 796.

96 *Harkness, like many foreigners*   Hahn, *China to Me*, p. 118. Hahn remembered with horror the sight of her chair coolies in Sichuan. "They breathed in loud, stertorous gasps before we were halfway up to the first zigzag in the road," she wrote. "I saw how their shoulders had been warped into great lumps from the carrying poles, and their legs looked foreshortened and squashed with all their muscles, from being pressed downward."

97 *These unhappy souls*   Spence, *Search for Modern China*, p. 382.

97 *What it took to survive*   Dong, *Shanghai*, p. 162.

97 *swaggering strong man*   Harkness, *Lady and the Panda*, pp. 130–31.

98 *If she were in their situation*   Harkness to Perkins, n.d., Oct. 1936.

98 *"Last night's Inn"*   Harkness to Perkins, 21 Oct. 1936.

100 *bandit gangs as large as armies*   Dong, *Shanghai*, p. 116.

101 *Up a ladder*   Harkness, "How I Caught the Rare Giant Panda," confirms two days to Guanxian.

101 *It was Campbell*   Harkness, "How I Caught the Rare Giant Panda," part 2.

CHAPTER FIVE: RIVALRY AND ROMANCE

105 *As Harkness traveled*   Smith, letter/document, 12 Oct. 1937, Floyd Tangier Smith Papers, Library of Congress. It is unclear whether Russell was near Harkness in the field and reporting information back in letters, or if Russell merely brought Smith up to date when he returned to Shanghai.

105 *Beyond field-intelligence*   Russell to Reynolds, 1 Apr. 1965. Russell states of Harkness and the capture of her panda: "What actually occurred 15 miles from Chaopo I do not know as I was in another area." And *China Journal*, Apr. 1937, places him at the Tibetan border, in "Wassu country" in Sikong.

105 *if he had been up to it*   Elizabeth Smith to Ruth Woodhull Tangier Smith, 23 Dec. 1936, Smith Papers. She says all this took place two months before the letter.

105 *Unaware of any espionage*   Harkness as told to Adamson, "How I Caught the Rare Giant Panda," part 1, "Led by Tibetan, Mrs. Harkness Finds Prize in Frigid Wilds," *New York American*, 14 Feb. 1937.

106 *Overjoyed that*   Details of soldier incident from Ibid.

106 *Cavaliere really would*   Harkness to Perkins, 17 Oct. 1936.

106 *They shared cigarettes*   Ruth Harkness, "In a Tibetan Lamasery," *Gourmet*, Mar. 1944, p. 57.

107 *Somehow a handful*   Harkness: *Baby Giant Panda*, pp. 35–36.

107 *She once used chopsticks*   Harkness to Perkins, 17 Oct. 1936.

108 *His impulse proved*   Harkness, *Lady and the Panda*, p. 137.

108 *It sat at the foot*   Author's observation, 29 Oct. 2002.

108 *The enchanted hamlet*   Ibid.; and Sheldon, *Wilderness Home*, p. 24.

108 *Their odd, semiautonomous*   Dr. Ming-ke Wang, Institute of History and Philology at the Academia Sinica, e-mail correspondence between Professor Sarah Queen (Connecticut College) and Dr. Ming-ke Wang, 17 Dec. 2002; Schaller, *Last Panda*, p. 132; Catton, *Pandas*, p. 16.

108 *The royal men*   Sheldon, *Wilderness Home*, p. 22.

108 *Wenchuan, it turned out*   Harkness, "How I Caught the Rare Giant Panda," part 1.

109 *But the military men*   Abend, "Rare 4-Pound 'Giant' Panda."

110 *"when you yourself are right"*   Lin Yutang, *Moment in Peking* (New York: John Day, 1939), p. 7.

110 *Saluting her back*   Abend, "Rare 4-Pound 'Giant' Panda."

111 *He was the headman*   Details from Harkness as told to Adamson, "How I Caught the Rare Giant Panda," part 2, "Mrs. Harkness' Thrilling Story of Her Hunt in Asian Wilds," *New York American*, 21 Feb. 1937.

112 *"a perpetual twilight"*   Abend, "Rare 4-Pound 'Giant' Panda."

112 *New droppings*   Schaller, *Last Panda*, p. 4.

113 *Her predecessor*   Sheldon, *Wilderness Home*, pp. 4, 5, 16, 19, 41, 76, 106, 129.

113 *The diggers lived*   *Pandas of the Sleeping Dragon*, PBS Nature documentary, 1 Mar. 1996.

115 *said to be five hundred*   Sheldon, *Wilderness Home*, p. 62.

115 *Exhausted, Harkness and Young*   Schell, *Virtual Tibet*, p. 4.

116 *The depictions were so graphic*   Torrance, *Journal of the West China Border Research Society*, 1932.

116 *The botanist E. H. Wilson*   Wilson, *A Naturalist in Western China*, p. 168.

116 *The deities seemed proud*   Schell, *Virtual Tibet*, p. 21.

116 *Harkness, who loved the "frankness"*   Harkness to Perkins, 24 Sept. 1937.

116 *Something must have stirred*   Although Harkness never actually revealed the romance publicly, she left poetic and sometimes rather obvious hints of it in the book she was to write later. Young went one step further; as an old man, he confirmed the relationship with reporter Michael Kiefer, and over time even told him where and when the liaison started. See Kiefer, *Chasing the Panda*.

117 *But the issue had fascinated*   Harkness to Perkins, 16 June 1936.

117 *Emily Hahn and the poet*   Sergeant, *Shanghai*, p. 293.

117 *There were rooms for ancestor*   Harkness to Perkins and others, 17 Oct. 1936.

117 *Still, both whites and Chinese*   Dong, *Shanghai*, p. 28.

119 *Sage had written extensively*   Sage, Jr., "In Quest," p. 312.

119 *"lonely, wild"*   Harkness, *Lady and the Panda*, p. 171.

119 *in her silk sleeping bag*   Ibid., p. 193.

120 *"Hurry up"*   Ibid., p. 180.

120 *Young strode down*   Ibid., p. 181.

121 *Not only were they climbing*   Schaller, *Last Panda*, pp. 85–86, 26. As the stoic field biologist George Schaller would declare many years later, "The essence of panda tracking was discomfort."

121 *"Picture, if you can"*   Harkness, "How I Caught the Rare Giant Panda," part 1.

121 *Evidence too*   William Theodore de Bary, Wing-Tsit Chan, and Burton Watson, eds., *Sources of Chinese Tradition*, vol. 1 (New York: Columbia University Press, 1960), from "Pao-p'u Tzu," p. 259.

122 *In this foggy region*   Harkness, "How I Caught the Rare Giant Panda," part 1.

122 *All along the route*   Ibid.

122 *Full of natural history data*   Anne Birrell, trans., *The Classic of Mountains and Seas* (London: Penguin Books, 1999), pp. 25, 124.

123 *Here in the mountains*   Schaller, *Last Panda*, pp. 61–62.

123 *In general, though*   Morris and Morris, *Men and Pandas*, pp. 28–30.

123 *Now, in the cold of November*   Susan Lumpkin and John Seidensticker, *The Smithsonian Book of Giant Pandas* (Washington, D.C.: Smithsonian Institution, 2002), p. 66.

123 *For a male in the vicinity*   Ibid., pp. 79–80.

123 *Precisely who she was* "Chemical Communication in Giant Pandas," "Panda 2000, Conservation Priorities for the New Millennium," workshop at the San Diego Zoo, Oct. 2000, http://www.sandiegozoo.org/conservation/fieldproject_panda2000.html.

123 *On this night, not far from Camp Two* Lumpkin and Seidensticker, *Smithsonian Book of Giant Pandas*, p. 76. A tree of this age is usually required for a hollow big enough.

123 *her two-month-old baby* Estimate of age from panda experts at Zoo Atlanta, from viewing photographs of Su-Lin.

123 *Next to his mother* Lumpkin and Seidensticker, *Smithsonian Book of Giant Pandas*, p. 89. Panda babies weigh about 3.5 ounces.

CHAPTER SIX: A GIFT FROM THE SPIRITS

125 *When Harkness first awoke* Harkness as told to Adamson, "How I Caught the Rare Giant Panda," part 1, "Led by Tibetan, Mrs. Harkness Finds Prize in Frigid Wilds," *New York American*, 14 Feb. 1937.

125 *She ate a spartan breakfast* Ibid.

126 *The visibility was poor* *North China Daily News*, 28 Nov. 1936.

126 *In the dense fog* Abend, "Rare 4-Pound 'Giant' Panda," 20 Dec. 1936.

126 *Stumbling on* Harkness as told to Adamson, "How I Caught the Rare Giant Panda," part 2, "Mrs. Harkness' Thrilling Story of Her Hunt in Asian Wilds," *New York American*, 21 Feb. 1937.

126 *When he quickly surrendered* Ibid., parts 2 and 3.

127 *At the bottom of Young's Tibetan trunk* Harkness as told to Adamson, "How I Caught the Rare Giant Panda," part 3, "How Mrs. Harkness Kept the Baby Panda Alive," *New York American*, 28 Feb. 1937.

127 *Sitting outside the tent* Harkness, *Baby Giant Panda*, p. 32.

128 *Harkness would report later* Harkness, "How I Caught the Rare Giant Panda," part 3.

129 *"or sprawled"* Harkness, *Lady and the Panda*, p. 224.

129 *Even his whimpering* Harkness, "How I Caught the Rare Giant Panda," part 2.

129 *gaze on his placid* Harkness, *Lady and the Panda*, p. 197.

129 *"the most precious thing"* Ibid., p. 211.

129 *Because there was no external scrotum* Su-Lin was discovered to be a male during dissection, reported in *Time*, 1 May 1939; and in *Field Museum News*, p. 7, n.d. but must be May 1938.

129 *"a week or two old"* Harkness, "How I Caught the Rare Giant Panda," part 2; and Harkness, *Baby Giant Panda*, p. 31.

129 *actually about eight or nine weeks* Consensus of panda experts at Zoo Atlanta, examining photos of Su-Lin, Mar. 2003. Pictures brought to zoo by

Jolly Young. Experts included zoo's veterinarian and the director of the Chengdu panda-breeding facility.

130 *fashioned a comfortable cradle*   Harkness, *Baby Giant Panda*, p. 31.

130 *Hudson Bay blanket*   Harkness, "How I Caught the Rare Giant Panda," part 3.

130 *They did everything to keep*   *North China Daily News,* 28 Nov. 1936.

130 *It had all gone to their heads*   Harkness, *Lady and the Panda*, p. 191.

130 *"The thing I most wanted"*   Ibid.

130 *Life was so good here*   Harkness, *Baby Giant Panda*, p. 31.

130 *the Immortals of Daoist belief*   Edward L. Shaughnessy, ed., *China: Empire and Civilization* (Oxford: Oxford University Press, 2000), pp. 91, 95.

130 *"Heaven is my bed"*   Chang Heng, "The Bones of Chuang Tzu," *Anthology of Chinese Literature: From Early Times to the Fourteenth Century,* ed. Cyril Birch (New York: Grove Press, 1965), p. 178.

131 *Rain and sleet*   Harkness, "How I Caught the Rare Giant Panda," part 3.

131 *The panda was cuddled*   Ibid.

132 *Firecrackers exploded*   Ruth Harkness, "In a Tibetan Lamasery," *Gourmet,* Mar. 1944, p. 58.

132 *They sometimes lived in temples*   Harkness, *Baby Giant Panda*, p. 36.

133 *Wisely, Su-Lin*   Ibid., pp. 36–39.

134 *After her days in the mountains*   Harkness, "How I Caught the Rare Giant Panda," part 3.

134 *She kept Baby close*   *North China Daily News,* 28 Nov. 1936.

134 *A vigilant mother*   Harkness, "How I Caught the Rare Giant Panda," part 3.

134 *For the journey to Guanxian*   Harkness, *Baby Giant Panda*, pp. 39–40.

135 *Instead, Harkness pressed*   Abend, "Rare 4-Pound 'Giant' Panda."

135 *At first light*   Ibid.; also, the picture of Harkness with Hosie in *North China Daily News,* 29 Nov. 1936.

136 *Lady Hosie was the daughter*   "Lady Dorothea Hosie, Lecturer on Chinese, Found Typhoon of Wit," *China Press,* 28 July 1936; and "Lady Hosie," *North China Herald,* 29 July 1936.

136 *The chance encounter*   *North China Daily News,* 29 Nov. 1936.

136 *The very British*   Dorothea Hosie, *Brave New China* (London: Hodder and Stoughton, 1938), pp. 138–39.

137 *When he came to a stop*   Harkness, "How I Caught the Rare Giant Panda," part 3.

137 *He was spending the night*   Ibid.

138 *Ruth Harkness felt it was*   Lin Yutang, *Moment in Peking* (New York: John Day, 1939), p. 9.

138 *The next morning, November 17*   The *China Press,* which met her at the airport, says she got into Shanghai on 17 Nov. (3 Dec. edition). *New York Times,* 18 Nov. 1936, says she arrived in Chengdu on 17 Nov., and we know she spent one night there.

138 *Douglas fourteen-passenger airplane*   From "Improvement of CNAC Air-

ways," "Tales of Old Shanghai" website. CNAC added another fourteen-passenger Douglas to its fleet in 1935 to ensure one-day travel between Shanghai and Chengdu. Leaving at 7 A.M., one could reach Chengdu by 3:30 P.M.

138 *November marked*   W. Langhorne Bond, *Wings for an Embattled China*, ed. James E. Ellis (Bethlehem, Penn.: Lehigh University Press, 2001), p. 87.

CHAPTER SEVEN: THE BATTLE ROYAL

139 *The sound of droning engines*   China National Aviation Corporation website, http://www.CNAC.org.

139 *Captain Mac, who had draped*   Harkness, *Baby Giant Panda*, p. 47 (Kyatang says a porter carried the basket).

140 *"The animal is believed"*   *New York Times*, 18 Nov. 1936.

140 *The flashed message*   "Baby Giant," *Time*, 7 Dec. 1936.

140 *She would do this*   "Battle Over, Panda and Captor Sail," *China Press*, 3 Dec. 1936.

140 *She wanted to make sure*   *Shanghai Evening Post and Mercury*, 2 Dec. 1936, talks about her heading out over the Yellow Sea, but maps from *National Geographic* (big map from 1933) and small, detailed map on p. 491, of Oct. 1937, indicate East China Sea.

140 *Since the airport*   Baum, *Shanghai '37*.

141 *As one of the heads of Standard Oil*   Jane Reib Pollock (Reib's daughter), conversation with author, 2 Dec. 2003. Reib even lived across the street from T. V. Soong, onetime minister of finance and brother-in-law of Chiang Kai-shek.

141 *cuddling tiny Su-Lin*   Harkness, *Lady and the Panda*, p. 227.

141 *"She has personality"*   Harkness, *Baby Giant Panda*, p. 48.

141 *"broken all the rules"*   Harkness, *Lady and the Panda*, p. 223.

141 *"naughty child"*   Ibid., p. 224.

141 *And as* The New York Times   "Baby Panda Here, Enjoys Its Bottle," *New York Times*, 24 Dec. 1936.

141 *After feeding Su-Lin*   Harkness, *Baby Giant Panda*, p. 48.

141 *She comforted*   Peggy McCleskey, interview by author, 29 Aug. 2002 and e-mail correspondence, 28 Aug. 2002.

141 *At first*   Peggy McCleskey e-mail.

142 *The panda grew stronger*   *North China Daily News*, 28 Nov. 1936.

142 *Nance went home*   Harkness as told to Adamson, "How I Caught the Rare Giant Panda," part 3, "How Mrs. Harkness Kept the Baby Panda Alive," *New York American*, 28 Feb. 1937.

142 *The next day*   Postal telegraph received at 299 Main St., Danbury, Conn., from Shanghai, 18 Nov. 1936.

142 *She would shortly afterward*   Abend, "Rare 4-Pound 'Giant' Panda."

142   *he recommended that*   Harkness, *Lady and the Panda*, p. 228.

142   *She was the hush-hush*   *China Press*, 28 Nov. 1936.

142   *In the mountains*   *North China Daily News*, 28 Nov. 1936.

142   *In the town*   Harkness, *Baby Giant Panda*, pp. 55, 67.

143   *Su-Lin's circle*   Elizabeth Smith to Ruth Woodhull Tangier Smith, 8 Dec. 1936, Floyd Tangier Smith Papers, Library of Congress.

143   *They became Su-Lin's*   *North China Daily News*, 28 Nov. 1936.

143   *Hardenbrooke, a Kodak*   "Tibetan Border New Quiet," *North China Herald*, 26 Aug. 1936.

144   *Given Harkness's inner circle*   Harkness, "How I Caught the Rare Giant Panda," part 3.

144   *In each case*   *China Press*, 3 Dec. 1936.

144   *"an influential person"*   Harkness, *Lady and the Panda*, pp. 230–32.

144   *The earliest liner*   "Foreign Sailings," *China Press*, 28 Nov. 1936.

144   *As the holiday approached*   *China Press*, 21 Nov. 1936.

144   *Once, in a dark moment*   Harkness, *Lady and the Panda*, p. 235.

145   *She gave up her time*   Harkness, *Baby Giant Panda*, p. 32.

145   *Long afterward*   *New Mexico State Tribune Company* stamped on undated article headlined "Sought Pandas Because Few White Men Caught Them," Feb. 1938.

145   *She became determined*   Harkness, *Baby Giant Panda*, p. 32.

145   *A piece of film*   Abend, "Rare 4-Pound 'Giant' Panda."

145   *Arthur de Carle Sowerby*   Jonathan Edwards Sinton, "Arthur de Carle Sowerby: A Naturalist in Republican China," (thesis, Harvard University, Mar. 1986).

145   *The gray-haired naturalist*   Harkness, *Lady and the Panda*, p. 238.

145   *"eminently fitting"*   "A Baby Panda Comes to Town," *China Journal*, Dec. 1936, p. 339.

145   *opening his eyes*   Harkness, *Lady and the Panda*, p. 233.

145   *And, as accomplished as Sowerby*   *China Journal*, Dec. 1936, p. 337.

145   *December issue of* The China Journal   "Baby Panda Comes to Town," pp. 335, 337.

146   *She would send*   *China Press*, 28 Nov. 1936.

146   *With Reib out of commission*   Ibid., 3 Dec. 1936. Reib's cold from Harkness, *Lady and the Panda*, p. 242.

146   *When the door was thrown open*   *North China Daily News*, 28 Nov. 1936.

147   *She told them that she owed*   Ibid.

147   *Sowerby noted*   *China Journal*, Dec. 1936, pp. 337, 338. Of course, the papers printed some of what she said, but they did not accord the same respect to Quentin Young as they did to Ruth Harkness, the least of it being that she was "Mrs. Harkness" in print, and he was referred to by the more familiar "Quentin."

147 *But before the launch*   *China Press*, 29 Nov. 1936.

147 *officials suddenly appeared*   Harkness, *Baby Giant Panda*, p. 59.

148 *Temperatures in the unheated*   *China Press*, 28 Nov. 1936, p. 1; and "Customs Holds Baby Panda; Tibetan Cub Fails to Sail for America with Mistress," *Shanghai Post and Mercury*, 28 Nov. 1936.

148 *Harkness was stopped*   *China Press*, 29 Nov. 1936.

148 *Harkness was nearly hysterical*   *New York Times*, 28 Nov. 1936.

148 *They wondered now*   Harkness to Perkins, 13 Aug. 1937.

148 *Officials told the American*   Harkness, "How I Caught the Rare Giant Panda," part 3.

149 *"This valuable find"*   *China Press*, 28 Nov. 1936.

149 *Floyd James made his way*   "Panda's Trip to America Is Held Up," *China Press*, 29 Nov. 1936.

149 *Dan Reib*   *New York Times*, 29 Nov. 1936.

149 *Before noon*   *China Press*, 29 Nov. 1936.

150 *a conference of Harkness supporters*   Harkness, *Lady and the Panda*, p. 249.

150 *Harkness, however, was showing*   *China Press*, 29 Nov. 1936.

150 *Harkness's insistence*   Schaller, *Last Panda*, p. 84.

150 *On Sunday two New York papers*   *New York Times*, 29 Nov. 1936.

151 *In Shanghai, where the local newspapers*   *China Journal*, July 1937.

151 *The China Press was told*   *China Press*, 29 Nov. 1936.

151 *All she had to do*   *New York Times*, 29 Nov. 1936.

151 *First, officials*   Moore, "Cosmopolitan Shanghai," p. 335.

151 *"smouldering fury"*   Buck, *My Several Worlds*, p. 52.

151 *"The only danger"*   *New York Times*, 29 Nov. 1936.

152 The New York Times *was one*   *New York Times*, 28 Nov. 1936.

152 *The* China Press *had placed*   *China Press*, 28 Nov. 1936; *Shanghai Evening Post and Mercury*, 2 Dec. 1936; and *Shanghai Times*, 3 Dec. 1936.

152 *"the most valuable"*   *China Press*, 3 Dec. 1936.

152 *Sowerby, her ally*   *China Journal*, Dec. 1936, p. 338.

152 *The* China Press *held*   *China Press*, 3 Dec. 1936.

152 *She had sunk every penny*   Ibid., 29 Nov. 1936.

152 *But now that the panda*   Smith document/letter, 12 Oct. 1937, Smith Papers.

153 *Their meeting would be brief*   "Mrs. Harkness Got His Panda, Explorer 'Ajax' Smith Charges," *China Press*, 4 Dec. 1936; and "Panda Problem Stirs Up Local Explorers," *Shanghai Evening Post and Mercury*, 4 Dec. 1936.

153 *the details of the route*   Smith, letter/document, 12 Mar. 1937: "She told me the truth about the route she had followed, but appeared not to know where it had led her," and appeared, he said, not to realize it led straight to his camp. Library of Congress.

153 *On Monday, November 30*   *China Press*, 3 Dec. 1936, p. 1.

153 *The bumpy and bleak*   Ibid., 30 Nov. 1936.

153   *On Tuesday, Harkness was still*   Ibid., 1 Dec. 1936.

153   *"Panda May Not"*   North China Daily News, 1 Dec. 1936.

153   *"One day the papers"*   Harkness, *Lady and the Panda*, p. 250.

153   *Its reporter heard*   New York Times, 1 Dec. 1936.

153   *As the highest scientific research*   "Panda Emigration May Fall Through," Shanghai Evening Post and Mercury, 1 Dec. 1936.

153   *There were persistent*   China Press, 1 Dec. 1936.

153   *A breakthrough came*   North China Daily News, 3 Dec. 1936.

153   The New York Times   New York Times, 2 Dec. 1936, p. 29.

153   Time *magazine said*   "Baby Giant," Time, 7 Dec. 1936.

154   *Much later she would tell*   "Sought Pandas Because Few White Men."

154   *Sowerby praised*   China Journal, Dec. 1937, p. 335.

154   *In holding the baby close*   Abend, "Rare 4-Pound 'Giant' Panda." Abend also says that Harkness never let the panda out of her sight.

154   The New York Times *reported*   New York Times, 2 Dec. 1936.

154   *While her journalist*   Telegram from Shanghai, unsigned, to Hazel Perkins, Danbury, Conn., 1 Dec. 1936.

155   *The* China Press   China Press, 2 Dec. 1936.

155   *Woo Kyatang recorded*   Ibid., 3 Dec. 1936.

155   *With all the interested players*   Shanghai Post and Mercury, 2 Dec. 1936.

155   *The staff was instructed*   China Press, 3 Dec. 1936.

155   *"Mrs. Harkness looked"*   "Panda Given Clearing Papers for U.S. at Last Moment," Shanghai Times, 3 Dec. 1936.

155   *Harkness was being so cautious*   North China Daily News, 3 Dec. 1936. The passenger list for the *President McKinley* does not contain her name. And China Press, 3 Dec. 1936, reports the deletion.

155   *On Wednesday, December 2*   "Rare Baby Panda Claws Mistress and Takes a Nap," Chicago Tribune, 23 Dec. 1936.

155   *Harkness, who had grown fond*   China Press, 3 Dec. 1936; North China Daily News, 3 Dec. 1936; and Shanghai Post and Mercury, 2 Dec. 1936.

155   *Just after 10:30 A.M.*   China Press, 3 Dec. 1936.

155   *express trans-Pacific liner*   "Shipping Green," China Press, 2 Dec. 1936.

155   *pulled away from the lower buoys*   North China Daily News, 2 Dec. 1936.

156   *last batch of Christmas mail*   "Shipping Green," China Press, 2 Dec. 1936.

156   *It was a brisk*   North China Daily News, 3 Dec. 1936; Shanghai Post and Mercury, 2 Dec. 1936; and Shanghai Times, 2 Dec. 1936.

156   *Harkness locked Baby*   Harkness, *Baby Giant Panda*, p. 68.

156   *"the quiet, unheeded"*   Harkness, *Lady and the Panda*, p. 238.

156   *"China is generous"*   Ibid., p. 68.

156   *Su-Lin was*   Harkness, "How I Caught the Rare Giant Panda," part 3.

156   *As Harkness was catching her last*   Morris and Morris, *Men and Pandas*, p. 73.

CHAPTER EIGHT: ANIMAL OF THE CENTURY

157 *The stages in darkness* A poem by Harkness's friend Charles Appleton, which was printed in part in "Su Lin, Panda Baby, Checks In at the Biltmore," the *New York Herald Tribune*, 24 Dec. 1936.

157 *slept for what seemed like days* Harkness, *Lady and the Panda*, p. 254.

157 *Smith claimed to a reporter* "Mrs. Harkness Got His Panda, Explorer 'Ajax' Smith Charges," *China Press*, 4 Dec. 1936.

158 *After the revelations* "Panda Problem Stirs Up Local Explorers," *Shanghai Evening Post and Mercury*, 4 Dec. 1936.

158 *He wrote that when Harkness left* Floyd Tangier Smith, letter to the editor, *North China Daily News*, 7 Dec. 1936.

159 *At the same time* Floyd Tangier Smith, "Hunting the Giant Panda," *Listener Rack*, fall 1937.

159 *His accusations* In his initial confusion, Smith wasn't quite sure whom to blame. He wondered if Quentin Young had misled Harkness about their bearings and led her without her knowledge into Wassu-land. In a letter from Elizabeth Smith to Floyd's sister, early in the controversy, she said, "Of course, Floyd thinks [Harkness] is perfectly innocent, but I am beginning to doubt that. Soon enough, he was conflicted. In his communiqué to the *China Press*, signed "F. T. Ajax Smith," he said Harkness's "invasion" was unintentional, but he felt that Harkness had avoided him in Shanghai because she was guilty. In short order, though, Smith would come around entirely to Elizabeth's way of thinking.

But the bulk of Smith's charges, and the pivotal point from which he would never waiver, was that Harkness had trespassed in a region that belonged to him. However, he would snare himself again in the tangle of this argument.

In his lengthy manifesto on the subject, he claimed that the notion of Wassu being "his territory" was an invention of the press. He would never have made such a claim, he said. "Those words are not mine," he demurred, "but constitute an expression that the newspapers considered justifiable." It was them, not me, making the charges against Harkness, would be a familiar refrain. And yet while he wrote this on page 3, on page 5 of the same document, he presented what he said was the text of the agreement he had drawn up for Harkness to keep her out of the kingdom of Wassu. In it, remarkably, was the very phrase he vowed he had never used—with quotes for emphasis; "I trust that . . . you will not 'invade my territory' and garner the grain that I have sowed." On one page asserting he would never, ever use such an imperialistic phrase, and then documenting his earlier use of it on another was an awfully clumsy move on Smith's part.

Whether or not Smith had actually drawn up this form for Harkness, which appears retrofitted to suit his later arguments, it is clear that he assumed he had made plain to Harkness that she would not approach this region, for which he felt he had proprietary rights.

During her stay in Chengdu, had Harkness told the experienced Cavaliere that she had agreed with Smith to avoid all of Wassu as well as the area surrounding it, he would have been aghast. Wassu territory was especially rich in wildlife, particularly the giant panda. In fact, every recent success in panda hunting—those of Wiegold, Sage, and Brocklehurst—had taken place there. It did not belong to Smith or any other man, white or Chinese or Tibetan.

When Harkness couldn't go south from Chengdu, heading north was a perfectly reasonable alternative. Smith had certainly not tried to bar other men—including another ex-partner, Russell—from "his territory." And the fact was that he had even actively helped at least one of them. Dean Sage's party—just the year before—was aided by Smith, who went so far as to provide shelter there, giving Sage keys to an old Catholic mission he owned to hole up in.

Yet, obviously, Smith did feel that where Harkness was concerned, all of Wassu land and beyond was prohibited. As unfair as this was, he was unembarrassed to explain publicly that he had extracted just such an agreement from the lady explorer through Russell. The pact was so important to Smith that when Harkness's association with Russell ended, he said, he sent Harkness a follow-up letter reminding her not to approach the whole region known as the kingdom of Wassu. Sources: Floyd Tangier Smith, letter to the editor, *North China Daily News*, 7 Dec. 1936; Elizabeth Smith to Ruth Woodhull Tangier Smith, 8 Dec. 1936; and Smith, letter/document 12 Oct. 1937, Floyd Tangier Smith Papers, Library of Congress. Arthur de Carle Sowerby, "The Natural History of West China," *China Journal*, Apr. 1937; Morris and Morris, *Men and Pandas*, p. 53; Sheldon, *Wilderness Home*, p. xviii; Floyd Tangier Smith, document/letter, 12 Mar. 1937, Smith Papers.

159   *But right afterward*   Smith, document/letter, 12 Mar. 1937.

159   *Somehow, with no recognition*   Smith, letter to the editor, *North China Daily News*, 7 Dec. 1936. He also says in his 12 Oct. 1937 letter/document that "I got the story of Mrs. Harkness movements from Mrs. Harkness herself."

159   *"impossible"*   Smith, letter to the editor, *North China Daily News*, 7 Dec. 1936.

159   *Yet he did write*   Smith, document/letter, 12 Oct. 1937.

159   *He said that she was*   Smith, document/letter, 12 Mar. 1937, Smith Papers.

159   *He had wanted to give*   Ibid.

159   *"quite amicably terminated"*   Smith, letter to the editor, *North China Daily News*, 7 Dec. 1936.

160   *The bottom line*   Elizabeth Smith to Ruth Woodhull Tangier Smith, 8 Dec. 1936.

160 *Years before* Floyd Tangier Smith to Ruth Woodhull Tangier Smith, 3 Feb. 1932, Smith Papers.

160 *Now he was the one* "Mrs. Harkness Got His Panda, Explorer 'Ajax' Smith Charges," *China Press*, 4 Dec. 1936.

160 *Her achievement* Smith, document/letter, 12 Mar. 1937.

161 *The easiest to dismiss* Phone conversation with Richard Reynolds in which he said he had letters from some missionaries who saw Harkness purchase the panda in Chengdu. Catton, *Pandas*, p. 18, reports of a missionary who said Harkness bought the panda not in Chengdu but in Guanxian. And Smith says he was told the panda was purchased in Chaopo.

161 *in pictures* Picture of Harkness with Lady Hosie, *North China Daily News*, 29 Nov. 1936; also Harkness's own photos of Wenchuan, at the threshold to Chaopo.

161 *and letters* Harkness to Perkins, various dates; Smith, letter to the editor, *North China Daily News*, 7 Dec. 1936.

161 *the notion occasionally* Morris and Morris, *Men and Pandas*, p. 78; and Catton, *Pandas*, pp. 18–19.

161 *He was "terribly cut up"* Elizabeth Smith to Ruth Woodhull Tangier Smith, 8 Dec. 1936. Elizabeth nursed an extra grudge against Harkness. She believed that had the widow not entertained the notion of an expedition, months before, the Smiths would have been saved financial calamity. Her husband, she felt, would have disbanded his camps in order to return to the United States, though given Smith's collecting aspirations, this would seem highly unlikely.

161 *By the magic* "Charges Hunters Took Baby Panda by Deception," *New York Times*, 4 Dec. 1936; and wireless to *New York Times* from Shanghai, 3 Dec. 1936.

161 *The few American papers* "Baby Panda Here from Tibet," *New York Sun*, 23 Dec. 1936, does not mention Smith by name.

161 *On the rare occasions* "Baby Panda Here, Enjoys Its Bottle," *New York Times*, 24 Dec. 1936; and "Mrs. Harkness Returns, Her 'Baby' in Her Arms; She Feeds Her Little Giant Panda from a Bottle," New York newspaper clipping, no ID, 23 or 24 Dec. 1936.

161 *"Whether the baby"* *Shanghai Evening Post and Mercury*, 4 Dec. 1936.

162 *"I knew her at last"* Smith, document/letter, 12 Oct. 1937.

162 *He was stuck fast* Elizabeth Smith to Ruth Woodhull Tangier Smith, 8 Dec. 1936.

162 *All of it fueled* *China Journal*, Nov. 1938, p. 267.

162 *"second wind"* Harkness, *Lady and the Panda*, p. 254.

162 *Even before she landed* "Baby Giant," *Time*, 7 Dec. 1936.

162 *Like most other American* "Baby Panda Here from Tibet" did mention Smith's charges, but briefly, and without naming him.

162 *On his arrival* Kiefer, *Chasing the Panda*, pp. 148–50.

163   *It was the greatest*   "Only One in Captivity: Mrs. Harkness Kidnaps Panda," *San Francisco Examiner,* 18 Dec. 1936.

163   *On a crisp morning*   Harkness, *Lady and the Panda,* p. 260. Harkness reports that after all the questions, and after dealing with customs, she "went lunchless," so it must have taken up her morning into the afternoon.

163   *They nearly swamped*   "Only One in Captivity."

163   *A wall of newshounds*   Harkness, *Lady and the Panda,* p. 259.

163   *"America was like a boxer"*   *"John Steinbeck: America and Americans and Selected Nonfiction,"* eds. Susan Schillinglaw and Jackson J. Benson (New York: Viking, 2002), p. 25.

163   *Everything seemed out of balance*   The American Experience, "If you would like to have your heart broken, just come out here," reporter Ernie Pyle had written from the Kansas-Oklahoma border that summer. WGBH-Boston. "Surviving the Dust Bowl."

164   *"That was fame"*   Poore, "Books of the Times."

164   The Times *had already*   Abend, "Rare 4-Pound 'Giant' Panda."

164   *It was "the most"*   Brookfield Zoo informational paper on the giant panda, 1 Dec. 1939, Brookfield Zoo archives.

164   *"control publicity"*   Harkness, *Lady and the Panda,* p. 259.

164   *She bristled at*   Ibid., pp. 259–60.

164   *And she hated*   "Only One in Captivity"; and Bruce Perkins, (Hazel Perkins's son), interview by author, Cleveland, Aug. 2001.

165   *A few days later*   "Rare Baby Panda Claws Mistress and Takes a Nap," *Chicago Tribune,* 23 Dec. 1936.

165   *At the Palmer House*   "Many Zoos Now Seek to Buy Famous Baby from Woman Captor," Associated Press, 23 Dec.; and official *Guide Book* of the Chicago Zoological Park, Su-Lin and Mei Mei Edition, 1938.

165   *Bean made his desire*   "Many Zoos Now Seek to Buy."

165   *Su-Lin would be headed for the Bronx*   New York Times, 2 Dec. 1936.

165   *"Don't Close Negotiations"*   Harkness to Perkins, 8 Dec. 1936.

165   *She made clear*   "Rare Baby Panda Claws Mistress."

165   *At 9:47 A.M.*   "Baby Panda Here from Tibet," *New York Sun,* Dec. 23, 1936.

165   *otter-fur coat*   "Baby Panda Here, Enjoys Its Bottle."

165   *"baby girl"*   "Many Zoos Now Seek to Buy."

165   *stepped up to the registration desk*   "Baby Panda Here from Tibet," and "Su Lin, Panda Baby, Checks in at the Biltmore," *New York Herald Tribune,* 24 Dec. 1936.

165   *"All that seemed lacking"*   Poore, "Books of the Times."

166   *Along with excited friends*   Harkness as told to Adamson, "How I Caught the Rare Giant Panda," part 4; "Baby Panda's Fate in the Balance—May Return to Jungle," *New York American,* 7 Mar. 1937; and "Baby Panda Here from Tibet."

166   *The panda too grew irritated*   Harkness, "How I Caught the Rare Giant Panda," part 4.

166   *Harkness was determined*   "Baby Panda Here from Tibet."

167   *In a large room*   "Baby Panda Here, Enjoys Its Bottle."

167   *"I keep the radiators"*   Abend, "Rare 4-Pound 'Giant' Panda."

167   *The chain-smoker*   "Baby Panda Here from Tibet."

167   *She settled herself*   "Su Lin, Panda Baby, Checks In."

167   *A tray with pots*   *Life*, 18 Dec. 1936.

167   *"knew by heart"*   Harkness, *Lady and the Panda*, p. 266.

167   *was Su-Lin housebroken*   Ibid., p. 266.

167   *"smartest panda"*   "Su Lin, Panda Baby, Checks In."

167   *To questions of Smith's charges*   "Mrs. Harkness Returns."

167   *When another reporter asked*   "Su Lin, Panda Baby, Checks In"; and "Mrs. Harkness Returns."

167   *The panda was so adorable*   "Su Lin, Panda Baby, Checks In."

168   *His eye patches*   Ibid.; and "Baby Panda Here from Tibet."

168   Time *magazine called*   "Su-lin In," *Time*, 4 Jan. 1937.

168   *"the most famous animal"*   Morris and Morris, *Men and Pandas*, p. 71.

168   *The baby panda*   Abend, "Rare 4-Pound 'Giant' Panda."

168   *The* Sun *reported*   "Baby Panda Here from Tibet."

168   *She would tell the press*   Harkness, "How I Caught the Rare Giant Panda," part 4.

168   *Charles Appleton*   "Su Lin, Panda Baby, Checks In."

168   *A few big guns*   "Baby Panda Here, Enjoys Its Bottle."

168   *Throughout the day*   Harkness as told to Adamson, "How I Caught the Rare Giant Panda," part 1; "Led by Tibetan, Mrs. Harkness Finds Prize in Frigid Wilds," *New York American*, 17 Feb. 1937.

169   *Though she may have downplayed*   "Baby Panda Here from Tibet."

169   *She made clear to the press*   "Baby Panda Here, Enjoys Its Bottle."

169   *Once the press*   "Baby Panda Here from Tibet." Also listed in 23/24 Dec. New York clipping with no ID. *New York Times*, 16 Jan. 1937, says Appleton tells reporter Harkness's address is 15 East Fifty-fifth Street.

169   *she was lonely*   Harkness, *Lady and the Panda*, p. 268.

170   *Harkness wanted the same amount*   "Baby Giant," *Time*, 7 Dec. 1936; also "Su-lin In."

170   *She had said as much*   Abend, "Rare 4-Pound 'Giant' Panda."

170   *Monkeys could be had*   From correspondence and price lists between Frank Buck and the Brookfield Zoo, May and Dec. 1936, Brookfield Zoo archives.

170   *The director*   "Everything Is Fine 'n Danda! S.F.'s Finally Got a Panda," *San Francisco Chronicle* morgue, stamped 19 Dec. 1936, but no paper affiliation on clipping.

170   *Blair complained*   Abend, "Rare 4-Pound 'Giant' Panda."

170   *Furthermore, Blair told*   John O'Reilly, "Infant Giant Panda Just an Item in Long 'First of Their Kind' List of Animals on Exhibition Here," *New York Herald Tribune*, 27 Dec. 1936.

170 *The Bronx, apparently* Harkness, *Lady and the Panda*, p. 270.

170 *all the windows rolled down* Harkness, "How I Caught the Rare Giant Panda," part 4.

171 *She wondered* Harkness, *Lady and the Panda*, p. 272.

171 *Her bank account* Ibid., p. 273.

171 *Harkness may have been downhearted* Harkness, "How I Caught the Rare Giant Panda," part 4.

171 *Among others, there were author* Schell, *Virtual Tibet*, p. 241.

171 *coming daily to sketch Su Lin* Poore, "Books of the Times."

171 *Brooke Dolan* Harkness, *Lady and the Panda*, p. 275.

171 *Theodore Roosevelt, Jr., arrived* Harkness, "How I Caught the Rare Giant Panda," part 4. This piece does not mention Kermit being there (pp. 271–72), but Harkness's *Lady and the Panda* does. The quotes differ very slightly in the book and the article. I have chosen the article's version.

172 *"And this," Harkness said* Harkness, *Lady and the Panda*, p. 275.

172 *As one Harvard* Vicki Croke, "Museum Quality," *The Boston Globe*, 31 March 2001. Quote from Glover M. Allen, Harvard University's Museum of Comparative Zoology.

172 *On Saturday evening* "Baby Panda Cries at Debut on Radio: Mrs. Harkness Holds It Up to Microphone at Dinner of the Explorers Club//Its Health Is Guarded//Rare Animal Rests in Air-Cooled Room While Waiting to Start the Broadcast," *New York Times*, 17 Jan. 1937.

172 *"They couldn't very well"* Harkness, *Lady and the Panda*, p. 274.

172 *Though they were forced* "Baby Panda Cries at Debut."

172 *sea of hundreds* Harkness, *Lady and the Panda*, p. 273, says 500 men.

172 *with their cocktails and cigars* "Baby Panda Cries at Debut."

173 *During dinner* Ibid.

173 *Before the broadcast ended* Ibid.

173 *For the series* Harkness as told to Adamson, "How I Caught the Rare Giant Panda," part 3; "How Mrs. Harkness Kept the Baby Panda Alive," *New York American*, 28 Feb. 1937.

173 *Though ragged* Harkness, "How I Caught the Rare Giant Panda," part 4.

174 *Late in the afternoon* Harkness, *Lady and the Panda*, p. 277.

174 *Her friends saw her off* All references of the time are to Grand Central Terminal, not Station. This one is from *New York American*, Mar. 1937.

174 *roses and violets* Harkness, *Lady and the Panda*, p. 277.

174 *She would stay one week* Ibid., p. 282.

174 *He was kept* Harkness, "How I Caught the Rare Giant Panda," part 4. "Baby Panda's Fate."

174 *Robert Bean, the curator* Robert Bean biography from the Brookfield Zoo archives.

174 *took the night shift* Mary Bean to Ruth Harkness, 10 Mar. 1937, Brookfield Zoo archives.

174   *Lloyd's of London*   Harkness, *Lady and the Panda*, p. 281; and Poore, "Books of the Times."

174   *the most valuable in the world*   Pathé News synopsis, 8 May 1937, Brookfield Zoo archives.

174   *in a large room*   Harkness, "How I Caught the Rare Giant Panda," part 4; "Baby Panda's Fate."

174   *He would be fed*   "Baby Su-Lin's Daily Diet," 10 Mar. 1937, records of Brookfield Zoo.

175   *Carrots, celery, lettuce*   Mary Bean to Harkness. 10 Mar. 1937.

175   *"but for whom or what"*   Harkness, *Lady and the Panda*, p. 282.

175   *Harkness returned to New York*   Her stationery from 15 Feb. 1937, lists her address as 15 East Fifty-fifth Street, New York City, Plaza 3-3465.

175   *"There are times"*   Harkness, "How I Caught the Rare Giant Panda," part 4

176   *kept off exhibit*   Harkness, *Lady and the Panda*, p. 285.

176   *It would pay Harkness $8,750*   "Su-Lin Greets Sister with a Poke on Nose; Then 2 Pandas Kiss and Make Up at Zoo," *Chicago Daily Tribune*, 19 Feb. 1938; and Brookfield Zoo archives. Sowerby, letter to the editor, *North China Daily News*, 28 July 1937, says Harkness told him $8,760. "Panda, Pet of Zoo Is Dead in Chicago," *New York Times*, 1 Apr. 1938, says $8,750. "Su-Lin Likes It at Brookfield; So She'll Stay," *Chicago Daily Tribune*, 20 Apr. 1937, reports $10,000.

176   *So, in mid-April*   "Su-Lin Likes It." By now her exploits were important enough to lure along the wildly witty Alexander Woollcott, famous for lines such as the one in which he described himself as "always a godfather, never a god."

176   *That day, April 20*   Ibid.

176   *Tens of thousands*   "Panda Becomes Gay Hostess When Guests Arrive," Associated Press, in *Joliet [Ill.] Herald News*, 18 July 1937, Brookfield Zoo archives.

176   *World Series games*   *Baseball Almanac*, http://www.baseball-almanac.com.

177   *The Bronx Zoo*   H. R. Mitchell, manager of the New York Zoological Park, to Edward Bean, director of the Brookfield Zoo, 20 Feb. 1937.

177   *Back in Shanghai*   *China Journal*, Apr. 1937, p. 190, says Russell left Shanghai for America in late March.

177   *Floyd Tangier Smith*   Russell to Reynolds, 1 Apr. 1965, says he met with Smith before leaving the country.

177   *Looking skeletal*   Floyd Tangier Smith to Ruth Woodhull Tangier Smith, 22 Apr. 1937, Smith Papers.

177   *Russell found*   Russell to Reynolds, 1 Apr. 1965.

177   *Smith had been*   From Elizabeth Smith to Ruth Woodhull Tangier Smith, 23 and 28 Dec. 1936, we know it started at Christmastime, and from his own letter to his sister, 12 Mar. 1937, we know it lasted until then. Smith Papers.

177   *Just before Christmas*   Elizabeth Smith to Ruth Woodhull Tangier Smith, 23 and 28 Dec., 1936.

177 *"financially embarrassed"* Ibid.

177 *"all gone phut"* Floyd Tangier Smith to Ruth Woodhull Tangier Smith, 22 Apr. 1937.

177 *Smith confided* Ibid.

177 *Instead of continued life* Fragment of letter, Smith to Ruth Woodhull Tangier Smith, n.d. but by information contained in letter, it must have been written in fall 1937 from, most likely, London. Smith Papers.

177 *From winter into spring* Smith to Ruth Woodhull Tangier Smith, 22 Apr. 1937.

178 *As if it hadn't* Elizabeth Smith to Ruth Woodhull Tangier Smith, 23 Dec. 1936; and Smith, document/letter, 12 Mar. 1937.

178 *After this* Smith, document/letter, 12 Mar. 1937.

178 *The irony was* Ibid.

178 *It is almost certain* Russell to Reynolds, 1 Apr. 1965, says he met with Smith before leaving the country.

178 *But Russell had another* "Another Live Giant Panda," *China Journal*, Apr. 1937, p. 190; and Arthur de Carle Sowerby, "The Natural History of West China," *China Journal*, Apr. 1937, p. 202.

179 *It was enough to daunt* Harkness to Perkins, 13 Aug. 1937.

179 *As for Smith* Smith to Ruth Woodhull Tangier Smith, 22 Apr. 1937.

179 *One of the most important* Ibid.

179 *Harkness and Smith* Harkness in Chicago on Mon. 19 Apr., according to *Chicago Tribune*; Smith writing of plans to sister Thurs. 22 Apr.

180 *Captain Brocklehurst* "Captain Brocklehurst Completes West China Expedition," *China Journal*, Apr. 1937, p. 190.

180 *Even with an expedition* *China Press*, 12 Aug. 1937, says Harkness completed both manuscripts before coming to China. This is the only reference I have to the actual writing of the books.

180 *"I shall return"* Harkness, *Lady and the Panda*, p. 288.

180 *"Again there were"* Ibid., p. 287.

CHAPTER 9: BOMBS RAIN FROM THE HEAVENS

181 *Ruth Harkness entered* Harkness to Perkins, 11 Aug. 1936 (mismarked 11 July 1936); and *China Press*, 12 Aug. 1937.

181 *Harkness knew of the danger* *China Press*, Shipping section, 12 Aug. 1937.

181 *Now, crowded up on deck* Dong, *Shanghai*, p. 252.

181 *It had backup too* *North China Daily News*, 12 Aug. 1937.

182 *As her ship drew* *China Press*, Shipping section, 12 Aug. 1937.

182 *Japan and China* Spence, *Search for Modern China*, p. 251.

182 *the Japanese making* *North China Daily News*, 12 Aug. 1937.

182 *Outside the International* *China Press*, 13 Aug. 1937.

182   *The clash that resulted*   Spence, *Search for Modern China*, pp. 420–21.

182   *Just that past December*   Roberts, *Concise History*, p. 240.

182   *By deflecting*   Tuchman, *Stilwell*, p. 168.

183   *"numbers, hate"*   Ibid., p. 161.

183   *She scrawled*   Harkness to Perkins, 11 Aug. 1936. Aboard the boat, she had been all good humor and jokes in her correspondence. At one point, she had responded to a cabled tease of Perkie's —"You are wrong. I wasn't having a cocktail when your telegram arrived; I was having a whisky with plain water."

183   *The next day, Arthur de Carle Sowerby*   "Modern Diana Returns," *North China Herald*, 18 Aug. 1937, says tea was on Thurs. afternoon.

183   *Despite the city's anxiety*   China Press, 11 Aug. 1937, with picture, "Returning."

183   *"Modern Diana Returns"*   North China Herald, 18 Aug. 1937.

183   *"Pres. Hoover Brings"*   China Press, Shipping section, 12 Aug. 1937.

183   *It couldn't help but amuse*   Harkness to Perkins, 11 Aug. 1936.

183   *Through her correspondence*   In her first letter home on 11 Aug., she expresses concern that Young is not around, but says she's not worried. *China Press*, 12 Aug. 1937, says "her first move will be to get in contact with" Quentin Young. Even by Sept., *China Journal* was reporting that Harkness "was to have met Mr. Quentin Young somewhere in South China," *China Journal*, "Travel and Exploration Notes," Sept. 1937, p. 145. And Harkness to Edward Bean, 24 Sept. 1937, Brookfield Zoo archives.

184   *Among all the cards*   Harkness to Perkins, 11 Aug. 1936.

184   *"I can't find"*   Ibid., 13 Aug. 1937.

184   *She was in the dark*   Ibid., 11 Aug. 1936.

184   *Many years later*   Quentin Young, interview by Michael Kiefer, in "I Need Time to Recuperate," *San Diego Weekly Reader* 19, no. 47 (29 Nov. 1990), p. 16.

184   *As Harkness stepped ashore*   "Ruth Harkness Completes West China Expedition," *China Journal*, "Travel and Exploration Notes," Jan. 1938, p. 37.

184   *his already pregnant wife*   Diana Chen had to have been pregnant because she gave birth in November (Harkness to Perkins, 10 Dec. 1937); and Young's presence in Hong Kong from Kiefer, *Chasing the Panda*, p. 150.

185   *In June, hunters*   "Second Live Panda Leaves China," *China Journal*, Aug. 1937.

185   *The young adult female*   "Food Problems of Giant Panda," *Shanghai Sunday Times*, 3 Oct. 1937.

185   *she boarded the* Andre Lebon   "Giant Panda en Route to U.S.," *North China Daily News*, 25 July 1937.

185   *There were rumors*   Harkness to Perkins, 13 and 23 Aug. 1937.

185   *He would admit*   "Food Problems."

185   *He sailed eventually*   "Mr. F. T. Smith Leaves Shanghai with Panda on Journey to London Zoo," *Shanghai Sunday Times*, 25 July 1937.

185 *The poor panda*   *China Journal*, "Travel and Exploration Notes," Jan. 1938, p. 38, says the panda was dead *before* Singapore; and *Shanghai Sunday Times*, 3 Oct. 1937, says she died before Saigon.

186 *Harkness would hear*   Harkness to Pierce and Perkins, 23 Aug. 1937, from aboard the *Aramis*.

186 *Pandaless, Smith continued*   "Food Problems" says he is in London then.

186 *Sowerby had amassed*   Harkness to Perkins, 13 Aug. 1937.

186 *"Such slander"*   Harkness to Perkins and Pierce, 23 Aug. 1937. Sifting through the stories, she saw that some missionaries had taken "pot shots" at her too. Many of them were on Smith's side, as he maintained strong ties with their community at the West China Union University in Chengdu. Somehow, though, the missionary rumbling struck Harkness as comic, and she shrugged it off. "Notorious character you have for a friend," she wrote home to Perkins.

186 *An inveterate writer*   The *Herald* was a round-up version of the *Daily News*, and Sowerby's letter, dated 26 July, appeared in the *Daily News* on 28 July, and in the *Herald* 11 Aug.

186 *With a tone of calm authority*   *North China Daily News*, 28 July 1937; and *North China Herald*, 11 Aug. 1937.

187 *Smith, in England*   Smith, document/letter, 12 Oct. 1937, Smith Papers, Library of Congress.

187 *Even though the writer-naturalist*   "Giant Pandas in the News," *China Journal*, "Scientific Notes and Reviews," July 1937.

187 *In September*   *China Journal*, Sept. 1937.

187 *He would point out*   Ibid., Oct. 1937, p. 210. The text says "included" instead of "inclined," a clear error.

188 *"The whole story told"*   "Ruth Harkness Here to Fulfill Mission She Holds 'Sacred,' " *China Press*, 12 Aug. 1937.

188 *She disliked having*   Ibid.

188 *Her fortunes*   Harkness to Perkins, 25 July 1937, mentions cable from "Jerry" asking her to wait for him in Chicago.

188 *It would appear*   In a later letter (10 Oct. 1937), Harkness reports meeting a missionary lady outside Chengdu who says that Russell received word of the captured panda, and had the hunters kill it and bring him the pelt.

189 *In torrents*   Dong, *Shanghai*, p. 252.

189 *"Wide thoroughfares"*   *North China Herald*, 18 Aug. 1937, dispatch dated 13 Aug. 1937.

189 *The frantic refugees*   Harkness to Perkins, 13 Aug. 1937.

189 *Many could stake out*   *China Press*, 13 Aug. 1937.

189 *The big North Station*   Ibid., 14 Aug. 1937.

189 *Settlement authorities*   Sergeant, *Shanghai*, p. 297.

189 *By Saturday morning*   *North China Daily News*, 15 Aug. 1937.

189 *Relying on information*   Harkness to Perkins and Pierce, 23 Aug. 1937.

189 *under Chiang Kai-shek's orders*   Spence, *Search for Modern China*, p. 422.

189 *Chinese biplanes* *North China Herald*, dispatch dated 16 Aug. 1937.

189 *After each raid* *North China Daily News*, 15 Aug. 1937.

189 *"Half-thrilled"* *China Press*, 15 Aug. 1937.

189 *In the late afternoon all hell* Dong, *Shanghai*.

190 *When the smoke lifted* *North China Daily News*, 15 Aug. 1937.

190 *Minutes later* Dong, *Shanghai*.

190 *In a flash* *North China Daily News*, 15 Aug. 1937.

191 *"Death from little bombs"* *China Press*, 15 Aug. 1937.

191 *"All told"* Dong, *Shanghai*. Number of dead also in "One Year of Undeclared War on China," *China Journal*, July 1938, p. 6.

191 *"I naturally"* Harkness to Perkins, 23 Aug. 1937.

191 *"Do not worry"* Dan Reib to Hazel Perkins, 5 Oct. 1937.

191 *A lights-out curfew* *China Press*, 16 Aug. 1937.

192 *By Tuesday* *North China Herald*, 25 Aug. 1937, dispatch dated 17 Aug. 1937.

192 *With heavy Japanese fire* *North China Herald*, 25 Aug. 1937, dispatch dated 18 Aug. and 25 Aug. 1937, dispatch dated 19 Aug.

192 *Harkness was not interested* Harkness to Perkins, 27 Oct. 1937.

192 *Ever more determined* Sergeant, *Shanghai*, p. 301.

192 *The "incessant bombing"* Harkness to Pierce and Perkins, 23 Aug. 1937. "Machine guns," has a typo and reads as "machibe guns."

192 *And, yes* Ibid., though she more than once refers to "the 1941 belief."

192 *"I know that this War"* Harkness to Perkins, 17 Aug. 1937.

193 The China Journal *China Journal*, "Travel and Exploration Notes," Sept. 1937, p. 145.

193 *But weeks later* Ruth Harkness to Edward Bean and family, 24 Sept. 1937.

193 *a burning* *North China Daily News*, 21 Aug. 1937, features pictures of billowing black smoke coming up out of Yangtzepoo.

193 *and battered* "Vessels Leaving," *North China Daily News*, 20 Aug. 1937.

193 *The launch* Harkness, "In a Tibetan Lamasery," p. 10. We find out they are leather from the dispatch she writes from Vietnam after the train wreck, Sept. 4–6.

193 *The horror would* Tuchman, *Stilwell*, p. 169; and Spence, *Search for Modern China*, pp. 422–423.

193 *Harkness was scrambling* "Ruth Harkness Completes West China Expedition," "Travel and Exploration Notes," *China Journal*, Jan. 1938, p. 37.

193 *Aboard the coast-hugging* "MM" is "Messageries Maritimes."

193 *While she had never* Harkness to Pierce and Perkins, 23 Aug. 1937.

CHAPTER 10: SAIGON TO CHENGDU

195 *Inscribe on your heart* Juan Chi (210–263), "Poems of My Heart," in *Anthology of Chinese Literature: From Early Times to the Fourteenth Century*, ed. Cyril Birch (New York: Grove Press, 1965), p. 179.

195 *After a brief stop* "Aramis Due To-Day," *South China Morning Post,* 24 Aug. 1937,

195 *Yet she turned* Harkness to Perkins, 15 Sept. 1937.

195 *She had several letters* Harkness to Pierce and Perkins, 25 Aug. 1937.

195 *Right away in Saigon* Ibid., 1 Sept. 1937.

196 *She was drawn* Robert J. Casey, "Four Faces of Siva: The Mystery of Angkor," *National Geographic,* Sept. 1928.

197 *The great place* W. Robert Moore, "Along the Old Mandarin Road of Indo-China," *National Geographic,* Aug. 1931.

197 *Spreading out* Barry Zwick, "Destination: Cambodia," *Los Angeles Times,* 23 Mar. 2003.

197 *The stone was known* Moore, "Old Mandarin Road."

197 *"funny little train"* Harkness to Perkins, 2 Sept. 1937.

197 *"an oasis"* Maynard Owen Williams, "By Motor Trail Across French Indo-China," *National Geographic,* Oct. 1935.

197 *But the passing scenes* Harkness to Perkins, 2 Sept. 1937.

198 *Her feelings of general foreboding* Ibid., 6 Sept. 1937; On 4 Sept. 1937, Harkness wrote in detail of a train wreck in Vietnam in a dispatch she hoped would be published back home:

> The brave little engine that screamed and whistled so courageously all of last night thru the jungle has been defeated—by the jungle. Her lights are twisted and buried in mud; her smoke stack is wreathed in twisted lianas, her little nose peers out from the fallen bamboo and bananas. She leans at a crazy but almost debonair angle, her wheels buried deep in mud; her whole expression is almost a malicious "I told you so." Even the little engine knows that the jungle is hard to defeat.
>
> Ahead is just the narrow line of steel tracks thru endless green; to the left steep wet green shooting abruptly upward, the red dripping earth torn up by the landslide is a raw wound in the hillside. From my compartment window the other side offers masses of ragged banana trees whose roots are washed by the Fleuve Rouge—it is brick red—that churns by in full flood, the muddy reddish color broken by masses of driftwood and debris. And then jungle, jungle. Low hills with masses of steamy clouds settling at their feet as if too heavy or too tired to rise again. Or perhaps beaten down by the straight heavy rain that covers the train, the jungle and the river with a gray curtain.
>
> There was only a series of jerking movements at five o'clock this morning. That had been going on all night so I merely turned over and went to sleep. We were to have changed trains at Lao Kay at six o'clock this morning, so it wasn't until I was up and dressed that I knew we were wrecked. I found someone who spoke English (I am

the only American on this train, the rest are Colonial French, Anna-
mite, Chinese or Tonkinese) and we walked up ahead to look at our
engine in the ignominious defeat. Monsieur le Directeur of this line
who is also making the journey stood in his bedroom slippers,
wrapped in a raincoat, sadly shaking his head. "Ah Madame," he said
as I approached, "we may be here indefinitely; the only diversion
here would be tigre hunting." He waved his arms in a vague Gallic
gesture. "There are plenty here in this jungle."

So I am here on a silly little train deep in the jungle, for how long
I do not know. The situation is somewhat complicated by the fact that
there is no dining car. I have had for my breakfast a glass of beer, but
food there is not. Novelists and people out here are fond of saying
"Anything can happen in the East" and one does find oneself in fantastic situations at times.

198 *"a night which I shall"*   Harkness, 4 Sept. dispatch.
198 *A certain blackness*   Ibid.
198 *a fancy Michelin train*   Harkness to Perkins, 6 Sept. 1937.
199 *She arrived at the hotel*   Ibid.
199 *She was alone*   Ibid., 6 and 10 Sept. 1937.
199 *Smoking and drinking*   Harkness to Perkins, 6 Sept. 1937.
201 *nimble little Stinsons*   Harkness to Perkins, 10 Sept. 1937; 7 Oct. description
lists five passengers on her Stinson to Chengdu.
201 *Things were jumbled*   Telegram, Edward H. Bean to Ruth Harkness, 9 Sept.
1937.
201 *In fact, matters weren't very good*   Tuchman, *Stilwell*, p. 172.
201 *While Jones gladly pledged*   Harkness to Perkins, 10 Sept. 1937.
201 *In fact, while she thought*   Ruth Harkness to Hazel Perkins, 1 Dec. 1937.
201 *her departure date from Shanghai*   Mrs. Robert McCombs to Brookfield
Zoo—"Dear Sirs"—8 Sept. 1937.
202 *Hazel Perkins had wired*   Telegram, Hazel Perkins to Edward Bean, 9 Sept.
1937, Brookfield Zoo archives.
202 *Harkness received Perkie's*   Telegram, Edward Bean to Hazel Perkins, 9 Sept.
1937.
202 *She found that he*   "Study Mystery of Su-Lin's Death," *Chicago Daily Tribune*,
2 Apr. 1938.
202 *"I really got it"*   Harkness to Perkins, 10 Sept. 1937.
202 *"For the first time in months"*   Ibid.
202 *She said her roundabout route*   Ibid.
202 *Later to the Beans in Chicago*   Harkness to Edward Bean and family, 24 Sept.
1937, Brookfield Zoo archives.
203 *Chengdu was yet another*   Harkness to Perkins, 15 Sept. 1937.
203 *It contained a massive bed*   Harkness to Perkins, 5 Oct. 1937.

203 *She had been trying*   Tuchman, *Stilwell*, p. 63.

204 *If it were possible*   Harkness to Perkins, 24 Sept. 1937.

204 *"Kay God dams"*   Ibid.

204 *"sun helmet"*   Ruth Harkness, "Our correspondent in China," unpublished dispatch, 7 Oct. 1937.

205 *"I find myself sunk"*   Harkness to Perkins, 5 Oct. 1937.

205 *She had her very best*   Harkness to Edward Bean and family, 24 Sept. 1937.

205 *Cavaliere uncorked a bottle*   Harkness to Perkins, 18 Oct. 1937.

205 *In part too*   Full name taken from back of photo in Ruth Harkness family archive. It reads: "Wang Whai Hsin my one servant."

205 *Still, by muddling through*   "Second Baby Giant Panda Caught Alive Arrives Here," *China Press*, 14 Jan. 1938, p. 1.

205 *Harkness so indulged*   Harkness to Perkins, 5 Oct. 1937.

207 *But as weeks passed*   Harkness to Perkins, 24 Sept. 1937.

CHAPTER 11: HIGH-ALTITUDE HELL

209 *The Face of the autumn moon freezes*   *Poems of the Late T'ang*, trans. and with an introduction by A. C. Graham (Middlesex, Eng.: Penguin Books, 1965; reprint 1970), p. 68.

209 *A miserable, drenching rain*   Harkness to Perkins, 10 Oct. 1937.

209 *She and Wang*   "New Trip Planned by Mrs. Harkness," *New York Times*, 27 Feb. 1938, says there were ten porters and "squads of carrying porters."

210 *Pulling the page*   Harkness to Perkins, 10 Oct. 1937.

210 *Many friends called*   Ibid., 18 Oct. 1937.

210 *One night, a familiar hunter*   Harkness to Perkins, 10 Oct. 1937.

210 *As a staging area*   "Panda Hunter Tells Story of Patient Quest," *Chicago Sunday Tribune*, 20 Feb. 1938.

210 *Here Harkness and Wang*   Harkness to Perkins, 15 Nov. 1937.

210 *"no bigger than a boy"*   Harkness, "In a Tibetan Lamasery," p. 10.

210 *Seeing him now*   Harkness to Perkins, 15 Nov. 1937.

211 *In the shadow*   Harkness to Perkins, 5 Nov. 1937.

211 *Set against a stubbled*   Harkness to Perkins, 15 Nov. 1937.

211 *They scrambled up*   Harkness, "In a Tibetan Lamasery," p. 58.

211 *There were battered*   Harkness, *Lady and the Panda*, p. 159.

211 *"ancient, spicy odor"*   Harkness, "In a Tibetan Lamasery," p. 10.

212 *The adventurer*   Ibid.

212 *A small terrace*   "New Trip Planned."

212 *Containing a small*   Harkness, "In a Tibetan Lamasery," p. 10.

212 *Harkness rummaged*   Harkness to Perkins, 24 Oct. 1937.

212 *She would decorate*   Harkness to Perkins, 15 Nov. 1937.

213 *As night fell*   Harkness, *Lady and the Panda*, p. 159.

213 *Some days Tibetan*   Harkness to Perkins, 27 Oct. 1937.

213   *Often they came to sell food*   Harkness "In a Tibetan Lamasery," p. 57.

213   *Sometimes people would hike*   Harkness to Perkins, 5 Nov. 1937.

213   *Through it all, a surprising number*   Harkness to Pierce, 10 Dec. 1937; and Harkness, "In a Tibetan Lamasery," p. 10.

213   *"They come, lift up*   Harkness to Pierce, 10 Dec. 1937.

213   *The people were achingly poor*   Harkness, "In a Tibetan Lamasery," p. 57.

214   *An opium addict*   Harkness to Perkins, 15 Nov. 1937.

214   *Harkness spent time*   Per Kvaerne, professor of the history of religions and Tibetology, University of Oslo, author of *The Bon Religion of Tibet*, e-mail correspondence with author, May 2004.

214   *Lying among*   Harkness, *Lady and the Panda*, p. 159.

214   *There might be a serene*   Schell, *Virtual Tibet*, p. 20.

214   *Harkness loved these*   Three of these cards archived by Linda Ash. One card bears a note in Harkness's handwriting, above and below the prayer: "November 1937/The Ruined Castle/Tsaopo"—and below, "Tibetan Border/China."

215   *Sometimes she would*   Harkness, "In a Tibetan Lamasery."

215   *squash, Chinese turnips, cabbage soup*   Harkness to Perkins, 15 Nov. 1937.

215   *pheasant, and a few times a week, chicken*   Harkness, "In a Tibetan Lamasery."

215   *And he cooked*   Ibid.

215   *If something was lost*   Harkness to Perkins, 27 Oct. 1937.

215   *Wang, who was married*   Harkness to Perkins, 5 Nov. 1937.

215   *his two-piece wives*   Harkness to Perkins, 15 Nov. 1937.

215   *There were no bed*   Ibid.

215   *At its center*   Harkness to Perkins, 21 Oct. 1937.

216   *As he would go off*   Harkness to Perkins, 27 Oct. 1937.

216   *The kindness and loyalty*   Ibid.

216   *It was the first step*   Harkness to Perkins, 24 Oct. 1937 (many typos that I have not put in).

216   *Her typewriter*   Harkness to Perkins, 5 Nov. 1937.

217   *Even though mail*   Harkness to Perkins, 2 Nov. 1937.

217   *Her first words to Hazel Perkins*   Harkness to Perkins, 24 Oct. 1937.

217   *She said the renovated*   Ruth Harkness to "Danbury Title Company" (Hazel Perkins), 27 Oct. 1937.

217   *She also pored over*   Harkness to Perkins, 24 Oct. 1937.

217   *Standing out on the balcony*   Harkness to Perkins, 27 Oct. 1937.

217   *Wang remained optimistic*   Harkness to Perkins, 27 Oct. 1937 and 15 Nov. 1937.

218   *Combing the ridges*   Harkness to Perkins, 1 Dec. 1937.

218   *Occasionally, though*   Harkness to Perkins, 5 Nov. 1937.

218   *Years later, Harkness would*   Harkness, "In a Tibetan Lamasery," pp. 10, 58.

218   *After the drop-off*   Ibid., p. 10.

219   *Harkness was overjoyed*   Harkness, *Lady and the Panda*, p. 167.

219   *"With no companionship"*   Harkness to Perkins, 2 Nov. 1937.

219   *There was a clipping*   Harkness to Perkins, 27 Oct. 1937.

219   *She clambered through*   Harkness to Perkins, 15 Nov. 1937.

219   *Collapsing into bed*   Harkness to Perkins, 27 Oct. 1937.

219   *In the morning, as light*   Ibid.

220   *Days of laziness*   Harkness to Perkins, 2 Nov. 1937.

220   *set in a beautiful forest*   Harkness to Perkins, 22 Aug. 1936. She was then calling it "Panther Stones." The manuscript-in-progress was presently locked up with clothes and ammunition in the bank in Shanghai.

220   *The drizzly nights*   Harkness to Perkins, 2 Nov. 1937.

220   *By this time*   Harkness to Perkins, 5 Nov. 1937.

221   *Wang arranged with the hunters*   Harkness to Perkins, 15 Nov. 1937.

222   *"he came rushing"*   Harkness to Perkins, 5 Nov. 1937.

222   *As for a trip into the forest*   Ibid.

222   *With all the preparations*   Harkness to Perkins, 15 Nov. 1937.

222   *By mid-November*   Harkness to Perkins, 15 Nov. 1937.

222   *Her humor blackened*   Harkness to Perkins, 5 Nov. 1937.

222   *She feared*   Harkness to Perkins, 27 Oct. 1937.

223   *"This year I'm"*   Harkness to Pierce, 10 Dec. 1937.

223   *a bowl of pale tea*   Harkness, "In a Tibetan Lamasery," p. 57.

223   *tiger balm*   Ibid., p. 10.

223   *and stoke the fire*   Harkness to Perkins, 15 Nov. 1937.

223   *Sometimes it was comforting*   Harkness to Perkins, 2 Nov. 1937.

223   *horrible images*   Harkness to Perkins, July, n.d., 1938.

223   *He must have been reproaching*   Harkness to Perkins, July 1938.

223   *She felt that*   Harkness to Perkins, 2 Nov. 1937.

224   *What she saw was real*   Schaller, *Last Panda*, p. 98.

224   *One night, the rhythms*   Harkness to Perkins, 2 Nov. 1937.

224   *Out here, she had faith*   Harkness to Perkins, 5 Nov. 1937.

224   *In this mood*   Harkness to Perkins, 1 Dec. 1937; and 24 Oct. 1937, says she knows what she is going to do with Nya-Nya; she mentions the story again to Perkie in letter of 10 Dec. 1937.

224   *Her agent would*   Harkness to Pierce and Perkins, 16 Dec. 1937.

224   *It was fresh*   Harkness to Perkins, 15 Nov. 1937.

225   *In a dark corner*   *China Press*, 16 Jan. 1938, gives Su-Lin's weight at the time as seventy-five pounds. Yin was said to be Su-Lin's size.

225   *The sorry state*   Harkness to Perkins, 1 Dec. 1937.

225   *But Yin wanted*   Ibid.

226   *He told her*   Harkness to Perkins, 10 Dec. 1937.

226   *"Really I can't describe"*   Harkness to Perkins, 1 Dec. 1937.

226   *At least poor Yin finally*   Ibid.

227   *The bamboo-obsessed*   Lumpkin and Seidensticker, *Smithsonian Book of Giant Pandas*, p. 79. George Schaller, in conversation with author, 19 Apr. 2004, says both males and females display this behavior. E-mail from biologist

Devra Kleiman, 23 July 2004: "I don't know whether you are speaking of headstands or handstands; it is the latter that pandas use when they scent mark. Males do most of these behaviors, but females also do so very occasionally. Pandas stand on their heads during other behaviors, in my experience, but not during scent marking."

227 *Since she couldn't go* Harkness to Perkins, 1 Dec. 1937.

227 *The new, loftlike* Ibid.

227 *So she moved in* Ibid.

227 *Through experimentation* Harkness to Pierce and Perkins, 16 Dec. 1937.

228 *With fewer comforts* Harkness to Perkins, 10 Dec. 1937.

228 *If she failed* Harkness to Pierce, 10 Dec. 1937.

228 *"I've been plotting"* Harkness to Pierce and Perkins, 16 Dec. 1937.

228 *Cavaliere had begun* Harkness to Perkins, 1 Dec. 1937.

228 *What she was hearing* Harkness to Perkins, 27 Oct. 1937.

228 *On November 11* Spence, *Search for Modern China*, p. 423.

228 *But within no time* Tuchman, *Stilwell*, pp. 176, 177.

228 *She would find a way* Harkness to Perkins, 1 Dec. 1937.

228 *In the meantime* Harkness to Perkins, 27 Oct. 1937.

229 *She mentioned the capture* Pierce to Perkins, dated only "Tuesday," probably from Jan. 1938, though filed in Dec. folder because it makes reference to Harkness's letter of 10 Dec. 1937.

229 *Harkness didn't seem* Harkness to Perkins, 1 Dec. 1937.

229 *Within weeks* Harkness to Perkins, 10 Dec. 1937.

229 *Her letters were peppered* Harkness to Pierce, 10 Dec. 1937.

229 *Quaker Oats* Harkness to Perkins, 10 Dec. 1937.

229 *Seven panels* *Anadarko Oklahoma News*, 11 Nov. 1937; and *Palestine (Tex.) Advocate*, 5 Nov. 1937.

229 *Two American women* "Su-Lin Doesn't Mind Winter at All," *Martinsville (Ill.) Planet*, 23 Dec. 1938. One of hundreds of similar articles kept in the Brookfield Zoo archives. Same article, headline, and photo in papers from Montana, Iowa, Ohio, Missouri, Brookfield Zoo archives.

229 *fifty-cent children's book* Ruth Ann Waring and Helen Wells, *Su-Lin* (New York: Rand McNally, 1937).

230 *A clothing company* Newspaper ad from the Brookfield Zoo archives—no date or company name, but ad encourages readers to visit Su-Lin at Brookfield.

230 *Calvert whiskey* Harkness to Perkins, 1 Dec. 1937, refers to ad; author has a copy of one from *Chicago Tribune*, 6 Apr. 1938.

230 *There was a jointed* "Baby Panda Here Has Own Amah, Passport," *China Press*, 16 Jan. 1938; also newspaper ad from the Brookfield Zoo archives.

230 *By Christmastime* "Study Mystery of Su-Lin's Death," *Chicago Daily Tribune*, 2 Apr. 1938.

230 *Dionne quintuplets* Correspondence between the Brookfield Zoo and the

Dionne Quintuplet Guardianship, 15 Dec. 1937 and 26 Mar. 1938, Brookfield Zoo archives.

230 *None of the profits* "Panda Andy," article from an unidentified newspaper, Brookfield Zoo archives.

230 *Adding in the money* Harkness to Pierce and Perkins, 16 Dec. 1937.

231 *She gauged the competition* Harkness to Pierce, 10 Dec. 1937.

231 *Although Smith had not* "Floyd Smith in China to Hunt Elusive Panda," *Washington Post,* 29 Dec. 1937.

231 *His indignation* Fragment of letter from Floyd Tangier Smith to his sister Ruth, n.d., but must have been written in fall 1937 from, most likely, London, Floyd Tangier Smith Papers, Library of Congress. See also Floyd Tangier Smith, "Collecting a Zoo in China," *Home and Empire,* Nov. 1937, p. 6, Smith Papers.

231 *With his latest associations* Floyd Tangier Smith, "Hunting the Giant Panda," *Listener Rack,* Smith Papers.

231 *He was even feeling upbeat* Smith, "Collecting a Zoo in China," p. 6.

231 *And in another article* Smith, "Hunting the Giant Panda."

231 *He said the giant panda* Ibid.

231 *"contented, well fed brood sow"* Smith, document/letter 12 Oct. 1937, Smith Papers.

231 *He could not* Smith, "Collecting a Zoo in China," p. 6.

232 *Things began to look up* Harkness to Pierce and Perkins, 16 Dec. 1937.

232 *Despite the mood-lifting* Harkness, *Lady and the Panda,* p. 19.

232 *She still believed* Harkness to Pierce and Perkins, 16 Dec. 1937.

232 *Once she had made up* Ibid.

CHAPTER 12: ONE GRAND THRILL

235 *Ruth Harkness's days* "Panda Is Bored by Jap Air Raid," Associated Press, dateline Hankow, China, 6 Jan. 1937, Brookfield Zoo archives; and "Su-Lin's Baby Sister Braves Hanchow [*sic*] Raid on Way Here," *Chicago Daily News,* 7 Jan. 1938, Brookfield Zoo archives.

235 *Resplendent in a turban* "Second Baby Giant Panda Caught Alive Arrives Here," *China Press,* 14 Jan. 1938, with many pictures of Ruth and Su-Lin, one on ship.

235 *Japanese air raid hit* "Japanese Air Raids on Hankow, Many Fires Blaze, Hospital Wrecked by Planes' Bombs," *South China Morning Post,* 7 Jan. 1938.

235 *A sortie of pursuit planes* "Su-Lin's Baby Sister Braves Hanchow [*sic*] Raid."

235 *As Harkness emerged* "Another Baby Giant Panda Found by Mrs. Harkness in West China," *New York Times,* 8 Jan. 1938.

235 *United Press* "Chicago Giant Panda to Get a 'Sister' Soon," United Press item, no newspaper affiliation attached, Brookfield Zoo archives.

236 *The bloodshed* "Panda Is Bored."

236 *Beginning on December 13* Spence, *Search for Modern China*, p. 423; and Iris Chang, *The Rape of Nanking: The Forgotten Holocaust of World War II* (New York: Penguin Books, 1997), p. 3.

236 *On December 18* *New York Times*, 8 Jan. 1938.

236 *a hidden adult panda* *China Press*, 14 Jan. 1938.

236 *As the animal fled* "Panda Hunter Tells Story of Patient Quest," *Chicago Sunday Tribune*, 20 Feb. 1938.

236 *The days without* "New Trip Planned by Mrs. Harkness," *New York Times*, 27 Feb. 1938.

238 *In the big city* Ruth Harkness, "In a Tibetan Lamasery," Harkness says this party was thrown in the beautifully appointed home of her American hostess.

238 The China Journal *China Journal*, "Travel and Exploration Notes," Jan. 1938, p. 38.

239 *She was convinced* Harkness to Edward Bean, 3 May 1938, Brookfield Zoo archives.

239 *Harkness had come* Tuchman, *Stilwell*, p. 180.

239 *upper reaches of government* "Baby Panda Here Has Own Amah, Passport," *China Press*, 16 Jan. 1938.

239 *Later, this one too* Morris and Morris, *Men and Pandas*.

239 *Officials in Hankou* *New York Times*, 9 Jan. 1938, reports Harkness arrives by plane in Hong Kong from Hankow on Sun., 8 Jan. 1938. Says she plans to sail for U.S. Mon. Also "Panda Is Bored."

239 *"the queerest passenger"* "Baby Panda Here; Curious Air Passenger Arrives from Hankow" *South China Morning Post*, 10 Jan. 1938; and "Panda Playmate for Su-Lin Starts Long Trip to Chicago Zoo," *Chicago Tribune*, 9 Jan. 1938, Brookfield Zoo Archives. Called Mei-Mei here. See also *South China Morning Post*, 10 Jan. 1938; "Giant Panda Expected in Colony To-day," *Hong Kong Telegraph*, 8 Jan. 1938, p. 1; and "Su Lin and Friend," *Chicago Times* 9 Jan. 1938, Brookfield Zoo archives (called Diana).

240 *"the dark, sharp features"* "Second Baby Giant Panda Caught Alive Arrives Here," *China Press*, 14 Jan. 1938.

240 *Understanding just what they* "Panda Hunter Tells Story of Patient Quest," *Chicago Sunday Tribune*, 20 Feb. 1938.

241 *The city was still* Dong, *Shanghai*, p. 256.

241 *The International Settlement* "Canadian Pacific and Dollar Ships Resume Shanghai Calls Soon, Empress of Asia Due from Vancouver Monday," *China Press*, 20 Jan. 1938; and *North China Daily News*, 26 Jan. 1938.

241 *plate glass in its front* Dong, *Shanghai*, p. 257.

241 *Ernie Kaai's* Ad from *China Press*, 20 Jan. 1938.

241 *And the movies* " 'The Good Earth,' Epic Film of China, Opens at Nanking

Tonight," *China Press*, 6 Jan. 1938; and "Great Picture Opens Tonight at Metropole; Gala Premiere of 'Lost Horizon,' Starring Ronald Colman," *China Press*, 27 Jan. 1938.

241 *Fights broke out* " 'Incident' Mars Evening of Night-Lifers at Ballroom," *China Press*, 15 Jan. 1938; and "Four Japanese Cause Trouble in Dance Hall; Want to Fight Patrons, Hostesses in Great Eastern Ballrooms," *China Press*, 20 Jan. 1938.

241 *The Japanese were beginning* "Whither Shanghai? The Conquerors Show Their Authority," *Hong Kong Daily Press*, 8 Jan. 1938.

241 *the papers would report* "Terrorists Hurl 4 Bombs in Foreign Areas Within Hour," *China Press*, 28 Jan. 1938.

241 *To cope* "Baby Panda Here Has Own Amah," *North China Daily News*, 23 Jan. 1938; and *China Press*, 23 Jan. 1938.

241 *Photographs of the woman* "Exhibited to Aid Refugees," *Shanghai Times*, 27 Jan. 1938.

241 *But with Diana* "Baby Panda Here Has Own Amah."

241 *Harkness's celebrity* "Sea Voyage of a Baby Panda," *Christian Science Monitor*, 1 June 1938, p. 10.

242 *With the publication* "Lady & Pandas," *Time*, 24 Jan. 1938.

242 *The New York Times Book* "The Adventurous Lady Who Captured the Panda," *New York Times Book Review*, 16 Jan. 1938.

242 *For better or worse* Poore, "Books of the Times."

242 *And* The Christian Science "Lady and Panda: Book News of the Day," *Christian Science Monitor*, 18 Jan. 1938, p. 20.

242 Time *grumbled* "Lady & Pandas."

242 *Because she didn't write* Poore, "Books of the Times."

242 *What no one could miss* Ibid.

242 *And its Sunday* *New York Times Book Review*, 16 Jan. 1938.

243 *While a winter chill* "Baby Giant Panda Slated for 'Personal Appearance' Here," *China Press*, 22 Jan. 1938.

243 *The upending of everything* Mu Soeng, *The Diamond Sutra: Transforming the Way We Perceive the World* (Boston: Wisdom Publications, 2000).

243 *While the press* "Panda Hunter Tells Story."

243 *When she first wired* Telegram, Ruth Harkness to Brookfield Zoo, 30 Dec. 1937. Full text reads: HAPPY NEW YEAR SMALL SISTER NO HUSBAND, and is signed HARKNESS, Brookfield Zoo archives.

243 *"Su-Lin" had wired back* Telegram, Brookfield Zoo to Ruth Harkness, 1 Jan. 1938, Brookfield Zoo archives.

243 *The* Chicago Times "Sorry, Su-Lin. It's a Girl! Love Hopes of Giant Panda Blasted," *Chicago Times*, 7 Jan. 1938, Brookfield Zoo archives.

244 *The* Chicago American "Here's Chance to Get Rich, Find Su-Lin a Playmate," *Chicago American*, 20 Jan. 1938, Brookfield Zoo archives.

244 *Even without Dan Reib*   Jane Reib Pollock (Reib's daughter), telephone conversation with author, 2 Dec. 2003.

244 *Sowerby showed*   "Baby Giant Panda Invades Sanctum of Shanghai Club Bar," *China Press*, 25 Jan. 1938; *China Journal*, Feb. 1938, p. 97, reports the date as Sat., 22 Jan. 1938; "Baby Panda Here Has Own Amah"; and "Second Baby Panda Leaves for America," *China Press*, 29 Jan. 1938. Visit at noon on the day of Harkness's departure.

244 *Under the sponsorship*   "Baby Giant Panda Slated for 'Personal Appearance' "; "Baby Panda Earns Lot [sic] of Money," *Shanghai Times*, 28 Jan. 1938; ad that ran in the local papers, including *North China Daily News* and *Shanghai Post and Mercury*, and *China Journal*, Feb. 1938, p. 97.

244 *From 5 to 7 P.M.*   All the ads said from 5–7 P.M., but *China Press* reported it lasted three hours—from 4 P.M. to 7 P.M. "Panda's Debut Here Attracts Large Crowd," *China Press*, 27 Jan. 1938. Later Harkness told an American reporter that the event was two hours, "Mei-Mei Entertains Self by Playing with Plumbing," unidentified clip. Albuquerque paper, Feb. 1938.

244 *Diana alternately sprawled*   "Ruth Harkness Completes West China Expedition," *China Press*, 27 Jan. 1938; "Travel and Exploration Notes," *China Journal*, Jan. 1938, p. 37; and *Shanghai Times*, 28 Jan. 1938.

244 *This time her visit*   "Baby Giant Panda Invades Sanctum."

244 *Thinking of Smith's fiasco*   "Second Baby Panda Leaves for America," *China Press*, 29 Jan. 1938; "Baby Giant Panda Slated for 'Personal Appearance.' " Also Associated Press, 29 Jan. 1938, says Seattle, and that it departs on the 29th; *China Journal*, Feb. 1938, says Vancouver. It was a Canadian line; historical information about the ship suggests that Vancouver must have been the destination.

245 *At 5 P.M. on Friday*   *China Press*, 29 Jan. 1938.

245 *Within minutes*   "Sails with Baby Panda," *New York Times*, 30 Jan. 1938.

245 *Out on the Huangpu*   "Shanghai Experiences First Snowfall of This Winter," *China Press*, 29 Jan. 1938.

245 *It would be good*   "Season's First Snowfall a Happy Omen for New Year," *Shanghai Times*, 30 Jan. 1938.

245 *The press was certain*   Herschell Brickell, "How a Dress Designer Became the World's Best Panda-Catcher," "Books on Our Table," no publication on clip, but Brickell wrote for *New York Herald Tribune*, *New York Evening Post*, and *Saturday Review of Literature*. Clip has to be from January, by reference to Diana. Also "Lady & Pandas."

CHAPTER 13: HELLO, I MUST BE GOING

247 *After she docked*   "Baby Panda Coming Here by Plane," clip from an unidentified San Francisco paper; "Baby Panda Arrives—Beds in Tub," San Fran-

cisco paper, 15 Feb. 1938; and "Mei-Mei Entertains Self by Playing with Plumbing," in unidentified Albuquerque paper, Feb. 1938.

247 *before boarding* "Sought Pandas Because Few White Men Caught Them," undated article stamped "New Mexico State Tribune Company," Feb. 1938; "Mei-Mei Entertains Self"; and "Su-Lin Greets Sister with a Poke on Nose; Then 2 Pandas Kiss and Make Up at Zoo," *Chicago Daily Tribune,* 19 Feb. 1938.

247 *At every stop* "Sought Pandas Because Few White Men"; "Panda's New 'Boy Friend' Is a Girl!" *Seattle Post-Intelligencer,* 12 Feb. 1938; and picture from unidentified San Francisco paper, marked 14 Feb. 1938.

247 *As the two sat* "Baby Panda in Chicago After 15,000-Mile Trip," *Chicago Daily Tribune,* 19 Feb. 1938, Associated Press, dateline Chicago, 18 Feb. 1938.

248 *Before the assembled crowd* *Chicago Daily Tribune,* 19 Feb. 1938; some details from photographs of the scene from Mary Lobisco's family archives.

249 *During the course* *Chicago Daily Tribune,* 19 Feb. 1938.

249 *That bound her to the Chinese* Ibid.

249 *The group was soon* "Baby Panda in Chicago"; "Panda Hunter Tells Story of Patient Quest," *Chicago Sunday Tribune,* 20 Feb. 1938.

250 *The newsreels covered* "Mei-Mei Entertains Self."

250 *Appearing with staff members* Robert Bean to Ruth Harkness, 5 Mar. 1938, Brookfield Zoo archives.

250 *At first, Su-Lin* *Chicago Daily Tribune,* 19 Feb. 1938.

250 *Su-Lin, known* Edward Bean to Harkness, 9 Dec. 1937, Brookfield Zoo archives.

250 *By now Diana* "Giant Panda Expected in Colony Today," Associated Press, 6 Jan. 1938; Associated Press report dateline Hong Kong, 8 Jan. 1938; *Hong Kong Telegraph,* 8 Jan. 1938. According to *China Press, New York Times* (14 Jan. 1938), *North China Daily News,* ad, 25 or 26 Jan. 1938, *Shanghai Times,* 27 Jan. 1938; "Panda Flies to San Francisco," *New York Times,* 13 Feb. 1938.

250 *Taking a suite* "Panda Hunter Tells Story."

250 *Zoo life seemed* Harkness to Perkins, on Stevens Hotel Chicago stationery, dated "Tuesday."

250 *In light of his continuing* "Study Mystery of Su-Lin's Death," *Chicago Daily Tribune,* 2 Apr. 1938.

250 *Harkness owned him* *Chicago Daily Tribune,* 19 Feb. 1938.

250 *When she swept* "New Trip Planned by Mrs. Harkness," *New York Times,* 27 Feb. 1938, sec. 2.

251 *"a grand bedfellow"* Harkness to Robert Bean, 7 Mar. 1938, Brookfield Zoo archives.

251 *She felt duty-bound* "New Trip Planned by Mrs. Harkness."

251 *If she was successful* Ibid.

251 *After the endless nights* Harkness to Perkins, Harkness has marked "Tuesday," and in handwriting, someone has noted "3/3/38" (which was not a Tuesday).

251 *That Tuesday* Harkness to Perkins, "Tuesday" (must be 1 Mar. 1938). Invitation to Perkins to join her, telegram, 24 Feb. 1938.

251 *She asked for a chance* Harkness to Perkins, Tuesday, or "3/3/38."

252 *Her patient friend* In ibid., Harkness says she will be moving into an apartment at 10 West Tenth Street. And when Perkie visits, Harkness is clearly doing the cooking and cleaning, but all correspondence afterward is on Algonquin Hotel stationery, and letters to her carry that address, such as her 7 Mar. to Robert Bean, and Robert Bean to Harkness, 13 Apr. 1938, Harkness to Edward Bean 20 Apr. and 3 May 1938; Edward Bean to Harkness, 18 May 1938.

252 *As a host* Another letter from Harkness to Perkins, marked "Tuesday." From clue in letter of 1 Mar. (invitation), likely 15 Mar. 1938.

252 *In March she* Hedda Hopper, "In Hollywood," *Washington Post*, 25 Mar. 1938; "11 Women Are Chosen As the 'Best Dressed': Medals Awarded by Designers to Leaders in Various Fields of United States Life," clip from unidentified newspaper, Harkness family files.

252 *Alongside several exotic* "Lone Woman Explorer on the Trail of the Panda, Rarest of Quadrupeds," *New York Times*, 27 Mar. 1938, rotogravure picture sec.

252 *She gave lectures* "Lewis Makes Plea for 'Ivory Tower,' " *New York Times*, 31 Mar. 1938.

252 *The next day* "Books Published Today," *New York Times*, 31 Mar. 1938; *Washington Post*, "Book of the Week," 5 June 1938.

252 *The illness appeared* Robert Bean to Harkness, 7 Apr. 1938, Brookfield Zoo archives.

253 *Mary Bean found* Ibid.

253 *It had not been there* "Panda's Death a Mystery" Associated Press, 2 Apr. 1938: "The black and white panda, which died yesterday, was supposed to have been suffering from a throat infection after choking on an oak twig Sunday."

253 *His health deteriorated* "Study Mystery of Su-Lin's Death," *Chicago Daily Tribune*, 2 Apr. 1938.

253 *Distraught zoo officials* "Pandas Galore," *Time*, 11 Apr. 1938.

253 *On Friday the Beans* Edward Bean to Harkness, 14 Apr. 1938, Brookfield Zoo archives.

253 *Telegrams of condolence* *Chicago Daily Tribune*, 2 Apr. 1938.

253 *color photograph of Su-Lin* *Chicago Tribune*, 15 May 1938, Brookfield Zoo archives.

253 *As his popularity* "Panda's Death a Mystery."

253 *But "of her countless"* "Su-Lin, America's Favorite Animal, Dies of Quinsy in Chicago Zoo," *Life*, 11 Apr. 1938.

253 *Reached with the news* *Chicago Daily Tribune*, 2 Apr. 1938.

254 *"could not feel"* "Panda, Pet of Zoo, Is Dead in Chicago," *New York Times*, 1 Apr. 1938.

254   *The Beans assured*   Edward Bean to Harkness, 14 Apr. 1938.

254   *A distinguished panel*   *Field Museum News* 9, no. 7 (July 1938), Field Museum archives.

254   *The cursory postmortem*   "Panda's Death a Mystery"; *New York Times*, 3 Apr. 1938, p. 23.

254   *The body*   "Cause of Su-Lin's Death Sought in Post-Mortem," *Chicago Tribune*, 3 Apr. 1938.

254   *That meant that the altitude*   Herbert E. Bradley, atty. and member of the zoo's animal committee, to Wilfred Osgood, Field Museum, 6 June 1938; and return letter from Osgood and D. D. Davis, 7 June 1938, Brookfield Zoo archives.

254   *Analyzed sections*   O. H. Robertson, M.D., Department of Medicine at the University of Chicago, to Wilfred Osgood, Field Museum, 11 May 1938; and Clifford C. Gregg, Field Museum, to Herbert E. Bradley, 10 June 1938, Brookfield Zoo archives.

254   *The press was agitating*   "Su-Lin Victim of Pneumonia, Museum Holds," *Chicago Daily Tribune*, 14 Apr. 1938.

254   *In fact, it would take*   Su-Lin discovered to be a male during dissection, reported in *Time*, 1 May 1939. And in *Field Museum News*, n.d., but must be May 1938, p. 7; *Chicago Daily Tribune*, 14 Apr. 1938; *Field Museum News* 9, no. 7 (July 1938); and *Chicago Daily News*, rough copy dated 1 Dec. 1939, Brookfield Zoo archives.

254   *A taxidermist*   *Field Museum News* 9, no. 7, (July 1938).

255   *Elizabeth Smith was telling*   "Four Giant Pandas Are Captured by Floyd Smith in Western China," *New York Times*, 4 Apr. 1938.

255   *Papers everywhere*   "Panda Market Wabbles [sic]; Four More Found," *Chicago Tribune*, 4 Apr. 1938.

255   Time *magazine*   *Time*, 11 Apr. 1938.

255   *The* Chicago Tribune   *Chicago Tribune*, 4 Apr. 1938.

255   *And* The New York Times   "Four Giant Pandas."

255   *Francis E. Manierre*   *Chicago Tribune*, 4 Apr. 1938.

255   *The zoo had*   "Panda Hunter Tells Story."

255   *Besides, the zoo*   Robert Bean to Harkness, 13 Apr. 1938.

255   *The first day*   Robert Bean to Harkness, 23 Mar. 1938.

255   *A poll conducted*   "Diz and the Panda Tie as Attractions," *Washington Post*, 3 June 1938.

255   *The zoo's slight*   Robert Bean to Harkness, 13 Apr. 1938; and "Pandas Galore," *Time*, 11 Apr. 1938.

256   *"turned cold"*   Harkness to Perkins, 22 June 1938.

256   *On previous occasions*   Harkness to Robert Bean, 7 Mar. 1938.

256   *Now she became*   Harkness to Edward Bean, 3 May 1938.

256   *"the very nature of pandas"*   Edward Bean to Harkness, 14 Apr. 1938.

256 *The zoo had* "Pandas Galore." *Time*, 11 Apr. 1938.

256 *At a luncheon* "Mrs. Harkness to Hunt Panda," *New York Times*, 13 Apr. 1938, p. 27.

256 *She was playing her cards* Young's May cable telling her that he had two pandas for her had to have been part of an already settled arrangement.

257 *The Bronx Zoo* "Panda on Way to U.S.," *New York Times*, 20 May 1938; and "1st Giant Panda in City Destined for Bronx Zoo," *New York Herald Tribune*, 22 May 1938.

257 *The animal, named Pandora* "City's First Panda Due Here Friday," *New York Times*, 7 June 1938; and "The Latest Panda News," *China Journal*, "Scientific Notes and Reviews" July 1938, p. 60.

257 *After all the wrangling* *New York Times*, 7 June 1938.

257 *a bargain-basement price* Pierce to Perkins, sometime in 1938.

257 *Simultaneously* "Giant Panda Imports Look Up, Bronx May See Five at a Time," *New York Herald Tribune*, 5 June 1938.

257 *Though there would be* "Mrs. Harkness Relates Adventure; Temperamental Panda Is Returned to Native Mountains by Explorer," *China Press*, 28 July 1938. The death of this little male is also mentioned in a letter from Harkness to Pierce on 16 June 1938.

257 *Her pandas were* Harkness to Pierce and Perkins, 25 May 1938, from aboard the *China Clipper*.

257 *Even her spirits* Harkness to Pierce and Perkins, 25 May 1938.

CHAPTER 14: THE BACK OF BEYOND

259 *From behind the great* Harkness to Pierce, 16 June 1938.

259 *A tame goose* Harkness to Pierce, 10 June 1938.

259 *She could take a sip* Ibid.

260 *From the theater* Harkness to Perkins, 22 June 1938.

260 *"a certain peace"* Harkness to Perkins, 10 and 22 June 1938.

260 *The flooding* Tuchman, *Stillwell*, p. 187; and Spence, *Search for Modern China*, pp. 424–25.

260 *Harkness had arrived* Arrived in Hong Kong on 1 June 1938, and expected to fly to Chengdu on 3 June, according to "For Baby Panda; Mrs. Harkness Comes to Colony from US; On Third Visit," *South China Morning Post*, 2 June 1938.

260 *He had promised* Harkness to Pierce, 16 June 1938.

260 *Together they cared* Harkness to Pierce, 10 June 1938.

260 *"high and mighty"* Harkness to Pierce, 8 July 1938.

261 *"the sort of companionship"* Harkness to Pierce, 8 July 1938.

261 *He still bristled* Quentin Young, interview by Michael Kiefer, in "I Need Time to Recuperate," *San Diego Weekly Reader* 19, no. 47 (29 Nov. 1990).

261 *After days shared*   Harkness to Pierce, 10 June 1938.

261 *She thought she would*   Harkness to Perkins, 22 June 1938; and "For Baby Panda; Mrs. Harkness Comes."

263 *But Harkness did not*   Hopkirk, *Trespassers*, p. 222.

263 *"Did she rub"*   Harkness to Pierce, 10 June 1938.

263 *When Harkness*   Ibid.

263 *"Everything I owned"*   Ruth Harkness, travel club speech, 1939.

263 *It sliced up*   Harkness to Perkins, 10 June 1938.

263 *"This baby will"*   Harkness to Perkins, 4 July 1938.

263 *She was a pistol*   Harkness to Pierce, 10 June 1938.

263 *What she got into*   Harkness, travel club speech, 1939.

263 *"The vixen"*   Harkness to Pierce, 16 June 1938.

264 *On rainy days*   Ibid.

264 *"little hellion"*   Harkness to Perkins, 22 June 1938.

264 *Then Harkness*   Harkness to Pierce, 16 June 1938.

264 *"I wish you could"*   Harkness to Pierce, 16 June 1938.

264 *The houses*   Harkness to Pierce, 10 June 1938.

264 *None of the talk*   Harkness, travel club speech, 1939.

265 *Without much luck*   "The Latest Panda News," *China Journal*, "Scientific Notes and Reviews," July 1938, p. 60.

265 *As soon as Harkness*   Harkness to Perkins, 22 June 1938.

265 *Suffering from tuberculosis*   Harkness to Pierce, 10 June 1938.

265 *a common therapy*   Colin Blakemore, *The Oxford Companion to the Body* (Oxford: Oxford University Press, 2001), p. 697.

265 *"I can't feel"*   Harkness to Perkins, 22 June 1938.

265 *A legion of hunters*   Harkness to Pierce, 8 July 1938.

265 *"He is simply"*   Harkness to Perkins, 22 June 1938.

265 *She heard that on this trip*   Harkness to Pierce, 16 June 1938, says five; Harkness to Perkins, 22 June 1938, is updated to six.

265 *"He keeps them"*   Harkness to Pierce, 10 June 1938.

265 *He had such*   "The Latest Panda News," *China Journal*, "Scientific Notes and Reviews," July 1938, p. 60.

266 *Graham never killed*   Morris and Morris, *Men and Pandas*, pp. 54, 92–93.

266 *Young had told*   Harkness to Perkins, 22 June 1938.

266 *A rare and not too*   "Live Giant Pandas Leave Hongkong for London," *China Journal*, "Scientific Notes and Reviews," Dec. 1938, p. 334.

266 *By April*   "China Bans Panda Hunting to Save Dwindling Species," 25 Apr. 1939.

266 *The mercurial Madame*   Harkness to Pierce, 16 June 1938.

266 *"I hadn't been here"*   Ibid.

267 *Rather than roll*   Ibid.

267 *The United States was*   Tuchman, *Stilwell*, pp. 173, 175, 206.

267 *In Chengdu* Harkness to Perkins, 22 June 1938. Perkins family has a photo of Harkness with the dog.

267 *Su-Sen, on the other hand* Harkness to Perkins, 22 June 1938.

268 *As for the practical* Ibid.

268 *Air travel had* Tuchman, *Stilwell*.

268 *Seats had to be booked* Harkness to Pierce, 8 July 1938. Stilwell's experience agrees—in the fall, when he tried to get a reservation, he was told the next vacancy was in February, Tuchman, *Stilwell*, p. 197.

268 *Worse, the Chinese* Harkness to Perkins, 22 June 1938.

268 *Harkness wondered* Harkness to Perkins, 4 July 1938.

269 *"There seemed to be something"* Harkness to Pierce, 8 July 1938.

269 *"We made no sacrifice"* Ibid.

269 *If there really were ghosts* Ibid.

270 *Her chances of success* Ibid.

270 *Just days earlier* "Around the World in News, Science," *Washington Post*, 26 June 1938.

270 *Harkness's intent* Harkness to Pierce, 8 July 1938; and Harkness to Perkins, 4 July 1938.

271 *"She too gets herself"* Harkness to Perkins, 22 June 1938.

271 *The animal* Harkness to Perkins, 4 July 1938.

271 *Harkness was not worried* Ibid.

271 *A bright, buzzing* Harkness to Pierce, 8 July 1938.

271 *"Publicity"* Harkness to Perkins, 19 Dec. 1938.

271 *With bundles of incense* Harkness to Pierce, 8 July 1938.

272 *"Wang came wandering"* Ibid.

272 *He had spent* Harkness, travel club speech, 1939.

272 *With the liquor* Harkness to Pierce, 8 July 1938.

272 *In no time* Harkness to Pierce, 8 July 1938.

273 *Summer was* Schaller, *Last Panda*, pp. 77, 82.

273 *Harkness and Wang* Harkness to Pierce, 8 July 1938; and Harkness to Perkins, 4 July 1938.

273 *at an altitude* Harkness to Perkins and Pierce, n.d. but about 10 July 1938. In travel club speech, 1939, she says 10,000 feet. Harkness to sister Helen from Jan. 1939, says 10,000 feet.

273 *She had gone* Ruth Harkness, *Pangoan Diary* (New York: Creative Age Press, 1942), p. 6.

273 *"at the back of beyond"* Ruth Harkness letter, not addressed to anyone but kept in the Hazel Perkins family archives.

273 *Their entire stay* Harkness to home, Perkins family archives.

273 *"My one quilt"* Harkness to Perkins and Pierce, n.d. but about 10 July 1938.

274 *She had lost* Ibid.

274   *Some mornings they*   Ruth Harkness, "In a Tibetan Lamasery," *Gourmet,* Mar. 1944, p. 10.

274   *She plunged*   Harkness to Pierce, 8 July 1938; and Harkness to Perkins, 4 July 1938.

274   *"She wandered off"*   Harkness, travel club speech, 1939.

274   *It was a rare moment*   Ibid.

274   *"There we lived"*   Harkness, *Pangoan Diary,* p. 6.

274   *Each evening*   Harkness to Pierce, 8 July 1938; and Harkness to Perkins, 4 July 1938.

275   *She had to rush*   Harkness to home, Perkins family archives.

275   *Stumbling back*   Harkness, travel club speech, 1939.

275   *The two campers*   Harkness to home, Perkins family archives.

275   *"swearing a blue"*   Harkness, travel club speech, 1939.

275   *She hadn't been*   Ibid.

276   *Angry enough*   Harkness to home, Perkins family archives.

276   *Instead, he turned*   Harkness, travel club speech, 1939.

276   *"Wang still had"*   Ibid.

276   *With that settled*   Ibid.

276   *In the instant*   Ibid.

276   *"ran as fast"*   Harkness, *Pangoan Diary,* p. 6.

277   *Streams were so*   Harkness, travel club speech, 1939.

EPILOGUE: SONG OF THE SOUL

280   *We were headed*   Harkness, *Lady and the Panda,* p. 21.

281   *Where she gratefully*   Ibid., p. 137.

281   *Yet her choices*   Spence, *Search for Modern China,* p. 425.

281   *ports, railroads, and big cities*   Tuchman, *Stilwell,* p. 195.

282   *Harkness watched*   Ristaino, *Port of Last Resort,* p. 103.

282   *She entered the hospital*   Harkness to Perkins, 9 Sept. 1938.

282   *Then with nothing to do*   Harkness to Perkins, 27 Aug. 1938.

282   *Toying with*   Harkness to Perkins, end of July 1938.

282   *had an intense*   Harkness to Perkins, 27 Aug. 1938.

282   *Fredi Guthmann*   I discovered his identity when author Jeffrey Moussaieff Masson read the manuscript in New Zealand and led me to Natacha Guthmann, Fredi's widow, who confirmed the affair between the then-single Guthmann and Harkness.

282   *Darjeeling*   "The High Road in Sikkim," *New York Times,* 30 Nov. 2003.

282   *"It is beautiful"*   Harkness to Perkins, 22 Nov. 1938.

282   *"For the first time"*   Ibid.

282   *In her hotel room*   Harkness to Perkins, 22 Nov. and 14 Dec. 1938.

282   *Restless*   Ruth Harkness, travel club speech, 1939.

282   *the 14,200-foot*   Sir Evan Nepean, obituary, *New York Times,* 6 Apr. 2002.

282   *"We passed caravan"*   Harkness, travel club speech, 1939.

283   *On her return*   Harkness to Perkins, 29 Dec. 1938.

283   *With renewed vigor*   Harkness to Perkins, 29 Dec. 1938, 14 Jan. 1939; and 5 Feb. 1939.

283   *Harkness would reach*   According to Harkness's letter to Perkins, 14 Jan. 1939, she would sail out of Liverpool on 16 Feb. 1939; "Five Giant Pandas at London Zoo," *Daily Mail,* 23 Dec. 1938; "5 Pandas Loose in Linter," *London Daily Telegraph,* 23 Dec. 1938; "Woman Risked Death from Bandits to Bring Rare Animal from China to Zoo," *London Evening Standard,* 23 Dec. 1938, all from the Smith Papers, Library of Congress.

283   *She survived*   Floyd Tangier Smith, "Bringing Them Back Alive: How We Captured Giant Pandas," *Home and Empire,* Feb. 1939; and "Rare Animals: Leaving by Antenor for England: Pandas for Zoos," *South China Morning Post,* 14 Nov. 1938.

284   *Minus one panda*   "Woman Risked Death."

284   *In mid-July*   "F. T. Smith," *Chicago Tribune,* 14 July 1939; "Floyd T. Smith, Zoologist and Explorer Dies: Sent Several Giant Pandas to U.S. During Scientific Expeditions in Far East," *New York Herald Tribune,* 14 July 1939, dateline Mastick, L.I., 13 July.

284   *The quick year*   Harkness, *Pangoan Diary,* pp. 3, 28.

284   *The world at large*   David M. Kennedy, *Freedom from Fear: The American People in Depression and War, 1929–1945* (Oxford: Oxford University Press, 1999); and Tuchman, *Stilwell.*

284   *The benched explorer*   Harkness to family, Jan. 1939.

284   *In the early fall*   "Program Seeks Funds for Chinese Civilians," *New York Times,* 22 Oct. 1939.

284   *Using "The Alton Railroad"*   Harkness to Perkins, 4 Nov. 1939.

284   *Back home*   Harkness, *Pangoan Diary,* p. 3.

285   *In that frame*   Ibid., p. 2.

285   *On February 23*   "Woman Explorer to Study the Incas," *New York Times,* 24 Feb. 1940.

285   *In Lima*   From the online autobiography of Carl Ingman Aslakson, "Earth Measurer," 1980, http://www.lib.noaa.gov/edocs/AslaksonBio.html.

285   *Harkness, the ultimate urbanite*   Harkness, *Pangoan Diary,* pp. 12, 19.

285   *They would travel*   Name of town corroborated in letter from Lyn Smith Manduley, a friend of Harkness's in Lima, to Manduley's mother, 22 June 1942, Lyn Smith Manduley Letters, Latin American Library, Tulane University.

285   *With his help*   Ruth Harkness, "Saludos," *Gourmet,* Feb. 1944. One reference to one rental is 76 cents a month; another, in the book *Pangoan Diary,* is 67 cents a month.

285   *She learned to cook*   Harkness, *Pangoan Diary*, pp. 134, 194, 205, 211, 254, 277; the making of *masato*, pp. 58–59.

285   *Days were taken*   Ibid. pp. 155–66.

286   *Frequent bouts*   Ruth Harkness, "Mexican Mornings," *Gourmet*, July 1947.

286   *she wrote home to Perkie*   Harkness to Perkins, either 13 Sept. or 13 Dec. 1940.

286   *"Sometimes an intense"*   Harkness, *Pangoan Diary*, pp. 92, 93.

286   *"This feeling exists"*   All from Yogi Ramacharaka, *Fourteen Lessons in Yogi Philosophy* (Yogi Publication Society, orig. 1903, repr. 1931), recommended by Harkness to Perkins in a letter from Peru in the early 1940s.

286   *By the time Harkness*   "Woman Scientist Seeks Peru Panda," Associated Press dateline Miami, FL, 12 Jan. 1942.

286   *Admitted to the hospital*   Lyn Smith Manduley to Manduley's mother, 24 Mar. 1942.

287   *On the Fourth of July*   "Hendrik van Loon Dies in Home at 62," *New York Times*, 12 Mar. 1944.

287   *As soon as Harkness*   Ruth Harkness to Helen Sioussat, 8 Jan. 1947, Library of American Broadcasting archives, College Park, MD.

288   *During quiet days*   "Mrs. Van Loon Is Dead," *New York Times*, 9 Nov. 1958.

288   *Ready to pitch*   "Mrs. Harkness Dies Suddenly in Pittsburgh," *Titusville (Penn.) Herald*, 21 July 1947.

288   *"feeling lousy"*   Helen Criswell, diary entry, 12 Oct., 1946, Cornell University archives.

288   *Through it all*   Harkness to Sioussat, 14 and 27 July 1946, Library of American Broadcasting archives.

288   *The problem was extreme*   Siglinde Ash, telephone interview by author, 12 Sept. 2002.

288   *In the face*   Helen Criswell, diary entry, 3 May 1947, Cornell University archives.

288   *Harkness ended up*   Harkness to Sioussat, July 1947, carries Fulton as the return address, and this is where her sister lived, according to "Woman Explorer, Former Erieite."

288   *famously bohemian Chelsea Hotel*   "Explorer's Widow Dies Unexpectedly in Hotel Bath," *Pittsburgh Post-Gazette*, 21 July 1947; and *Pittsburgh Post-Gazette*, 18, 19, 21, and 24 July 1947. She listed the Chelsea as her address.

288   *At almost midnight*   "Ruth Harkness, 46, Explorer, Is Dead," *New York Times*, 21 July 1947, dateline Pittsburgh, 20 July. "Woman Explorer, Former Erieite," says she checked in on Thurs. *Erie Dispatch*, 21 July 1947, agrees with Associated Press report—she checked in Fri. *Titusville (Penn.) Herald*, 21 July 1947, also says Fri. for check-in.

288   *When by midnight*   "Woman Explorer, Former Erieite."

288   *Greer used his master key*   "Ruth Harkness Death Probed," Associated Press, dateline 20 July 1947.

288 *The bedcovers* "Mrs. Harkness to Be Buried in Union Cemetery," *Titusville (Penn.) Herald,* 22 July 1947.

289 *In the opinion* "Harkness Death Probed."

289 *The officers searched* "Mrs. Ruth Harkness Dies at 46; Brought Giant Panda to U.S.," *New York Herald Tribune,* 21 July 1947.

289 *suspect foul play* *Erie Daily Times,* 21 July 1947.

289 *T. R. Helmbold* "Mrs. Ruth Harkness Dies at 46."

289 *She was cremated* "Woman Explorer, Former Erieite."

289 *The simple services* *Titusville (Penn.) Herald,* 21 July 1947.

289 *The family* Copy of funeral bill, Tracy Home of Funerals, 120 E. Main Street, Titusville, Penn.: "Titusville's Finest."

289 *"a heavy loss"* Quentin Young to Harriet Anderson, 5 Mar. 1974, from family archives.

289 *Unlike his resilient* Kiefer, *Chasing the Panda,* p. 196.

291 *Kiefer would write* Ibid., p. 196.

291 *In 1974* Two letters—both to Mary Lobisco, who was working at the time for a U.S. congressman—make this clear. One from Quentin Young, 30 Nov. 1974, the other from the wife of his former boss, Hazel Good, 25 Nov. 1974.

291 *He not only presented* Quentin Young letter to the editor, *Smithsonian,* 13 Dec. 1983, Harkness family archives.

291 *In the first letter* Young to Anderson, 15 Jan. 1974, Ruth Harkness family archives.

292 *The two would be* Kiefer, *Chasing the Panda,* p. 210.

293 *Just miles away* Schaller, *Last Panda,* p. xi.

293 *In Sichuan Province* World Wildlife Fund, 15 Feb. 2001, 40th anniversary report.

294 *While dozens of reserves* World Wildlife Fund's China division, correspondence from George Schaller, July 2004

INDEX

Page numbers in *italics* indicate photographs

VICKI CONSTANTINE CROKE has been covering pets and wildlife for more than twenty years. She wrote the "Animal Beat" column for *The Boston Globe*, which was carried internationally by *The New York Times* News Service.

She has been a contributor reporting for the National Public Radio environment show *Living on Earth* on everything from conservation in Madagascar to a coyote vasectomy. She consults on film and television projects, most recently a two-hour documentary on gorillas for the A&E Channel.

Her highly praised first book, *The Modern Ark: The Story of Zoos: Past, Present and Future*, a comprehensive look at zoos, was published by Scribner's in 1997.

Croke has also written for *Time, People, The Washington Post, Popular Science, Gourmet, Discover National Wildlife, International Wildlife,* and *The Atlanta Journal-Constitution*. She was also a news writer and producer for CNN in Atlanta.